AMERICAN DEMAGOGUE

AMERICAN DEMAGOGUE

*The Great Awakening and the
Rise and Fall of Populism*

J. D. DICKEY

PEGASUS BOOKS
NEW YORK LONDON

AMERICAN DEMAGOGUE

Pegasus Books Ltd.
148 W 37th Street, 13th Floor
New York, NY 10018

Copyright © 2019 by J. D. Dickey

First Pegasus Books edition November 2019

Interior design by Maria Fernandez

Library of Congress Cataloging-in-Publication Data is available.

ISBN: 978-1-64313-219-8

10 9 8 7 6 5 4 3 2 1

Printed in the United States of America
Distributed by W. W. Norton & Company

"Liberty without obedience is confusion, and obedience without liberty is slavery."

—William Penn

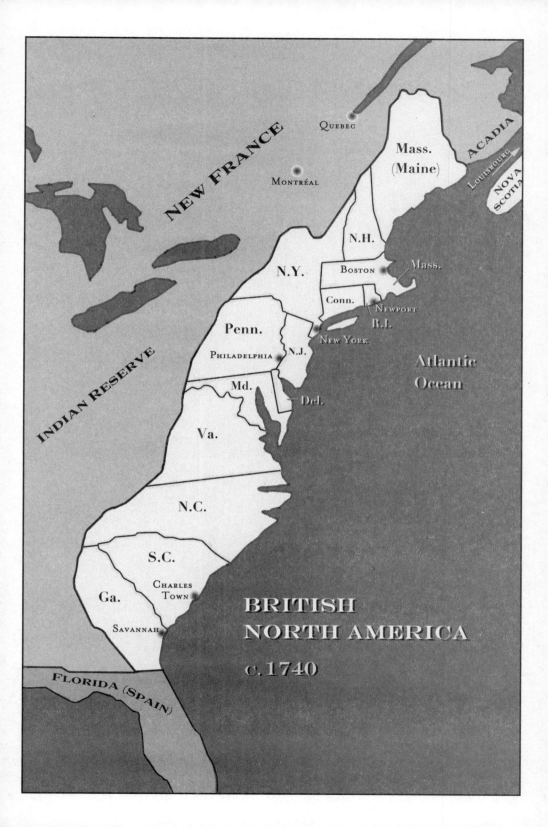

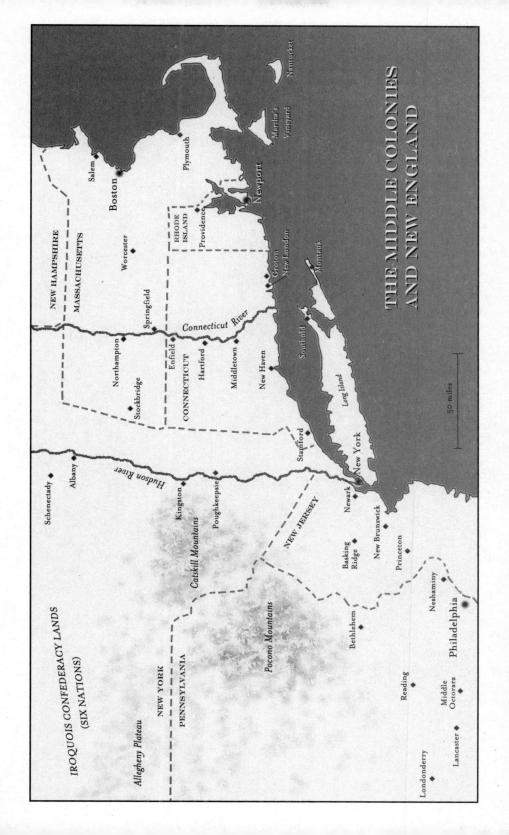

THE MIDDLE COLONIES
AND NEW ENGLAND

IROQUOIS CONFEDERACY LANDS
(SIX NATIONS)

Allegheny Plateau

NEW YORK

PENNSYLVANIA

Catskill Mountains

Pocono Mountains

NEW JERSEY

Hudson River

Schenectady
Albany
Kingston
Poughkeepsie

Stamford

New York

Long Island

Newark
Basking Ridge
New Brunswick
Princeton

Bethlehem
Neshaminy

Reading

Middle Octorara

Londonderry
Lancaster

Philadelphia

NEW HAMPSHIRE

MASSACHUSETTS

Salem
Boston

Worcester

Springfield

Northampton
Stockbridge
Enfield

CONNECTICUT

Hartford
Middletown
New Haven

Southold
Montauk

Plymouth

RHODE ISLAND

Providence
Newport

Groton
New London

Connecticut River

Martha's Vineyard

Nantucket

50 miles

CONTENTS

INTRODUCTION

WHAT IS A DEMAGOGUE?

For students of history or political science, it seems self-evident: A demagogue is a politician or ruler who incites his audience through appeals to emotion, denigration of his enemies, blatant lies and insults, and impossible promises of a greater world to come. He may also call for a return to a mythical past, in which strength and tradition held sway before the modern world ruined everything with corruption and weakness. A demagogue can be merely a public agitator and gadfly, or he can evolve into a murderous dictator, depending on how much power he can accrue through public opinion, mass propaganda, government bureaucracy, and armed force.

Though there are exceptions, demagogues are almost always men. They may rise to notoriety through elected office, corporations, the media, the military, or simply appear out of nowhere—magnetic personalities blessed with the gift of oratory that attract a mass of followers and build a cult of personality. Our Western understanding of them goes back to ancient Greece and Rome and continues with today's politicians. Such firebrands represent all that is combustible and dangerous in public life, and demagoguery is said to be like an electric shock to the body politic.

Defining who is a demagogue can be a challenge, as the term has been used as an "attack word" for hundreds of years. In the context of Western democracies, its meaning is fluid and subject to interpretation. For one person's menace to society may be another's tribune of the people; and scabrous rhetoric to the ears of an enemy may sound like common-sense wisdom to an ally. The judgment about who is and isn't demagogic is based as much on human emotion and tribal loyalties as it is on partisan politics. The reaction of the heart to such a public figure—whether it be praise or revulsion—matters more than the rational judgment of the brain.

At present, Donald Trump has the reputation of being the architect of contemporary demagoguery. And indeed, he shows many of the characteristics: the emotional harangues delivered to mass audiences, the attacks on minorities like Hispanic immigrants, talk of conspiracies like the "deep state" bureaucracy, the barrage of fake news (either denounced or defended), juvenile insults against his foes, and the slogan Make America Great Again emblazoned on a wide range of affordably priced merchandise. He heralds a return to the halcyon days of the mid-20th century, or perhaps the mid-19th century, and condemns the various opposition politicians, reporters, judges, veterans, statesmen, world leaders, and common citizens who have questioned or criticized him. Indeed, to his opponents, Trump is such an ideal example of a demagogue that it stands as a wonder he does not read or study history, since so much of what makes him typical of demagoguery has appeared again and again in the annals of American life. Huey Long, Father Coughlin, Joseph McCarthy, the Know-Nothings, the Dixiecrats . . . the list goes on.

That said, demagoguery is not confined to a single person or political party. Although few leaders exhibit as many characteristics of the incendiary style as Trump, there are a number of individuals on the political left and right who inflame public opinion in pursuit of money and votes. Some of them warn against a sinister cabal of billionaires who would rob common people of their dignity and delight in their misery, all to make a quick buck. Others claim to speak for average Americans, whoever they might be, and imagine themselves as their champion against the wicked designs of those who would oppress them—i.e., members of the other party. Still others go for the rhetorical throat and employ weasel words to defame one minority group or another, using terms like "welfare queens" or "international bankers" or "immoral deviants" to summon outrage and inspire their audience to offer more campaign donations, often at the same time. The variety of hateful, instigating language in public life is almost endless, though the reaction to it is often the same: offense from those attacked, followed by a hardening of tribal loyalties and a greater schism between factions.

Demagogues were present in American public life even before there was an America—and the notion that a figure like Trump could only emerge from our technology-saturated, hyperconnected world is false. A contemporary demagogue might use that hyperconnectivity to better spread his message to his followers, but such figures have always seemed to possess a unique insight into how to use technology to their benefit, regardless of how advanced that technology may have been. What an angry tweet is to the 21st century, an angry pamphlet was to the 18th: a method of mass communication that enabled the demagogue to target his audience in the quickest and most effective fashion.

For hundreds of years, the demagogue's methods have been consistent. He uses fear and terror to agitate his followers, denounces his enemies with stirring and dramatic rhetoric, and finds new and groundbreaking ways to build his reputation and power. He glories in controversy and never backs down from a fight. He inspires passion, breeds division, turns friends into enemies, and leaves society reeling. He is bold and clever and adroit, and can spread turmoil with ease, but can never seem to master the forces he unleashes. For while the demagogue plays a key role in any social upheaval, sparking it and feeding its flames, he is often consumed by it when the fires became too hot to be contained.

Which brings us to the Great Awakening.

Firebrand ministers were essential to the growth and spread of this religious movement. They built their reputation through mass communications and exhausting travels over hundreds of miles, proclaiming the beauty of the "New Birth" in Jesus Christ and denigrating those who resisted it. Using powerful rhetoric, they compared their foes to agents of Satan and the Antichrist, yet they also inspired such devotion in their followers that their preaching tours had a joyful, carnivalesque quality. They outraged their enemies, and divided Christian denominations into hostile factions. They lionized the antique Puritan past and criticized the failings of 18th-century contemporary life, but also promised a bold new future of piety and transcendence. Above all else, they were fundamentally American and set a precedent for the kind of political religion, or religious politics, that is still with us in the 21st century.

Surprisingly, their story is little known today. Indeed, discussions of the movement rarely take place outside of religious studies, colonial American history, and evangelical Christianity. When the revival does appear in textbooks, it is often mentioned solely as a forerunner to the more familiar Second Great Awakening of the 19th century, or as an example of the kind of late-period Puritanism that reveled in hellfire and brimstone. But to those who study this period, the truth is much richer. The Great Awakening was a transformative event that opened a chasm between the stodgy traditions of the colonial world of the early 18th century, and the trailblazing, tumultuous nation of the Revolution. It represented a boundary change in how Americans thought of themselves, or even that they thought of themselves as American at all, instead of simply being British.

Consider: Before the Awakening, American religion was clearly on the decline. In the Middle Colonies like Pennsylvania, New Jersey, and New York, there were too few clergymen to attend to the needs of their parishes—and some parishes lacked ministers entirely. As ordination in Europe was a requirement for many faiths, and many pastors refused to come to the New World, or had to be cajoled with the equivalent of hardship pay. In New England, churches had become insular and hidebound, and delayed or denied admission to those who wanted to become new members. This caused many parishes to be hollowed out, as community meetinghouses became increasingly cliquish and suspicious of those who might have enlivened the faith or populated the pews.

Ministers themselves stood at a distance from their flocks. Unlike the clerics of Europe, who drew their income from state-supported churches, American pastors had to fight and scrape for their income from skinflint congregations, whose coffers were often too threadbare to provide for a fair wage and whose members resisted paying that wage. Pastors were paid so little, they couldn't even provide for their families. Parishioners lobbed accusations of greed, immorality, and incompetence at men who were supposed to be their spiritual leaders. In return, ministers charged the members of their flock of being sinful and depraved. They worried that overseas trade and imported goods gave laypeople a taste for luxury and consumerism. They accused them of having more interest in acquiring wealth and possessions than in living a virtuous life and caring for the sick and the poor—of which there were increasing numbers in a world plagued with social inequality.

At the same time, the colonies attracted waves of new migrants from Northern Ireland, Scotland, and the German states, many of them looking to practice their faith as they had across the Atlantic, or to find new faith in a community that would welcome them to the fold. Too often they found neither. Not only were there scant pastors to care for them, but the pastors they did encounter typically delivered dry, airless sermons that argued the finer points of theology when most of their congregants were looking to learn more about their own salvation. The "legalism" they preached had more to do with church members behaving well and following proper doctrine than it did with helping them find God's grace, and it made Christian worship a drab and formal ritual deprived of color, life, and energy. As a result, people started to drift away from the churches or became indifferent in their beliefs, and faith in America looked ready to become just as institutional and declining as it was in the Old World. As one historian put it, "organized religion seemed on the verge of collapse when the Great Awakening . . . rescued the floundering churches."

The Great Awakening had a broad and turbulent effect—though no one at the time called it by that name. Historian Joseph Tracy invented this term for the movement in 1842, a century late and long after most of the chaos of the era had been forgotten. Mid-18th-century colonists knew it as the "revival" or "revivals," or used one of several other terms, and a few theologians like Jonathan Edwards wrote of a "general awakening," though the term was not widespread. It began with a few isolated events in the 1720s in which communities experienced a spiritual rebirth; achieved a measure of fame around Northampton, Massachusetts, in the mid-1730s; and exploded throughout America in the early 1740s before collapsing and transforming later in the decade into a different kind of movement. However, before attempting to further explain the characteristics of the revival, it's worth clarifying what the revival *wasn't*.

Namely, we have to put aside our 21st-century notions of what social change and conflict look like. We're used to sharp-edged partisan battles between ultraconservative Christians and secular leftists fighting each other over school prayer, abortion rights, gay rights, gun rights, and socialism, among other issues. We might be tempted to assume the same warring sides had direct equivalents in the 18th century—say, with Ben Franklin playing the liberal Deist role against Jonathan Edwards the fundamentalist. But once you realize that Franklin actually helped create the Great Awakening through his print operation, and that Edwards both supported and questioned the movement, the assumption begins to weaken. It further weakens with the understanding that some of the most ardent critics of the revival were fierce defenders of tradition and hierarchy (and the attendant economic inequality) and the most extreme revivalists preached against slavery, the rule of the wealthy, and the oppression of workers and the poor. And the assumption altogether vanishes upon realizing that those groups with little to no political authority in British North America—women, enslaved blacks, and Christian Indians—became some of the revival's greatest supporters and gave powerful testimony to God in the most zealous congregations. Far from a bastion of the political right, radical Christianity in mid-18th-century America was a daring and unsettling force for social change and contributed in no small part to the psychological transformation that led Americans of all kinds toward the Revolution.

This book attempts to explain the Great Awakening through the lens of populism. The idea of populism in its classic American form relates to the revolt of rural Midwesterners against the plutocratic two-party system of the Gilded Age. But the elements of that movement are also evident in the earliest roots of populism in the mid-18th century. They include a broad appeal to common workers and the middle class, praise for tradition and homespun religion, a return to a simpler time before moral laxity and corruption set in, furious attacks on economic privation, social inequality, and cultural elites, and brilliant orators who sometimes had the reputation of demagogues. William Jennings Bryan was the symbol of the populist revolt in the late 19th century; a century-and-a-half earlier, it was George Whitefield.

Whitefield was both a catalyst for the revival and a skillful provocateur—to his friends and allies a pious crusader who converted thousands of people to be reborn in Christ, and to his enemies a fearsome zealot who wielded a unique power to destroy social convention. At his apex, on his second tour of America from 1739 to 1741, Whitefield achieved fame as a masterful evangelizer, his travels reported and publicized in the press, his pamphlets and sermons selling thousands of copies, his name and notoriety increasing with each stop on his relentless tour. Historian Harry Stout wrote, "he can rightly be labeled Anglo-America's first modern celebrity."

Whitefield is still adored in evangelical circles and for good reason—he brought to America a new kind of passionate, emotional, individual style of worship by speaking to the common desires and interests of ordinary Christians. He was devout and earnest in what he preached, and he crafted the template for the frontier preachers, tent-show evangelists and circuit-riding ministers of the 19th century, and charismatic revivalists like Billy Sunday and Billy Graham of the 20th. But at the outset of the Great Awakening, Whitefield inspired much more dissension than any of those figures, and reveled in it.

He had all the hallmarks of a controversialist: provoking public fights with adversaries in his own Anglican church, achieving a cult of personality by comparing aspects of his own life to that of Jesus Christ, causing schism between his followers and detractors, and showing a stunning hypocrisy on issues like slavery, publicly arguing for the education and kind treatment of the enslaved while privately seeking to profit from their labors. On his later trips to America after the peak of the revival, he adopted a moderate tone and sought to mend fences with those he offended, and established a reputation in some quarters as a near-saintly agent of God's grace. However, at the turn of the 1740s, when his social impact was at its greatest, Whitefield also trafficked in demagoguery. The first section of this book, "Fathers," concerns his influential tour of British North America and the widespread influence he had over the hearts and minds of colonists.

Whitefield's journeys led to a spiritual revolution. His friend and ally Gilbert Tennent followed up on his work by demanding his listeners be reborn in Christ and excoriating his enemies with a venomous tongue and spine-chilling rhetoric. Whereas Whitefield inspired greater love than hate, Tennent mainly trafficked in fear. His itinerant ministry had a galvanizing effect on those who witnessed it, and he enflamed souls from Pennsylvania to New Hampshire, and helped divide his own Presbyterian church into warring camps. Many Christian sects became similarly split over the right way to worship, with the so-called New Lights championing the revival and Old Lights fighting it vigorously. Jonathan Edwards, who had sparked revivals long before Whitefield ever came to America, used the power of his pen and pulpit to offer a thoughtful view of how God's grace could transform a human soul, and a frightening view of how his wrath could destroy it. Ben Franklin also promoted the revival, for reasons both ethical and financial, and delivered the revivalists' message to new audiences through his newspaper and print operation—despite his own misgivings about the harsh Calvinism of such preachers.

The second section, "Sons," describes how radical forces grew out of the revival and transformed it into a movement with shocking social implications. Evangelists like James Davenport and Andrew Croswell stunned royal authorities with their wild behavior and threats against the hierarchy. They and other preachers encouraged the exhortations and testimony of those who had been silenced in most churches—Indians on the frontier, enslaved blacks, and women. Notably, Sarah Osborn (née Wheaten) rose to prominence as a religious leader and teacher, despite being stricken with poverty and physical ailments. Other women expressed divine revelations, or forecast the apocalypse, or claimed to see heaven in their mystical journeys. As this kind of radical enthusiasm spread and Americans from all stations of life joined the uprising, the original revivalists found that the movement had escaped their control. The demagoguery they used to stir people up had altered the colonial mind in ways they didn't expect and could not have imagined.

The enthusiasm of worshippers and the extremism of some revivalists brought a backlash. Traditionalists like Charles Chauncy castigated the revival and its emotional displays and frenzied worship. They catalogued the errors of the radicals and accused them of inciting anarchy and encouraging blasphemy. Americans found themselves divided into mutually hostile camps: the supporters of the old traditions, the promoters of the new faith, and the iconoclasts who began to question all orthodox beliefs. Like the traveling preachers who began the movement, colonists developed an aggressive style of civic discourse, one that used caustic language to corrode long-held ideas of civility. The peak of the movement had passed, but the methods its leaders used were still employed by all sides.

The most surprising result of the revival, however, was what it did to Americans' view of the British. No longer willing to accept unjust imperial actions, and trained by a half-decade of battling each other over religion, colonists in the late 1740s turned to public protest and riots against policies like naval impressment, repression of religious liberty and speech, and conversions of non-Anglicans. Aiding these efforts were Samuel Adams, the son of a Boston maltster who published contentious pamphlets, and Jonathan Mayhew, who agitated an entire region with his religious liberalism and his preaching against English tyrants.

Section three, "Spirits," explores the aftermath of the Great Awakening: the later lives of the revivalists, the early crusade against slavery, and the struggle against Great Britain. It discusses how Chauncy and Mayhew transformed from opponents of the revival into firebrands against imperial rule, uniting even their former evangelical enemies in a campaign for religious liberty and colonial rights. This "Black Regiment" of clergymen provided godly sanction for revolutionary activities and produced some of the most vehement anti-imperial sermons American colonists had ever heard. They bridged the gap between the sectarian battles of the revival and nationalist resistance to the mother country.

The role of the Great Awakening in the story of the Revolution is one focus of this book, but doesn't exclude other, more familiar causes of the drive for independence. These include Americans' participation in, and reaction to, multiple rounds of imperial warfare and the outrage over the taxation and trade policies of Parliament. Also important are the liberal philosophies of the European Enlightenment advanced by Rousseau, Locke, Smith, Montesquieu, and others, who provided the intellectual backbone for the theory of government that Thomas Jefferson, James Madison, and the Founders championed.

These ideas form the basis for the classical scholarship of the Revolution, though it should be noted that a revolution cannot be waged by men of wealth and status alone, and the other side of the story has its roots in the artisans, the shipyard workers, the female teachers and seamstresses, the urban poor, and the enslaved who made up a much greater part of the polity of colonial America. The common people would not have fought so vigorously in American armies against the British, would not have sacrificed their lives and livelihoods, only on behalf of Enlightenment philosophies, or anger over taxation, or dislike for trade mandates. They brought so much zeal and passion to the fight because many of them saw it in a cosmic, often apocalyptic light—as a struggle for religious liberty against forces of oppression, as a battle between dissenting Christians and the Church of England, and as a war between God's armies and those of Satan.

These ideas make some of us uncomfortable in the modern age. The notion that the United States didn't just evolve out of the genteel philosophies of Western Europe, but also out of uneducated, homegrown wildcat evangelism seems vaguely unacceptable, a breach of decorum, an uncomfortable assertion. But the scholarly research on the subject over the last half-century has proved to be convincing. Ever since Alan Heimert's monumental 1966 study, *Religion and the American Mind,* we have begun to appreciate how much the creation of an independent America owes to the religious upheaval. Scholars have followed up on Heimert's work and broadened it with significant research in the five decades since, and the evidence has only increased that there is a clear link between the "psychological earthquake" of the Great Awakening and the political tempest of the Revolution.

This book validates that argument, showing that an upsurge in Christian evangelism, first using the tools of demagoguery, brought forth a powerful counterreaction that created a climate of anger and dissension. After the revival peaked, those strong emotions lingered and became redirected into protests over British imperial policy—often led by the same figures who had battled during the revival—and eventually warfare. In the process, the minds of Americans changed, from valuing social cohesion and unity to valorizing political and religious liberty, even at the cost of violence. As

John Adams himself wrote, "the Revolution was effected before the war commenced. The Revolution was in the minds and hearts of the people. A change in their religious sentiments of their duties and obligations."

Americans had once been loyal and complacent subjects of the king, offering their affection and servility in exchange for his protection. But once he violated their trust, they turned on him with a skill for revolt honed from years of practice, and they expressed outrage that he had exceeded his authority and infringed on their liberties. As Adams wrote, "this radical change in the principles, opinions, sentiments and affection of the people was the real American Revolution."

AMERICAN DEMAGOGUE

FATHERS

ONE

DISSECTING THE HEART

The newspapers from London all carried the story. A strange, exuberant figure had been transforming the faith of His Majesty's kingdom. The reports said he was barely twenty-five years of age, sported a baby face, and cried real tears of passion. He told stories of hope and rage, of fear and damnation, and the beauty of eternal salvation. He offered the promise of love and peace at the right hand of Jesus Christ and encouraged his listeners to confess their sins and allow God's grace to transform them, in a great moment of conversion he called the "New Birth." Bringing his audience to fits of joy and excitement, he incited an uproar throughout Britain.

The tales almost seemed too outlandish to believe. This young Anglican priest, George Whitefield, was said to have preached to some 20,000 people near Bristol, and 80,000 in Hyde Park. With the doors of many established churches closed to him, he took his message to open fields and meadows, or wherever people could hear him, including "table tops, open windows, courtyards, hills, wagons, and marketplaces"—even a "Tomb-Stone in Islington Church Yard," with his audience dangling from tree limbs to hear his words.

His followers called him the "Grand Itinerant" for his inspired wanderings to offer his testimony wherever the spirit led him. He called his approach "preaching without doors" and, whether in a church or a forest clearing, he spoke without notes and delivered his gospel homilies off the cuff, in great dramatic bursts of inspiration. Newspapers claimed he preached to upwards of a million Britons over the summer of 1739, which gave him a reputation as a spellbinding orator who could transform the lives of his listeners and improve their spirits and, perhaps, their souls.

The reports crossed the Atlantic Ocean and drew the interest of thousands of American colonists eager to read about the gospel of Whitefield and perhaps even experience it for themselves. One publisher who knew this was a story too compelling to keep from his readers was Benjamin Franklin.

Franklin had been printing the tales of Whitefield in his *Pennsylvania Gazette* for several years, though he regarded them as potentially exaggerated. He had heard talk of country preachers tantalizing crowds and performing miracles before, but these stories typically carried the air of folklore. Franklin was too wise, and certainly too wary, to accept such reports at face value, but he remained intrigued by the man's traveling ministry. Some 80,000 listeners in one venue . . . a million overall . . . these were colossal numbers that, even if overblown, could not be imagined in the parks and meetinghouses of the colonies.

He understood why so many of his readers had become transfixed: Whitefield had tapped into something deeper in people's hearts, something beyond conventional Christianity, perhaps even beyond religion. So despite whatever doubts he may have had, as the summer came, Franklin resolved to heighten the young priest's profile even further. Soon enough, all his readers would know the life and legend of the Grand Itinerant, what he preached, and how he preached it, and that he would be arriving in the colonies the following November.

Yet Whitefield's religion was not Ben Franklin's religion. This was not to say that Franklin had no religion, simply that he went his own way. He thought he knew God. He thought he understood him, had reconciled with him, even made an ally of him. As a rational thirty-three-year-old newspaper publisher and entrepreneur, Franklin embraced the idea of God, along with the social utility of religion, for its salutary effects on people's behavior. He imagined Whitefield might encourage such effects, even if the preacher's traditional views clashed with Franklin's own idiosyncratic perspective.

Franklin envisioned the Lord not as a raging, vindictive tyrant, as some orthodox believers did, but simply as a wise and skillful "Creator of the Universe" who had made the earth and "govern'd it by his Providence." He created immortal souls, punished vice and rewarded virtue, and established those fundamental principles that Franklin had come to live by in life and business: truth, sincerity, and integrity. And while he didn't know God personally, because surely he didn't, at least he could articulate the deity's purpose and praise his ennobling effect on his fellow Pennsylvanians.

This knowledge did not come without struggle. Throughout his youth Franklin had chafed at his education in the Presbyterian Church, whose "peculiar doctrines . . . were all to me very dry, uninteresting and unedifying." Instead he created a detailed moral inventory, a list of attainable virtues, which included thirteen key traits ranging from temperance and cleanliness to chastity and humility. And he measured his actions every day on a graph to plot how closely he upheld or deviated from his personal standard for ideal behavior. This was his "bold and arduous project of arriving at moral Perfection"—his own handcrafted religion.

Franklin's philosophy served him well and gave him a sense of duty to achieve success and a determination to uplift the character of the colony's citizens, just as he had improved his own. From the time he arrived in Philadelphia at 17, he had been advancing his reputation. He set type and kept the books for print houses, helped found one of the colonies' first subscription libraries and volunteer fire companies, and printed the currency for New Jersey, Delaware, and Pennsylvania. He also began to investigate the workings of the natural world with scientific experiments and formed a social club for moral and educational improvement called the Junto. But more than anything, publishing the *Pennsylvania Gazette* brought him much of his early notoriety.

In his newspaper, he wrote witty and incisive commentary on politics and society—often under assumed names—sold advertising, ran classified ads, and reprinted news from abroad. However, though the *Gazette* had become the most popular publication in the colony, he faced real competition from

Andrew Bradford and his *American Weekly Mercury*. While Franklin saw its articles as a collection of shopworn ideas by hidebound authors, he took his contest with Bradford seriously, and had recently trumped his rival by displacing him as postmaster—thus giving him an advantage in distributing his publications across the colonies. He had also created a juggernaut with *Poor Richard's Almanack*, in which Franklin recycled a series of popular proverbs from other sources in new American packaging, encouraging thrift, modesty, humility, frugality, and other virtues that he revered.

Though Franklin had gained over Bradford in ways large and small, he knew success could be fleeting and complacency could lead to failure. He channeled his energy into finding new avenues for attracting public interest, driving the print operation forward, trying to reach more subscribers, more advertisers, more readers. How could the *Gazette* finally eclipse the *Mercury*? Where could he expand his business? And how could he enchant the public while uplifting their morality? He thought he might have found the answer to all these questions in George Whitefield.

Typically, Franklin would have been wary of such a man, especially if he followed the unforgiving doctrine of Calvinism, as so many others did throughout the colonies. As an arch Calvinist, Whitefield saw human beings as fundamentally base and depraved creatures, whose only hope of salvation was to confess their sins before Christ and submit to him in unquestioning faith and devotion. But there was a catch: even with such a confession and submission, only God knew for certain whether any individual would be saved, for he had predestined only a sliver of humanity to sit with him in heaven at the Lord's Table. Everyone else was damned, regardless of how many good works they undertook, or how devout they were, or how spotless their reputation might be. God favored only the Elect, and only he knew who they were.

How much ink had Franklin spilled attempting to disprove the link between that kind of faith, of which there was too much, and morality, of which there was too little? He had inveighed against orthodoxy for years in the *Gazette*, but only saw incremental progress in the advance of reason and morality against the dull tide of devout conformity. Yet here was a preacher whose message was just as rigid and pious as that of any dogmatic Christian—yet Franklin was intrigued by him.

The logic made a certain kind of sense. While Whitefield's system of belief had almost nothing to do with Franklin's own philosophy, he appreciated the preacher's call to good behavior. The public certainly needed no instruction in drinking, stealing, and gambling, and some of its members had proven quite adept in those lowly arts. Rather, it needed guidance in moral philosophy and a teacher who could steer them on a proper course, away from vice and indulgence and toward ethical behavior and civil conduct. So regardless of whether Whitefield proclaimed Calvinism or some other baleful theology, if he could encourage a sense of virtue, honor, and responsibility in his audience, Franklin would do all he could to advance his message.

Beyond religious belief, Franklin faced a more fundamental problem with Whitefield. Namely, he knew what a good businessman the preacher was, and that he was no rube in negotiating a good rate for publishing his works. Indeed, the minister had converted the appeal of his message into brisk sales of his sermons and journals in Britain. This could be a very lucrative business too, since the printed words of clergymen often became best sellers in bookstores in Europe and the colonies, and the evangelical publisher James Hutton had achieved a signal success in gaining the exclusive right in Britain to publish the first Whitefield journal of his travels.

Franklin knew Whitefield had recently arranged for the publication of his sermons in serial form, sending subscribers a weekly sermon for the price of two pence over the course of twenty weeks. This clever arrangement locked in paying readers for the preacher's message and guaranteed him an audience. It also helped that he and his press agent William Seward had created a transnational publicity network to advertise his appearances, relying on letters to sympathetic preachers, handbills and public notices, and even ads in newspapers to rouse a growing audience to attend his revival events and purchase his tracts. In short, Whitefield was a businessman on par with even Franklin himself, and he had to cut a deal with him.

Franklin wondered how great an investment he could make in the preacher. Though he had achieved various recent successes, Franklin had also put his hard-earned cash into ventures that had foundered. From the colonial doctor who wrote of the "Disease of Virginia" to a divinity series by one Magnus Falconar, Franklin's would-be authors had failed to draw an audience for their subscription plans and had cost him no small amount of money. Would the same be true of Whitefield? He wasn't sure. But considering the stakes, he knew he had to cut a deal with Whitefield before Andrew Bradford did.

Even before the Grand Itinerant arrived in America, Franklin arranged a contract with his agents for their mutual benefit. While he would not get exclusive rights to Whitefield's sermons, Franklin would be able to offer his readers a chance to subscribe to their serial publication, and thus be given the first opportunity to own them. He would also be the primary publisher of Whitefield's journals, at prices five times that of the sermons, which would allow Franklin to capitalize on his investment if it bore fruit. If it did not, Whitefield would be yet another European attraction who failed to translate his success overseas, and Franklin's scheme would fail. But if he did succeed, Whitefield could become a transatlantic phenomenon and Franklin could pummel Bradford at the newsstand. It seemed like a worthy gamble.

On this way to America, George Whitefield felt sick in body and spirit. It had been more than two months since the Anglican priest had spied land, and the convulsions of nautical travel mixed with the frailty of his constitution had rendered him pallid and heaving. Few knew of his dire condition. He performed his duties, held public prayers, delivered the sacrament to the ship's crew, and shared with them the spirit of Christ in a great "love-feast." But in private he struggled, and not merely with infirmity.

He knew that as a man he was base and wicked, cursed with a "polluted, proud, and treacherous heart." Was this not the condition of all men? Scripture said it was, and he could never help but be reminded of his depravity, especially during those evenings in which he, risen from sleep, felt "inexpressible agonies of soul" that would last for several days "at the remembrance of my sins, and the bitter consequences of them." He recoiled at the memory of his youthful villainy, at the thought of the time before he was saved, and compared himself to Adam chucked out of paradise, or David convicted of adultery, or Peter denying Jesus. These thoughts plagued him, wrenched his stomach, and twisted his heart to despair. He knew he was a sinner and deserved to suffer.

The miseries onboard the ship lasted until late October, when he disembarked at Lewis Town, 150 miles from Philadelphia, his next destination. Upon his journey to that city, he felt his spirits improve as he traveled over the rough, pristine landscape—his constitution settled and delight rose in him, as the "remembrance of my humiliations is sweet unto my soul, and the freedom which God has given me over some darling failings, fills me with joy unspeakable and full of glory."

He spoke of God's grace to the inhabitants of the countryside and ate a meal at a humble tavern: unleavened bread, cider, and eggs. And he marveled at how his lord deigned to make his presence felt even in such low and mean conditions—"Amazing that the High and Lofty One that inhabiteth eternity should condescend to dwell in earthly tabernacles!" And with that, he filled his belly, had a restful sleep, and rose the next day to begin his deeper exploration of America.

Upon his further travels, he saw a great number of colonists, of varying rank and status, race and provenance, and especially religion and creed: Congregationalists, Baptists, and Presbyterians, among others. How teeming the country was with dissenters! In Britain they might have been made to answer for their beliefs, or restricted in their worship by the Crown. But here in Pennsylvania, they evaded any such punishment, and practiced their faith openly and without restriction. The much-persecuted Quaker sect even ran the colony, naming it after the father of one of their own, William Penn.

Such nonconformists rejected the teaching of the Anglican Church. In Britain that stance had made the government suspicious of them, and wary of their effect on the social order. The century before, the forerunner of Congregationalists—famously known as Puritans—had declared war on the king, executed him, crushed the state religion, and upended English society. When the Crown restored its power, it punished them for their transgressions.

Despite their reputation, Reverend Whitefield found a strange kind of sympathy for the dissenters. Though he was not one of them, he helped lead a reform movement in the Church of England that some called Methodism. Designed to purify worship and root out moral corruption, Methodists often found themselves enduring as much abuse as the dissenters. Anglican churchmen called them "young quacks" and fanatics, and they endured heckling and public scorn for their fiery preaching and challenge to the authorities. Whitefield wasn't a true dissenter, but he understood the meaning of the term, and spoke to the colonists as potential allies and genuine seekers of God's mercy. He resolved to preach to them all, regardless of sect. He would tell them of their sins and guide them toward the New Birth. He would be open and affectionate and accept these people without judgment or derision—or at least be kinder to them than they were toward each other.

The Americans did not worship in harmony. Whitefield had heard tell of their fearsome disagreements and bitter contests and knew the challenge of proclaiming the message of Christ here. Many shared his philosophy of Calvinism—emphasizing man's helplessness in the face of God's omniscient power—while others believed in free will, including many Anglicans and Methodists. But beyond theological divisions, practical matters also vexed American churches. Some parishioners might argue with their ministers over matters of long-held doctrine; others might challenge his salary or refuse to pay for his support; and still others might threaten to abandon their parish if they were insufficiently enlightened by him. As one wag said, this place was "heaven for farmers, paradise for artisans, and hell for officials and preachers." Yet Whitefield felt no fear in spreading the gospel here. He had convinced himself he could marshal the Holy Spirit and bring about a great revival in his travels. Philadelphia would surely be an excellent place to start.

His friend William Seward had spread the word of his journey, writing hundreds, perhaps thousands of letters to sympathetic men and women willing to hear the story of Whitefield. Mr. Seward sought out the colonial weeklies to provide reports of his travels, and at each stop along Whitefield's way, the crowds grew and the interest in his gospel swelled, until much of William Penn's colony yearned to see the Grand Itinerant in the flesh.

Whitefield gained approval to speak at Christ Church by the commissary of Pennsylvania, Archibald Cummings, who represented the local authority in the Church of England. Cummings received him civilly and offered Whitefield the pulpit, and for this he was grateful. How many bishops and other officials had locked him out of their churches in Britain? How many had kept him from conveying the word of Christ simply because he lacked his own parish? And how many times had he fought them, and had to preach in barns and fields, just to bring the gospel to the great mass of British sinners? He had lost count.

On November 8, 1739, Whitefield spoke at Christ Church. He delivered his homilies with the usual vigor, but there were more parishioners who longed to hear his gospel than there were seats to accommodate them. So after he spoke, hundreds of people demanded he address them in a grander forum more suitable to his reputation. And so Whitefield chose to speak outside, on a blustery Thursday evening. As he climbed the steps of the courthouse on Market Street, he looked out on a crowd of 6,000 people—half the number of the entire city. He had preached to greater numbers, but never in a place so unfamiliar.

They had come by word of mouth, hearing of the Itinerant's travels in the New World. They had come by way of broadsides scattered throughout the streets that offered the promise of salvation to those with a mind to be saved. They had come after seeing newspaper advertisements, or reading his sermons, or receiving letters from his emissaries, or just by dint of pure curiosity. They had come because they wanted to be transformed, illuminated, blessed, and entertained, and Whitefield knew he could not disappoint them. And so he did not.

He spoke without notes, gently at first, then rising in pitch and volume until his voice rang out over the assembled congregants. Some said he could be heard on the shore of New Jersey, others at least to the city wharves, clearly and without difficulty, hundreds of feet away.

He began to tell them the story of Abraham and Isaac, a familiar one to any Christian or Jew. But instead of dryly repeating the story's moral lessons, Whitefield surprised them. For as he stood before them, he spoke not as a preacher but as an performer, delivering lines written by God.

In his youth he had been a budding actor, and a skilled one indeed, performing various roles in school performances and immersing himself in the English stage. And though God directed him toward the ministry instead of the theater, he had preserved his talent, and Whitefield took advantage of the gift.

First he took the role of the stoic patriarch Abraham, unquestioning servant of the Lord, called by his master to do the impossible—"Take now thy son, and offer him up for a burnt offering."

This shocked Abraham. In the role, Whitefield reacted with terror at the thought of killing his own kin. He paused and trembled and wrestled with his faith, he became overcome with fear, and he resisted the holy command to murder. But he also trusted in God's wisdom, and in the end chose to prepare the sacrifice.

Then Whitefield became Isaac, knowing nothing, the picture of innocence being led to his death. Whitefield conveyed the boy's ignorance and confusion. Looking not much older than the boy himself, Whitefield inhabited the spirit of the child, a picture of fear and misery—asking to know why his father was taking him to a land three days' distant. The audience felt a chill.

And then Whitefield was the father again, whispering and crying out, with words describing how God demanded a lamb for slaughter.

With tears in his eyes, he said, "You are to be the lamb, my son!"

Abraham's emotions washed over his son, "Adieu, adieu, my son; the Lord gave you to me, and the Lord calls you away." He produced the knife and held it to the boy's throat.

Whitefield wept, his voice choked with emotion, his robes damp with sweat. He paused and let the terror of the moment sink in, the imaginary knife held to his own throat. The crowd held its breath, awaiting God's verdict.

Abraham clutched the knife and prepared the slaughter. But just as he moved to cut the flesh and make the offering—

"The angel of the Lord called unto him from heaven and said, 'Abraham, Abraham,'" in the sweetest and most powerful tones Whitefield could muster. Abraham answered, and the angel said, "Lay not thine hand upon the lad, neither do thou anything unto him; for now know I that thou fearest God, seeing thou has not withheld thy son, thine only son from me."

The audience gasped. Many in the crowd cried as he did, overcome with pathos, standing transfixed and silent in the face of his oratory. The story they knew all too well had become vivid and electrifying in the performance of this traveling preacher.

Before he concluded, Whitefield offered his thoughts on the story of Abraham. He praised the patriarch's decision to obey God, and he announced that the choice of Abraham was the choice all must make: whether to follow one's faith and accept the word of the Lord, or to follow one's conscience and reject it. But to devout Christians, there was really no choice. There was only the word of God, and nothing else. Faith and salvation were paramount, and no amount of questioning or equivocation could change that. And if God called a man to commit murder, he had to obey. If he listened to his conscience, he did not deserve to sit at the Lord's Table.

The crowd exploded with joy and exaltation. Whitefield had lit the fuse of revival.

Ben Franklin stood in the crowd at one of Whitefield's later sermons in Philadelphia and could hear his voice with clarion precision. He marveled at the minister's vocal stylings and skill in projection, and resolved to discover how many people might have heard his words. He moved back to position himself nearer the river and imagined the Itinerant to be in the center of a semicircle, with the distance between himself and the preacher as its radius. Allotting two square feet per each of the audience members, "I computed that he might well be heard by more than thirty-thousand"—five times the number of people actually present.

Franklin was delighted by the calculation, for it meant that Whitefield might well have drawn upwards of 25,000 people or more to his British sermons, as the press had reported, and could draw up to half that number in the more thinly populated cities of America. Franklin did the math and found it reasonable to assume that Whitefield's appeal would only broaden, and that the audience for the minister's sermons and journals could be huge. He might become as colossal a phenomenon in America as in Britain.

Franklin made plans to publish twenty-four volumes of Whitefield's sermons in two volumes, as well as the first two of his journals. Initial orders were brisk, and Franklin saw his faith in the firebrand justified. He would show his commitment to the gospel of Whitefield by featuring him regularly in the *Gazette*, in both news and opinion pieces, and by previewing each stop on his upcoming tour. This would feed enthusiasm for his appearances well before he ever arrived at a given city, hamlet, or coach stop.

This was one of Franklin's greatest entrepreneurial risks to date, and one of his largest investments of any sort. It would provide Whitefield with a forum far greater than any other preacher, or any colonist, had yet attained, and it would give Franklin a lucrative source of income and a clear advantage in his publishing war with his rival. Andrew Bradford would have to find his own Grand Itinerant.

Franklin was curious to meet this preaching dynamo, so he arranged a meeting in which they could discuss their shared interests and business affairs. Upon meeting Whitefield, Franklin found him to be much less imposing than he seemed from a distance. He was, to be sure, tall and stately, if a bit stooped over, with somewhat gentle features. He appeared soft and childlike, befitting his youth, and had a curious lazy eye that made him appear cross-eyed. This was, his followers claimed, so he could keep one eye on God and the other on the devil.

Whitefield's curious appearance and dramatic oratory, along with the growing number of female converts among his followers, made him a target for British critics. They claimed that with his soft features, effusive tears, and "clear and musical voice," he incarnated not the spirit of God, but any common woman. His adversaries in the church dismissed the "feminine" qualities of his ministry, and one Anglican church weekly even sniped, "Hark! He talks of a sensible New Birth—then belike he is in labour, and the good women around him are come to his assistance. He dilates himself, cries out [and] is at last delivered."

Franklin could not have disagreed more with such carping. In Whitefield's powerful ministry, Franklin saw a beacon of revival—the kind he encouraged. He sealed his business arrangement with the preacher in Philadelphia, witnessed more of his sermons, and delighted over "the extraordinary influence of his oratory on his hearers." He wrote, "it was wonderful to see the change soon made in the manners of our inhabitants; from being thoughtless or indifferent about religion, it seemed as if all the world were growing religious; so that one could not walk through the town in an evening without hearing psalms sung in different families of every street."

Whitefield stayed in Philadelphia for a week before beginning the next leg of his journey. He found during his travels around New Jersey, Pennsylvania, and New York—the Middle Colonies, as they were known—that word of his preaching had preceded him. When he returned to Philadelphia in late November, Franklin marveled at the spectacle the preacher brought with him to the pulpit, along with his sense of integrity. He seemed to be a fair and honest man, wholly committed to his revival efforts, and had the audacity to criticize the Anglican Church in which he was ordained. Such boldness incurred the wrath of high churchmen and reminded Franklin of his own struggles against the formal, hierarchical Presbyterian Church in which he had been raised.

Franklin had a broad and open-minded view of spirituality, and wrote, "I esteemed the essentials of every religion, and being to be found in all the religions we had in our country I respected them all." He detected a similar ecumenical spirit in Whitefield, evident from his ministry to all individuals—from Jews and Quakers to Congregationalists and Baptists—and his lack of hauteur, which so many other ministers from the high church in Britain seemed to have. All this made Franklin consider him an ally, as well as a friend. He even offered his home to Whitefield during one visit to Philadelphia: "You know my house, if you can make shift with its scanty accommodations you will be most heartily welcome. [Whitefield] replied, that if I made that kind offer for Christ's sake, I should not miss of a reward—And I returned, *Don't let me be mistaken: it was not for Christ's sake, but for your sake.*"

Upon getting to know the minister better, Franklin had learned his purpose was not simply to save souls. He also had a mind to raise donations for an orphanage he was planning to complete in the southern colonies. This seemed like a noble enough cause, and for Franklin it was the very defini-tion of charity and good-heartedness. But he could only wonder, why not Philadelphia instead? The Pennsylvania capital was surely a worthy spot to host an institution for indigent children, of which there were many, and it would help give the city a reputation for philanthropy and a generous spirit. But the preacher balked at such conventional notions. He would build his orphanage in the swamps of Georgia!

As Franklin saw the settlement of that forlorn colony:

> [T]he only people fit for such an enterprise, it was with families
> of broken shopkeepers and other insolvent debtors, many of
> indolent and idle habits, taken out of the [jails], who being set
> down in the woods, unqualified for clearing land, and unable to

endure the hardships of a new settlement, perished in numbers, leaving many helpless children unprovided for.

Only established a few years before, Georgia had begun as an experimental farming colony for its proprietor James Oglethorpe, but struggled to succeed in its early years. It was simply too isolated and too poorly sited—on the boundary of unfriendly Spanish Florida—for any but the most risk-taking farmers to want to live there. As for civilization of any sort, the colony was lacking. The culture, industry, and entertainments of British North America stopped at Charles Town (modern Charleston) in South Carolina and advanced no farther south.

Yet Whitefield persisted. He recalled the evangelism of his fellow Methodists John and Charles Wesley, who had come to Georgia several years before to convert souls and build a mission to the native Indians. Although they failed in their attempt, Whitefield respected their efforts. He followed their example and came to Georgia for his first brief trip to North America in 1738—but unlike them, he kept a foothold in it. He was now laying the groundwork for his institution, for which he had solicited money during his preaching tours in Britain. He would do the same in America and was already beseeching Pennsylvanians to open their hearts and pocketbooks for his great endeavor.

While Franklin could not be convinced that a Georgia orphanage was the best use of Whitefield's efforts, he was happy to help him raise funds for it. He published in the *Gazette* an article describing the various goods Englishmen had donated to the cause—everything from brass candlesticks, nails, duck and goose shot, to rugs and blankets, buttons and silk—and how the auction of those goods in Philadelphia would be used to support the orphanage. He had no plans to donate his own goods or money to the cause, of course, because the enterprise was clearly a fool's errand. Franklin even watched Whitefield ask for money from his congregants during one of his sermons, and "I silently resolved he should get nothing from me."

His resolve didn't last long. As he listened to Whitefield's oratory, Franklin quickly changed his mind and gave a handful of copper coins to his ministry. Upon further reflection, Franklin decided he had been miserly, and so offered up the silver coins as well. By the end of the sermon, the preacher's words had so moved Franklin that "I emptied my pocket wholly into the collector's dish, gold and all."

Another parishioner, knowing of Whitefield's power, had decided to protect himself against being lured into generosity and left his pockets bare before attending the sermon. By the end of it, he too was overcome with charity, and begged a neighbor to lend him money for the collection plate. The neighbor, however, was a Quaker known for his frugality. He responded, "At any other time, Friend Hopkinson, I would lend to thee freely; but not now, for thee seems to be out of thy right senses."

George Whitefield felt eager to explore America, and to find sympathetic Christians with whom he could discuss the workings of the Lord. The first opportunity came two days after his success on the courthouse steps in Philadelphia. He chanced to meet a wizened but influential figure of the Presbyterian Church, William Tennent. He was an "old, grey-headed disciple and soldier of Jesus Christ. . . . both he and his sons are secretly despised by the generality of the Synod." Whitefield enjoyed meeting a fellow pariah, for the established Presbyterian Synod was as much an adversary to Tennent as the established Church of England was to Methodist reformers like himself.

Through his conversation with Tennent, he began to appreciate that danger lurked not only in the darkness of the sinful human heart, but in the very churches of which they were ministers. Great scheming evil had polluted the hearts of men, and Tennent described how the wickedness of powerful clerics had abused good and honest Christians and had made them pawns in the grip of Satan. He told Whitefield that high churchmen of many faiths had allowed reason and religion of the mind to debase their thinking. They privileged morality, ethics, and good works over the singular faith in God that was the only true path to heaven. And such vile clerics dismissed the energy that Whitefield brought to the pulpit and the emotional bond he formed with worshippers. They mocked the New Birth and called Whitefield's converts "enthusiasts"—a grave insult suggesting frenzy and madness!

The words of Tennent struck Whitefield with force and made him realize dissenting Americans like this old man were engaged in spiritual combat throughout the Middle Colonies. Though Whitefield had brought words of joy and beauty to the New World, he now realized more was at stake.

He became convinced of the truth of William Tennent's words, and wrote, "Though we are but few, and stand alone . . . the Lord will appear to us, as He did for [Elijah], and make us more than conquerors."

William Tennent guided him to New Brunswick, New Jersey, to meet his son, Gilbert. A man a half-generation older than Whitefield, Gilbert Tennent was a controversial figure and well known among dissenters of the Presbyterian Synod. He and his father and his three brothers had fought for many years over the proper role of the Presbyterian Church, the education of its ministers, and the actions of those ministers to spread the message of Christ. It didn't take long for Whitefield to see Gilbert's power. He bonded with him immediately over matters of faith and "what God had done for our souls." Soon he became "my worthy brother" and a man deservedly among the greatest ministers in America, along with his other family members. "The devil and carnal secure ministers rage horribly against them."

Gilbert planned to introduce Whitefield to an army of dissenters and iconoclasts who had fought the doctrines of their respective churches—men whose expressions were hardened but who remained undaunted in the face of threats from clerical authorities. For years Gilbert and his allies had battled to bring the power of the New Birth to their parishioners, to melt their hearts in Christ and to enflame the next revival throughout the colonies. They had no use for church formalities and bureaucracies—not when a great war of the spirit was underway, not when the fate of souls lay in the balance. And they wanted Whitefield to aid them in their cause.

Whitefield, however, feared he would disappoint them. He struggled to summon the energy even to preach at times, let alone to battle the authorities in a land he barely knew. He often felt sick and violently ill, especially before his sermons, and had contracted terrible diseases onboard ships crossing the Atlantic and in unfamiliar places. Moreover, he had no idea that even when he spoke with a measure of success, the clerics of his own church were busy trying to undermine him.

For one, the commissary of Philadelphia, Archibald Cummings, who had allowed him use of Christ Church in that city, now plotted against him. In a letter to other Anglican officials, he claimed Whitefield was no scholar or gentleman, but was skilled mainly in "railing against the regular clergy" in promoting his causes. If he were not constrained, his menace might spread and encourage his listeners to behave with unhinged emotion and demonic energy. Whitefield threatened to bring about such lunacy in his followers, for he was "enthusiastically mad."

Whitefield did not at first realize he had been undermined. So when he came to ask Commissary William Vesey for the use of his Trinity Church in New York, Vesey ambushed him. Not only was he furious at Whitefield, he denied him use of his pulpit, and demanded to see his Letter of Orders in the church as well as his preaching license. Whitefield, however, refused to show him any of those things, which incurred the commissary's wrath even more. The high church official charged him with violating canon law by preaching without a license, and Whitefield felt cornered. He responded that Vesey himself violated canon law by frequenting low establishments like tavern houses, as everyone knew! The Grand Itinerant thus made himself a powerful new enemy.

Following Vesey's denial of the Trinity Church pulpit, another Anglican minister, Jonathan Arnold of Staten Island, added to the insult by publishing an open attack on Whitefield, whom he had just met. He went a step further than Vesey and called his theology and manners dubious, his ignorance and pride indisputable, and his attack on the clergy intolerable. He was nothing less than "an open enemy to religion."

Whitefield now saw the battle joined. It seemed as if the words of the Tennents had been proven true—there was a war underway within Christianity, and Whitefield would have to help fight it. In response, he criticized those who had received him in New York and later had his disparaging journal entries published throughout the colonies. He wrote, "What manner of spirit are the generality of the clergy possessed with? Is this the spirit of the meek Lamb of God? Are these the fruits of the Holy Ghost? . . . Their bigotry, if it was nothing else, in time would destroy them."

Whitefield began to voice these sentiments from the pulpit, too, denouncing sinners in high places, and the crowds welcomed his indictments. His feelings of persecution and oppression, of being threatened and cornered, of facing a growing list of enemies—all of it fueled his ministry and added to his power of his sermons, which now featured as much anger as they did joy.

The commissaries and other local church leaders clearly saw the danger of Whitefield, as did the Bishop of London, who oversaw Anglican churches in the colonies. They feared his methods as well as his message—especially his means of delivering it. Itinerancy held bad stock with the authorities, be they Anglican or Presbyterian or any other faith that valued organization and control. To them, parish boundaries dictated that only an officially licensed minister be allowed to preach in a given area; his parishioners would look to him for guidance in spiritual matters, and he would be free to interpret the Bible without interlopers challenging him on it. But men like Whitefield did just that.

Throughout Britain, he paid little heed to respecting such boundaries, and willfully intruded upon them. To the clergy, this was a violation of canon law, of proper order, of the very foundation of the Church. Yet Whitefield persisted—if he were denied a pulpit, he would find one for himself, whether it be in an old barn, or a desolate moor, or a barren field, or a graveyard. And his listeners would follow wherever he led them.

Now feeling as persecuted in America as he had been in Britain, Whitefield returned to the method he had perfected. If church doors were closed to him, his followers would rush to him en masse into fields and meadows or wherever he spoke. He would tell them to follow their heart, to allow the grace of God to invest and uplift them, and to confess and renounce their sins and accept conversion to the true faith. If he met resistance from authorities, he would persist. If the gentry refused to worship with the "lower orders," he would deride them. If parents tried to keep their children from him, he would tell the kids to "go to Heaven without them!" And if anyone called him a rouser of hordes and mobs, he would embrace the role. This made Whitefield a clear threat to the colonial order—which valued peace, reason, good conduct, and rigid hierarchy—and he reveled in it.

He spoke in a range of settings, from the grand Wall Street Presbyterian Church in New York, to an array of small towns and waysides. Anywhere from 1,000 to 3,000 people might show up, crowding the dirt lanes, the woods, the cemeteries to witness his gospel. And Whitefield had no problem speaking atop wagons or out of windows or balconies or even over tombstones to express his message of the New Birth and condemn those who resisted it. The souls from the city and the country flocked to him, as he tried to change what the Middle Colonists believed and how they expressed their faith.

All the while, his energy and power grew. Even if he felt his innards heaving or his soul wavering or his sins multiplying, he would still exhort his listeners with tears and sweat and energy and volume. Whitefield was a warrior in the pulpit, and his enemies had no sound defense when he invaded their turf.

In his New York travels, Whitefield had a kindred spirit to accompany him. Gilbert Tennent had been guiding him throughout the Middle Colonies, finding new allies for him to meet, and instructing him on local politics and controversies. Gilbert also fed his enmity for the established churches, until the two men were united as rebels in Christ against the unjust actions of their foes. To further express his feelings, Gilbert found a meetinghouse in which to preach, and Whitefield witnessed his friend in action for the first time. The sermon stunned him.

Gilbert spoke with gravity, strength, and conviction, his loud voice booming out across the hall. He wasted no time in attacking the enemies of God and those who tried to shackle his gospel. He fulminated against sinners and the enfeebled preachers that he claimed had corrupted the church. He made no gentle entreaties to his audience as Whitefield did; instead he made bold demands of them, questioning their courage and fidelity to Christ. And he not only requested, he outright demanded that those who preached the word of God experience it in their hearts. Whitefield realized he had "never before heard such a searching sermon."

The gospel of Gilbert Tennent shook Whitefield deeply. It made him recognize his own flaws and the gravity of his sins, and how much more he must do to advance the message of Christ. For Gilbert "has learned experimentally to dissect the heart of a natural man. Hypocrites must either soon be converted or enraged at his preaching. He is a son of thunder, and does not fear the faces of men."

Whitefield could not resist the man's message. He quickly learned to appreciate him not only as a friend, but as a teacher and a guiding light. "My soul was humbled and melted down with a sense of God's mercies, and I found more and more what a babe and novice I was in the things of God."

His first conversion had been in Britain, to the ministry of Jesus Christ. His second came in America, to the method of Gilbert Tennent. He realized he had been too soft on his listeners, too gentle against his nemeses, too mild when he should have been forceful—and he resolved to do better.

He would soon bring his own thunder to the pulpit.

TWO

THE WAY TO IMPERIAL HEAVEN

Gilbert Tennent carried the force of God. He was not God, but as he preached he could feel that power coursing within him—demanding sinners repent, castigating the wicked, proclaiming the glory of the Kingdom to come. Had his voice ever thundered with such clarity? Had his audience ever trembled before him with such fear? He knew they had not. For the moment had come in his crusade to purify the church. God had chosen this moment to send him a soldier—God had chosen George Whitefield to help him fight the war.

What a scene it had been when Whitefield spoke! He had somehow drawn 6,000 people to Germantown, Pennsylvania, for a rousing sermon that left people weeping for nearly two hours. Members of some fifteen different sects watched him orate, many of them Swiss and German who couldn't even speak English, yet who knew the power of the Itinerant's gospel. They nearly mobbed him after the sermon, describing their own conversions to Christ, and sharing their experiences as dissenters or nonconformists or outcasts. And Whitefield welcomed them all to the fold, as new Christians, new converts to the New Birth, new subscribers to his works, new friends in the New World.

Whitefield called his brand of devotion "experimental piety."

This was the religion of the heart in its full convulsive, cataclysmic power, offering the promise of salvation to sinners, showing the fire of Christianity—and aiding Gilbert in his struggle to defy the Philadelphia Synod and foment revolution in the church.

Gilbert's journey to rebellion had taken half a lifetime. In 1718 his father William had brought him and his three brothers to America from County Armagh in Northern Ireland, all of them refugees from the authority of the Church of Ireland, which was associated with the Church of England. They were part of a growing wave of Protestant newcomers—Scots-Irish like them, as well as Germans, Swedes, Dutch, Swiss, and others looking to practice their religion free from restraint.

While a settlement with the Crown had made Presbyterianism the established church of Scotland, in Ireland the British government still freely persecuted the sect. Presbyterians and other nonconformists could not hold public office, graduate from universities, teach school, or take part in other aspects of community life that members of the established church took for granted. William Tennent saw such policies as odious, and looked to America to practice his faith, since a distance of 3,000 miles gave him sufficient space from oppressive monarchs and high churchmen.

Even better for him, the establishment of the Church of England was weak in the Middle Colonies. Colonies like New York and New Jersey provided fertile ground for the rise of the Presbyterian Church, and within that denomination, immigrants from the British Isles came to dominate the most prominent synod, based in Philadelphia. It should have been a successful pairing between the Scots-Irish Synod and the Scots-Irish Tennents. But William Tennent became a pariah.

Almost as soon as he arrived in Philadelphia, his beliefs came into question. Members of the Synod questioned his sincerity and fitness to be a minister. The conflicts only got worse as the decades passed and the Tennent patriarch clashed with the official rules on the education and ordination of ministers, and the role of faith and revival in spiritual practice. He chafed at their regulations and simmered with anger at their treatment of him.

The leaders who vexed him came from the "Old Side," comprising Scottish and Irish immigrants who valued rules and conformity to Scottish standards above all else. They encouraged education in established colleges for theology, and rigorous examination of ministerial candidates to root out heresy. Men like William Tennent countered them on the "New Side." They were less willing to conform to church law and argued faith and conversion should be paramount, not grilling would-be ministers about how orthodox they were.

After years of fighting to deliver the gospel his way, William Tennent's frustrations had grown and his grievances had multiplied. He began to defy any doctrine he found disagreeable, and to challenge the authority of the church hierarchy. The Old Side did not speak for him—it spoke for the kind of hidebound, institutional religion that had crippled the souls of Europe. The religion of the New World had to be proud, assertive, and emotional, and reach depths of devotion that could never be attained with dry formalism. Tennent realized the only way to ensure that his kind of religion became the dominant one was to educate young pastors himself, as he saw fit. So he created his own school, called the Log College.

Built in the woods of Neshaminy, Pennsylvania, it was a school Ben Franklin described in the *Pennsylvania Gazette* as a log house measuring twenty-by-twenty feet, "and to me it seemed to resemble the school of the old prophets; for their habitations were mean. . . . From this despised place, seven or eight worthy ministers of Jesus have lately been sent forth." Among them were the Tennent boys, and especially Gilbert, the most promising of the siblings and certainly the most committed. Despite the meager conditions of his father's school, he gained an education in logic, philosophy, theology, Latin, and some Greek and Hebrew. The local Philadelphia presbytery granted him a license to preach at the age of twenty-two. He later found a pulpit in the New Brunswick presbytery in New Jersey.

Gilbert Tennent entered the ministry transformed. Guided by his father, he had not only learned the catechism of Protestant faith and Calvinism, he was reborn in Christ and found the experience overwhelming and irresistible. God demanded that Gilbert spread the gospel to all who would listen, and many who would not.

Gilbert could testify to the New Birth better than almost anyone. As he had experienced it, when the Lord wished to extend his grace to a miserable sinner and the sinner accepted that grace, the force of the Almighty devastated his heart, lacerated him, dissolved and crushed him. God rebuilt the heart and soul of a person—he didn't just tinker with his mind or persuade him salvation was a good idea. He overpowered him with force.

He had seen this in his brother John's conversion:

> His conviction of his sin, danger, and misery, was the most violent in degree, of any I ever saw. For several days and nights together, he was made to cry out in the most dolorous and affecting manner, almost every moment. The words which he used in his soul-agony were these, "O my bloody, lost soul! What shall I do? Have mercy on me, O God, for Christ's sake." Sometimes, he was brought to the very brink of despair, and would conclude, "surely God would never have mercy on such a great sinner as he was."

Yet John Tennent hardly sinned at all, except to lose his temper occasionally. So if God could level an innocent boy with such violent effect, what could he do to the heart of a committed sinner? Gilbert dared to imagine.

Throughout the 1730s, a spirit of antagonism grew in Gilbert, just as it had in his father. He had seen how the Old Siders repeatedly attacked and undermined the Log College. He had watched them try to thwart the ordination of his brother, Charles. And he had witnessed them drafting rules to prevent ministers like himself from preaching in vacant churches outside their jurisdictions, and how they kept his New Brunswick presbytery confined, shackled, and red-taped into submission. But despite their power, he would not yield to it. He had already faced the ferocity of the Lord, so he hardly feared breaking the rules of the Philadelphia Synod.

Gilbert asserted that his family's Old Side adversaries knew nothing of God or godliness. They preached from ignorance, cast rules from decadent wisdom, and neutered the beauty, passion, and terror of true belief. And when he looked out at the spiritual landscape of the Middle Colonies, everywhere he saw Pharisees. They were men of the cloth, wigged and robed, speaking eloquently upon matters both earthly and sublime. They praised good works and rational belief and proper conduct. They lauded the latest philosophies from Europe. They read books and professed knowledge and played the role of wise counselors of law, reason, and benevolence. And he was convinced most of them were going to hell.

Who were these men? Who had given them license to preach? And how many of them had riddled and corrupted the soul of the Presbyterian Church? These questions raised his righteous anger to a boil. And what of the souls of their parishioners? For the sake of good works and rationalism, their ministers were steering them toward damnation. He could not accept it. He would not abide it. He had been battling it since he had taken his vows.

Gilbert Tennent's own theology was just as combative as his views of the Synod. With evidence from his own conversion, he was certain that "no person became a true believer without first experiencing the terror of sin, the searching of the soul, and the resulting realization that one was not a Christian." Only through pain and misery could the path to salvation be found, and he accepted this idea as gospel.

From the Dutch Reformed minister Theodorus Frelinghuysen, who led revivals in the 1720s, Gilbert had learned to scare his parishioners out of their "presumptuous security" and into a state of fearful excitement. The examples were many:

- "Sluggish souls are overgrown with corruptions, deprived of the robes of the redeemers' righteousness, and can expect nothing but shame and contempt." That was the fate of lazy people.
- "Would it not cause intolerable pain to have one of your arms broken and crushed to pieces, and while the bones jarred and ripped against each other, to have it pulled off by the shoulder blade?" That was what sinning was like.
- "But is it not still more dreadful to have the breast dug and opened, and the heart that seat of life, and spring of motion, violently tore out of it, having first broke all these vital, bleeding cords, by which it was united to the body, and then to have the precordium (or skin that covers it) flayed off and the caul rent from it?" That's what happened when God became jealous.

Gilbert Tennent's reliance on terror became an essential and contro-versial part of his ministry. He laid out his dark view of humanity in the 1735 sermon, *A Solemn Warning to the Secure World, from the God of Terrible Majesty*, in which he identified righteous, complacent behavior as the fundamental sin against God, including "ignorance, negligence, self-love, inconsideration, pride, pretensions to perfection, palliatives for imperfec-tions, and false conceits to all Christian graces" and described the draconian punishments that awaited anyone who committed such sins, in vehement and scorching language. In short, "Men must be frightened out of hell with the law [of God] and lured into heaven with the gospel."

The Tennent family used deep-seated fear of the deity to keep their parishioners obedient to the gospel as they taught it. Other Calvinists also employed fear to control their congregants, but only Gilbert Tennent raised the practice to an art, inventing clever new ways men and women might be tortured for their errors, and describing such horrors in rich detail. As he described the path to salvation: "terrors first, comfort second."

He realized his message was grim, but he thought the earthly fears he aroused could not compare to the torture awaiting fallen souls in hell. He scoffed at his critics who preached tolerance and moderation: Why offer a salve for sinners when they needed to be horrified into compliance with God's law? If anything, he needed to preach more terrors, to save even more souls, to lift them out of base earthly depravity.

For all of its shock value, Gilbert found popular success with his ver-sion of the gospel. His published sermons appealed to a growing audience, who seemed to appreciate his lurid imagery and would pay a fair price for it. Some even enjoyed learning about the fate that awaited sinners in hell, which attracted readers who may not have witnessed his sermons in person and elevated him to be one of the best-known Presbyterian ministers in the Middle Colonies.

Notoriety, however, did not translate into success in his battles against the Synod. He remained another dissenting voice in a secondary presbytery in New Jersey, well away from the powerful pulpits of the major cities. He remained steadfast to the challenge, though, and began to see his earthly conflicts as a reflection in miniature of the cosmic struggle between Satan and God—a holy war in which he was a foot soldier. In one famous sermon, he praised "The Necessity of Religious Violence" and said, "We have a description of the way to the Imperial Heaven, and the violent take it by force."

He could not defeat Satan in battle, but he had more hope in his war against the church hierarchy. He had been sharpening his strategy for many years, planning his attack, and waiting for the right moment to unleash it. In November 1739, that moment came when George Whitefield arrived in America.

On his recent tour of the Middle Colonies, Whitefield had seen the spiritual landscape of America through the lens of the Tennent family. To the Itinerant it was a providential pairing; to the family it was part of a carefully cultivated plan. Thus, it was no accident that William Tennent had sought out Whitefield so quickly when he arrived in Philadelphia. He directed him to visit New Brunswick, and Gilbert not only befriended Whitefield there, he helped him navigate the Middle Colonies, where to go and whom to meet.

Most of the controversy of the trip focused on the Anglican preacher's clashes with commissaries like Jonathan Arnold and William Vesey, but Gilbert knew that, while Whitefield enjoyed delivering sermons in fields, he would still need proper meetinghouses to preach in and pulpits to preach from. And he had a few key dissenters in hand who could loan them.

Again, this was no accident. Pastors like Ebenezer Pemberton and Jonathan Dickinson weren't just friendly well-wishers who could open their churches to him. They were important members of the Synod whom Gilbert was trying to convert to the New Side in his battles against the hierarchy. The influential Dickinson had a reputation as a moderate and had called the harsh rhetoric of revivalists like the Tennents "a dead fly in the apothecaries ointment." Still, despite the criticism, Gilbert needed every ally he could find. Whitefield appeared at the perfect moment.

Pemberton and Dickinson came away impressed, even astounded, by the effect Whitefield had on his listeners. His marshaling of the Holy Spirit for the cause of worshippers' salvation was unprecedented and convinced them and other Presbyterian ministers that the momentum had shifted to the New Side, to the Tennents, in the growing conflict within the church.

An added benefit: While Presbyterian ministers like Gilbert were limited by church law to preach only in their presbyteries, Whitefield could preach anywhere he liked. The Grand Itinerant respected no boundaries and could spread his gospel—or that of the Tennents—into any place that had a spare church, barn, field, or cemetery. His potential was unlimited, and Gilbert could only imagine the possibilities now that he had so potent a weapon as Whitefield in his arsenal.

A few hundred miles away on horseback, George Whitefield felt a bit sad to have to leave his new friends in the Middle Colonies. Gilbert Tennent wrote to him, "your sermons have much confirmed the truths of Christ which have been preached here for many years." He wrote back, "I love and honor you in the bowels of Jesus Christ. You are seldom out of my thoughts." Whitefield hated to go, but he knew there was more work to be done, more souls to be saved, in the southern part of America. He was making his way down the Eastern Seaboard toward Georgia, to oversee the creation of his orphanage.

In the Upper South colonies of Virginia and Maryland, he found a stronger Anglican presence in community life, but in neither colony did his experimental piety draw the mass attention or the conversions he had seen in the Middle Colonies. Perhaps the locals had read about him in the colonial weeklies, but that didn't encourage more than a few hundred of them to turn up at meetinghouses where he spoke. The population was too scattered across the countryside to assemble in groups any larger.

He noticed his greatest appeal lay among dissenters, and his least among members of his own church. No doubt they had heard how he denounced the commissaries in the Northeast and railed against Anglican corruption. While nonconformists might enjoy this kind of rhetoric, it did not make him popular with his fellow clergymen. A few opened their doors to him, but more often he engaged in skirmishes with clerics who were unimpressed with his animated style and confrontational message, which only seemed to incite division and pit parishioners against one another for no clear reason.

One layman of the Church of England, Stephen Bordley, saw White-field preach in Annapolis. While taken by his good teeth, handsome presence, pleasant voice, and excellent pronunciation, he had harsh words for everything else: "[H]is language is mean and groveling, without the least elegance; and his method of discourse is ten times worse than his language, or rather he has no method at all." He found Whitefield's study of divinity suspect, his anticlerical attitude unfounded, and his rhetoric brutish. In short, "he is a very wretched divine. . . . If he is sincere, he certainly is a violent enthusiast. If not, he is a most vain and arrogant hypocrite."

Whitefield remained steadfast in the face of his critics, and he looked forward to seeing Georgia again, and escaping the Upper South as soon as he could. As he wrote in a letter to Gilbert, "in these parts Satan seems to lead people captive at his will."

He began to take a closer look at the landscape of the South and its social and racial divides. In the same letter, he came to realize "Here there are no great towns, as in other provinces, and the commonality is made up of Negroes and convicts" who faced abuse at the hands of their respective masters, and endless demands to work ever harder.

By the end of the year he pushed on into North Carolina, crossing on horseback over rivers and swamps swollen by winter rains, past meager townships and hamlets in the thinly populated colony, where he found more dancing masters than ministers. The Christian revival had not ignited here, and Whitefield's preaching didn't spark it. His heart sank to witness "what an indifferent manner everything was carried on."

Now isolated from his allies in the Middle Colonies and Britain, a spirit of desolation crept in. The old familiar doubts, the fears, the sadness were made worse by his spending Christmas in such a barren place. "I cried mightily to the Lord in my secret devotions, and in the afternoon when I read prayers and preached." A poor local woman's offer of a free holiday dinner cheered him up a bit.

Aside from the camaraderie of his traveling associates, he had few real friends and "virtually no local or private life," as he preached up to fifty hours a week. He could dispense homilies and biblical wisdom, but he found it difficult to share confidences with old friends or make new ones. And like other Methodist reformers, Whitefield felt uncomfortable with the idea of romantic love. He could praise a couple's shared admiration and worship of Christ, but anything further seemed to tempt carnality and moral depravity. He did become fixated on a woman, Elizabeth Delamotte, but agonized over his feelings for her, which seemed to invite physical desire, and that he could not allow. Still, since he could not be seen as a celibate priest, he soon proposed marriage to her in a letter. He offered that upon their matrimony, she would oversee the Georgia orphanage in his absence, and he would treat her "uprightly" like a sister, without resort to lust or physical indulgence of any kind. She rejected his proposal.

Whitefield reached South Carolina on New Year's Day, 1740, but his spirits did not brighten after a few strained encounters with the locals. At dusk he came to a tavern where a local woman danced a jig to lively folk tunes. The Itinerant informed her such activity was sinful and suggested "how well pleased the devil was with every step she took." He implored her and the musicians to abandon their frivolity with a lecture on their wantonness and ungodly behavior. He thought he had convinced them of their folly and went to bed, only to hear the same lively tunes and the stamping of dancers' feet once more. Their saucy defiance brought him to anger. He asked God to "suffer them not to go on in such a carnal security till they lift up their eyes in torment!" But petty curses brought him no satisfaction. He began to miss Pennsylvania dearly.

There was so much about these dark and treacherous bottomlands that he did not understand. The few people he met did not respond to the Lord's call with joy in their hearts. A great number of residents were either destitute and living off charity or bound to servitude and lives of misery. The Anglican gentry either reveled in idleness, or engaged in horse racing and pastimes like cockfighting and gambling, or gloried in gluttony and drunkenness. Human barbarity was a constant sight.

Masters reigned over their bondsmen with depraved cruelty, using severe punishment and outright torture to keep them in a state of terror. Even worse in Whitefield's view was the lack of spiritual instruction given to slaves, whose masters kept them from experiencing such sacraments as baptism and the Eucharist. They separated men from their wives, sold their children to the highest bidder, and debauched the very idea of marriage and the family. Such realities nauseated him and deepened his vow to bring the message of Christ to all men and women, be they slaves or free.

Yet Whitefield resisted any greater liberties for the enslaved. During his first trip to Georgia in 1738, he had argued slavery should be made legal—since it had been banned by the colony's trustees—to make the colony economically competitive. He differed with fellow Methodists John and Charles Wesley, who saw the practice as an abomination. Like most other Anglican ministers, Whitefield rejected the idea of abolition. Indeed, the few American churchmen who had done so were largely Quakers, and he would no more accept their idea of the equality of the races than he would their other "false and unscriptural" beliefs, which he criticized in his letters.

Moreover, Whitefield feared to encounter black people. In January at a South Carolina plantation, the owner offered him accommodation. In the vicinity he saw a "hut full of negroes," which scared him and made him quicken his pace, only to see "another nest of such negroes . . . and one of my friends at a distance observed them dancing round the fire." He decided these were the same sort of rebels who had launched an insurrection in the colony a few months before and were doubtless fugitives who might attack him and his friends, "in great peril of our lives." When Whitefield and company returned to the plantation, the owner assured them of their safety. It didn't matter—Whitefield thanked the Lord he had survived.

On January 10, he reached Savannah, Georgia, completing a journey on foot, on horseback, and by canoe over 1,200 miles—a rare feat for anyone, let alone someone preaching the whole way. Surprisingly, Whitefield's stamina only seemed to increase with his labors, and he intended to marshal his energy to build his orphanage, which he called Bethesda. He meant it to be an example of Christian charity, where destitute and abandoned children could receive shelter and nourishment while they worked on a plantation picking cotton. They would also receive five daily hours of catechism modeled on his own Calvinist theology. He thought it to be a fine solution to their material and spiritual poverty, and a worthy cause for which he had been raising funds for several years—the very essence of his public ministry.

Yet he encountered confusion and hostility as soon as he arrived. The trustees of the colony questioned his plans for religious instruction, accusing him of trying to raise servile youth for a Methodist ministry and causing problems for Anglican leaders. They also made little progress on building him a proper church in Savannah, where he was due to act as the parish priest. One trustee even thought Whitefield to be a raving, enthusiastic fool. All of it frustrated and enraged him. He threatened to denounce the trustees publicly for administering their colony so poorly and wasting his orphanage funds. They responded by calling him a menace.

The problems mounted: Whitefield could not escape his critics' demands that he provide an account of the expenses for his holy endeavor, how he had raised funds and where he had allocated them. In response, he provided a full list of contributors, but failed to break down how much had gone to his institution and how much into his own pockets, only showing debits for "sundry provisions" that were never detailed. His foes charged him with purloining the funds and stealing charity from the mouths of orphans. They claimed he was little more than a merchandiser of religion, a "retailer of trifles" and a "pedlar of divinity"—essentially a traveling huckster who fired people up, swiped their cash, and moved on to the next town before anyone wised up.

Such accusations only served to stiffen Whitefield's spine; he responded to his enemies with the same sharp language. He reasoned that if these bitter contests were meant to advance God's cause, then God's cause had prospered very much indeed. He wrote to an ally, "It often pleases me to reflect how Christ's kingdom is securely carried on in spite of men and devils."

Yet the battles had also given him a reputation as a troublemaker and demagogue as much as a healer and evangelist. He felt torn by the need to spread love in the pulpit and to rip apart his foes at the same time. In a letter to a fellow Welsh revivalist, he admitted the toll such conflicts had taken on him: "I have not had much enlargement in preaching, since I have been here; but my heart is often weighed down, and torn to pieces with a sense of my desperately wicked and evil heart. . . . I sometimes think my heart is more vicious and perverse than anyone's; and yet Jesus Christ will come and dwell in me." As long as the Lord granted him favor, he would continue to wage the war.

On his travels he found many targets for his criticism. British North America seemed to be a world riven into a small number of wealthy men, who dominated industry and society, and the beleaguered masses who suffered under their heel. It especially galled him that such men of means refused to contribute to charity—especially his—and instead hoarded treasure for themselves and their heirs. He laid out the case in a sermon, "The Great Duty of Charity Recommended," blasting the wealthy as a scourge in God's eyes:

> Our great men had much rather spend their money in a playhouse, at a ball, an assembly, or a masquerade, than relieve a poor distressed servant of Jesus Christ. They had rather spend their estates on their hawks and hounds, on their whores, and earthly, sensual, devilish pleasures, than comfort, nourish, or receive one of their distressed fellow creatures. . . . You will not be excused because you have had a great estate, a fine house, and lived in all the pleasures that earth could afford you; no, these things will be one means of your condemnation.

These elites might control the fate of the colonies and hold sway over societies and governments, but Whitefield told his parishioners that only made them subject to God's curse: "Go on now, you rich men, weep and howl for your miseries that shall come upon you: your riches are corrupted, your garments are moth-eaten, your gold and silver is cankered, and the rust of them shall be a witness against you, and shall eat your flesh as it were fire. . . . [These sins] shall be as a worm to your souls, and gnaw your consciences to all eternity."

Whitefield said that such elites were not found only in dancing halls and theaters, but in the churches themselves. He called out sin and corruption among the ministers of America, and especially in his own Church of England. It seemed even worse in places like Virginia and South Carolina, where even the church's establishment by law, and the duty of all citizens to support it financially, seemed to bear no fruit in converting people to Christ. In South Carolina, the planter Hugh Bryan even told him the writings of the theologian John Tillotson—a legend among Anglicans—had thwarted his understanding of the Bible; and Whitefield saw that many Christians followed his philosophy of good works at the expense of real faith.

Yet how could he counter such beliefs, with so many Anglican pulpits closed to him? The local church in Charles Town, St. Philip's, had barred him from speaking there when he visited in January, and other institutions would doubtless follow its example. However, it was the Carolinians, perhaps more than any other colonists, who he felt desperately needed to hear his words. He resolved to try to preach again, with more vigor, when he revisited South Carolina in March 1740.

He found the environment in Charles Town more combustible upon his return. Dissent had begun openly breaking out in nonconforming pulpits against the dominance of Anglicanism. The old patrician gentry were uneasy with the waves of newcomers, among them French Huguenot Protestants driven out of Europe, and new Baptist and Congregational churches took root in defiance of official rules. Adding to the tension were recent smallpox and yellow fever epidemics, an economic recession, and the looming memory of the previous year's Stono Rebellion, in which one hundred slaves fought for liberty and against inhuman conditions, killed twenty whites, and met defeat at the hands of the colonial militia. For those rebels not executed in battle, the authorities had their heads cut off and placed on pikes along roadsides as a warning to other slaves who wanted to flee their bonds.

The colonial hierarchy, then, was in no mood to compromise with Whitefield. His bellicose words threatened the church hierarchy. His racial sympathies threatened plantation owners. His appeal to the masses threatened the caste system. And his denunciation of gambling and dancing threatened the pleasures of the elite. Not surprisingly, his rise to fame alarmed several powerful figures in the southern colonies—and few were as powerful as Alexander Garden.

The commissary of South Carolina, Garden had received Whitefield cordially in 1738, when they first met. Whitefield came away impressed by his fortitude, describing him as "a good soldier of Jesus Christ." Since March, however, Garden had been using an assumed name to condemn the Grand Itinerant in the *South Carolina Gazette* as a threat to the colonial order who trafficked in the ignorance of his parishioners and exploited division to achieve public acclaim. He claimed he judged others harshly who differed with him, preached dubious theology, and abused scripture to serve his own ends. Worse, Garden was known for his rapier wit, being as "conservative as Dr. Johnston [sic], as vehement as Swift, and as satirical as only a Scot in poor health can be." For once, Whitefield hadn't crossed swords with a blundering functionary; he had angered one of the church's sharpest and most caustic minds, who wished to see his name blackened, and his reputation destroyed.

Whitefield felt stunned by Garden's accusations. Had he not accurately represented the gospel of Jesus Christ? If he launched a diatribe on occasion from the pulpit or raised his voice in support of the Lord's agenda, then surely he could not be blamed for it. After all, Whitefield reasoned, his foes within the church were the ones who had twisted the message of Christ. They dismissed the beauty of the New Birth and said it produced "an arrant jumble of contradiction and confusion" that may have owed to "a warm, frantic, enthusiastic brain." But the Itinerant knew that such a deep and emotional connection to God was the only valid one, and to think otherwise made one a Roman Catholic, a Deist, or a lunatic.

When Whitefield met Garden again in the latter's home, the accusations only mounted, this time with increased venom, and to his face. The commissary called him an enthusiast, a troublemaker, an inciter of disorder, and a preacher of false doctrine. Garden's rage stemmed not only from Whitefield's attacks on the clergy, but from his dismissal of Anglican protocol like following the Book of Common Prayer for church services. Instead of obeying tradition, Whitefield disregarded the book and preached whatever he felt like. Garden threatened him with violations of canon law and barred him from preaching in any church in the colony. Whitefield told him he gave any such command the same respect as an edict from the pope.

Whitefield added to the insult by questioning why Garden had allowed decadent public balls and "midnight assemblies" to occur in Charles Town instead of censuring them. The commissary said he saw no harm in such amusements. In return, Whitefield vowed to speak against such sinful frivolities, and to denounce Garden publicly for encouraging them.

The commissary responded, "Get you out of my house."

It should have been a shameful moment, but Whitefield didn't see it that way. Instead he felt pity for the commissary, as well as a sudden jolt of energy. Invigorated by the confrontation, he accepted the invitations of Congregational and Baptist ministers to preach in their meetinghouses and to speak truth to their worshippers. He felt God's power running through him, and it only deepened his commitment to fight the Anglican power structure and authorities like Alexander Garden with every spiritual tool he had.

Whitefield felt so confident of his righteousness that he even attended church where Garden preached and listened to the commissary denounce him as a Pharisee from the pulpit. Garden claimed the Itinerant placed himself above other men, and thanked God for his elevation over them. In short, he was nothing less than a smug hypocrite.

The words stung Whitefield, and made him physically ill—but it would take more than insults to crush his spirit. He would remember all the slanders of his enemies, all their baseless charges and tyrannical behavior, and in his journals he would let the rest of the world know about it. But Garden too would find success on the public stage, and in Whitefield he would discover an ideal target for everything he thought wrong with the growing revival.

In Philadelphia, Benjamin Franklin had found success publishing the works of George Whitefield far beyond his expectation. Even as the preacher struggled in the South, his presence still loomed large in the Middle Colonies—and readers of Franklin's publications could hardly avoid it. By spring 1740 Franklin had brought to the public almost everything the Grand Itinerant could produce: descriptions of his church services, reprints of his sermons, ads for his books and treatises, and his increasingly popular journals. Franklin made sure three-quarters of the *Pennsylvania Gazette*'s issues included at least a mention of the Itinerant, and he devoted one-quarter of the column text to him and featured him on the cover no fewer than eight times. It was remarkable, for the *Gazette* had hardly featured religion before Whitefield arrived in the colonies, and news of the British priest now dominated it.

Franklin knew that Whitefield, despite his rigid theology, had built his appeal on the comfort he brought to his audiences, the drama of his oratory, and the simplicity of his Bible narratives—and his readers could not resist it. Subscribers had made Franklin's gamble an unquestioned triumph, with 2,500 volumes ordered in the colonies, and some buyers ordering full sets and multiple copies. He had never seen anything like it and was delighted that fortune had once again favored his enterprise.

The investment in Whitefield also broadened his advantage over Andrew Bradford. While Franklin had shown the foresight to cut a deal with the Itinerant when he appeared in the colonies, Bradford had hesitated, and only printed two of his sermons after he arrived. *The American Weekly Mercury* not only failed to showcase Whitefield's revival tours, it focused on the attacks of his critics. Franklin had no such desire to print such vitriol, and instead smothered his pages with news of the revival. A few wags even said Franklin acted as a sort of press agent for Whitefield, instead of maintaining an independent view. At first, Franklin ignored such claims, but when his bias became too obvious, he was forced to deny the charges.

On May 1, for example, the *Gazette* printed a story from Whitefield's publicity agent William Seward in which he claimed he had quelled the "devilish diversions" of a music and dancing troupe in Philadelphia because the public no longer approved of such amusements. In fact, he had rented the troupe's ballroom in advance and locked it without their permission, then claimed he had done the Lord's work by imploring the dancers to quit their revels. In any case, the performers' season had actually ended and they in no way intended to be swayed by the hectoring of the minister's press flack. The hall's owner condemned Seward's "low craft" of a publicity stunt to "spread his master's fame" and other critics of Whitefield's eviscerated the false account in the *Gazette*. Franklin retorted with a hairsplitting defense of his actions: "the article is allowed to be literally true, yet by the manner of expression 'tis thought to insinuate something that is not true." This convinced no one that Franklin and Whitefield weren't in cahoots.

Indeed, Franklin's bias was impossible to hide. For not only was religious news pushing out current events and political stories, Franklin had lessened the amount of ink he gave to the innovative novels, ideas, and philosophies of the day—the very fruit of the Enlightenment. He saw the public preferring "books of piety and devotion" over secular tomes, and psalms and hymns over "idle songs and ballads." Since November, the revival had spread even further into Pennsylvanian life, invigorating religion in a way Franklin had never seen, and he meant to take advantage of it.

The New Birth had unquestionably altered the fabric of colonial society. Inspired by Whitefield, many congregations offered their pulpits to ministers who could bring drama to their sermons. Other parishioners questioned why their own pastors couldn't preach in a more vigorous manner. Were they afraid to talk about about their relationship to Christ? Why couldn't they express their devotion with greater passion, or describe how God had changed their hearts? Why couldn't they be more like the Grand Itinerant?

Franklin appreciated the spread of the movement. It inspired better behavior and made people more virtuous. But he stopped at the New Birth. He would no more convert to the revival than he would renounce the money he had made from it. Yet Whitefield kept trying to make him change his mind. "Apply to God," he wrote to him, and "be willing to do the divine will, and you shall know it."

Franklin wasn't surprised at Whitefield's persistence. He knew the Itinerant would "pray for my conversion, but never had the satisfaction of believing that his prayers were heard." Mysteries like the Incarnation of Christ, and dogma like predestination and justification by faith, did not interest Franklin as matters of belief, and in any case had nothing to do with his quest for perfect moral conduct, in which Jesus was a model, not a messiah.

Although Whitefield's demands for Franklin to convert were met with indifference, the printer had to admit the preacher appealed to him. He saw him as a worthy fellow, a trailblazing spirit, and a pillar of high-mindedness. And he felt the friendship growing between them. Their bond transcended religion, and profits, and cynicism. Upon Whitefield's visits to Philadelphia, he would be a guest in Franklin's own home, and the printer was happy to introduce him to his family and friends, or to anyone who might need to hear a good word or two.

How different this clergyman was from the others he had known. Instead of offering bombast and pretension, Franklin found Whitefield to be a genuine man of the cloth and a philanthropist. His ideas of salvation were not palliatives meant to soothe the consciences of rich and powerful men. Instead they applied to everyone, including many people so often ignored in holy discourses: women, orphans, the poor, and especially slaves. Franklin appreciated the broad scope of his friend's ministry, even while he recognized Whitefield's limits—as well as his own.

Franklin was no abolitionist. He owned several slaves in his early life and advertised them for sale in the *Gazette*. However, he acknowledged the ugliness associated with the practice, especially in his private letters. In January, Franklin learned the preacher had written a public letter, addressed to the residents of the South, that had incensed the plantation owners there because he condemned the barbarity of slavery.

> [Some slaves] have been, upon the most trifling provocation, cut with knives, and have forks thrown into their flesh: not to mention what numbers have been given up to the inhuman usage of cruel task-masters, who, by their unrelenting scourges, have ploughed upon their backs, and made long furrows, and, at length, brought them even to death itself. . . . And, though I pray God the slaves may never be permitted to get the upper hand, yet, should such a thing be permitted by Providence, all good men must acknowledge the judgment would be just.

Whitefield cursed the slave owners just as he cursed all powerful and greedy men. Indeed, ever since the Itinerant's tour of the Middle Colonies, he had grown quite belligerent toward his foes, and his critiques went beyond doctrine or theology. They cast doubt into many corners of American life and threatened to undermine the social order and civility that Franklin had worked so hard to advance.

Along with the wealthy planters, Whitefield attacked the religious authorities with a newfound ferocity. He no doubt remembered what Alexander Garden had said about him—and from the pulpit no less!—and planned to lacerate any clerics with similar ideas. In a recent winter sermon in Savannah, he had described his fellow clergymen as "slothful shepherds and dumb dogs" for their poor theology, and around the same time, he made his greatest attack yet—on an icon of the Church of England.

Franklin learned Whitefield had targeted Archbishop John Tillotson. This was no humble pastor, but a well-known theologian who had died a half-century before, whose writings were more influential to the church and sold more copies to missionaries than any other volumes aside from the Bible itself. They exalted human reason and wisdom, guided parishioners to pursue good conduct and morals, gave a thoroughly Anglican understanding of the sacrifice of Christ, and steered away from Calvinist ideas like justification by faith alone.

To Whitefield this doctrine was anathema. In traveling throughout the colonies, he learned of the still-great influence the late archbishop wielded over the church and resolved to undermine it. In several letters, sermons and a pamphlet, he took aim at Tillotson in the most bracing and uncompromising language he could muster.

He said Tillotson's theology was specious and his followers "have built their hopes of salvation on a false bottom" of anti-Christian "sorceries." His works did not convert a single soul amid their "false divinity and fundamental errors." He had no knowledge of God's grace, of original sin, of justification by faith, or any other holy truths, and he "knew no more of true Christianity than Mahomet." He was, in short, a fraud, and no true believer should have anything to do with reading his books or praising someone who was "no real Christian at heart."

Such an attack troubled Franklin. For this was no mere dead clergyman with equally dead ideas. He was someone who provided rational spiritual guidance to countless people, who blended faith with reason, and brought hope to many—including Franklin himself. Some of the archbishop's quips Franklin used to illustrate a point (such as "I never knew any good to come from the meetings of priests") and his very mission aligned with Franklin's own: exhorting good moral conduct, respecting the mystery and beauty of divine creation, allowing for the value of good works as well as faith, and rejecting severe and intemperate philosophies. In fact, Franklin "admired Tillotson more than any other theologian."

But what to do about Whitefield's attack? It was clearly uncharitable, for the spirit of Tillotson was peaceable and did not invite abuse of that sort. It was also misdirected, for it was less about Tillotson than it was about the churchmen who admired him and belittled Whitefield. And it was unabashedly self-promoting, as Whitefield himself admitted: "You may make what use you will of it. I care not if the contents are published upon the house top." The material had already been published in Charles Town, where it had caused a stir within the church, and Whitefield had plans to publish the screed in London and New York, and would doubtless want it printed in

Philadelphia as well. In sum, it would be a verbal assault on someone revered by the church of which Whitefield was a minister, and would thus guarantee a sizable audience for the Itinerant's visit to the Middle Colonies in April.

Franklin knew the anti-Tillotson tracts would be hugely profitable, but would also run directly counter to his own ideas. They would expand the audience for Whitefield's sermons and journals and make him into a publishing sensation without compare. They would also influence countless people to reject reason, logic and a hospitable faith in the Lord and replace it with uncontrolled emotion, anger, and passion. Franklin recognized the stakes of his decision, whether to publish the material, and was torn between devotion to his philosophy and promotion of his business. But in the end he did the only logical thing. He chose the latter.

On April 10, Franklin gave the entire front page of the *Gazette* to the Tillotson attack. He followed with another full-page display two weeks later, and bound the articles, the pamphlet and other material into a single volume that he sold to his readers soon after. With Whitefield's return to the Middle Colonies imminent, the public response was an unprecedented success, as Franklin knew it would be. A firestorm erupted between the Church of England and its detractors, with Whitefield as the spark—and the beneficiary. The slandering of John Tillotson made for good business, and excellent publicity for the coming season of revival.

In fact, Whitefield's latest controversy might have been the only thing most Pennsylvanians would have wanted to talk about, if not for the uproar Gilbert Tennent had already unleashed in their colony a few weeks before.

THREE

INCREDIBLE RHAPSODIES

Gilbert Tennent needed more soldiers to fight for the New Birth. He had zeal and passion on the New Side, but not enough believers to transform his battles against the Presbyterian elite into a full-scale war. So he came to Nottingham, Pennsylvania, to support the work of the Reverend Samuel Blair, a graduate of the Log College who had achieved a measure of fame for his inspired evangelism. Blair had recently led a revival in Londonderry Township, in the heart of the conservative southwest part of the colony, a stronghold of Scots-Irish Old Siders and named after a city in Northern Ireland. Despite the region's hostility to the revival, Blair had worked his magic here, bringing his parishioners to fits of weeping and fainting, and experiencing "unusual bodily motions" under the influence of the Holy Spirit. Word had spread into New York and New Jersey about the wonders Blair had effected, and numerous revivalists traveled to the region to discover more about it and spread the flames however they could. If their crusade could triumph in this region, it could work anywhere in the Middle Colonies.

Nottingham was a test case: twenty miles from Londonderry, it lacked a minister after the previous one had died and was split between rival

Presbyterian factions. Many people seemed ripe for swaying to the New Side, but still maintained ties to the traditional church and its respect for order and hierarchy. Gilbert wanted to change this. He knew the power of the revival lay in its emotional appeal, tapping into people's deepest hopes and fears, their ecstasy and misery. He could not deploy subtle logic and meticulous theology to win them over; he had to overpower them with the strongest force he had. And on March 8, 1740, he delivered it.

Most of the Nottingham worshippers had never seen a preacher quite like him. He rose to the pulpit not wearing a wig and clerical robes, but sporting a huge coat that was tied in the middle with a leather girdle, his hair flowing freely. His striking, untamed appearance made him resemble a "New Testament prophet of Christ's coming," not unlike John the Baptist. And like the oracles of old, he cast a dramatic spell over his audience.

He began by telling them he knew he was going to stir up trouble and wasn't happy about it. In fact he was quite sad, riddled with "grief for the injuries that have been done to the Church of God by natural ministers, that has extorted such acrimony from my pen." He could not be blamed for the terrible words he was about to speak; his foes drove him to it.

He turned to a familiar theme: the depravity of his enemies: "An ungodly ministry is a great curse and judgment: These caterpillars labor to devour every green thing." Those who had fought against the gospel of the revivalists were no better than insects. He also compared them to the "heaps of Pharisee-teachers" from the Bible who taught wisdom and law, but rejected Jesus. They might be educated, they might hold powerful offices, but "they had no experience of the New Birth. O sad!"

Gilbert was just getting started. He pitched his voice to a commanding tone and harrowed his audience with the horrors of sin. He told them the enemies of Christ were the *unconverted ministers*—those who had not been reborn like himself. Like the Pharisees, these vile men were "polished with wit and rhetoric" and marked with their "zeal, fidelity, peace, good order, and unity." But none of those things guaranteed salvation, only uncompromising faith in God.

He issued a list of the blasphemies he blamed for the decline in modern piety: the emphasis on rationality and logic, and the celebration of ethics and good works as a way to achieve salvation. Enemy pastors promoted such heresies in their teachings, which "are cold and sapless, and as it were freeze between their lips. . . . They have not the courage, or honesty, to thrust the nail of terror into sleeping souls."

But if they would not, Gilbert was happy to. He pushed the nail of his argument into the heart of his listeners and celebrated the turmoil that resulted. He told them it was a myth that Jesus brought tranquility to the world. No, Gilbert said, "our blessed Lord informs us that he came not to send peace on earth, but rather a sword, variance, fire, and division, and that even among relations." Jesus was a warrior, and so was Gilbert Tennent. That gave him license to fight a war for the imperial heaven.

Gilbert now thundered at the congregation. He accused his foes in the church of being "doubtlessly damnably wicked in their manner of performance, and do deserve the wrath and curse of a sin-avenging GOD." These enemies of Christ were everywhere—among them in the pews, preaching from pulpits, walking in the street—and faithful Christians must learn to identify them: "While some are sincere servants of God, are not many servants of Satan under a religious mask?"

Your neighbor could be a friend of God or an agent of the devil. Even worse, your dutiful minister, who preached at your community meeting-house where you had been baptized and took communion, might very well be hell-bound himself. So it was *your* responsibility as a Christian to judge between the saintly and the damned, especially those in high pulpits. "Does not the spiritual man judge all things? Though he cannot know the states of subtle hypocrites infallibly; yet may he not give a near guess[?]" Gilbert didn't have to guess; he knew who the damned were.

Devout Christians should demand nothing less than that their leaders be reborn! They should inquire into the condition of their pastors' souls, and reject them if they were found lacking. The old wicked unredeemed ministers should be cast out and replaced with fresh new ones who had been reborn—even if those ministers had just wandered into their parishes as itinerants, without seeking permission.

He concluded that the pious should no more spend time in the meetinghouses of false ministers than they should in the company of the devil. With this, Gilbert encouraged his listeners to flee the churches of those who opposed the revival, and to "let those who live under the ministry of dead men, whether they have the form of religion or not, repair to the living where they may be edified."

Thus Gilbert Tennent launched his greatest salvo against the Old Side, and he did so in Nottingham, well outside his own presbytery. Almost immediately, his powerful message and bracing imagery made the sermon famous. When word got out he had compared his enemies to corpses, devils, bugs and heathens, many in the established church were aghast. But more damaging they thought was how he goaded parishioners to cause trouble in the pews: to demand a level of holiness most ministers did not have, to reject well-qualified pastors who hadn't been converted, to embrace the traveling preachers who spread conflict and division, and to undermine the entire clerical system by abandoning their parishes.

The Old Side despised Gilbert Tennent and how he used the Bible as a weapon. They also feared the discord he had brought to the church, and in recent months had been making small concessions to repair some of the damage. But now they could no sooner turn away from Gilbert's challenge than they could accept his demands for all ministers to be reborn in Christ. They would fight him church by church, measure for measure, because they had no choice after Nottingham. Even the title of Gilbert's sermon was a clear threat: *The Danger of an Unconverted Ministry*.

The dissension in the pews emboldened Gilbert, and his increasingly aggressive preaching forced his audience to take a side. He had already adapted the style of George Whitefield to heighten the dramatic power of his words, and those words now echoed throughout the Middle Colonies. He imagined his influence only growing later in the spring when Whitefield planned to join him for a spring revival tour: What momentum they would have with the newly returned Itinerant in tow! And he looked forward to the *Danger* sermon finding a fresh new audience later in the year, when Ben Franklin published it throughout the colonies.

George Whitefield returned to Pennsylvania in April 1740, welcoming a respite from the hostile climate in the South and eager to see his friends again. The timing was opportune, for Ben Franklin had just published his attack on Archbishop Tillotson. *The Pennsylvania Gazette* fed the controversy and forced colonists to take sides in the battle between Whitefield and the Church of England. Was the Itinerant justified in shredding the reputation of an esteemed cleric who couldn't defend himself? Or had he finally gone too far? Such questions not only pitted people against each other, they made for excellent publicity for Whitefield's next round of colonial travels.

He spent ten days in and around Philadelphia and found that his appeal to the crowds had not diminished since the previous November. Some of his allies had even erected a stage for him upon Society Hill, where he could preach to some of the largest crowds he had ever seen in America. Depending on the day, 15,000 or even 20,000 worshippers came to hear him orate about the New Birth and the glory of souls "graciously melted" for Christ.

Whitefield had great plans for Pennsylvania. One of them involved a project north of Philadelphia that he called Nazareth. On 5,000 acres of land, he looked to erect a school and housing for slaves, which German Moravians—dissenting immigrant Christians—would build after they relocated to the tract. He envisioned it as an island of godliness in the wilderness, and his biggest enterprise yet. He sent his agent William Seward back to England to arrange financial matters for the new project and enlisted the aid of evangelicals in the region who wanted to assist him. But not everyone was pleased by his plans for the colony, or by his presence.

He had no sooner set foot in the City of Brotherly Love than he found a former friend had become an enemy: Archibald Cummings, the city's Anglican commissary who had once allowed him use of Christ Church, now barred him from the pulpit and expressed his disdain for the Itinerant's message and the way he delivered it. Whitefield was surprised to hear such a complaint. Hadn't he been forthright in his opinions and civil in his differences with the likes of Cummings and other officials? Indeed he had, but he had also attacked the wrong archbishop in John Tillotson, and thereby lost all credit with Anglican authorities.

Commissary Cummings was happy to advertise his changed feelings. Through Andrew Bradford, he published a pamphlet entitled, *Faith Absolutely Necessary, but Not Sufficient to Salvation Without Good Works*. He condemned the idea that faith alone would allow Christians to jettison good works and moral behavior—"What wild, distracted notions are these? Into what dangerous mazes may they lead well-meaning credulous souls?" He accused Whitefield of besmirching a good man in Tillotson, and violating his vows: "Such vile and slanderous invectives are crimes doubtless." And for the first time, a man of Cummings's stature warned of the contagion that might envelop parishioners overcome by the zealots of the New Birth:

> Some they have made stark mad, they have set the nearest and dearest relations at variance, disturbed the quiet of families, nay thrown whole neighborhoods and parishes into confusion by casting like Solomon's madman, firebrands, arrows and death; nay disgorging themselves in flames of fire and brimstone; threatening Hell and everlasting damnation against all, that would not implicitly believe their incredible rhapsodies.

It was as sharp and damning an attack as Whitefield had yet seen in print. But the challenge did not sway him; it only strengthened his resolve and increased his power. He wrote, "Little do my enemies think what service they do me. If they did, one would think, out of spite they would even desist from opposing me." His battle with his own church only made him more popular on the revival circuit and gave credibility to his mission among the dissenters who had become his closest allies.

In his *Journals*, he wrote passages designed to enrage his critics further, adding even bolder invective against John Tillotson: "I do not despair of seeing people bring his works, as they once brought the books of curious arts [i.e., sorcery], and burn them before all men." With Whitefield thus comparing the archbishop to a necromancer, he set out to meet the Tennents.

He visited the elder William Tennent in his Neshaminy meetinghouse and preached to some 5,000 people there. He felt honored to testify to the glory of God in one of the tinderboxes where the revival had been enflamed. Afterward, Whitefield continued on to eastern New Jersey and greeted Gilbert Tennent and a few other allies. With his *Danger* sermon, Gilbert had achieved the status of pariah among the Presbyterian hierarchy, and some of his associates had become even more despised than he was. One of them was John Rowland, to whom the Philadelphia Synod had denied ordination, but who had been ordained anyway through Gilbert's defiance.

Rowland and other rebels had waited years for their moment to upend the church, and Whitefield's grand tour of America gave them the opportunity.

Thus, the Itinerant wasn't just fighting a battle within the Church of England; he was waging a war by proxy among the Presbyterians. Every tract he published, every speech he gave, could be seen as a salvo in these conflicts. The arguments that ensued raged in print and in the pulpits and often became as petty as they were exhausting.

After multiple rounds of fending off the attacks of his enemies and launching his own, Whitefield came to realize all of this emotional labor had done foul things to his health. He frequently found himself ailing and laid up in bed, sometimes convulsed in body, other times in spirit. He began to have a hard time buoying his energy, and flagged in the spring heat, fatigued from his duties and in need of sleep. Sometimes it was difficult even to mount the stage to deliver his homilies, but inevitably he felt the Holy Spirit pulling, dragging him forward.

He also felt antagonism curdling in his heart. Whether due to poor health or the influence of the Tennents, his spirit took a bilious turn by the end of April. As he wrote to a friend in London, he had become disgusted by all the adversaries he was collecting in America—"[c]ovetous, proud boasters, self-willed blasphemers," among other wretches who rejected his mission. He said such men had sowed strife and division, and he had merely defended himself from their onslaught, but his moderation would soon cease. As he wrote, "I abhor controversy and disputation; but *my Master's glory now calls me to be more explicit than I have been yet.*"

He condemned the clergymen who locked their church doors to him and forced him to preach in fields and barns. He spoke against the "bigoted, self-righteous Quakers [who] now also begin to spit out a little of the venom of the serpent . . . One of their head teachers called original sin original nonsense." He even attacked his dissenter allies, who could speak well of Calvinist theology, "but never truly *felt* it in their hearts." He knew they had sinned as much as anyone, but if he dared to critique their devotion, they "*shoot out their arrows, even bitter words.*"

Again he felt alone, stranded in a strange continent, surrounded by adversaries, at war with the agents of Satan and the ignorant and the depraved and the doomed. But he knew such opposition could be a source of comfort, and proof of his valor. He would not relent; he would not retreat; and, yes, he welcomed their enmity. For "the more I am opposed, the more joy I feel."

He shared this joy of confrontation with the Tennents. Only they seemed to fully grasp the stakes of the battles they fought and the spiritual campaigns they waged. But the Tennents had gone well beyond other revivalists into the realm of the ethereal: They saw divine intervention in their ministries, miracles in their daily lives, and holy apparitions of their mortality—the Reverend John Tennent had even forecasted his own death in 1732.

Other reborn Christians came to believe they spoke directly to God, and saw visions of the afterlife and angels and heavenly spirits among them. The more radical seers "imagined themselves as direct participants in an unfolding cosmic drama that was rapidly drawing to its apocalyptic close." Such ideas were textbook "enthusiasm" that establishment clerics condemned, and many revivalists fought hard to rebut. Critics called such behavior a sign of madness or, worse to Protestants, akin to the miracles and superstitions of the Roman Catholic Church.

Whitefield came to understand this mystical side of the Tennents better when he went to New York City and met William Tennent Jr., namesake of the family patriarch. Unlike his brother Gilbert, this Tennent was a more relaxed soul, quieter and more hospitable, with a voice "mellowed by a sense of the divine pity." Whitefield took to him immediately, when William "refreshed my heart" speaking of revival successes, and they enjoyed long, intense discussions into the night about salvation and the electric presence of God in a reborn soul. As Whitefield wrote of his encounter, "our hearts burn within us when we opened the Scriptures, and communicated our experiences to each other." But William's experiences were like no other preacher Whitefield had known.

THE NARRATIVE OF WILLIAM TENNENT JR.

As a young man, William Tennent Jr. had died and been reborn—not metaphorically, but literally. He was only a student then, a minister in training under the tutelage of his brother Gilbert in New Jersey. He devoted his mind to the theology he learned, and his heart as a person reborn in Christ. But his studies were so rigorous, they caused "a pain in his breast, and a slight hectic." In short order he took ill and became emaciated, little more than "a walking skeleton." Death came quickly, and he passed away to the great grief of his family.

They laid him out on a rough board, making plans for his funeral. Hearing of the tragedy, the town folk in New Brunswick gathered to pray for his soul on its journey heavenward, but the attending physician interceded before the body could be buried. He examined the corpse and thought a bit of warmth issued from its armpit. He put the body to bed and asked that the young man's funeral be canceled. Gilbert, however, would have none of it, "the eyes being sunk, the lips discolored, and the whole body cold and stiff." He wanted to bury his brother. Instead, they all waited.

They persisted in watching over the corpse for three days, until its protruding tongue swelled, and the entire spectacle took a turn for the grotesque. The doctor even tried to feed the body, to Gilbert's horror—"It is shameful to be feeding a lifeless corpse"—but at that moment, William opened his eyes and groaned. He descended back into lifeless paralysis, but the glimmer of life gave his family hope. He returned to gasp and breathe again an hour later and stayed dimly, distantly alive. That was more than his family could have ever hoped for. The town folk were shocked by the news and chastened in their doubts, especially those "who had been ridiculing the idea of restoring to life a dead body."

After much praying and cajoling, over the course of days William regained a greater whisper of life, and over the course of a year, through much trial and pain, he slowly regained his health. Remembering his deathly experience, William recalled how he had walked with the Lord. "I saw an innumerable host of happy beings," he said, "I heard things unutterable. . . . I felt joy unutterable and full of glory." It was then that an angel tapped him on the shoulder and bade him return to earth. "This seemed like a sword through my heart," he recounted. Death was preferable to living, but God still had plans for him on Earth, and so he returned to his mortal coil.

After that, William enjoyed an otherworldly kind of faith. He felt overcome by the divine presence and had searing visions of God in heaven and the afterlife. His mysticism also bred suspicion and a host of enemies. In one case he found himself accused of perjury, in an absurd accusation involving a clerical imposter and a stolen horse. The court case threatened his freedom, but before he could be convicted of the crime, a Pennsylvania couple had a dream he was endangered, and they traveled from Pennsylvania to New Jersey to corroborate his testimony and secure his acquittal.

But if God protected him through prophecy on some occasions, the devil attacked him on others. In one particularly lurid episode, William awoke from sleep to find his toes neatly severed. They bled profusely, though he had experienced no pain in their amputation, nor was there any physical evidence an animal or criminal had amputated them. He could only believe "the injury was done by the prince of darkness, of whose power and malice he was deeply convinced." Thus, William lived his life as a holy pawn between Christ and Satan, and could only trust in the grace of the Lord, as revealed in his fantastical dreams and visions.

William's example influenced the beliefs of his brothers and father. He channeled his mystical experiences into his ministry and developed a deep understanding of salvation and heaven. He assumed control of his recently deceased brother John's pulpit in 1733 and continued a revival in Freehold, New Jersey, and brought the power of divine intervention toward saving souls. He made the Tennent family's battles against their foes not merely earthbound and political, but universal and cosmic.

Inspired by the words of William Tennent Jr., Whitefield preached in Freehold to 3,000 people, sending them to fits of sorrow, ecstasy, terror, and delight. In his oratory, Whitefield felt the spirits of the family rising in him, with holy Providence transforming the lives of sinners, as "the power of God was much manifested."

After his encounter with William Tennent Jr., Whitefield met new allies of the Tennent family, clergymen who seemed more like revolutionaries than pastors. Foremost among them was James Davenport, who had already acquired a reputation as a fervent visionary and uncompromising revivalist. In Southold, in far eastern Long Island, he had led his parishioners to experience the New Birth through desperate confessions of sin and fiery, cathartic conversions. Whitefield wrote, "God has lately highly honored [him]" by giving him the power to transform souls. Davenport had even brought children as young as eleven years of age to recount their failings and accept God's grace and be reborn.

Davenport spoke with a style few had ever seen: he shouted with abandon, he groaned in pain, he sang with joy, he spat out words in a frenzy, he used rough language, and he rejected the old style of sermonizing that American ministers had been using for at least a hundred years. Surprisingly, he had been properly trained at Yale and graduated at the top of his class, but something about the revival bred a strange new spirit in him, one that many people found tantalizing and irresistible.

But such behavior also bred enmity in his adversaries. Whitefield reported, "[He] is looked upon as an enthusiast and a madman by many of his reverend pharisaical brethren." Increasingly, Anglican commissaries and Old Side Presbyterians denounced Davenport and other such radical ministers as wild-eyed fanatics, as dangers to spiritual harmony and social stability, as well as the gravest accusation of all, "antinomians."

Simply put, antinomians believed that God's grace, and unquestioning faith in him, gave them license to do as they pleased, without regard to good works or proper conduct. Those who were saved could behave any way they wished, since God had already guaranteed their heavenly reward. Although few people claimed to be antinomian (meaning, "against the law"), in a few cases, thieves and other scoundrels had defended their actions with the excuse they had been sanctified by God. And now Davenport, the Tennents, and Whitefield were charged with doing the same thing: acting with unjust liberty to undermine the foundations of society. Whitefield knew this was a lie, but he had a hard time disproving it, since the evidence of his innocence was in his heart, not his words. As he wrote, "I abhor the thoughts of it."

Even as the accusations mounted against him, Whitefield felt himself energized by the response to his revival tour. He returned to Philadelphia a few days later and brought about an outpouring of emotion in his sermons.

Many in his audience, free whites and blacks as well as slaves, erupted with outbursts of ecstasy, even interrupting him. As the shouts and cries and cacophony of voices rose, the tumult increased to such a pitch that some worshippers "seemed affected as those that are in fits." He had seen nothing like it before, and worried about what it meant. The people in the crowd seemed stricken with mania, possessed by confusion more than salvation, and he began to doubt whether their outpourings of spirit were truly divine. "Some such-like bodily agonies, I believe, are from the devil" and would only serve to embarrass the revival and lend credence to his critics.

This was not the America he knew on his previous trip in 1738. Then, congregants sat in respectful, often sleepy, silence as their ministers spoke, and they deferred to authority even if they didn't respect it. Disorder in the pews was unheard of and conformity of worship a necessity. But since then, a surge in religious passion had overwhelmed the colonies, as parishioners found their voices and expressed themselves with abandon. The feelings the revival had unleashed were both invigorating and frightening, and at times White-field couldn't tell whether they issued from the hand of God or the paw of Satan. Whatever questions he may have had, though, he had no choice but to welcome the conversions of his listeners and accept whatever form they took.

The next day, he attended Christ Church and heard Archibald Cummings denounce him in person as a zealous ignoramus—another blunt insult from an Anglican cleric. He refused to acknowledge the criticism and instead spoke to some 20,000 people on Society Hill, which became one of his greatest successes to date. He also offered special praise to the Tennents, who were the "most worthy preachers of our dear Lord Jesus," and his bosom allies in a world still largely unfamiliar, and sometimes quite hostile, to him.

These days it often seemed Whitefield spent as much time doing the bidding of the Tennent clan as he did promoting the revival. He preached where they preached, their allies were his allies, their enemies were his enemies, until he became as much a warrior for the New Side Presbyterians as they were. But unlike them, he also had to battle with the Church of England, whose colonial officials belittled and undermined him whenever they could, and sapped his strength to fight two wars at once. Still, he persisted; his passionate crowds of supporters always gave him fresh energy.

Whitefield marshaled that energy when he traveled to the very place where Gilbert had given his *Danger* sermon: Nottingham, Pennsylvania. He wasted no time following up on his friend's work, preaching outdoors to some 12,000 people. The worshippers had come from all around western Pennsylvania to watch him play out his Bible stories, and they responded with breathless enthusiasm. He wrote, "thousands cried out, so that they almost drowned my voice. . . . Some fainted; and when they had got a little strength, they would hear and faint again. Others cried out in a manner, almost, as if they were in the sharpest agonies of death!"

Nottingham was another success and confirmed the region as newly conquered territory for the New Siders. Whitefield was overcome with delight and spent the rest of the night traveling to Samuel Blair's house happily singing psalms and hymns, scarcely tired after the long day.

The following day he preached in Londonderry Township, to a crowd nearly as large and chaotic. He wrote, "some were struck pale as death, others wringing their hands, others lying on the ground, others sinking into the arms of friends, and most lifting up their eyes towards heaven, and crying to God!" It made Whitefield imagine what the final days would be like, for "they seemed like persons awakened by the last trump, and coming out of their graves to judgment." But as he contemplated this, he was rudely interrupted.

A certain Reverend Francis Alison rose to challenge Whitefield. He charged him with misquoting and misunderstanding the Bible, and was prepared to argue with him verse by verse. Shocked by the intrusion on his carefully crafted drama, Whitefield tried to defend himself, but the fellow kept after him. How did he know who had been saved and who hadn't? Didn't the Book of Isaiah say a person could be saved and not know it? And if this were the case, how could Whitefield judge anyone, since he wasn't God?

This made Whitefield angry, but instead of debating the man or trying to defend himself, he issued a few sharp words and quickly mounted his horse. This villain had tried to ruin his great moment, and he could not forgive the insult. "I believe he was an enemy to God" he wrote. Later that night over dinner, still upset over the memory of the slight, Whitefield brewed with ill feeling: "I hate to have communion with ungodly unconverted ministers." In fact, that minister was a champion of the Old Side, and a sworn enemy of Gilbert Tennent. He had ambushed Whitefield in order to embarrass him, and to remind him just how many enemies he was collecting, whether or not he even realized it.

That was Whitefield's last major stop before he boarded a sloop and left for the South. Pleased with his work, the Tennents and his other friends bade him an emotional farewell, but the exhausted Whitefield could only return their love with a sigh of affection. Aboard the boat, he felt ashamed that he hadn't been grateful enough for everything his friends had done for him. He resolved to do better, and asked God to grant him a humble heart.

Nine days later, still at sea, Whitefield pondered over how he had prospered in America despite the challenges, aided by so many friends who supported the revival and were willing to fight for it. He wrote, "Sometimes I think it best to stay here, where we all think and speak the same thing: The work goes on without divisions, and with more success, because all employed in it are of one mind."

He was inspired to write to his fellow Methodist John Wesley, a close ally for many years and the original reason he had set sail for the New World in 1738. But now he meant to chastise him. He rebuked him for his resistance to Calvinism, and warned him, "I dread your coming over to America, because the work of God is carried on here (and that in a most glorious manner) by doctrines quite opposite to those you hold. . . . Here are many worthy experienced ministers, who would oppose your principles to the utmost." He had once tolerated philosophical differences with his friends, but now felt empowered to scold them, even at the cost of their friendship.

Whitefield arrived in Savannah with a new commitment to his mission. He inspected the physical condition of the Bethesda orphanage and the spiritual condition of its residents and found them both improving. The institution now cared for forty young souls, and one hundred people overall, and he set them to work. He wrote, "The children are industrious. We have now in the house near one hundred yards of cloth spun and weaved." Even better, they proved to be a captive audience for his gospel.

On one occasion, after telling them of the fearsome power of the Lord, and the dreadful "weight of their sins," some of the orphans had been shocked, even horrified. They cried and moaned in the night, worrying about their accursed condition. Whitefield saw how "they are even now in frequent agonies, when lying and groaning under the sense of their original and actual sins. The next day after this awakening, for near two hours, they cried out as violently as they did the night before." He saw this as a great success, and a path to their salvation.

The Georgia trustees, however, did not agree. Not only were they worried the orphanage might become a school for budding dissenting ministers, they were troubled by the way Whitefield made the children work and pray almost constantly during their waking hours. John Percival, Earl of Egmont, reported "not a moment of innocent recreation, though necessary to the health and strengthening of growing children, is allowed in the whole day, but much public and private prayer with frequent singing of psalms and hymns . . . [is] required. The whole discipline appears to be too strict." The trustees tried to investigate Whitefield's use of the funds he collected for the orphanage, only to have the Itinerant rebuff them. He would neither give an account of his finances nor consult with the trustees' secretary on how best to assist the poor. He ignored their inquiries because he thought he knew best how to make the enterprise succeed—and he harbored scorn for them.

Feeling confident about Bethesda's prospects, Whitefield planned to enlist the help of Jonathan Barber, an ally of James Davenport, to run the operation. With Barber's reputation as an ardent revivalist, many Anglican critics openly worried the orphanage would be in the hands of a "parcel of wild enthusiasts." But Whitefield cared little for their concerns, and regularly visited South Carolina to find new allies to add to his parcel.

One of them was the wealthy planter Hugh Bryan. Under his influence, Whitefield had written the tracts denouncing Archbishop Tillotson, and now Whitefield relied on him to aid the financing of Bethesda, as well as to build a school in Charles Town for the education of black children. Whitefield had personally converted Bryan and several of his close family members, and oversaw Bryan on his path to righteousness. After converting, Bryan began to have mystical visions, experiencing "raptures of joy from the rays of divine light and love" and informing others of his newfound ecstasy. This incurred the suspicions of some of his neighbors, who began to wonder just what kind of ideas Whitefield was preaching.

No one had greater doubts than Commissary Alexander Garden, who had been nursing his grievances against Whitefield since he left for the Middle

Colonies in the spring. Now that the Itinerant had returned, Garden had no intention of letting his quarry escape him again.

On July 13 Whitefield attended St. Philip's in Charles Town to hear Garden's sermon. But as Commissary Cummings had done in Philadelphia, Garden surprised him, attacking him personally as he sat in the pews. Whitefield wrote, "had some infernal spirit been sent to draw my picture, I think it scarcely possible he could paint me in more horrid colors. . . . The commissary seemed to ransack church history for instances of enthusiasm and grace abused." Garden not only accused Whitefield of being akin to nonconformists like Quakers, he compared him to social radicals like the Ranters of 17th-century England, who went about naked in public; the fanatical "French Prophets," who luridly warned of the end of the world; and the Dutartre family of South Carolina, who were "guilty of the most notorious incests and murders."

Garden had already refused Whitefield the sacrament of communion, and the next day, he surprised him again by issuing a writ for him to appear in ecclesiastical court. The charge claimed his soul was in peril and demanded "the reformation and correction of his manners and excesses." Whitefield and his attorney duly appeared in court the day after, and said Garden had no jurisdiction over him since he had previously acted as the parish priest of Savannah in Georgia, not South Carolina. The court gave him a year to appeal the case, and Whitefield and Garden waited for word from the Bishop of London, who administered the colonies. This ensured the case would not be resolved any time soon.

Upon reflection, Whitefield assumed Garden's enmity grew from jealousy or confusion. He felt pity for him and asked people not to scorn him, but to pray for his soul. A few days later, he attended church once more at St. Philip's. Garden again derided him from the pulpit, if not quite as viciously as before. Whitefield resolved to leave Charles Town, but not before having one last conference with the commissary.

The next day the men debated the finer points of scripture and laid out their differences, but in the end agreed on very little. Garden would not retract his insults, and Whitefield wouldn't change his style of preaching. The Itinerant grew disgusted with the commissary, and no longer felt as much pity for him as contempt. He told him he was "an unregenerate man, an enemy to God, and of a like spirit with the persecutor Saul." With that he left, and told his followers, "since the gospel was not preached in the church, to go and hear it in the meetinghouses" of the dissenters. He was finished with the commissary, or so he thought. He would later learn that such a deeply devoted enemy would not relent so easily.

Whitefield sometimes wondered why he had ever brought his ministry to the South. Though he remained committed to the success of the orphanage, the hostility he encountered from the Georgia trustees and Anglican clerics had been unrelenting. Had he really become such an outcast in the region? The passionate crowds at his sermons told him otherwise, but the corrupt establishment tried to thwart him at every turn. He knew he could not relent in the face of their rancor. He had to be stronger and bolder in sparking the greater revival and must quell any fears that plagued him. God expected wondrous things from him, and he could not fail his creator.

In mid-September Whitefield planned to bring his revival tour to New England. There he would be among like minds: fervent Calvinists whose orthodoxy was pure and unquestioned. The region was home to New Hampshire, Rhode Island, Connecticut, and Massachusetts; the latter two had established Congregationalism as the official church and supported it with public taxation. That made the Church of England a *dissenting* sect, which should have put him out of place as one of its priests, but considering how his ministry had flourished among nonconformists, he knew he would be among friends.

Whitefield had written to several of the region's key ministers in the months before his embarkation. One of them, Jonathan Edwards, was known for leading a revival at Northampton a half-decade before and writing about it in *A Faithful Narrative of the Surprising Work of God*, which had made his name famous in the colonies. Edwards was the consummate intellectual, and Whitefield had respectfully written to him and another important cleric, Benjamin Colman, with hopes of borrowing their pulpits. Both men responded positively and led Whitefield to think his preaching would find a happy home in New England.

He was right: News of his travels had spread throughout region, with Ben Franklin and other publishers ensuring his name and controversies would be familiar to anyone reading a newspaper or visiting a bookstore. Boston ministers took sides for or against the Grand Itinerant, and weeklies carried extensive coverage of the revival—much of it written by William Seward or Whitefield himself—including inspiring stories of worshippers redeemed, souls saved, and critics repudiated.

Showing his ecumenical side, Whitefield first dropped anchor in Newport, Rhode Island, the notorious hotbed of dissent and freethinking that Anglican critics called "fertile soil of heresy and schism" and old-fashioned Congregationalists denounced as "the sewer of New England." Yet his initial encounters in Newport were auspicious, and the city seemed to reflect the soul of the region. He wrote that one of the first ministers he met "looked like a good old Puritan, and gave me an idea of what stamp those men were, who first settled New England."

As Whitefield and other ministers knew, the Puritans had been blessed with a legendary history. They had had settled here as dissenters from the state church, founded the colleges of Harvard and Yale, raised icons like John Winthrop and Cotton Mather, and built thriving societies on what had once been windswept scrubland. No wonder so many Britons and Anglicans still distrusted them. They had crafted a theocracy from the native soil, and made it grow.

Whitefield's visit to Boston began well, as he "perceived fresh emanations of divine light [to] break in upon and refresh my soul." God himself seemed to encourage Whitefield to spread the word of Christ in the fabled city of 17,000. While Boston was no longer the economic driver of the colonies, it retained a measure of piety and a good amount of orthodoxy that seemed irresistible to him. Yet before he could raise a revival, he had to contend with more hostile clergymen.

He met with five Anglican missionaries, including the local commissary Timothy Cutler. They had heard all about Whitefield's controversies in South Carolina, how he had tangled with the fearsome Alexander Garden, and had faced his withering attacks—which had not ceased since Whitefield left the colony. The missionaries picked up where Garden left off, questioning his methods and philosophy, wondering why he had allied with such troublemakers as the Tennents, and asking why he had called them "faithful ministers of Jesus Christ." Whitefield replied, "I believed they were." He would not apologize for the family or their ideas because he had fully taken them to heart and made them his own.

Commissary Cutler grilled him further. He quizzed him on his knowledge of the Bible and his familiarity with the finer points of theology, but his essential question was, "Can you see regeneration with your eyes?" He didn't believe Whitefield had any right to weigh the condition of the human heart, for only God could judge. But Whitefield claimed he could, too. He saw it in the pews, in the fields, in the barns where he preached—rebirth in Christ before his eyes, by the power of God's grace. Sins confessed, hearts melted, souls rebuilt, salvation achieved.

Whitefield finished the combative interview. He had held his own against Cutler and the missionaries, defended his friends, and praised the New Birth without reservation. With that, he thundered into Boston.

Welcomed by Benjamin Colman and other important clergymen, Whitefield preached with great power from the outset. His audiences grew as fast as they had in Philadelphia: 4,000 people in Colman's own meetinghouse, 6,000 in Samuel Sewall's, 8,000 in Thomas Foxcroft's, and then 15,000 on Boston Common! It was on the Common where he made the greatest impression, as he "roamed around the portable field pulpit at will, amazing his audience with the sheer pathos and passion of his delivery." He channeled his ecstasy, sorrow, wrath, joy and fury into what was his best and most inspired performance in America to date. He wrote, "I felt much of the divine presence in my own soul."

The furor of revival began to overwhelm him. He wrote in his *Journal* of the deep feelings he stirred and released:

> There was more of the presence of God through the whole visitation than ever I had known at one time through the whole course of my life. Justly it might have been said of that place, it was no other than the House of God and the Gate of Heaven! . . . The spirit of God, indeed, seemed to be moving upon the face of the waters at that time, and who knows, but that to a great many souls, God was pleased to say, *Let there be light, and there was light.*

Thus the Lord had not merely sanctioned Whitefield's revival, he had reenacted the first words of the Bible to prove it.

Now the spirit came to affect Whitefield in body as well. He cried with those who wept deeply, and convulsed with those who felt trauma: "The Spirit of the Lord was upon them all. It made intercession with groanings that cannot be uttered"—possibly a sign of speaking in tongues, or other mysterious blessings. The passions crippled him for a spell, and he felt "ragged and becoming extremely ill, violently vomiting between sermons. He was feverish, dehydrated, and sweating profusely." Yet he persisted, for his gospel had catalyzed the Holy Spirit as he had never seen it, and he would not allow illness to hamper him.

Tragedy would not stop him, either. On the afternoon of September 22, he planned to preach at Reverend Samuel Checkley's meetinghouse. Though it was designed to hold only a few thousand people, the crowds on this day numbered many more, and they surged into the building without restraint. As Whitefield was preparing his sermon, a floorboard cracked, and panic ensued.

People plunged from the galleries, unleashing a mass of screaming and terrified parishioners, all running for their lives. Fueled by panic, they jumped out of the pews and leapt from the windows, and "many (especially women) were thrown down and trod upon by those that were crowding out, no regard being had to the sensible screeches and outcries of those in danger of their lives, or others."

Five people died in the melee, and the moans of parishioners came not from the New Birth, but from sorrow and horror. Whitefield was stunned by the chaos and carnage of the scene, even walking by several lifeless bodies on the ground, and he blamed the devil for the tragedy. But he would not be deterred.

He led the remainder of the crowd away from the terrible scene and felt strangely at ease. "God was pleased to give me presence of mind," he wrote, and "I gave notice I would immediately preach upon the Common."

To the surprise of nearly everyone, Whitefield did not postpone his sermon, and instead spoke in a torrent of rain. He would not be daunted by the weather, or chastened by death, or defeated by Satan. He thundered on through the storm.

FOUR

THE BURNING AND SHINING LIGHTS

Jonathan Mayhew had only been enrolled at Harvard for a month when George Whitefield came to town. Like his peers, he had followed the reports of the English revivalist making his way to Massachusetts, and he was eager to take a break from his studies and watch him preach. Whitefield, too, was eager to visit the school, which he called "the chief college for training up the sons of the prophets in all New England," after hearing of its divinity training and scholarship.

It was a rainy Wednesday when Whitefield spoke to 7,000 listeners, including Mayhew, and captivated the students with his oratory. "The Holy Spirit melted many hearts," Whitefield wrote. "The Word was attended with manifest power." After his sermon, he met the president and the leaders of the school and some of its students, toured the grounds, and perused the library. It was a gracious welcome for the Itinerant and one that any revivalist might have appreciated. But he found it lacking.

What Mayhew and the other students and faculty didn't realize was that, while Whitefield was polite and respectful to them in person, in his *Journals* he showed another face. When his writings were published a short time later, they were stunned to read that he looked down on their institution: it was tiny compared to Oxford (his alma mater), its students were undisciplined (and possibly unconverted), their morals were suspect (despite their reputation), and its library contained numerous "Bad Books"—including the works of John Tillotson.

Whitefield's censure of the school angered its faculty. Based on a short visit, he had judged the college harshly, dishonored its tutors, and insulted its students. He even condemned the books in its library, though the great majority had been penned by authors whose orthodoxy was above reproach. The Itinerant seemed to care more for attracting controversy than for offering a fair critique and showed a mean and peevish side that few had expected.

Still, while Whitefield's attacks enraged the academics, they only enhanced his popularity on the revival circuit. Most of Whitefield's listeners had not been to Harvard, or college of any kind, and either did not understand what it taught or thought it was a bastion of heresy. Whitefield was happy to encourage their distrust of the institution and the elites who sent their sons there, and to rouse their suspicions about the education of the mind instead of the heart.

Despite the controversy over Whitefield's trip to Harvard, Mayhew found inspiration in his preaching. This was partly because he embraced a sense of Christian piety—he prayed daily with a small group of friends—and partly because he did not fit the stereotype Whitefield criticized. For one, he was almost twenty when he entered Harvard. Compared to his peers, he was both too old and too poor. Most of the other students were three or more years younger than him, the firstborn sons of local aristocrats or well-heeled merchants who had been groomed by their parents since childhood to attend the best college in New England. By contrast, Jonathan's father, Experience Mayhew, could scarcely afford to pay for his studies. He had sacrificed for decades as a missionary and now struggled to provide for his family. He had managed to send his oldest son Nathan to Harvard to study for the ministry, but two years after the boy's graduation, he met an untimely death—as did Experience's first wife Thankful, his second wife Remembrance (Jonathan's mother), and his daughter Reliance. Death had cut a swath through the Mayhew family, and financial troubles ensured the survivors would continue to face hardship.

The twice-widowed Experience had sold off much of the family's land holdings to raise money, but it wasn't enough. Now, for him to send Jonathan to school, he had to ask the General Court to grant him title to unappropriated lands that he could use to scrape together the funds for tuition. The court granted the request, awarding him six hundred acres of land and a small economic stipend, but it did not issue the grant from a sense of charity. Instead it acknowledged the sacrifices Experience had made as he worked for little reward to spread Protestantism in the hinterlands of New England, a thankless and exhausting task that he had labored at for decades.

The members of the court also realized that, though the Mayhews lacked money, their family name still carried a certain prestige. During the first great wave of Puritan migration to the Bay Colony in the 1630s, their ancestor Thomas Mayhew had used his business and political acumen to secure title to an obscure island that later became known as Martha's Vineyard. He styled himself "Governour Mayhew," and he and his grandson Matthew ruled over the island as "Joint Lords of the Manor of Tisbury"—a rare feudal estate permitted to exist in the British North America. Although the province of Massachusetts Bay eventually assumed control of their holdings, their land hierarchy persisted in token form until 1732. By this time, the power of the Mayhews had vanished, and their successors were mainly known for proselytizing to Indians on the colonial frontier.

Experience became one of the most successful missionaries, bringing the gospel to the Wampanoag people and Christianizing a number of them. He even composed a psalter that translated books of the Bible into Native languages. For his record of accomplishment, Harvard granted him a Master of Arts—one of the first honorary degrees it ever awarded. By 1740, Experience was still hard at work as a missionary, even though he had been doing it for nearly a half-century and was sixty-eight years old.

His son Jonathan, however, did not follow in the steps of his father. Nor did he know what he wanted to do with his life. He loved to read and study the classics, he became fluent in Latin and conversant in Greek and had an interest in theology and other pursuits. Experience recognized how perceptive he was, and how anything less than an education at Harvard—with its broad curriculum that included rhetoric, geography, ethics, metaphysics, astronomy, and math—would do him a disservice. He secured his tuition with the help of the court and sent his son to Cambridge.

Jonathan entered Harvard in the late summer, after passing a rigorous entrance exam, and became part of a class that included such future worthies as Samuel Cooper, James Otis Jr., and James Warren, as well as Samuel Adams. Unlike his friends, though, Jonathan had to ask for grants and jobs from the college to make ends meet and always faced the danger of running out of money before he could graduate.

All of this made Jonathan a poor target for Whitefield's accusations, but it didn't keep him from becoming engaged in the revival. Soon after Whitefield's visit, the spiritual climate began to change, and the college became consumed by the New Birth. The same sons of the elite who wanted to use their Harvard education as a stepping stone to a respectable career now found themselves overcome with piety, loudly praising God and worshipping with fervent devotion, including fasting. Many students asked the question, "What shall I do to be saved?" as did other converts who had been shaken by Whitefield's message.

Anxiety spread on campus, too, as the students worried over the fate of their souls, and whether the scholarship they had been taught by their faculty would send them to hell. A climate of fear gripped many of the students and made them unreceptive to anything that carried a hint of heresy or seemed even vaguely unorthodox. As the disquiet increased along with the revival, the students' concerns mounted until some of the faculty members worried, not about the students' souls, but their mental health. One tutor reported that most suffered from "extravagances and errors of a weak and warm imagination."

Whitefield contributed to their worries by blasting college life in his *Journals*. He accused institutions of higher learning of heretical thinking, and demanded they shun the philosophies of Tillotson and others that had drawn students toward rationalism and other menaces. "As for the universities," he wrote, "I believe it may be said, their light is become darkness, darkness that may be felt, and is complained of by the most godly ministers."

Jonathan knew about Whitefield's criticisms, but remained interested in all spiritual ideas, whether they derived from champions of the New

Birth or anti-Calvinist Anglicans. Within a year, though, he contracted a high fever from a dangerous illness and, upon his recovery, the ideas of the revival began to consume him. In 1741 he traveled seventy miles north of Boston to York, where a great religious upheaval was underway. This one featured the tears and moans and paralysis Whitefield had reported in his *Journals*, as well as new and even more enthusiastic outbursts. Some men and women writhed in pain as if cast into a furnace; others issued "hideous cryings and yellings, and all the distortions of body which the acutest torments could throw them into." Some looked on the verge of death; others belted out quasi-Biblical incantations such as "Comfort me with applies, slay me with flagons, for I am sick of love—This is my beloved and this is my friend, O ye daughters of Jerusalem!"

This behavior was unusual, even for the most devout. It was also different from that found in most New England meetinghouses, and the shock was palpable to the outsiders who witnessed it. But Jonathan took no issue with such outpourings of feelings, however extreme they might have appeared. By this time he had begun to respect the power of the evangelists, and even commended them for their work. Encouraged by their example, he wrote, "May our souls be more and more enflamed with the love of Christ, and grow warmer and warmer in our devotions to him."

Jonathan was smitten, his heart affected, if not yet melted. He tried to convert his brother Zachariah to the cause, but found little success. His father was even more resistant to Jonathan's newfound piety. Experience had proven true to his name and revealed to his son the checkered legacy of his own proselytizing, including his mission to the Wampanoag. He told Jonathan that the fervor of revivals could be short-lived and, without ongoing study and deepening faith, zealotry could lead to disappointment or even disbelief.

Experience also had little respect for Whitefield, calling him a "miserable enthusiast" laboring "under the power of Satanical delusions." Instead of studying scripture closely, the Itinerant used theatrical antics to force his audience into convulsions and false revelations, which could lead them astray. The tutors and faculty and president of Harvard, too, became bitter in their contempt for Whitefield, calling him "young, poorly educated, heedless of ecclesiastical order, intolerant, scornful of reason, dependent on histrionics"—the opposite of the kind of model they wanted the students to embrace.

Still, despite their criticisms, Jonathan remained under the influence of Whitefield and the revivalists. His heart was torn between the passion for Christ that he saw in the New Birth and the commitment to his father and his tutors who professed a more rational and analytical version of the gospel. He would ultimately have to choose one side of the argument, for this spiritual battle allowed for hardly any middle ground. Both factions thought they had God as an ally.

Farther west in Massachusetts, Jonathan Edwards looked to make a friend of George Whitefield. Months before, he had responded to the Grand Itinerant's introductory letter by inviting him to come preach in the church in Northampton where he was pastor. He happily blessed his success, "with an irresistible power bearing down all opposition! And may the gales of Hell never be able to prevail upon you!" He thought a great revival was overdue, and if Whitefield could bring it on his tour of New England, so much the better.

He lamented how the faith of his forefathers had declined. How the 17th-century heritage of John Winthrop, Increase and Cotton Mather, and the legendary Puritan divines had gone into eclipse. Religion had become rigid and institutional, its ministers dull and legalistic, and rationality of the mind held sway over devotion of the heart. Even within Calvinism, the great mass of people found their sins "no cause for anxiety nor any hindrance to social respectability." This was religion used to advance one's fortunes, and to succor the mind with abstract philosophies, and Edwards would have none of it.

Some considered Edwards the greatest theologian in America, as well as its most persuasive intellectual. But while he had gained acclaim for his writing, in his ministry he was riddled with vexations. It galled him that the morals of his congregants had decayed, since he had built his reputation on his evangelical triumphs. But that reputation now felt hollow, many of his conversions had failed, and he yearned to try again. He found in Whitefield a man who could bring back the holy fire.

◆

Ever since he was an adolescent, Reverend Edwards had been involved with revivals in New England. He had witnessed several of them in the company of his grandfather, the renowned pastor Solomon Stoddard. Under his grandfather's tutelage, he had graduated from Yale College at seventeen and learned how to assist conversions and lead spiritual upheavals that could uplift communities and wash away sin and the workings of the devil.

He saw the transformation of the heart, not the mind, as the key to redemption. God worked on a person's higher emotions, or the "affections," as Edwards called them. He could reach down to the miserable life of a sinner and extend his grace and give that poor soul a chance to be redeemed. Edwards himself had experienced this transformation as a young man. But his conversion was not full of agony and terror. God did not pound him into jelly or melt him down or trample over him. Instead, God offered him pleasure and delight, and an irresistible "inward sweetness."

> The appearance of every thing was altered: there seemed to be, as it were, a calm, sweet cast, or appearance of divine glory, in almost every thing. God's excellency, his wisdom, his purity and love, seemed to appear in every thing; in the sun, moon, and stars; in the clouds, and blue sky; in the grass, flowers, trees; in the water, and all nature.

When Edwards was thinking about the divine, and that ethereal world of perfect harmony and beauty, he found transcendence. Yet when he thought about his fellow human beings, he bristled with disgust. And he didn't need to look far to find examples of what he found wrong with his peers and the lives they led.

In Northampton, and in countless towns larger than it, he saw how farmers and merchants who had found material success reveled in their decadence: copious amounts of food and drink, elegant clothing, assorted luxuries, all the things necessary for "fashionable living." Even as they basked in their abundance, Edwards saw the other members of the congregation suffering, wearing tattered garments, eating meager fare, reduced to hunger and penury. And this sort of greed wasn't merely sinful in the biblical sense, it was destructive to the health of the community. Indeed, a "commercial frenzy" caused men to lust after wealth and consumer goods, allowing dishonesty and deceit to run rampant, and spiritual health to weaken.

In the prior century, the Puritan divines had established an oasis of godliness in America, but the vices of the outside world had now corroded it. Edwards saw Britain, in particular, as the root of "wickedness of almost every kind": its imported goods corrupted people's hearts; its selfish, secular philosophies did the same to their souls; and its economic practices exploited their land and debased their spirit. He thought that wealthy aristocrats were so lazy they "cease to any way be beneficial members to human society." And he imagined that, with their example, people might reject all faith and scruples of conduct, harm their neighbors for profit, aggressively lie and cheat and scheme, and behave "like wolves one to another," for "beastly lusts . . . will make men of a beastly disposition."

In 1734 he had tried to change the behavior of his neighbors before it was too late. Like other Congregational ministers, Edwards used the skill he had acquired from his grandfather to speak vividly to his congregants of hellfire and damnation. Solomon Stoddard was something of a legend for using terrible imagery of souls roasting in hell and the everlasting torment of sinners. Edwards adopted these techniques to make his parishioners aware of their sins and their helplessness before God. He preached the terrors to break them down to despair, so they could accept heavenly grace and follow a path to redemption.

Edwards's strategy had a galvanizing effect in his Northampton parish. He noticed more of his parishioners taking his message to heart and telling their friends to attend his sermons. Yet what they heard was nothing like a theatrical performance. Edwards spoke quietly and carefully, rarely raised his voice, and called attention to well-known sinners whose lives had been upended by the Holy Spirit and irresistibly changed for the better.

Edwards did not play out biblical roles or shout at full volume. He didn't insult other ministers or spit bile at a lengthy set of enemies. He kept his preaching simple and direct; even in all its fearsome power, he found that having a strong message persuaded many more people than delivering it with sideshow antics. Before long, the conversions in his parish increased and news spread of his powerful evangelism, which "seemed almost like a flash of lightning, upon the hearts of young people, all over the town, and upon many others."

A great outpouring of the spirit began to consume Northampton, as ideas of rebirth filled the conversations of the town folk, and outsiders came to learn more about the revival. Even those who visited to ridicule the events seemed stunned by them and underwent their own transformations. Edwards delighted in the success of his preaching and estimated that 300 souls had been saved through God's mercy—and that was only in Northampton. Later in the year, the revival traveled through the Connecticut River Valley and affected many of the towns and hamlets alongside the river—from Suffield and South Hadley—to more distant cities like New Haven and down into the Middle Colonies.

Edwards learned similar revivals were taking place in New Jersey from its dissenting clergymen, "especially the Rev. William Tennent [Jr.], a minister who seemed to have such things much at heart" and he discovered a "very considerable revival of religion in another place under the ministry of his brother the Rev. Mr. Gilbert Tennent." Thus, the Northampton revival paralleled and overlapped with other upheavals of the time, even though Edwards belonged to a different sect than the Tennents, and his methods were very different from theirs.

He saw the revival having universal consequences. It touched men and women equally, young and old, white and black, poor and rich, and crossed different regions and classes and boundaries with ease. Some of the reborn experienced the investment of the Holy Spirit like wildfire, writhing in pain or shrieking with delight, overcome with agony and remorse or inexpressible joy. Edwards also witnessed things he didn't understand. He saw people talking about spirits, visitations, emanations of the divine presence. In their visions, hell exploded in terror and sinners burned in everlasting torture, Christ bled on the cross and the blood ran richly from his wounds, and other revelations caused great excitement to those who experienced them.

Edwards tried to grasp what such visions meant. They seemed like the work of the Holy Spirit, but their extravagance troubled him. All he could do was try "to teach persons the difference between what is spiritual and what is merely imaginary." He would come to learn the line between the two could be very thin indeed.

He published his account of the revival in London in 1737, *A Faithful Narrative of the Surprising Word of God*, and described the manner in which the events had started at Northampton and the way they had spread. In his view, the eruption of the spirit was unexpected, it was wondrous, and it was welcome—but it wasn't unprecedented. As a minister, Edwards had seen revivals take place in many of the same regions, and he was hardly shocked by them. This one, though, seemed particularly heartfelt, and it gave him hope for a wider revival that would make God favor America once again as a beacon of piety.

Edwards's book became a sensation in both America and Britain. Some readers thought the events he described would lead to a new reformation. Others saw his work as a template for spiritual uprisings throughout the colonies. Yet even though his book became an inspiration to countless evangelicals and made its author well-known among dissenters, the one thing it could not do was keep its original participants converted. As declension set in, most drifted away from the light and returned to their previous sinful ways. Edwards knew it, and it crushed him. As he wrote in a letter to Benjamin Colman, "it is a great damp to that joy to consider how we decline, and what decays that lively spirit in religion suffers amongst us." The irony was cruel and bitter: He had found universal praise for spreading the fire of revival at the same time that fire had faded into embers.

He told private groups of his parishioners their hearts were "immensely harder than the hearts of idolaters, harlots, whoremongers, murderers, and sodomites," because at least some of those sinners might truly repent, whereas he had no hopes left in Northampton. He added that he would "rather go to Sodom and preach to the men of Sodom, than preach to you." He could only hope the next revival, whenever it came, would lead to a much greater reformation, a long-standing awakening for Christ, instead of the lightning flashes that had made his reputation.

George Whitefield had no illusions about the demise of the Northampton revival. In a neighboring town he saw how "people of God have complained of deadness and losing their first love" after years of falling away from faith. But Whitefield thought he could improve on Jonathan Edwards's work and quicken the pulse of the people in the name of Christ. If he could lead

Boston and Philadelphia to holiness—among the largest and most worldly cities in British North America—then surely he could do the same for a minor colonial hamlet.

Over the course of four sermons, Whitefield enchanted Northampton. Parishioners cried openly and "were filled, as it were, with new wine." Jonathan Edwards too sat in the pews, stunned by the effect of Whitefield's ministry on his wayward congregants, and he felt the emotions pouring out of him in a way they hadn't in many years. He wept continuously, unable to contain himself in the same way he did as a minister. And he realized the visiting Englishman might very well be blessed with a holy gift and lead an awakening that would be a godsend.

He gushed to his wife Sarah that he hoped the Itinerant's example could make him a better Christian, and that he might be imbued with passion and thus "become fervent, as a flame of fire in my work." Whitefield enjoyed the effect he had on Edwards, seeing him initially as "weak in body" but later appreciating the reverend's full heart and commitment to the revival. It was a joy to meet his family, too. He ministered to the Edwards children, and became quite taken with Edwards's wife Sarah, whom he saw as an ideal mate. In fact, Whitefield was so impressed with this "daughter of Abraham" that he desperately asked God to make the same gift to him, "that he would be pleased to send me a daughter of Abraham as my wife. . . . Lord, hear me, Lord, let my cry come unto thee."

Edwards brought Whitefield to East Windsor, his birthplace, where Whitefield preached in the church of Edwards's father Timothy. Along the way, Edwards saw Whitefield's sermons having a galvanic effect on his listeners—bringing them to extremes of ecstasy and agony, and summoning tears and laughter and other strong reactions. The crowd became a magnet for his passions: They praised God and newborn pious souls with the same intensity he did and condemned the devil and his works with the same aggression.

Edwards also heard the Itinerant denounce unconverted ministers with a ferocity that had only been building since he first met Gilbert Tennent. Whitefield called such men "the bane of the Christian church," and even extended his criticism to Edwards's own beloved grandfather, Solomon Stoddard. While Whitefield recognized the late minister's greatness, "I think he is much to be blamed for endeavoring to prove that unconverted men might be admitted into the ministry. . . . I think no solid arguments can be brought to defend such a cause."

Hearing Whitefield's latest criticisms, Edwards began to wonder if his fire burned a bit too hot. Were all of these scabrous words necessary to convert people to Christ? Perhaps unconverted ministers were merely sinners like everyone else, not worthy of special scorn. And perhaps faith guided by biblical study could be just as valuable as faith fueled by sudden emotions. The appeal to the heart did not mean reason had to be rejected, and Whitefield in all his theatrics sometimes threatened to do just that. So Edwards tried to correct some of his worst tendencies.

As Edwards later wrote, he "took an opportunity to talk with Mr. Whitefield alone about impulses . . . [and] I told him some reasons I had to think he gave too great heed to such things." Whitefield listened passively to him without making an argument in return. But Edwards knew his admonition had offended him: "I thought Mr. Whitefield liked me not so well, for my opposing these things."

Edwards returned home troubled by the encounter, wondering what to make of the English preacher's crusade. Whitefield doubtless had marked effects on his listeners and had sparked revival throughout the colonies in many places where he went. Yet Edwards could not quash his suspicions, and he had cause to worry.

He remembered how the decline of the Northampton revival had begun, and how the once-noble outpourings of spirit became sour and corrupted. Some people with pious reputations claimed they were divinely guided and tried to advise others on the condition of their souls, but they were really false prophets driven by their own bizarre delusions. Even worse, extreme and frightening behavior began to overcome people, as "Satan seemed to be more let loose, and raged in a dreadful manner. The first instance wherein it appeared, was a person's putting an end to his own life, by cutting his throat." This was a man who became so obsessed by the state of his soul, "[h]e was kept awake nights, meditating terror . . . he was scarcely well capable of managing his ordinary business, and was judged delirious by the coroner's inquest."

The suicide stunned the community and encouraged more parishioners to consider ending their own lives, "as if somebody had spoken to them, *Cut your own throat, now is a good opportunity.* Now, now!" One of them was Edwards's own uncle, who became so ridden with terror over the fate of his soul that he decided to slash his throat and perish rather than face any more agonizing fears. Shortly after this, instances of conversion in Northampton came to an end and "the Spirit of God not long after this time, appeared very sensibly withdrawing from all parts of the country."

Edwards meditated over this, and in November made his feelings known to his congregation. In a series of sermons based on the parable of the sower in the book of Matthew, he explained how certain preachers could attract great attention with the novelty of their subject matter, or the power of their presentation, or the loudness of their voice. But the emotions aroused by such techniques "produce not genuine convictions of conscience but greater hardness of heart." When the revival fades, such converts would return to their old ways, more embittered and sinful than ever. The process only accelerated when itinerant preachers left town after their fiery sermons, leaving it up to others (like Edwards) to carry the revival forward, or to pick up the broken pieces.

In the sermons of such preachers, Edwards wondered whether an outpouring of tears was worth anything. Even though he had cried fervently a month before in the pews, he now questioned such emotion. He said deceptive ministers were skilled at shedding tears and adept at exhibiting false joy. In fact, people "may shed a great many tears and yet be wholly ignorant" of a personal conversion to Christ. Rather than being the mark of a godly man, crying was simply the badge of a hypocrite.

Moreover, a preacher of the emotions could bring out the worst hypocrisy in his listeners, too, encouraging them to have a passionate, superficial reaction rather than a full understanding of faith. He might bludgeon his audience with "a very earnest and forceable manner" and an "air of sincerity and fervency," only to lead them toward false ecstasy and spiritual emptiness. Even worse, that preacher might lead congregants to think he is the divine leader instead of God, and to blindly obey his commands, "almost ready to follow the preacher to the ends of the earth." In this way the converts were not worshipping Christ, but *the preacher himself.* Such a demagogue of the spirit could lead only to wickedness and blasphemy.

Even though Edwards spoke in a parable, everyone knew who he was talking about.

George Whitefield left New England at the end of October, and though he had only been there for a month and a half, he managed to deliver 175 sermons, nearly four a day. He enjoyed his travels and wrote that the region "exceeds all other provinces in America, and, for the establishment of religion, perhaps all other parts of the world." But his congenial frame of mind did not last. As soon as he entered New York, he learned of the latest smear campaigns against him.

From South Carolina, his old nemesis Commissary Alexander Garden had been busy penning increasingly hateful letters that denounced him and everything he stood for. In the form of six letters bound in a pamphlet, Garden called him a poor theologian and a rabid enthusiast, an inciter of trouble within the Church of England, an antinomian who despised good works, and a fanatic who reveled in discord, disobedience, and slander. Whitefield's attacks on Archbishop Tillotson especially rankled Garden, and he wrote, "In your mountebank way you have David-like, as you fancy, slain your Goliath, but his works and memory will long survive after you and your dirty pamphlets are sunk into oblivion." He mocked his concern for the welfare of slaves, even as children in his own orphanage labored under his cruel hand, starving and subject to overlords who punished and abused them. And in a fresh swipe, Garden added that Whitefield's sermons were no more than "a medley of truth and falsehood, sense and nonsense, served up with pride and virulence, and other like saucy ingredients."

Whitefield did not reply directly, but his allies in the South answered the charges. He faced a much graver threat, however, from an anonymous document called *The Querists*. Published through the New Castle presbytery, it was the latest salvo from the Old Side Presbyterians against the revivalists. They took aim at the Itinerant because he had promoted Gilbert Tennent's baleful views, and "looked upon Whitefield no longer as an Anglican cleric, but as a cohort of the Log College men." They picked apart his *Journals* for every error and deviation from orthodoxy they could find, and interrogated him over his dodgy theology, his ecumenism, his extemporaneous preaching, his thoughts on "impulses" and enthusiasm, and his threats of church schism, which he seemed to encourage.

Amazingly, these sorts of attacks had almost become routine. Whitefield had only been in America for a little over a year, and he had already split the colonists into mutually hostile camps with his brand of experimental piety. He had aroused popular feeling against one church (Anglicanism), helped divide another (Presbyterianism), and threatened to do the same to a third (Congregationalism). He was as polarizing and loved and hated a figure as colonial America had ever seen, yet his understanding of the country was thin, and his life experience was short. He had polished himself into a brilliant lightning rod and enjoyed all the electric currents he channeled in society, but he had only a dim understanding of the force of the energy he wielded or what to properly do with it.

The Querists struck a nerve in a way few other polemics against Whitefield did, and the pamphlet had to be answered. First, Charles Tennent, Gilbert's brother, came to his defense with a short reply, then Whitefield himself answered the charges. Surprisingly, he admitted his errors and apologized for his lack of understanding about the finer points of Calvinism. He said, "I think it no dishonor to retract some expressions that have formerly dropped from my pen." But he rejected the charge of being divisive, and he defended how he preached spontaneously and welcomed all faiths to hear his message. His words were humble, his tone mild, and he gave the impression of being a properly chastened sinner. But however penitent he might have appeared, he had no intention of changing his ways. If anything, *The Querists* only fueled his emotions and made him burn all the hotter.

On November 2, he delivered an impassioned oracle to New Yorkers before the wedding of a local couple. He unleashed a mass catharsis among his listeners, who felt the Lord's spirit arrive "like a mighty rushing wind, and carried all before it. Immediately the whole congregation was alarmed. Shrieking, crying, weeping, and wailing were to be heard in every corner. Men's hearts failing them for fear, and many falling into the arms of their friends." Even Whitefield was struck speechless after his spellbinding performance, and he collapsed after returning to bed. But he was called back to the wedding ceremony where "divine manifestations flowed in so fast, that my frail tabernacle was scarce able to sustain them." Stunned and overjoyed, he could only thank his enemies for bracing his spirit in this way: "God has remarkably revealed himself to my soul, ever since I have seen the pamphlet published by the Presbyterians against me."

This was only a foretaste of what was to come. Whitefield soon accrued a band of allies that may have been the most formidable collection of preaching talent the colonies had ever seen. From New England, a Harvard tutor named Daniel Rogers decided to leave his preparation for a Boston pulpit and join the Itinerant on his travels. He realized he was unconverted and waited for a sign of the grace of God. When it arrived at King's Bridge (later called the Bronx), he felt the presence of the Lord enrich his soul "with such joy in the Holy Ghost as I never experienced before."

Whitefield then encountered another ally, "my dear brother [James] Davenport from Long Island, by whose hands the blessed Jesus has of late done great things." Davenport had already preached with Whitefield in various outdoor venues in the Middle Colonies, though his methods of conversion were quite different from Whitefield's. He didn't amuse or entertain his parishioners. Instead he blasted them, gesticulating aggressively and distorting his body wildly to make a point. Some thought he was a holy man, not least for his strange behavior and unprecedented feats of preaching. A few months before, he had testified to the power of God for twenty-four hours before he collapsed. Another of his techniques was to split his parishioners into groups that he deemed either spiritually worthy or unworthy. To the former he gave all the benefits of church membership, while he denied the latter communion and refused to baptize their children.

These methods had made him notorious on Long Island, but when he came to other parishes to preach as an itinerant, his following only grew, along with the controversy. In recent days, he had been experimenting with taking Gilbert Tennent's attacks on unconverted ministers a step further, invading their parishes and accusing them *by name* of being wicked and unregenerate. He impelled them to submit to his inquiries about their spiritual condition. If found lacking, he demanded their congregants find a new minister to follow, such as himself.

Like Whitefield, Gilbert Tennent thought highly of Davenport and called him "one of the most heavenly men" he knew. All three preachers crossed paths on Staten Island, and they were joined by yet another minister named John Cross, a New Side Presbyterian who had led fervent revivals of his own. His congregation was in Basking Ridge, New Jersey, which became the troupe's destination, since Cross thought would be an excellent site for lighting the next spiritual fires.

When they arrived, Cross was proven correct: They witnessed some of the most intense mass conversions anyone had ever seen in the region. In the morning, Davenport proclaimed the gospel to 3,000 people and spoke with such fury that people cried out in the crowd and broke down in tears. One eight-year-old boy became so overwhelmed with piteous weeping ("as though his little heart would break") that Cross urged him to preach to the crowd. The child responded by praising the divine power, which only increased the passion of the worshippers, who now cried out louder in their own exhortations.

In the evening, the crowd retired to a barn where the revival continued. First Gilbert gave a sermon, then Whitefield. The Itinerant had barely spoken for six minutes before people began shouting at him—"He is come! He is come!" and "I have found him!"—and then the evening took an even more tumultuous turn. Daniel Rogers was stunned to witness the mass of worshippers now "weeping, sighing, groaning, sobbing, screeching, crying out" until many doubled over from exhaustion. The power of God's grace, and the spontaneous redemption of sinners, seemed forceful, alive, irresistible, and agonizing. Even after Whitefield retired to sleep, the event did not end. The tireless Davenport and Rogers kept it going nearly until dawn, and they led more outbreaks of the Holy Spirit to anyone still standing.

Whitefield couldn't have been more pleased with the blazing success of the day, and despite his fatigue, he felt a note of triumph. The troupe of evangelists returned to New Brunswick, New Jersey, site of Gilbert Tennent's presbytery. Whitefield knew they all had to part and he would soon have to return to Britain. His heart swelled with love for Gilbert, of whom he wrote, "May I follow him as he does Christ. . . . [He is] our Mouth to God. He prayed in the Holy Ghost." The Itinerant knew how critical the Tennents had been to the success of the revival in America, and he persuaded Gilbert to carry on his work in New England over the winter, knowing "he will be a burning and a shining light."

Whitefield also wrote to Jonathan Belcher, governor of Massachusetts Bay Colony. He informed Belcher that Gilbert would soon be on his way to his region "to blow up the divine fire," and he asked for Belcher's support. For he knew that much depended on the success of the revival in New England, the birthplace of American dissent. He wrote, "the welfare of dear Boston people, especially the welfare of your own soul, lies upon me night and day." Whitefield saw himself as an agent of God's will on earth, and he accepted the weight of that cosmic responsibility.

His alliance with the Lord would soon be tested by earthly matters. After stopping in Philadelphia to visit the commodious New Building, which had been erected for his preaching, Whitefield encountered several people who had accepted Christ into their hearts after hearing his preaching, but now threatened to lapse back into sin. Some fell into misery or madness, such as one woman who wanted his counsel and asked him to baptize her child. Whitefield did not make time do so, and she became consumed by terror, and went home, "and there the devil would fain have persuaded her to cut the child's throat with a pair of scissors." In the end, she called on Christ to help her, and she did not commit the murder. However, the incident showed that even the most ardent converts could slip back into depravity without ongoing spiritual counsel—something Jonathan Edwards knew from his experience in Northampton, but Whitefield hadn't learned yet.

Whitefield spent several more weeks traveling in the Middle Colonies until he departed for the South in December. This was the final leg of his American journey, and he wished to end it with a visit to his Bethesda orphanage. He brought Jonathan Barber with him to administer the institution, and he spent Christmas in the company of his allies. However, life in Georgia remained grim, with few resources and much hardship. He wrote that the colony remained "in a very declining and piteous state" and almost met his death there after a worker accidentally fired a gun in his direction. This put the Itinerant in a morbid mood, but he reasoned "in the midst of life we are in death."

Even before he stopped in Savannah, he visited what was left of Charles Town, South Carolina, where a fire on November 18 had wiped out three hundred houses and a fair amount of the town's material infrastructure at a cost of 200,000 pounds. Whitefield felt pity for the victims of the fire, but also suspected it had come from a divine source. In the devastated town he preached to its people about the reasons for their misery: "I endeavored to show what were the sins which provoked God to punish the Israelites in that manner. I drew a parallel between them and the Charles-Town people."

Whitefield's friends struck an even more militant tone, demanding their listeners see the fire as an act of judgment by the Lord. Dissenting minister Josiah Smith preached a sermon entitled *The Burning of Sodom*, which echoed Whitefield's feelings about the destruction being justified because of the vices of South Carolinians. And Hugh Bryan, the plantation-owning convert and ally of Whitefield, claimed in a letter to his brother that the fire wasn't only justified, it was a warning that God was angry and might follow the conflagration "with more severe strokes of his displeasure." He castigated the Anglican clergy who had criticized Whitefield and predicted they would surely be condemned to hell for leading their parishioners astray. He broadened his attack to include not just the churchmen, but the civil authorities of the colony—and the king.

To publicize his feelings, Bryan thought it would be a good idea to have the letter published in the *South Carolina Gazette*. Whitefield reviewed the letter at Bethesda, editing it to increase its potency, and Bryan arranged for its publication. The newspaper printed it just a few days after Whitefield returned to Charles Town to take a ship back to Britain. Outrage ensued.

Alexander Garden condemned it as a "scurrilous libel," and the civil authorities treated it as a threat—not only as a sacrilege to God, but as a danger to the colony and the rule of law. They arrested Hugh Bryan and forced him to account for his writings. He in turn blamed Whitefield for editing and changing the document beyond what he had written. Soon the authorities arrested the Itinerant too, charging him with composing "a false, malicious, scandalous, and infamous libel against the clergy of this province, in contempt of His Majesty and his laws, and against the King's peace." Brought before magistrates for the second time in six months, Whitefield tried to explain himself before the court, then made bail and promised to appear again at the tribunal.

But though he had recanted his words, Whitefield made sure his followers knew he would not relent. His sermons became filled with invective against civil authorities and clergymen like Garden who persecuted him. He preached from the book of Kings, describing how Naboth had been falsely accused of blasphemy against God and the monarch, then was carried away to be stoned and killed. He compared Naboth to himself and hinted at the growing wickedness of earthly powers. He charged the "men in authority" with "the heinous sin of abusing the power which God had put into their hands." While Whitefield had previously directed his ire against unconverted churchmen and Anglican authorities, now he targeted colonial magistrates and rulers—a dangerous and potentially seditious turn for him.

Before any more controversy could erupt, he boarded the ship *Minerva* on January 16 and sailed home, still reeling from the chaotic final days of his trip. As North America began to disappear from view, he asked "God of the sea and the dry land [to] be with us on our voyage, and prepare me for the many perils and mercies that await me amongst my own countrymen."

It would be more than four years before Whitefield would return to the colonies. But his American tour was not forgotten, and the fires he had set would only burn hotter and expand in his absence. His attacks on the clergy, and his suffering for it, became especially influential to young revivalists. A budding minister named Andrew Croswell even wrote a response to Alexander Garden's *Six Letters* that not only defended the Grand Itinerant from his slanders, but accused the commissary of being a "meritmonger" and a liar, a slanderer with "virulent and unorthodox" doctrine whose "heart seemed full of choler and resentment." And he added a new twist, especially timely in light of Whitefield's recent arrest. He claimed these sins weren't just inherent to Garden, they were endemic to all the religious authorities who came from the Old World. For while average people in Europe were bound to that antique hierarchy, and "are generally so ignorant and weak as to hug the chains of the clergy," in the New World it was different.

> [T]he AMERICANS live in a freer air, more generally taste the sweets of liberty, and being nearer an equality of birth and wealth, there being land enough for every industrious person,

there are fewer among them in dependence on others, they are generally more knowing than the common people of EUROPE, and are not like for several ages, or as long as this near equality remains, to desire the dominion of the clergy over them.

Thus Andrew Croswell became one of the first of his kind to proclaim religious and political liberty, economic equality and personal industry, as hallmarks of a new American way, circa 1741.

SONS

FIVE

THE CREATURE IN THE EGG

D oubt plagued Sarah Wheaten. She considered herself a moral and upright woman, with an open heart and a searching soul, but still she couldn't allay her troubles. She longed for happiness and prayed for relief from her suffering, but she found little solace. She had accepted God's grace in her early twenties and had converted to Christ in a beautiful moment of transcendence, but her woes had only magnified since then, along with her doubts. "I knew I was a dreadful backslider, and had dealt treacherously with God," she wrote. She remained in a constant tumult, "some times revived, and sometimes sunk, and dejected."

Living in Newport, Rhode Island, and only twenty-six years old in 1740, Sarah had already endured a lifetime's worth of pain. Rheumatism made her hands ache terribly, she suffered from chronic headaches and fatigue, and she sometimes found it difficult to walk or even see. Doctors had prescribed everything from liquid mercury to "corrosive plasters," but those had not cured her. She endured bouts of vomiting and diarrhea and high fevers, which sometimes worsened with her medical treatment. And to this was added the pain of widowhood. She had married a sailor at seventeen, but he died soon after, and she now had to care for herself and her eight-year-old son.

She worked as a schoolteacher and housekeeper, but the money was always meager, never enough to survive, and too often she found herself indigent and dependent on public charity. The contrast between her life and those of her fellow citizens was stark. All around her were the fruits of Newport's commercial economy: a busy harbor, prosperous merchants, and prodigious wealth built on the shipbuilding industry and the transatlantic slave trade. Although some women became clerks and shopkeepers, and others sold dry goods and craftwork, Sarah's health made her unfit for most of these occupations, and what work she had was often exhausting.

Teaching school, keeping house, and raising a son might seem like a trial even for an able-bodied woman, yet Sarah did so despite her physical infirmities—and even managed to write, prolifically. She expressed her joy and fear and sorrow and hope on page after page of letters and notes and even a memoir she planned to write about her challenging existence. She described her simple pleasures of playing cards with friends, singing popular songs, and attending dances, while also revealing the ruinous state of her health and manifold fears for the future—and the way she understood the majesty of God.

In tolerant Rhode Island, she could worship at any Christian church she desired. But she chose to be a Congregationalist because her parents had raised her in the church and because this faith spoke to her. How else could she explain her life? What would otherwise account for the trials she had endured but her inherent sinning and her soul's perilous state? Calvinism provided the answer as no other theology could.

She knew friends who had been raised as Quakers, who worshipped in a great meetinghouse in the city. They rejected the idea of original sin and felt the essence of the divine within as an "inner light," and women could speak in their meetings. Her church elders told her such notions were heresy: the apostle Paul demanded that women be silent in the churches, and they would stand accused of "enthusiasm" should they act otherwise. Sarah did not dispute the point. Thus, while she had much to say, she confined her exultation of God to the written, not the spoken, word.

Such was her condition when George Whitefield came to Newport in September.

As she wrote, "God in mercy sent his dear servant Whitefield here, which in some measure stirred me up." The Itinerant brought his signature style of preaching laced with hope and joy and drama, and for a few months his memory enlivened her spirit. But by the winter it began to sink again—and that's when Gilbert Tennent arrived.

Unlike the wondrous drama Whitefield presented, Gilbert did not come to uplift or entertain his congregants. He came to shock them into submission. He delivered his sermons with blunt and angry words and rough, numbing cadences, his voice hectoring his listeners and mocking their claims to piety. As he saw it, they lived in hatred of God, and their devotions were false and corrupt. Their only hope was to confess their sins and plead for God's mercy, and pray that he would bestow it upon them. Otherwise they would spend eternity in the fiery furnace.

This message shocked Sarah and crushed her spirit. Perhaps this traveling minister was right, that her assorted miseries were just punishment for her crimes, her sins against God that she didn't even realize she had committed. "I questioned the truth of all I had experienced, and feared I had never yet passed through the pangs of the New Birth, or ever had one spark of grace."

Even though she had been reborn, she could not get away from the idea that her life had been one of defiance, not acceptance, of the Lord. Her spiritual mentor Reverend Nathaniel Clap—whom Whitefield had called "a good old Puritan"—had told her of her condition before God: "My sins, from my cradle, were ranked in order before my eyes, and they appeared dreadful. I saw the depravity of my nature; and how I was exposed to the infinite justice of an angry God." Gilbert Tennent reinforced her chronic sense of dread, and she could not abide it.

Thoughts of being a backslider and a hypocrite plagued her for months. By the time Gilbert returned to Newport at the end of winter, to preach the terrors twenty-one times in town, her fears began to overwhelm her. This time, he decried such menaces as "singing songs, dancing, and foolish jesting," with special scorn reserved for the "dancing Christian," who had no cause to be reveling when life was so short and miserable.

How many of these additional sins was she guilty of? How much incalculable damage to her soul had she done without fully understanding it? She did not know and could only respond to Gilbert's preaching with a new commitment to her faith: She resolved not to engage in any frivolous pursuits, and to redouble her commitment to spiritual purity. For a time this resolution sufficed, but still the menacing thoughts of hell and sin and damnation returned. Finally, in "very dark and melancholy circumstances," she wrote to the reverend and pleaded for help.

Gilbert wrote back presently. "I like your experiences well. They seem to me to be scriptural and encouraging," he wrote. For it was only natural to be distressed about sinning and it showed her commitment to holiness. Ultimately, the covenant God made with those reborn in him would not be broken, for "though they have played the harlot with many lovers; yet they may return to their first husband. Though God may hide his face for a little moment, yet with everlasting loving kindness will he return." She found solace in his words, and release at last from some of her lingering doubts. Gilbert had whipped her into a state of terror, but he also gave her just enough comfort to suggest that a kind and just God would eventually save her.

Eventually. But for the moment, the pain continued. Her brother soon died from an unexpected illness, and her teaching began to falter. "After this my business failed, and I found I could not keep my room where I lived; and which way to turn, I knew not." Now homeless and destitute, Sarah stood at the precipice of survival. But her cosmic fears had at least abated, and she "was persuaded God would point out some way for me."

Sarah wasn't alone in her suffering. An economic slump in New England had entered its third decade, with currency values plummeting and the cost of living rising ever higher. The price of wheat reached an all-time high—putting it out of reach as a food staple for many—and the real price in sterling of everything from butter and molasses to shoes, clothing, and firewood had doubled or tripled. Sailors, artisans, and laborers who had once competed for jobs now found themselves suited "only for the lower life." If they ended up in penury, they might be put to labor in a workhouse or, as in Boston, ejected from the city entirely. Despite this, growing numbers of paupers filled the streets and gave the city an air of destitution.

Native New Englanders worried over the waves of Scots-Irish and Germans arriving in America, many of them desperate for work and, the natives feared, looking to displace them from their jobs. Meanwhile, epidemics of diphtheria and malaria raged, and the death rate recently exceeded the birth rate in Boston. Grimmer news came from abroad in the War of Jenkins' Ear, as British armies fell in defeat to the Spanish at Cartagena, and most of the 3,500 men recruited from Massachusetts to fight for the Crown did not return.

The waves of bad news allowed fear and anxiety to spike in many towns, as parish preachers issued dire warnings of the end times, and an apocalyptic tone crept into their sermons. The economy, the war, the poverty, the decline in moral values—it all suggested divine punishment for their transgressions. And as time passed without relief, soon many started to believe the great New England experiment, and God's wondrous covenant with his people, would collapse in utter failure, and hardship and wickedness would achieve brutal success.

These were the conditions that Sarah Wheaten and other New Englanders faced as they witnessed Gilbert Tennent on his revival tour in the hard winter of 1741.

Persuaded to travel to the region by George Whitefield, Gilbert's itinerary was nothing less than heroic. He spent three months traveling from major cities like Boston to small outposts on the frontier. Often unable to go by horseback through the fearsome weather, he trudged through snow and ice—even in snowshoes—to get from one isolated village to another. With just a small entourage, including the young revivalist Daniel Rogers, he arrived at dissenting meetinghouses with little advance notice, much less the glowing newspaper reviews and testaments Whitefield had received. The nuances of the established Congregational Church eluded him as much as the snowbound geography. Still, despite the weather and his unfamiliarity with the region, in the frigid temperatures his preaching of terrors burned hot.

While Whitefield had primed New Englanders well for the New Birth, nothing prepared them for Gilbert's oratory. Over dozens of sermons, he spread his incendiary message over the northern colonies and left them reeling. Like Sarah, many who witnessed Gilbert on the stump were left spellbound, shocked, or shaken by his galvanic message.

He often began his discourse by insulting the piety of his congregants. He mocked them for pretending to be so devout, when he knew their hearts were dirty and corrupt. "You needn't boast of your dead hypocritical faith; you'll surely go to the Devil with it, if you get no better." He praised their Puritan ancestors, who had "the simplicity and power of the religion of Christ," and wondered why they—as modern enterprising people with so many advantages and luxuries—should fail in their duty before God. Their predecessors had made a covenant with the Lord and built a godly civilization out of heathen wilderness! And yet they had defiled it with their greed and rationalism and fashionable sense of ethics.

He called out the "Grandees" who acted as if material success guaranteed their place in heaven, but he claimed that this was really a sign of God's anger, not his favor. He said "their prosperity lifts them up, and makes them condemn God" and quoted scripture to devastating effect: "Are ye rich? Cursed are ye in the city and in the field. . . . Whatever conceit you have of your wit or wealth, you are nevertheless *wretched, poor, blind, miserable and naked.*"

Like Whitefield and Edwards, Gilbert brought a sharp economic edge to his preaching and condemned the notion that having a fancy estate, or worthy genealogy, or high social status had anything to do with securing God's favor. "What will your good parentage avail you, unless you walk in the steps of their simplicity, faith and holiness, but to aggravate your everlasting pains?" Without a confession of sin and rebirth in Christ, his listeners were doomed to roast in hell for eternity. He asked them: Could they summon the strength to admit they had allowed Satan to rule over their lives with perfidy and wickedness? Would they accept God's grace, and admit the full weight of their sins and transform their souls?

Gilbert's questions dissected the heart of New England. Daniel Rogers called one of his orations "the most awful awakening sermon I think I ever heard," which he meant as high praise. Many parishioners felt the same or greater agony of body and spirit they had upon hearing Whitefield's preaching—and expressed it with wailing and moaning, or conversely with laughter and joy.

From Benjamin Colman to Thomas Foxcroft, prominent Reformist ministers gave hearty approval to Gilbert's preaching, and his words found special appeal at Yale, where more than half the student body were said to convert after hearing his message. As word traveled of his successes, the crowds grew larger and hundreds more people became convinced of the perilous condition of their souls. One man spoke for many in calling himself "a self-righteous, self-ruined wretch . . . who deserved hell." He loved that Gilbert promised him rebirth.

Common pastors prospered by his ministry. One reported that, after his visit, he saw more converts in a week than he had in a career's worth of preaching. Among those who discovered the power of the Holy Ghost were "boys and girls, young men and women, Indians and Negroes, heads of families and aged persons" and almost anyone else who wanted to save their souls and be at peace with God instead of living under threat of his terrifying wrath.

But just as the praise and success for Gilbert's New England tour became widespread, the antipathy it aroused became more vocal. One of Whitefield's foes, Boston commissary Timothy Cutler, led the way by calling Gilbert "a monster! Impudent and noisy, and told them all they were *damned, damned, damned!* This charmed them! And in the dreadfullest winter that I ever saw, people wallowed in the snow night and day for the benefit of his beastly brayings, and many ended their days under these fatigues." As if being accused of causing suicides were not enough, Gilbert was attacked for unleashing mass hysteria and shattering clerical norms—his itinerant preaching violating parish boundaries, his oratory wild and uncontrolled, and his appearance without wig and robes offending custom and decency. Opponents of the revival spoke of him in ever more caustic language, claiming he provoked "animal convulsions" that would incite the lower orders of society, and they only increased their venom when his sermons met with greater success.

After Gilbert's tour, his groundbreaking *Danger of an Unconverted Ministry* sermon appeared in print for the first time in New England (a year after its Philadelphia printing). This intensified the momentum of his revival and provided a template for new evangelists to follow. In print his words in the pulpit echoed all the more powerfully, with sharp attacks on pastors who were "stone-blind and stone-dead" to the gospel truth. His solution: Evangelical churches would have to replace colleges like Harvard and Yale for training a new, more passionate kind of minister who possessed "plain evidences of experimental religion."

In the weeks and months that followed, 150 New England towns including Boston became swept up in his revival, with observers noticing outbreaks of piety in the streets and fervent worship in the pews. Many opponents of the revival lost their grip on long-held congregations, and laypeople demanded that converted men should minister to them, instead of the sinfully unredeemed preachers he had condemned. Power struggles erupted over the control of parishes, and frequently the congregants won, securing the leadership of more committed, zealous men to guide their souls. And when they didn't succeed, many worshippers defiantly formed their own churches, which started to divide friends and neighbors into warring camps, and "spelled doom for the Congregational monopoly in New England." The opposing sides took up names that expressed their cloven identity: the New Lights, the champions of Christian revival, versus the Old Lights, the protectors of order and tradition. And just as Whitefield had called Gilbert "a burning and shining light," now the preaching of the two men in just six months had sparked thousands more hot and radiant souls to follow their lead.

How thankful Gilbert was to Whitefield for the opportunity to go north! He wrote to him in England expressing his gratitude, exulting over the shock his ministry had caused, as "[m]ultitudes were awakened, and several had received great consolation." It was a massive social and spiritual upheaval, and in many respects Gilbert's greatest moment as a preacher. Yet it ended all too quickly, because soon after his tour finished, he returned to the Middle Colonies to find the Presbyterian establishment in revolt against him.

The cause was one Alexander Craighead. He was a Presbyterian of the New Side who sermonized at the Middle Octorara Church in frontier Pennsylvania's Lancaster County, where he was said to be "the first clergyman who preached west of the Susquehanna [River]." His parishioners knew him as a fiery proponent of the New Birth, someone who could provoke weeping in his audience and lead souls toward salvation with his fury. Yet he could also be strangely gentle. Craighead had joined Whitefield's entourage on his recent tour, and as they traveled to different small towns, "they made the woods ring, most sweetly singing and praising God."

The zeal of Craighead was unmatched, and when he felt pastors of neighboring congregations didn't preach with enough of it, he invaded their parishes to provide his own. He called out any parishioners he judged to be sinners and refused to baptize the infants of unconverted parents. His actions not only divided his own church into competing factions, they got him in trouble with the Donegal Presbytery that oversaw his ministry. In short order they referred him to trial and asked him to account for his actions. But Craighead would have none of it.

He cheerfully turned the proceeding into a circus. Even as the Old Sides who ran the presbytery adjudicated his case, Craighead held court outside the church in something he called a "tent"—really a wooden structure he had erected for his orations. There, throngs of listeners heard him declaim against his enemies on the court, accusing them by name of whoremongering, drinking excessively, lying, and breaking the Sabbath. He whipped his listeners up into such a frenzy that when the trial began, the courtroom burst into chaos, with Craighead spouting bile against the judges and the audience screaming and interrupting them "in the most scurrilous and opprobrious terms." The judges now accused Craighead of slander and incitement and suspended him from his ministry. Undeterred, he repaired to his "tent" and mounted his defenses with new attacks against his foes. This spurred his followers to interrupt subsequent meetings of the presbytery and to castigate the men who ruled it as drunks and blasphemers. The mayhem then spread throughout the area with the New and Old Siders calling each other "dead drones," "blackguard ruffians" and charlatans, liars, and heretics, among other choice insults.

The case attracted notoriety throughout the Presbyterian Church, and the Old Side planned to use it as a cudgel to force the revivalists into full conformance with their doctrine. The Synod had already struck a blow the year before by reducing the status of men educated by the Log College to second-class ministers—they could preach the word of Christ, but not be full members of the Synod—thus keeping control firmly in the hands of the establishment.

When the Synod met again in late May 1741, its leaders planned to finish the work of bringing the revivalists into line. The establishment pastors claimed to be "wounded and grieved at our very hearts, at the dreadful divisions, distractions, and convulsions, which all of a sudden have seized this infant church to such a degree." They blamed this condition on their rivals, and put forth a document called a protestation that laid out all of their flaws in detail, with special censure for Gilbert Tennent and his allies like Craighead.

In order to protect the integrity of the church, they demanded the revivalists desist in their actions. They charged Gilbert's own presbytery with violations of church law in the examination of ministerial candidates and transgressions of doctrine, rules, and order. In short, "the doctrines of the New Side men were heretical, their government anarchical, and their revival spurious."

Gilbert and the New Side were shocked, as the Old Siders not only condemned their practices, they threatened to expel them and their sympathizers from the Synod entirely. And in a sudden, narrow vote, that is what they did. They pronounced them "guilty of schism" and cast out Gilbert, the members of his presbytery, and the other proponents of the New Birth from the "true Presbyterian Church"—and they did so without a formal proceeding, without a proper trial, and without any warning.

The public galleries erupted in outrage. Some expected bad results from the meeting, but no one expected this. The Old Side had taken a controversial, possibly illegal action by ejecting their brethren from the church, and they had succeeded. And now the revivalists had no standing with official Presbyterianism and no communion with their former church members. It was an act of "supreme disorder," and the first major schism of a church in the colonies, though it would be far from the last.

Yet Gilbert remained undaunted. He quickly organized two new, independent presbyteries—his own at New Brunswick and a new one for Londonderry—that took in the cast-off ministers and tried to rebuild a new church in the face of their defeat. This included his father William Sr. and his brothers Charles and William Jr., as well as their controversial ally John Rowland, trailblazing evangelist Samuel Blair, and even Alexander Craighead, the spark for all the trouble. It was a misfit bunch upon which to build a new sect, but the men vowed to adhere to core tenets of Presbyterianism and mounted a public defense of their actions. And many of them took to the road.

Forcing their expulsion was the worst move the Old Side could have made. Whereas in earlier years, the revivalists were at least nominally bound to respect the parish boundaries of established preachers, now the rules were moot. Ejected from the church and barred from taking communion, men such as Rowland and Blair and the Tennents descended upon the countryside. They freely invaded the precincts of traditional ministers and made overt appeals to their congregants to cast off their corrupt authority.

They claimed such ministers were unredeemed, unbelieving, unrepentant wretches in the eyes of God. They warned their parishioners that following such pastors might lead them into hell, too. And they worked to pry these worshippers loose with the promise of salvation. The emotional appeal had a stirring effect.

Many of the Presbyterians they targeted did turn against their pastors, forcing them out of the pulpit or harassing them until they gave in to their demands to accept the New Birth. Others facing more resistance jettisoned their parish entirely and went over to a new revival meetinghouse in their area. All of this broadened the appeal of the schismatic ministers and gave the rogue congregants a sense of their own power. For they now enjoyed greater participation in church policy, more authority in judging the spiritual state of their ministers, and more excitement in the mass assemblies and dramatic sermons that Whitefield and the Tennents had pioneered.

The revivalists also surged into regions where no ministers had been ordained or where there were vacant pulpits, and they began to preach there to people who desperately wanted it. They occupied the New Building in Philadelphia, which had been erected so Whitefield could orate to thousands indoors, and turned it into the greatest advertisement for the New Birth in the Middle Colonies. Flocks of young men brought energy and zeal and ferocity to their roles as revival pastors, ardent in their defense of Calvinism and uncompromising in their contempt for their rivals.

They engaged in pamphlet wars in the press and dueling missives in newspapers with their foes, praising the beauty of being reborn in Christ and dismissing the wicked old "Pharisees" who opposed them. They spread their passion into new provinces and pushed the boundaries of Presbyterianism into regions where it had never gone. And they constantly made sure that, throughout the Middle Colonies at least, no one could remain neutral in this battle over faith and devotion. You were either on the side of the angels or the devils, and every good Christian had to choose.

Some observers decried the new, often menacing, state of affairs, riven with "turbulence, shattered and divided congregations, and a rash of slanderous reports against Old Side clergymen." They remembered how the church had been, at one time, a force for unity. Just twenty years earlier few of these divisions were apparent; the church had developed into one of the major intellectual and spiritual forces of British North America. But now, even before it could reach fruition, it had been undermined—the saboteurs either upholding or defying tradition, depending on one's perspective. And with this tumult rising in what had been one of the most traditional and hierarchical of all faiths, it could only be a portent of things to come for others.

By 1742, repeated attempts to heal the breach in the church failed, and with the division now looking permanent, the warring sides became more vehement in their denunciations of each other. The Old Side issued dictums on proper behavior and dogma, leveling threats at those who might stray from the doctrine. By contrast, New Side revivalists found their power in mass appeal, an ecumenical approach that allowed them to spread their gospel to whomever might embrace it, regardless of race, sex, occupation, or station in life.

The traditionalists now saw an even greater danger from their foes—not only in the church, but in society at large. They condemned the "wild rabble" who congregated for the revivals, and lampooned their writhing, screaming, blubbering, convulsing masses as subjects for both low comedy and high tragedy. In their view, Satan laughed with delight at such frenzies, which could only encourage blasphemy and depravity. And almost as bad, such "social leveling" threatened to collapse the hierarchy upon which colonial society was built, where the *best men* in business, law, state, and religion held sway over the rest of the populace, and everyone accepted this as part of God's natural plan.

But who were the *best men* now that so many in this new church were women, or Indians from the frontier, or black slaves held in bondage, or indentured white servants, or humble children or hungry laborers or paupers or vagabonds? They all testified to the spirit of the Lord at revival meetings and became the lifeblood of this new Presbyterian church. Such forces only strengthened when itinerant preachers brought their message to areas where it had never been and converted fresh waves of men and women who had been ignored by established churches, and caught these "multitudes in the gospel net" of the New Birth.

So a frightening specter faced the ministers of the Old Side. Their enemies had driven masses of parishioners toward the revival, giving them the power of judgment over their spiritual mentors and upending the rule of church law. The revivalists filled their converts with "contempt of their betters" and pitted "husbands against wives, children against parents, servants against masters." A sense of dread took hold, as the old powers grew despondent over the new divisions and the rise of common people who had no business determining the proper course of worship. One minister lamented this "exceeding difficult gloomy time" and mocked how "Every low-bred, illiterate person can resolve cases of conscience, and settle the most difficult points of divinity better than the most learned divines."

With the rising, muscular power of the New Side, Gilbert Tennent reached the moment when victory over his nemeses now seemed palpable. It should have given him cause for satisfaction, or at least tempted him with the sin of pride. But instead he felt fear creeping into his heart—not because of his opponents in the church, but because of his friends.

The revival movement he had started began to slip out of his control. He realized it immediately and questioned his own judgment, when not every minister allied with him proved to be reliable—or even stable—in his conduct. Alexander Craighead, perennial source of trouble, caused even more of it by demanding that the New Side adopt the Solemn League and Covenant, a bid to increase the sectarian power of Presbyterianism at the expense of other faiths. Gilbert worried that would repel potential allies and mix clerical and civic authority to a dangerous degree. Craighead didn't appreciate his argument, withdrew his church from the reformed presbyteries, and formed an "independent Covenanters movement," creating a schism within a schism. He also spread bile about Gilbert and his allies and proclaimed himself as the true leader of the new Presbyterian church.

More headaches arrived in the form of Count Nicolaus Zinzendorf, who led the Moravian denomination and, like Craighead, encouraged New Side parishioners to leave their pastors and worship under him as their bishop. More bizarrely, he claimed sin could be expiated by "the body's fermentation in the grave," and that Jesus paid ransom to the devil in a sort of cosmic blackmail, and he flirted with antinomianism—the idea that true faith allowed God's elect to behave however they liked on earth. Outraged at such heresy, Gilbert lambasted him and his beliefs in print, but Zinzendorf paid him little heed. He preached to growing crowds in Philadelphia and even maintained a strong ally in George Whitefield. To Gilbert's dismay, the Itinerant wrote to him, "Jesus Christ fights for the Moravian brethren," and refused to denounce the German evangelist no matter what sort of heresy he proclaimed.

There were worse problems to come. One of the revivalists' greatest allies, John Cross—whose congregation in Basking Ridge had been the scene of a frenetic all-night revival with Whitefield and other preachers—now stood accused of terrible and infamous acts. He was said to have seduced a young virgin who was a parishioner in his church, informing her she had to become a "notorious sinner" before she could be redeemed. "Whereupon the holy man, in the fear of the Lord, deflowered her, and for some time repeated the practice, until he had, by pregnancy, put her in the way to receive the Lord Jesus Christ." Cross fled before the case could be heard in court and became a fugitive from justice. It was a shocking embarrassment for the New Side, whose leaders could only condemn Cross now that the wayward preacher had vanished.

From New York and Connecticut, Gilbert also heard disturbing reports of James Davenport's latest actions: That his denunciation of unconverted ministers by name had become especially vehement. That his preaching had reached new levels of intensity, and potentially madness. And that he commanded a legion of unhinged followers who disrupted public order and made a clamor in the streets. Thus a man who had once been a bosom friend to the New Side, marked by a sense of holiness, now seemed to be blossoming into a demagogue.

Gilbert read these reports with concern, which the Old Side seized upon as evidence of the degeneracy of those they had expelled from the Synod. He duly defended his movement from their accusations. Such men as Craighead and Cross and Davenport were surely to be expected in a growing, passionate Christian revival, as outliers if nothing else. As long as the authority of converted ministers remained sacrosanct, and as long as those ministers trained in a proper school like the Log College or perhaps Yale, the cohesion and serenity of the church would persist.

Then Gilbert discovered that he himself had unleashed the greatest turmoil of all.

Gilbert's effect on New England had not ceased when he returned to the Middle Colonies. If anything, his fiery preaching and powerful orations had only strengthened his audience's commitment to the New Birth and gave rise to the New Lights who favored it. But the memory of his ministry had also emboldened men and women to challenge clerical authorities, rules, and customs in ways he could not have expected, and certainly didn't approve of.

Inspired by the gospel of Gilbert Tennent, a rash of lay exhorters—common people driven by the Holy Spirit—crossed the countryside as itinerants, proclaiming the power of the new gospel and declaring themselves to be its finest examples. They burst into church services without permission and challenged anyone to stop them. In some meetinghouses they popped up and occupied the deacon's seat, while in others they stood among the congregation, blasting their scorn at anyone they felt deserved it. Their behavior could get outrageous: "Frequently these 'guests' interrupted the proceedings to preach terrifying sermons, which set the listeners into 'hideous shrieks and outcries,' to shout charges of unconversion against the local pastor, and to urge the congregation to separate from him." They demanded men of the cloth become outwardly charismatic, passionate, and spellbinding—and if they did not, they denounced them as Pharisees.

This perverted Gilbert's message and made a mockery of his sermons! He could not understand why any sane Christian would take his principled stand against an unconverted ministry and transform it into such despicable behavior. It was freelance theology, mayhem in the meetinghouses, and he could not allow it. These lay exhorters had no proper training, no good cause, no reason whatsoever to interrupt the ordered praise of God. Although some of the reports he read had been overblown by his enemies, he had no choice but to write an impassioned critique assuming many of them to be true.

To the moderate revivalists of New England, whose commitment to the revival now seemed to waver, Gilbert wrote that his mission had been worthy, and he had never intended to cause anarchy in the churches. He said that proper revivals were necessary, but "for ignorant young converts to take upon them authoritatively to instruct and exhort publicly tends to introduce the greatest errors and the grossest anarchy and confusion." He also implored good Christians to "rise up and crush the enthusiastic creature in the egg."

He placated most of these ministers with his words, but his real targets weren't listening. They were too busy roaming across the countryside, spreading what they thought was his gospel, whether he wanted them to or not. They were common men and women, redeemed and transformed, lucid and visionary, fierce and burning. And among them was Andrew Croswell.

Only thirty-two years old, Croswell's origins were humble, and there was nothing unusual about his background that suggested he might become a radical evangelizer. As an aspirant to the clergy, he adhered to all the tenets of Congregationalism that were standard to eastern Connecticut. He had managed to gain entrance to Harvard to study divinity, yet unlike most of his peers there, he struggled to pay for it. He graduated while still in his teens and received a degree that would prepare him to become a minister, after which he was ordained in a parish in Groton, and became its pastor after the previous one decamped for the Anglican Church. (Croswell later denounced him as unconverted.)

His first acquaintance with the New Birth came in the mid-1730s, when Jonathan Edwards's great wave of Christian revival washed over Connecticut and swept him up in it. He admitted and renounced his sins, gave his heart to Christ, and promised to be faithful in his mission and recommit to spreading the gospel. Though his new faith was ardent, his Calvinist views were still relatively moderate and his profile obscure, at least until George Whitefield came to America.

The Itinerant brought great excitement to the world of Andrew Croswell, who not only enjoyed the great drama of his preaching, he came to appreciate how many adversaries there were in his own church. He experimented with denouncing them, in the way of his hero, and courted controversy with leading clerics for his remarks. He managed to offend academics at Harvard and Yale by amplifying Whitefield's attacks on them, calling out their presidents and instructors as champions of heresy and "enemies to the work of God." He encouraged students to ignore their teachers, demanded parents pull their children out of school and instruct them privately, and told anyone who cared to listen that an education aboard a British warship was better than that of a New England college. More than anything, though, Croswell really made his name when he read about Alexander Garden's attack on Whitefield and responded by calling him a vile "meritmonger."

His defense of the Itinerant gained him favor among the evangelists of the New Birth. It also lured the hair-trigger commissary into a war of words in print, as Garden vented his spleen against Croswell almost as much as he had against Whitefield. He compared him to a "zealous lady" overcome with the Holy Spirit moving within her, and chastised him for being foolish and delusional. He maligned the evangelical movement as "a harvest indeed for Romish missionaries!" and charged him with being in league with the pope—an absurd accusation trotted out with no evidence.

Having such a foe as Garden became a victory of sorts for Croswell. It enlarged his profile and emboldened him to denounce the corruption of the state church of Britain, which he increasingly saw as a nemesis to all Americans. He then extended his criticism to anyone who questioned the legitimacy of the New Lights, charging those critics with favoring good works over true faith and making an unholy alliance with the Church of England and, indeed, the Church of Rome.

Then James Davenport came to town.

Croswell was stunned to witness the fire of Davenport's ministry. Over a little more than a week, the brash evangelizer converted thirty-eight people in great displays of ecstasy. He writhed and convulsed in the pulpit—he shouted bold words to his congregants—he made them erupt in full. They felt the Holy Ghost coursing through them, breaking them down, rebuilding their souls, and lifting them up to sit beside the Lord in electric phantasmic visions. Croswell stood among them, impressed by the sway Davenport had over his listeners, for not only did they explode with joy in the meetinghouse, they carried their enthusiasm into the streets, where they sang hosannas to God and let everyone know they had been touched by the miracle of God's grace. Croswell wrote, "my former objections against singing were presently sung away."

Gilbert Tennent, of course, did not approve of such behavior, but radicals like Davenport increasingly cared little for what the Presbyterian minister thought. Such men took his attacks on unconverted ministers and magnified them, calling out the wicked souls in high pulpits and denouncing them by name in front of their own parishioners. After observing Davenport in action, Croswell came to embrace this idea, too. He took to the road as an itinerant to condemn unconverted pastors and lead their followers to the New Birth.

He soon became one of Davenport's firmest allies, working with him on plans to convert many more people in New England and even directing him to savage the enemies of God in Boston—"the great city Nineveh." He encouraged his followers to interrogate unredeemed ministers in their own churches and worked at "breeding up exhorters" to carry out the Lord's work. This made him notorious among settled parishes, where a visit from Croswell was seen as anything but a blessing and might be an invitation to anarchy. He set the template for such behavior at Plymouth.

He was only supposed to give a sacramental sermon for communion, but instead he decided to jar the parishioners with attacks on their character. In an especially incendiary sermon, he said, "I doubt not, but if you were to die tonight, three-quarters of you would be damned to Hell." He told them that he had once been unregenerate, that most of his followers were unregenerate, and—now shouting—that the church's leaders were unregenerate! He said, "a man may live in all the commandments and ordinances of the Lord blameless, and yet go to Hell at last." Then he pointed his finger at the church elders and community leaders seated across from him, and eviscerated them as "old, grey-headed sinners."

The congregation reacted with surprise and confusion. As one observer saw, "the fervors and frenzies of this teacher had answerable effects on the audience; where you might observe a general foaming or fainting, laughing or crying." Some in the crowd stood up to preach themselves hoarse, testifying to the glories of Christ. Parents bellowed from the pulpit, as their children preached from stools. When the spiritual exultation could no longer be contained in the room, the congregants burst out into the street, singing and laughing and shouting, "everyone delivering the yell he was particularly inspired with, joined with all the mad gestures and actions that frantics show, the Reverend Mr. Croswell leading the van."

The next day, none of Croswell's furious energy had left him. He spoke to assembled crowds in the street that "God hates every one of you, as he does the devils and damned spirits in Hell, and to one degree worse, inasmuch as they have never sinned against redeeming love and grace as you have." The crowds couldn't get enough of it.

Some of them followed Croswell to Charlestown, Massachusetts, his birthplace, where they saw an even more frenzied performance, as the evangelist spoke for consecutive nights, his passion never seeming to flag. This time he not only tore into unconverted ministers, he condemned the abusive treatment of prisoners and the horrors of slavery—a denunciation that few established ministers were willing to risk. The rotten edifice of the church and the corrupt society around it should be razed, Croswell demanded, and restitution made with the Lord for such sinful depravity.

In one church, he darted from pew to pew, scampering up to the high galleries, proclaiming the coming kingdom of God, then tearing out of the building and leading his audience into the streets with ecstatic singing and cries of salvation. On some occasions, Croswell repeated his performance with the added touch of stripping off his shirt, to preach salvation in his trousers.

This obviously went well beyond anything Whitefield or Gilbert Tennent had ever imagined. The church authorities didn't know what to do with Croswell. Some moderate revivalists claimed this behavior would lead to infamy, with such frightening zeal and uproar fit only for the devil. Another critic mockingly praised him for imbibing the Holy Spirit "by the quart or tankard" with a voice like a trumpet or conch shell; now he had become "a brother to dragons, and a companion to owls, when you wailed and howled, and were stripped, though not quite naked." Outraged by such activity, the

Old Lights called men like Croswell "wandering stars" and "red-hot comets" who spread chaos wherever they went.

Yet the critics also feared something else that went along with Croswell. Amid his masses of lay exhorters were black parishioners standing and shouting amid their white counterparts. There were women—some of them poor and destitute—exalting the glory of the Lord just as the men in wigs and robes did. And there were children, too, some barely old enough to raise their voice, but trying valiantly anyway, telling everyone who could hear them how God had reached down and brought beauty and power to their little lives.

Such social and racial mixing was anathema to the traditionalists, who mocked the evangelists for provoking it. Yet even their lampoons could not account for the rampant social leveling that had broken out with such powerful effect. The masses in all their ragged and untamed emotion, in all their heady spirits and unlearned ways, had become the firmest allies of the New Lights. With their visions and prophecies, their outbursts and exhortations, they were changing the face of the revival, seizing it from the men of the cloth without mercy or permission.

George Whitefield, Gilbert Tennent, and most of the original preachers of the New Birth did not see it coming. But Andrew Croswell did, and by the time March 1742 was finished, he and James Davenport had transformed the redemption movement into a social uprising. By their radical force, the power of the Holy Spirit overwhelmed hundreds, perhaps thousands, of people who experienced it. It charged them with energy, melted their hearts, and turned them into bold new *enthusiastic* Christians. And for a brief time, it even became too much for Croswell, who spent the end of winter in bed after preaching himself sick. For the moment, the glorious revolution of the spirit would have to go on without him.

SIX

ANIMAL SPIRITS

By 1742, Americans were bracing themselves against the rising tumult of a social and religious upheaval. Their anxieties had risen with the ministry of men like Gilbert Tennent and Andrew Croswell and worsened as economic desperation and poverty began to crack the veneer of polite society. Evangelical ministers and their lay exhorters freely invaded their enemies' parishes, while their foes responded with ever-greater anger and derision from the pulpit and in print.

This marked a dramatic change in the religious landscape. Just a few years before, members of a community would grow up and be baptized in the church of their parents, a local pastor would guide them in their parish, and they and their neighbors would share the same faith and help each other during times of crisis. Now those social bonds had been destroyed, and Christian churches stood under siege from both New Birth insurgents and the vehement defenders of the old dogma. Ideas of redemption, the promise of salvation, and faith itself now came into question: What doctrines should believers accept? How should they pray and behave? How could they expiate their sins? Which side should they choose, and would they suffer in the afterlife if they picked the wrong one? No one knew the right answers because no one knew the mind of God. Even pretending to know how he felt was itself a kind of sin. This lack of answers provided fuel for more anxieties.

In Philadelphia Benjamin Franklin featured the drama throughout the pages of his *Pennsylvania Gazette*, as he continued to profit from the zeal of the warring sides. Two years before, he had written that "the alteration in the face of religion here is altogether surprising," and that change had only become more severe in the time since.

The dividends from his bet on George Whitefield continued to multiply. His printing house now sold volumes on the life of Whitefield to explain and illuminate his ministry; sermons and journals to let devotees know how he preached and what he thought; descriptions of his orphan house and charity work to assure readers of his philanthropy; letters and pamphlets that belittled his old enemies and made controversial new ones; and a full range of paraphernalia like Whitefield portraits and mezzotints to go with a "great variety of Bibles, Testaments, Psalters, spelling books, primers, hornbooks, and other sorts of stationary [sic] ware." Franklin even published attacks on Whitefield like *The Querists*, and Whitefield's response to them. Indeed, whenever a dispute arose about the Grand Itinerant, Franklin made sure his readers knew about it, breaking the latest news on the conflict even though the preacher had sailed away more than a year before.

One third of everything he printed in the early 1740s concerned the evangelical revival. Along with the stories on Whitefield, Franklin highlighted the Presbyterian schism: the Old Side's attacks on the New Side, the New Side's defenses and its counterattacks, and vice versa, month after month. He printed a *Querists III* pamphlet attacking Gilbert Tennent and the Protestation that caused the expulsion of the New Side in the Synod. Then he printed Gilbert's response to the Protestation and his sermons touching on the subject and asked him to comment on *Querists III*. Gilbert passed on the offer because the pamphlet was "stuffed with satire and burlesque."

Franklin's promotion of the New Birth gave him an unquestioned advantage over Andrew Bradford. In 1741 alone he published forty-six books and pamphlets on the revival, whereas Bradford only printed ten. As postmaster,

Franklin had the opportunity to put his publications in the hands of more colonists, and to give his rival a long-awaited comeuppance—payback for earlier years when Bradford had been postmaster and refused to allow his mail carriers to deliver the *Gazette*.

Franklin was clever with his return gambit. Instead of refusing to distribute Bradford's *American Weekly Mercury,* he offered to carry it for free, with the understanding that his rival would have to settle his account later with a deputy postmaster. This scenario promised to make Bradford dependent on Franklin for distribution, which he could revoke on a whim if necessary. This fed Bradford's anger. Soon, a furious battle over the tactics and schemes of both men inked the pages of the *Mercury* and the *Gazette*, with each man (or his flacks) calling the other a schemer and a liar, and accusing him of transgressing the "rules of honor and the laws of humanity," among other things. Ultimately, the dust-up did little to prevent Bradford's decline. He had placed too little stock in covering the revival, and when he did, it was often from the point of view of the establishment.

Privately, Franklin's views were darker, and colored with pessimism. While he had allowed the pages of the *Gazette* to be filled with news of the Calvinist crusaders who were transforming the soul of the colonies, the revival began to vex him. What he originally saw as a long-overdue resurgence of morality and ethics had turned into a strange battle over clerical hierarchy and purity, with the threat of turmoil always looming. The clerics in conflict had brazenly violated six of his thirteen key virtues—silence, order, justice, moderation, tranquility, humility—and their lack of restraint alienated him further.

In the 1742 edition of *Poor Richard's Almanack*, he published a jaunty rhyme that described well his views of the current state of religion and the world:

> Among the divines there has been much debate,
> Concerning the world in its ancient estate;
> Some say 'twas once good, but now is grown bad,
> Some say 'tis reformed of the faults it once had:
> I say, 'tis the best world, this that we now live in,

Either to lend, or to spend, or to give in;
But to borrow, to beg, or to get a man's own,
It is the worst world that ever was known.

Franklin refused to fall into the trap of choosing a side in the conflict over faith. His own handcrafted religion had worked well for him—with his emphasis on Christian ethics stripped of the supernatural—and he resisted any efforts to change his mind. Although Whitefield continued to try to steer him toward orthodoxy in his letters from Britain, Franklin had little interest in returning to the fold. He recalled how, in his younger days in Boston, he had ceased going to services on Sunday, and became skeptical of organized religion, and instead embraced teachings that would later be labeled "Deist." Regardless of what it was called, Franklin's philosophy held good works, upright behavior, and ethical conduct to be paramount—and though it was not one of his official virtues, he would make public charity the guiding principle of his life.

It troubled him that few of these things seemed to matter in the warfare that had erupted between the sects. While divines argued who would run the churches and control their worshippers, public attention to virtue and morality had gone lacking. Franklin saw how Anglicans and Presbyterians and other hierarchical denominations "served principally to divide us and make us unfriendly to one another." Indeed, the spiritual combatants undercut the very Christian ethics they claimed to uphold. And this made him cynical to claims of holiness by the reborn, especially if they behaved abominably in pursuit of salvation. As he wrote, "morality or virtue is the end, faith only a means to obtain that end; and if the end be obtained, it is no matter by what means."

He knew he was an outlier in America for this stance. He had seen it all too clearly in the mid-1730s, during a time when Jonathan Edwards's Northampton revival was fully enflamed and the passion for piety burned hot. During this time, he came into conflict with the Synod over its accusations of heresy against the rationalist minister Samuel Hemphill, whose gospel of moral virtue influenced his own. He wrote that the pastor "delivered with a good voice, and apparently extempore, most excellent discourses. . . . I became one of his constant hearers, his sermons pleasing me, as they had little of the dogmatical kind, but inculcated strongly the practice of virtue, or what in the religious style are called good works."

But such a seemingly innocent ideology brought condemnation, since it deviated from orthodoxy as the Synod saw it, which made Hemphill "unqualified for any future exercise of his ministry within our bounds." The reverend also faced accusations of plagiarism for lifting words out of others' sermons, and of heterodoxy for "teaching of a religion based on the law of nature"—minimizing the role of justification by faith and divine revelation.

Such charges prompted Franklin to battle the Synod in the press. Not only did he defend Hemphill with vigor, both by name and anonymously, he called out such ministers as Robert Cross of Jamaica, Long Island, for persecuting him. (Cross would later help expel the New Side from the Synod.) It galled Franklin to see how those censorious zealots had hounded the poor fellow, interrogated him, and accused him so unfairly. Such an exercise of power only validated his feelings about the cruelty and excesses of dogma, and the way good men with sensible beliefs could be torn down by imperious institutions. It prompted him to write, "a virtuous heretic shall be saved before a wicked Christian."

He composed other tracts and did whatever he could to plead Hemphill's case in the press and to redeem his name from the blackened words the old-guard ministers had applied to it. In the end, though, Franklin's invective did little to help the minister's case, and he may have even hampered it. When it was clear the Synod would excommunicate Hemphill, Franklin composed a scabrous bit of doggerel about the clerical "authors" who composed the reverend's demise:

> Asses are grave and dull Animals,
> Our Authors are grave and dull Animals; therefore
> Our Authors are grave, dull, or if you will, Rev. Asses.

Ironically, seven years later, Franklin profited by many of those same asses. After the failure of his Hemphill campaign, he had learned to keep his opinions about religious revivals to himself, and to distance his emotions from the charged feelings on both sides. He remained friends with many of the men who despised each other, and even became a trustee in charge of the New Building, since he belonged to no sect and was respected for his neutrality in overseeing the hall for itinerant preachers. Yet while he was nonsectarian, he was not indifferent to all religion. The sect in the Middle Colonies that most appealed to him was the Society of Friends.

Many of Franklin's closest friends were Quakers, and he found much to admire in their frugality, tolerance, and practicality. While he was not a subscriber to their doctrine of the "inner light," he did approve of their moderate behavior, sensible ethics, and attention to good works. And with many of the leading Quakers controlling politics and government in the colony, Franklin found it useful to be allied with them, at least for now. However, though the Quakers came closer than any other sect did to his own philosophy, he could not embrace them fully. For they believed in the God within, and Franklin believed in a god . . . very far away.

His ideology allowed little room for a personal savior delivering him peace and comfort. He could not find succor, as the revivalists did, with religion of the heart, the transformation that lifted the reborn Christian up to a place of redemption. He did not feel, as Whitefield did, that God took an interest in his salvation or any of his personal affairs. He could only see the deity as a great designer and overseer of the universe, and a master craftsman of moral values. He might reward virtue and punish sin in the afterlife, but he would never reveal the true workings of the cosmos. And beseeching him for salvation or waiting for him to bestow his grace seemed like a fool's errand.

Franklin found it difficult to accept that such a divine figure could ever be actively involved in his life. His doubts about the presence of God in human affairs had only grown since his younger days, as he questioned not only the truth of the stories of the Bible, but basic Christian theology. The Incarnation, the Resurrection, the Ascension, the miracle stories—they all seemed so hard to accept. As Franklin aged, and the wars over belief enflamed around him, his doubts only strengthened.

Later in his life he wrote to Whitefield, dismissing the idea that God had much of any sway over human doings: "though the general government of the universe is well administered, our particular little affairs are perhaps below notice, and left to take the chance of human prudence or imprudence." In a different letter, he saw religion mainly as a tool to control human wickedness, for a great "proportion of mankind consists of weak and ignorant men and women . . . If men are so wicked as we now see them *with religion*, what would they be *if without it?*"

This level of doubt made Franklin an odd figure to be promoting a spiritual revival. While his newspaper was filled with stories of rebirth, his feelings about the church grew ever hollower, his cynicism ever deeper. He could only watch in silence as dissenting sects tore themselves apart, each faction accusing the other of reveling in sin and being in league with Satan. While their congregants hungered for assurance their souls would be delivered in the afterlife, many of their ministers preached terrors to them, mocked their ethics, and condemned them to hell, as if they held the keys to salvation instead of God. And all around them, even the secular news they read seemed to echo the bleak outlook of the direst Calvinists. Franklin printed the following stories during the era:

- In the winter the failure of the local currency exchange caused economic panic and led some merchants to refuse to accept orders until they could be paid in sterling. Bread riots broke out as Philadelphians couldn't buy the staple, with a mob smashing shop windows and raising havoc throughout the city. Order was only restored when the authorities forced the mob to relent.

- In May a biblical-style plague of "black worms or caterpillars" emerged from the earth to consume corn crops and ruin farmers' harvests, upon which their livelihoods depended. The fields soon became riddled with the insects, as "where no worms have been seen on one day, there have been millions the next."

- During an October election, a crowd of up to eighty sailors attacked magistrates and constables and chased people out of the voting sites. Armed with clubs, they beat and killed several people in the frenzy, in which "the confusion and terror was inexpressible." A group of angry townsfolk counterattacked and chased the sailors back to their ships, where they dragged them out one by one, throwing almost fifty of them into prison.

In this atmosphere, as division and hostility surged amid economic uncertainty and violence, one minister seemed to perfectly echo his times. The reputation of Jonathan Edwards reached its pinnacle.

Reverend Edwards was of two minds. He had become an ardent champion of the revival, but he also felt dismay at the economic and social conditions around him. The New Birth might prepare people's hearts for Christ, but it had done very little to make them more charitable or aid the poor. Many of his congregants lived with penury and desperation, and he looked to assign blame for their miseries.

Long before other revivalists attacked the cruelties of market society, Edwards saw wickedness hiding under its pious veneer. He noted how rich men trampled on the dignity of those below them, and repeatedly denounced the practice of theft—not only simple larceny and fraud, but the abuse of creditors by wealthy debtors, and the exorbitant pricing of goods by greedy merchants. He knew that commoners lusted after money just like the rich, and the economy had become ever more injurious to the poor even as the elite prospered by it. With the Crown forcing the retirement of Massachusetts's inflated currency in 1741, and no replacement for it in sight, Edwards saw the crisis throwing people into debt and creating "national calamities" that fed injustice and "threatens us with ruin." He would later remark that "God oftentimes gives those men that he hates great outward prosperity."

Looking across the Atlantic, Edwards saw another source of great sin: the mother country of Britain. Holding no affection for the colonial power, he saw little good coming from its shores. Its merchants and tradesmen stripped and exploited the riches of the New World to make worldly goods, then sold those goods back to Americans at high prices. Their ultimate goal: to make the unlucky colonists more like Britons: acquisitive, selfish, materialistic, and indifferent to God.

Britain's most popular recent export continued to be George Whitefield. His sermons and musings sold in great quantities, but Edwards cast a wary eye on his rendition of the gospel. As he had already told his congregation, the power of itinerant preachers could be ephemeral or even damaging, with the threat that such men might present themselves as God and lead their followers toward damnation. However, it could not be denied that

Whitefield had reignited the revival and gave it new life and color. Edwards felt some resentment at the effect he achieved: his theatrics, his impromptu passions, his lugubrious melodrama. And he resolved to do better.

Edwards had been invited to preach a sermon in Enfield, Connecticut, to a particularly hard-nosed congregation that rejected the New Birth. He prepared a text that he had already offered to his own parishioners in Northampton. But he continued to hone it, reasoning that he could incite a response more powerful than anything the theatrical preachers like Whitefield had achieved. He would show that clear logic, thoughtful argumentation, and cogent rhetoric could summon deep emotions and achieve lasting results, a far better outcome than merely entertaining a crowd with bombast and spectacle.

He knew his listeners in Enfield, and indeed throughout New England, needed such a lesson in the consequences of sin—they reveled in it, and took pride in their selfishness. So he aimed to convince them of the error of their ways by employing a rhythmic structure that repeated and reinforced his points, almost akin to literature. He would draw on scholarly research that showed how Newtonian physical gravity could reflect God's own emphasis on moral gravity and how John Locke's ideas about the importance of the senses could release inner feelings. He knew that a direct appeal to the heart was the strongest way for sinners to understand their dependence on Christ. He would later write that there could never be "any lively and vigorous exercise of the will or inclination of the soul, without some effect upon the body, in some alteration of the motion of its fluids, and especially of the animal spirits." And for him, the best way to activate such emotions was to preach terrors.

On July 8, 1741, Edwards came to the Enfield pulpit with a calm demeanor, a measured tone of voice, and a quiet intensity to lecture on Deuteronomy 32:35, "Their foot shall slide in due time"—by which he meant slide into hell.

He informed the congregation that most of them were damned. Not only were they damned, but God had made sure their roastings would commence soon: "the pit is prepared, the fire is made ready, the furnace is now hot, ready to receive them, the flames do now rage and glow." Just as the truth of it was unavoidable—God was furious at them for sinning—the physics of it were unquestionable: "Your wickedness makes you as it were heavy as lead, and to tend downwards with great weight and pressure towards hell." All God had to do was release his grip, and the sinners in the church would soon be burning. Even if they felt they were safe on earth, luxuriating in their pleasures, God could at his whim plunge them into the pit without warning.

Edwards told them they could die at any moment, and if sinning would face damnation. God's arrow of wrath was ready to strike at the heart, and only his "mere pleasure . . . keeps the arrow one moment from being made drunk with your blood." Moreover, he held the sinner in his hands like one might hold a spider—dangling by a thin thread over the chasm of hell, ready to be consumed by the flames for eternity.

The "greatest earthly potentates" would of course be condemned to the furnace with Satan, no matter their power on earth, but so too would the smallest children, who in their callow sins would "bear the dreadful wrath of that God that is now angry with you every day, and every night[.] Will you be content to be the children of the devil . . . ?" Ultimately, the only choice people had was to convert; to renounce their sins and repent before God; and pray that he might bestow his grace upon them and prevent them from suffering annihilation. And Edwards left the Enfielders with this thought: "The wrath of the almighty GOD is now undoubtedly hanging over [a] great part of this congregation: Let everyone fly out of Sodom: Haste and escape for your lives, look not behind you, escape to the mountain, lest you be consumed."

The congregants did not literally run for their lives, but they did fill the church with weeping and moaning, crying out "What must I do to be saved?" among other pleas. Word soon got out that the reverend had preached a particularly stirring and gut-wrenching homily, and within months people began seeking out the sermon to read for themselves. Edwards oversaw the publication of the work, titled *Sinners in the Hands of an Angry God*, within months after he delivered it, and it spread his message throughout the colonies. It also considerably advanced his name, as America's leading theologian and an evangelist without equal. With a soft voice and controlled rhetoric, he had outdone Whitefield for dramatic effect and provided more fuel for the revival to burn hotter.

A few months later, in September, Edwards had another opportunity to give a key sermon at Yale College when he gave the commencement address. In recent months the college had become a battleground between New and Old Light students over questions of piety, sin, and redemption. A Yale alumnus himself, Edwards prepared an oration addressing the tensions in the revival movement. He imagined himself as the bridge between those who distrusted the "awakening" and those who had experienced it. It would be a sober and thoughtful analysis, and a follow-up to the ideas in his *Sinners* sermon. But before he could get to New Haven to deliver it, James Davenport got there first.

From the time of his tour with George Whitefield, Davenport's methods had only become more extreme and eccentric. Routinely denied admittance into established churches, he railed at any minister who denied him entrance and said that his parishioners were better off consuming rat poison than listening to his sermons. He shouted and stamped his feet in furious tantrums, "roaring that thousands of persons roasting in the devil's kitchen" were there because the teachings of the targeted minister "had seduced them into hell."

In recent days he had resorted to holding church services that were unlike any New England had ever seen. After informing his parishioners of their many sins, he cast some of the worst offenders outside the church, only to run after them shouting "Come to Christ! Come to Christ!" He then rushed back inside to sing and preach in an outpouring of wild emotion, and his congregants followed his lead—"some praying, some exhorting and terrifying. Some singing, some screaming, some crying, some laughing and some scolding, [which] made the most amazing confusion that was ever heard." Newspapers like the *Boston Weekly Post-Boy* reacted in horror to the spectacle, but Davenport continued to gain followers with each new radical gesture.

Even before Davenport traveled to New Haven for commencement week, the locals had been warned of his excesses, but they welcomed him anyway, respecting his long family legacy. His ancestor John Davenport was the town's cofounder and its first pastor, and James himself had graduated from Yale at the top of his class and been one of its youngest attendees ever. And so, with deference, the minister of First Church, Joseph Noyes, allowed him access to his pulpit, and gave him all the professional courtesies to which he was entitled. Such sentiments, however, did not tame Davenport's wild nature.

As soon as he arrived, he singled out Reverend Noyes as "dead of heart, a blind leader of the blind" and a "wolf in sheep's clothing" and blasted college officials for their impiety and wickedness—to the delight of the New Light students who despised the old-guard minister and many of their teachers. Davenport thundered his contempt for the sinners at Yale and predicted their demise in Satan's lair. He encouraged his followers to erupt in praise of God before leading them into the streets singing and praying at top volume, well into the night.

Inspired by Davenport's example, the New Light students accused their tutors and leaders of being unredeemed and deaf to the word of God and demanded to be led by men of the New Birth. They openly revolted against the traditions and formalities of the institution, and put the authorities on notice that the school must cater to their needs and desires, instead of vice versa. With the tension at a high pitch on the day of commencement, the college trustees rushed through a rule that no student could say "the rector, either of the trustees or tutors are hypocrites, carnal or unconverted men" upon penalty of public confession and expulsion. This was the charged atmosphere that awaited Jonathan Edwards when he came to town.

When Edwards later published the text of his sermon, *The Distinguishing Marks of a Work of the Spirit of God*, it ran to more than 100 pages, and the reverend may have spoken for more than three hours. To the Old Light and moderate ministers who were appalled at the antics of Davenport and his kind, Edwards admitted that the frenzy that had erupted in recent months was alarming. He called the outbreaks of untamed emotion strange and unusual and saw how they could invite harsh judgment. He said "tears, trembling, groans, loud outcries, agonies of body, or the failing of bodily strength" were disturbing and not a reflection of whether a revival was the true work of God. His words placated the establishment ministers and college leaders and persuaded them that Edwards was on their side.

But then the reverend turned the argument. He said that in biblical times many "extraordinary effects on persons' bodies" occurred in the midst of spiritual conversions. While visions and prophecies, lay exhortations, and extreme emotions could indicate questionable behavior, all such things also followed a real revival. And he offered an interesting duality: "Grace dwells with so much corruption, and the new man and the old man subsist together in the same person; and the Kingdom of God and the Kingdom of the Devil remain for a while together in the same heart."

Even the wildest sort of enthusiasm had long been found in times of devotion to God, such as during the reign of Oliver Cromwell in England when "vital religion" held sway, and "in the beginning of New England, in her purest days, when vital piety flourished." Any frightening behavior, therefore, might be part of the Lord's design, and should not be shunned. For the true signs of righteousness would eventually outshine those of wickedness, and the heavenly plan would be made clear.

Thus Jonathan Edwards admitted the faults of the revival, but endorsed it anyway. For it was an extraordinary event "from the Spirit of God." Moreover, the results of the latest revival were more striking than what occurred six years before at Northampton, with its suicides and declension, miseries and backsliding. This new, more devout rebirth had forced people to admit their sins and expose their souls to the power of God's grace in a great beautiful swell of redemption and transformation.

Upon reading *Distinguishing Marks*, the New Light evangelists treated it as a personal endorsement of their work, and the sermon further elevated Edwards as the central figure of the revival. He was now known throughout the colonies, and across the Atlantic to London and Edinburgh, by virtue of his brilliant arguments and rhetoric, and his intellectual power; and he would continue to support this great work of God and ensure there would be many more converts to come.

Yet even as he accomplished so much, one thing Jonathan Edwards could not do was stop the chaos engulfing Yale College.

James Davenport's antics and Edwards's sermons empowered the radical students to action. They became ever more boisterous in their piety and issued more brazen insults against the school's tutors and leaders. The bar for moral purity rose, with radicals demanding higher standards of devotion and louder calls for conversion no matter the cost. Tension rose between those who had been saved and those they saw as unconverted, and thus damned. One of Edwards's own followers, David Brainerd, claimed a particular teacher had no more grace than a chair, and he was expelled. Another student said the preaching in New Haven was as chilly as the winter air, and he was fined. In this atmosphere, the authorities found it impossible to contain the disruptions from student protests, itinerant ministers and lay exhorters. Strident dissent and open disrespect of authority became common, and the tutors and their pupils became wary or even fearful of each other. Students began deserting Yale in greater numbers, and in April 1742 the rector, Thomas Clap, shut down the college altogether. It wouldn't reopen for another two months.

During Yale's closure, Davenport and his old college friend Timothy Allen began assembling plans for an institution to channel the zeal of converted students. They called it the Shepherd's Tent, and Allen set up classes on the second story of a convert's house while Davenport traveled throughout New England raising money for the school during his preaching tours, in the manner of Whitefield. Picking up anything from a few pounds to several pairs of socks, Davenport brought his donations back to New London and funneled them into his "Nursery of True Converts."

His school was nothing like Harvard or Yale. Admittance did not depend on one's station in society, family connections, or even sex or age. All the applicants had to do was to pass a rigorous screening process to weed out the unconverted and make sure they possessed a minimum level of holiness. The school had no divinity curriculum, no library, and no formal pedagogy, but what it lacked in structure it more than made up for in enthusiasm. Young male and female revivalists prayed together, exalted God and explored the nature of rebirth, and became part of Davenport's growing army of exhorters who brought the force of the gospel wherever he led them.

Critics decried New Light schools like Davenport's as "castles or colleges in the air" and tried to shut them down. The Connecticut authorities fined and punished the tutors of the Shepherd's Tent and even its president Timothy Allen, sending him to jail for several months. They weren't just worried over the enthusiasm bred there. The Shepherd's Tent represented a real threat to the legitimacy of classical education and the social hierarchy. Davenport already encouraged black and white, men and women, poor and rich, Indian and colonist, to pray together in his tumultuous open-air assemblies, and the Shepherd's Tent threatened to make him even more dangerous. But despite all the authorities did, they couldn't shut the school down. By the fall of 1742, it had moved on to Rhode Island and attracted ever more attention in the press and on the revival circuit.

During the time of his greatest activity, when James Davenport's trailblazing ministry was known throughout New England, Jonathan Edwards rarely mentioned him by name in his sermons. Edwards did critique him privately in his letters but took care not to denigrate such radicals in public because he didn't want to hamper the spread of the revival or get in a petty war of words with such men. But not all his fellow revivalists felt the same way. Gilbert Tennent, for one, had finally had enough.

Gilbert had grown familiar with being a source of controversy, but at least he had been the driving force behind it. With Davenport he could only watch helplessly as the Long Island minister committed acts that brought all the New Light revivalists into disrepute. Critics cast Whitefield, Tennent, and Davenport as part of one great hydra of chaos, threatening to collapse America into a maelstrom of screaming in the pews and singing in the streets.

Knowing how he had influenced the radicals, Gilbert wrote to his ally Jonathan Dickinson and admitted his failings. He owned up to his role in the breach with the Synod, writing that "I cannot justify the excessive heat of temper which has sometime appeared in my conduct." He confessed to "much spiritual desertion and distresses of various kinds" that forced his own self-examination, and he regretted his tendency toward division that had encouraged radical behavior. "Alas for it! My soul is sick for these things." And he added a postscript about his old friend turned bugbear James Davenport, whom he had once allowed to preach in his New Brunswick Presbytery and who now brought so much cacophony to the house of God.

He hammered Davenport's "damnable errors and confusions"—the way he claimed to be infallible in his knowledge of people's souls and how he called out unconverted ministers by name. He despised the way he encouraged lay exhorters "to bring the ministry into contempt, to cherish enthusiasm, and bring all into confusion," and how his acolytes warbled in the streets so offensively. In fact, "my soul is grieved for such enthusiastical fooleries. They portend much mischief to the poor church of God."

Reverend Dickinson knew Gilbert's private thoughts carried great critical weight. So instead of keeping the letter to himself, he sent it to Thomas Clap, rector of Yale turned critic of the revival, who in turn sent it on to the press.

The result was months of embarrassment. Old Light critics delighted in Gilbert's admission of the faults of the revival. They compared his criticisms to their own, and even held him up as an example of the purest sort of hypocrite. For how could he deride Davenport for attacking unconverted ministers when he had pioneered the practice himself? How could he champion order and unity when he had helped bring down one of the major churches in the colonies? Wasn't Davenport simply a more deranged version of Gilbert himself, and if so, why shouldn't he go ahead and admit guilt for everything he had done?

The letter offered Gilbert's critics the ammunition they had long awaited. They created a caricature of him as a merciless sadist, who laughed uproariously at his congregants' distress and promoted schism with his ugly rhetoric. One anonymous New Englander published a pamphlet titled *The Examiner; or Gilbert Against Tennent*, in which he arranged statements in columns marked "Gilbert" and "Tennent," and showed how almost all of his key arguments contradicted each other and made no sense. As one critic wrote, "Tennent has been severely censured in Boston where someone took all the arrows which he had sharpened for us and shot them at him."

Gilbert responded with *The Examiner, Examined; or Gilbert Tennent, Harmonious*, trying to reconcile his various positions on the revival, but the damage had been done. Added to this was his ongoing feud with the Moravian sect, whose leader Count Nicholas Zinzendorf had proven to be a formidable foe. Gilbert had already rebuked him and his group for antinomianism—claiming God's grace allowed them to disregard moral laws—and accused him of corrupting believers with lies and sowing discord. Worse, he said the Moravians had nothing to do with the real Christian revival, and instead preached "nonsense and contradiction" to the "ignorant and credulous" with ideas founded on "detestable mysteries" and "detestable doctrine."

This did not go over well with the New Lights, who had many friends among the Moravians. They painted Gilbert as a humorless, rigid, and prideful pedant who routinely spoke out of both sides of his mouth and became incensed when questioned about it. The anti-Moravian screed also put Gilbert in trouble with Whitefield, who from Britain had learned of his attacks and wrote him a disapproving note. Did he have to be so harsh and sectarian? And was it proper for him to judge the sect so harshly, when they were all God's children who strove to be "nearest the mind of Jesus Christ"? Gilbert wrote back denying he was a bigot, reminded Whitefield of the importance of doctrine, and snapped—"Your high opinion of the Moravians and attempts to join with them shocks me exceedingly and opens a scene of terror and distress." He implored Whitefield to renounce the sect of "enthusiastical heretics," as he had. Yet the Itinerant would not listen to Gilbert's counsel, and the latter could only feel more adrift and isolated from his old ally.

By this point it was clear that 1742 had become Gilbert's year of misery. His coreligionists had split from him, his fellow revivalists had questioned his ideology, and even his enemies had twisted his words and forced him into a desperate defense. But amid all this, the challenges became greater, as Gilbert's reputation, and that of all the revivalists, suffered once again from the continuing debacle that was the ministry of James Davenport.

THE FINAL NARRATIVE
OF JAMES DAVENPORT

By the spring of 1742 Reverend Davenport had been traveling through the Middle Colonies and New England for two years igniting spiritual fires in meetinghouses, fields, barns, and anywhere else the spirit led him to preach. His association with George Whitefield and Gilbert Tennent had given him initial credibility, but since then he had established his own brand of radical experimental piety, with the people of New London, Connecticut, as his current test subjects. No longer pleased to be the target of his abuse, the colony's Old Light pastors joined together to pressure the Connecticut Assembly to pass the first in a series of laws to cripple the ministry of men like him and his army of followers.

In May a new law outlawed itinerant preaching in the colony. No longer could traveling ministers expect to give sermons outside their parishes without permission from the governing pastor; no longer could lay exhorters and random strangers offer their testimony in the pulpit without the same permission; and no longer could one congregation allow its minister to preach in other jurisdictions without consequences. If found guilty of breaking the law, transgressors were subject to fines, arrest, and exile.

More laws were to come. Soon, the authorities forbade New Light separatist congregations from legal protection as religious dissenters. New seminaries like the Shepherd's Tent required legislative approval. Tests of religious orthodoxy became mandatory at Yale College, and ministers lacking a college degree were barred from teaching. And ministers of schismatic churches were forbidden to give communion or baptism to their congregants.

Critics reacted with outrage, charging that the lawmakers had tried to outlaw religious expression to protect a sinful and oppressive establishment. The revivalists in New England shuddered to imagine the next steps the authorities would take to shut down their movement. But despite the new challenges, James Davenport remained undaunted.

Just days after the passage of the anti-itinerant law, he boldly broke it in Stratford, Connecticut. The press followed his actions closely, and reported he preached angrily against unconverted ministers; pronounced damnation against his various enemies, "with hell-flames flashing in their faces"; imitated the agony and suffering of Christ; and created "shocking scenes of horror and confusion, under the name and pretext of religious devotion, as language can't describe."

The authorities drew up a legal complaint, which charged him with behaving in a "strange and unaccountable manner" to "affright and terrify the people, and put them into utmost confusion, contention, hate, and anger among themselves." A great public trial followed, in which Davenport and his allies stood accused of inciting public outrage and breaking the laws and disturbing the peace of the colony. After the first day's hearing, the reverend and his associates left the meetinghouse where the court heard their case, and he began shouting at the assembled crowd. Davenport blasted out invective about how the authorities had persecuted him and threatened his ministry. The sheriff grabbed his sleeve to take him away, after which Davenport fell to the ground invoking the protection of God: "Strike them, Lord! Strike them!" He was seconded by his allies, who promised the vengeance of God against their enemies. The crowd surged and attempted to release him from his bonds, but failed. That night, the masses mounted enough of a threat to try to free Davenport and ransack the town that forty militiamen had to be called out to restore order.

Yet despite the confusion Davenport had brought to Stratford, the court wanted to be rid of him more than punish him. In its decision, it concluded that the minister was "disturbed in the rational faculties of his mind, and therefore to be pitied and compassionated," instead of imprisoned. So it deported him from the colony and sent him back to his parish in Southold, Long Island.

Davenport was not finished with his mission, though. He next planned to visit Boston to attempt to ignite fervor in New England, a region that had proved so hospitable to men like Whitefield and Tennent. Fearing his plans, an association of ministers decided to bar him from their pulpits and requested that he refrain from any disruptive, impolite, or judgmental behavior. These pleas, of course, only encouraged him to stir up more trouble. As one of his associates said, "where any congregation is in peace, the devil is their ruler."

In midsummer Davenport burst into town with a vengeance, preaching to the masses on Boston Common and calling out a dozen preachers for being ungodly and unconverted. He declared these "miserable and wretched men" would soon be going to hell, and "were murdering souls by thousands and by millions" with their horrific carnal beliefs. He preached in fields and led mobs through the streets and incited his followers into what town leaders thought would surely be anarchy. One reporter saw a monstrous scene in which Davenport led his legions through the streets, "hands extended, his head thrown back, and his eyes staring up to heaven" with his followers more resembling "a company of Bacchanalians after a mad frolic than sober Christians who had been worshipping God." Another saw Davenport's spiritual army as "so red hot, that I verily believe they would make nothing to kill opposers."

The authorities reacted with alarm to these events, fearing not only for the protection of established religion, but also the stability of society. One minister in Salem wrote, "it is impossible to relate the convulsions into which the whole country is thrown by a set of enthusiasts that strole about haranguing the admiring vulgar in extempore nonsense, nor is it confined to these only, for men, women, children, servants and Negroes are now become (as they phrase it) exhorters."

Many ordinary workers and commoners now rose up in support of Davenport, among them common artisans and the downtrodden, to threaten the rule of law and the sanctity of private property. Many of the elite worried that once fully unleashed, the revivalists would make "strong attempts to destroy all property, to make all things common, wives as well as goods." Other saw disturbing parallels between the religious enthusiasts and revolutionaries like Oliver Cromwell, who had incited a civil war in England in the previous century and whose followers demanded the "leveling" of social classes. These assorted worries soon coalesced into legal action: Davenport was once again arrested and tried, declared insane, and removed from the colony.

When he returned to Southold in October, he did not receive a hero's welcome. Instead, his congregation censured him for spending so much time outside his parish ministering to outsiders. Within months after the judgment, Davenport took his followers to their refuge in New London, Connecticut—despite the colony's powerful anti-itinerancy law and despite the controversy that followed him wherever he went. By this time, Davenport suffered from inflammatory ulcers and bodily weakness that required him to employ an "armor-bearer" to help him walk. He ascribed his lame leg to the work of Satan and had fever dreams of being God's favorite and privy to his cosmic plans. He preached of the millennium and offered the promise that everyone would soon be engulfed in a fiery final judgment, because God had offered him "some extraordinary discovery and assurance of the very near approach of the end of the world . . . in a very short time all these things will be involved in devouring flames."

On March 2, 1743, he began organizing a church of New London separatists. God now gave him instructions in his dreams, and one such mission was to purge his followers of their wicked possessions—from wigs and cloaks to rings, jewels, and necklaces—and put them to flame. Four days later, another burning commenced, this time with a pile of books Davenport judged to be the works of the devil. Among them were classics by Puritan divines like Increase Mather and modern works by moderate revivalists like Benjamin Colman. The justification for the fires came from Acts 19:19—"Many of them also which used curious arts brought their books together, and burned them before all men"—and met with the excitement of the crowd, who shouted and sang "Hallelujah!" and "Glory to God!" and imagined their authors being tortured in hell.

Davenport again fueled the flames the next day, now demanding that his followers' own clothing be incinerated. Women hurled their "scarlet cloaks, velvet hoods, fine laces, and every thing that had two colors" while men torched their wigs and velvet collars, among other posh attire. Davenport crowned the ceremony by offering his own contribution—his breeches, which he whipped off and threw into the bonfire with aplomb. This action stripped his legs bare along with his power over the crowd.

One angry woman suddenly announced, "the calf you have made is too big" and took the smoldering breeches from the pyre and flung them at the minister's face. Another man agreed the bonfire was a golden calf that symbolized Davenport's pride and idolatry. Others claimed he had the devil inside himself and demanded he recant his actions. Shocked by their accusations, Davenport had no choice but to admit his error, claiming he was "under the influence of an evil spirit, and that God had left him."

This led to the demise of his worldly power. Appalled by the spectacle, most of his acolytes deserted him, as did his allies in the ministry. Press reports detailed the bonfires of books and clothing he had arranged, and pronounced him insane beyond redemption. His congregation had already dismissed him, and now even the radical New Lights kept him away—knowing that his name had become infamous to some, absurd to others. Ardent revivalists like Andrew Croswell denounced Davenport, seeing that his ministry meant to "drive learning out of the world, and to sow it thick with the dreadful errors" of heresy. Within weeks of the bonfire, the Shepherd's Tent closed and the spiritual army he had assembled seemed to vanish altogether.

What did not vanish were the consequences of Davenport's ministry. For the March 6 bonfire sputtered the momentum of the revivalists and threatened to undermine the redemptive force of the New Birth. In many ways the figure of James Davenport was the greatest gift the Old Lights and the other traditionalists could have received, for their accusations of lunacy, fraud, blasphemy, and terror against their foes now seemed borne out and proven beyond question. Davenport was the embodiment of everything unholy they saw in the revivalists, and now every one of them would have to account for it.

SEVEN

DAGGERS AND DRAWN SWORDS

A t the height of his mad trek through New England in 1742, James Davenport decided to pay a visit to the Reverend Charles Chauncy. Sharing a nickname with the First Church building where he preached, "Old Brick" Chauncy was the leader of Boston's Old Lights. As had become his method in recent months, Davenport thought he would use the visit as an excuse for one of his signature interrogations. After quizzing Reverend Chauncy on the state of his soul, Davenport would doubtless find it lacking and, barring a sudden confession, would then proceed to denounce him. On Boston Common or in a similar public venue, Davenport would muster every ounce of venom he could to publicly incriminate this foe of the revival and turn the people against him, perhaps even his own congregation.

Chauncy had not always been an enemy of the New Birth. In fact he had been intrigued by the revival at first, when it seemed to bring about a reawakening of faith among his parishioners and lead them toward more virtuous behavior. But as the movement progressed, he saw its perils: unsound forms of worship, itinerant ministers raising havoc, unchecked enthusiasm in the pews. And he realized one of the central figures behind these perils was Davenport. In his writings and sermons, Chauncy began to let his congregants and other Bostonians know his feelings—and soon enough, Davenport knew them too.

Chauncy wasn't surprised by Davenport's unannounced appearance at his door. He had been observing the man's tactics for some time and had prepared his defense. Davenport had barely begun his questioning when Chauncy gave him a verbal lashing. He blasted him for abandoning his congregation in Southold, for leading church services that descended into madness, and for bringing chaos to places like Boston. He thought him to be either a scheming charlatan who deluded the masses, or an outright lunatic with no control over his actions. In the end Chauncy opted for the latter and hoped that "if God ever gives you a sound mind, you will cry to him from the deeps, for this strange conduct you have unhappily fallen into."

He didn't stop there. To his own First Church congregation, Chauncy delivered a sermon, *Enthusiasm Described and Cautioned Against*, that used his encounter with Davenport to illustrate everything he saw as dangerous about such extremists. Most of the charges had been heard from the pulpits of other Old Lights, but Chauncy argued his points cogently and convinced many New Englanders that the revivalists were not only errant in their conduct, but insane. As he said, the disease of enthusiasm led people to follow "the blind impetus of a wild fancy" causing tortured visions and emotional outbursts, among other unfortunate effects. With this sermon and later works on the same topic, Chauncy became the central nemesis of the revival in the colonies and, not surprisingly, his books were some of the first Davenport torched at his 1743 bonfire in New London.

Chauncy found himself invigorated by the contest against the New Lights, writing letters and pamphlets against them, excoriating them from the pulpit, and unlike many of his brethren, taking to the road to quench the revival fire where it had spread. Chauncy undertook an exhausting 300-mile circuit from New England to the Middle Colonies, taking extensive notes at the meetinghouses he visited, gathering information about enthusiastic wildness and using it as evidence of the revival's excesses. His work led to a book, *Seasonable Thoughts on the State of Religion in New-England*, that not only provided the traditionalists with the foremost defense of the old faith they could imagine, but helped hamper the revival's progress and impugn the reputations of many of its champions.

George Whitefield and Gilbert Tennent especially came under scrutiny. Chauncy accused them and other, more radical figures of sowing division in the churches, muddling God's word in the pulpit, causing strife in parishes that were not their own, and whipping worshippers into a state of frenzy and terror. As he saw it, the whole New Light project had thrown churches into turmoil and caused good Christians to attack and abuse each other. And in true hypocritical fashion, after causing so much chaos and splitting decent Christians into factions, these cunning New Light schemers had the nerve to present themselves as pious and holy men!

On one occasion in his travels, Whitefield met Chauncy at random on a street in Boston. Whitefield knew Chauncy had tried to convince New England clerics to close their doors to him and to chastise him in print. But surprisingly, when they crossed paths, they offered a courteous bow to each other. Chauncy inquired as to his purpose in town; Whitefield said he had come in service of the Lord. "I am sorry to hear it," Chauncy said. Whitefield replied, "So is the devil!"

In a recent work, *Some Thoughts Concerning the Present Revival of Religion in New-England*, Jonathan Edwards had anticipated many of the Old Light arguments and admitted some aspects of revival—harsh judging of others' souls, censorious and extreme behavior, and claims of divine revelation—were false and disorderly. But such outcomes did not negate the outpouring of the Holy Spirit that had transformed souls and revived people's faith. However, Old Brick Chauncy could not accept this defense, and in *Seasonable Thoughts* spent page after more than 400 pages eviscerating the revival and its "strange effects upon the body, such as swooning away and falling to the ground . . . bitter shriekings and screamings; convulsion-like tremblings and agitations, strugglings and tumblings, which, in some instances, have been attended with indecencies I shan't mention."

Even after some of the revivalists began to retreat with the demise of Davenport, Chauncy did not relent in his attack. To him, the revival was a scourge that had few positive effects on people's faith, apart from those that God naturally bestowed. Its proponents were blackguards and mountebanks, and no good had come from undermining the power of the clergy. And while melodramatic orations like those of Davenport and Whitefield might be entertaining and fuel people's emotions, they did not lead to salvation or redemption from sin. The only thing that could accomplish that was good old-fashioned faith channeled through human reason—"the plain truth is, an enlightened mind, and not raised affections, ought always to be the guide of those who call themselves men."

Moreover, the lay congregants who dared to preach were no better than a rabble to Chauncy, who feared hordes of ignoramuses and fools polluting the meetinghouses and babbling incoherently about meeting Jesus and having divine revelations. Such enthusiasm threw the whole system of pastoral education, licensing, and ordination into question and forced the Old Light orators to compete with the more theatrical and thrilling Calvinist upstarts.

Furthermore, since the traditionalists represented many of the wealthier parishes in the colonies, they saw the evangelical churches as a magnet for "the lower sort" who had a mind to steal from their betters and tear down the traditional hierarchy and civil order. This could not be allowed to stand, and in his writings Chauncy painted the threat of mob rule with the darkest images he could. Because once the masses no longer respected their old ministers, customs, and loyalties, they might believe anything and accept any miscreant or tyrant to rule over them—and start burning books, or clothes, or even people.

He reserved a special animus for women. Proclaimed as truth-tellers and visionaries by many New Lights, women had, through the course of the revival, found their voice in the pews, and exhorted with vigor and passion in fields and meetinghouses to hundreds of souls. It was one of the most visible outcomes of the revival, and to opponents of the New Birth, it had to be stopped. Chauncy wrote, "It is a shame for WOMEN to speak in the church . . . 'Tis a plain case, these FEMALE EXHORTERS are condemned by the apostle [Paul]." Such an outrage as female ministers would lead to the perversion of the church and threaten the power of established ministers—all of them men like himself, in formal wigs and robes.

Sarah Wheaten knew most orthodox ministers felt the same way as Chauncy, and she knew better than to speak in church—and to suffer the consequences of it. She had been told at least once by her minister Nathaniel

Clap that the proper role for ladies in the house of the Lord was silence and solicitude of the gospel. She followed the edict and did not raise her voice in her worship, even as the great revival swept through Rhode Island around her.

Though silent in her pew, Sarah did not otherwise keep quiet about her faith. With her friends she discussed God, prayed, and sang hymns to him, read the Bible and pondered and worried over what it took to be a good Christian. Since the arrival of Gilbert Tennent in Newport, she had given up her interest in popular music and dancing and avoided all gratuitous pleasures. She dressed modestly and cast aside the old Sarah who enjoyed fun and frivolity and instead embraced a life of piety that could prove what a good and faithful follower of Christ she was. She had found rebirth through him, so she figured she should let it show.

Proper and upright did not mean passive and docile, however. The new Sarah began to speak publicly about her thoughts on the divine creator and created a women's gospel society in which she led Bible study and counseled those in need of spiritual guidance. With her "steady, prudent zeal and activity" she tried to inspire her group members with stories of the grace and beneficence of the Lord. For if she could find hope in God, anyone could.

Nothing came easy for Sarah. For many years, Sarah's life seemed to resemble the story of Job. But while God ultimately rewarded that famous biblical figure, he rarely seemed to take pity on her or provide an earthly reward for her troubles. Yet she still persisted through the pain and grief.

When she was younger, she thought of suicide as a release from her star-crossed existence. She wrote regularly in her journal of her hatred of her sins and sometimes of herself. But by 1743, she had become reconciled to her struggles, and made it part of her philosophy. For it was strangely comforting to see God as the author of her misery: it made her a better Christian and in some way proved that the divine creator existed. As one writer summed up Sarah's views, "If there was no divine providence in the world, but only fate or luck, then human life was sheer chaos, an abyss of meaninglessness that was even more frightening than hell. Either God controlled everything, including suffering, or there was no God." Sarah knew there was a God, for he continually brought her new obstacles to face and new burdens to shoulder. Even when the Lord showed her mercy, he did so in a curious way: "It pleased him to remove a dear friend by death, with whom I was very intimate." The loss of her friend allowed her to find work through the widower, which enabled her to subsist for a while longer. God offered his providence through her sorrow, and she thanked him for it.

The year before, shopkeeper Henry Osborn had proposed to her. He promised relief from her financial woes and a measure of loyalty and affection. But she wasn't convinced the pairing was a good idea. He was nearly thirty years older than her, he had three almost-grown children who were only a decade younger than she was, and she questioned whether she loved him. She took comfort that he seemed like a decent Christian, but she still struggled over whether to say yes. Henry brought many potential pitfalls and few benefits other than companionship and perhaps economic security. Somehow, though, she felt God encouraging the union, and since she always trusted in his will, she took Henry's hand in marriage and became Sarah Osborn.

Months later, the newly married couple were bankrupt. Henry's money had disappeared in a failed shipbuilding investment, his savings vanished for unknown reasons, hers were seized by creditors, and he sold all the goods in his shop at cut-rate prices. Unable to pay their debts, the couple sunk into the mire of poverty—with four children in need of care. Worse, Henry was suddenly struck with physical infirmities and could not hold a job, so Sarah was once again forced to work as a schoolteacher to survive and to pay the family's mounting bills, which sometimes seemed like an impossible task.

Once again cursed by fate, Sarah wondered how she could endure this as a proper Christian. She tried to understand God's motive behind this latest grim turn of events, and the sins for which she was being punished. She blamed it on her pride.

She lived in a world where fine linens, expensive clothing, and rich imported goods from Europe had tempted the souls of many New Englanders. While she did not covet such things, God must have thought she could not be trusted with even the hope of material comfort, much less good health and happiness, so he never let her have it. As she wrote, "I have often thought God has so ordered it throughout my days hitherto, that I should be in an afflicted, low condition, as to worldly circumstances, and inclined the hearts of others to relieve me in all my distress." God had meant for her to be poor and for others to take pity on her, and she had to deal with it.

Despite all the misery God heaped upon her, she refused to take pity on herself, and redoubled her commitment to being a good Christian and proclaiming her faith publicly. By the end of the year she finished her memoir, having endured a lifetime's worth of suffering despite only being thirty years old, and now wished for others to understand her struggle and what it meant. Just as "I have always reaped much benefit myself, by reading the lives and experiences of others," so too would Newport and the world beyond come to know what it meant to be Sarah Osborn, and how she had profited in the eyes of God by the hardships he inflicted on her.

Women who were not Sarah Osborn struggled in colonial America and faced countless obstacles, too. They could not study for the ministry, they could not go to college or vote for the assembly, and they could not own property independently of their husbands. They had fewer rights than their eldest sons to their estate, and they received a fraction of the inheritance of their male siblings. Viewed by some quarters of society as "a more advanced child," an adult woman had less power and fewer rights in the eighteenth century than she had in the previous one. As Sarah discovered, one of the few outlets a woman had was religion.

For most of the century, women dramatically outnumbered men in the pews. In one church in New London, Connecticut, where James Davenport had an influence, there were nearly three times as many women as men. Some parishes showed greater parity at the height of the revival, but for the most part the majority of congregants were women and nearly all the ministers were men. The few exceptions were in Quaker meetinghouses, where during quiet prayer a woman might be inspired to speak out and channel a divine message, but in other sects, women were told to keep silent and not interfere with the workings of the Holy Spirit.

Jonathan Edwards and other Congregationalist ministers saw some women, including his wife, as exemplary in their faith, but many other preachers did not, and blamed them for the world's assorted ills. One English pamphlet condemned "lewd women that are no whores, and yet are ten times worse" because their devilish spirit derived from the very first sinner,

Eve. And in a society where original sin had wide-ranging power over the minds of men, such a charge was a grave one—"as the world grew in years, so women grew in wickedness, each age being worse than the preceding." Some churches had such a baleful view of women that they didn't even allow them to read their stories of conversion aloud. For Sarah, the task was done by Reverend Clap.

Now that the revival had come, however, many women broke the silence. In New Light meetinghouses and outdoors in the fields, they raised their voices to praise the Lord. They shouted from the galleries, gave their testimony in the pews, and summoned the Holy Spirit in the streets. Daniel Rogers, acolyte of Whitefield, recognized the power of the revival for women as early as 1741, when during a spiritual meeting he saw how "the Spirit of God came down in an astonishing manner—two or three screamed out—it spread like fire." Rogers came away so impressed by women's testimony that he vigorously defended their exhorting and preaching the gospel, often in the face of hostile rebukes from other ministers.

The radical women of the New Birth did not stop there. Some found so much power in their conversions in Christ, they no longer feared reprisal from the clergymen who demanded their silence. They broke from their old churches and led splinter congregations. And when those congregations evolved into Separatist churches, they took major roles in their operation, and used their power as laypeople to hire ministers of the New Birth. As one writer put it, "evangelical religion offered women a faith that explicitly embraced feminine qualities. From its emotional rhetoric to its ecstatic conversions," this new spirituality gave women the opportunity to find strength in the house of God that they had not known before.

The men in wigs and robes condemned them for it. Charles Chauncy and the Old Lights inveighed against female enthusiasts who should have known their place, while other ministers worried women would fall prey to lusty itinerants who would use them for their own pleasures, or that they would usurp men's role in the church and the family. Such critics warned that if this happened, women would subject their husbands to unjust authority, and they would lose their status and be reduced to an effeminate role—as women became "queens for life." Even Jonathan Edwards, otherwise sympathetic to the revival, worried that "women and children might feel themselves inclined to break forth and scream aloud to great congregations, warning and exhorting the whole multitude, and to go forth and halloo and scream in the streets, or to leave the families they belong to, and go from house to house earnestly exhorting others."

While Sarah Osborn had no interest in hallooing and screaming, she did become increasingly vocal in her faith. Through her women's group, she drew listeners and followers for her thoughts on the gospel. She offered strength and even a hint of martyrdom to give them comfort through their trials and provided counsel to those who stood wracked by fear and guilt that they were on their way to hell. Offering herself as an example, she explained how salvation could be attained through suffering, and how God's grace could arrive in unexpected ways.

This prompted a reaction from her neighbors. They questioned her surety that she had been picked by the Lord for redemption and dismissed her thoughts on religion as those of an ignorant pauper. Ultimately, they wanted her to cease her improvised ministry and to keep quiet as she had once done. But she refused, for she saw her struggles as proof of God's power, and wrote, "Should I altogether hold my peace? . . . It appeared to me such a monstrous piece of ingratitude that it seemed as if the very stones might cry out against me."

She acquired a reputation in Newport as an arrogant evangelical, someone so convinced of her righteousness that she impinged on the judgment of God. One minister even preached against her and other revivalists in church—one of the first times she was considered important enough to be the object of public derision, instead of pity. But she would not relent in her mission to tout the gospel as she knew it. She had suffered too much, and endured too many miseries, to turn back from her true calling and lose favor in the eyes of her creator. As she wrote defiantly in defense of her actions, "God must cease to be God if he damned me."

Sarah's religious study group attracted women drawn by her self-assurance, and who were in need of comfort from their fears and anxieties. One such example was Sarah's friend Susanna Anthony, who, though a dozen years younger than Sarah and still a teenager, would remain her closest confidante over the decades. "Susa," as Sarah called her, had suffered the loss of her sister and other traumas, and felt her torments multiplying and enveloping her.

Susa's troubles began in earnest with the arrival in Newport of George Whitefield in 1740. Shortly after she saw the Itinerant in action, she experienced a great spiritual uplift, only to come crashing back down when Satan began to trouble her. The infernal beast taught her to despise herself and all she was, and she became consumed with paralyzing terror and self-hatred. She wrote, "I believe a bloody inhuman butcher would have been more welcome to my tortured breast than a reprieve to a tortured criminal. For Satan began to persuade me that I was a devil incarnate." The wicked one convinced her she was a mere plaything in God's hands, her soul broken at his whim, and an example to others of his taste for revenge upon sinners.

These torments went on for months, as Susa saw herself as "one of the worst of monsters; and often wished that I might be annihilated" for her baleful thoughts and actions. When Gilbert Tennent arrived the following year, he made things worse. Now the visions of hell, and Gilbert's vivid preaching of terrors, became more palpable and irresistible to Susa's young heart. She contemplated suicide to avoid the suffering she had been forced to endure; she begged Christ for mercy, and sometimes received it, only to be thrown into distress again with new and more fearsome attacks of the beast. The agony often became too much, and "through the violence of my distress, I wrung my hands, twisted every joint, and strained every nerve; biting my flesh; gnashing my teeth; throwing myself on the floor." God eventually rescued her from such horrors, but Satan remained ever present and ready to strike.

Sarah Osborn had endured more hardship than Susa, but she took pity on her friend's ravaged heart and did what she could to relieve her suffering. Others in Sarah's study group also struggled between light and darkness and wondered if the Lord would ever offer them mercy from their troubles. Sarah could not answer such questions. She could only tell them of the grace of God and the promise of salvation, and the possibility their sins would be expiated by Christ's loving sacrifice. She would become their teacher, their counselor, their confessor. Indeed, while Sarah may not have worn a pulpit gown or have earned a divinity degree, she did more to help her friends find God than any of their own ministers ever had.

◆

In more radical sects, some women went even further. Not only did they exhort and preach to worshippers, they revealed fantastic visions and prophecies. They described vivid scenes of Satan and Christ, images of warring demons and angels, messages from God and missives from the underworld. As a wave of mystical faith swept over the land, newspapers described how such women lapsed into trances and spoke directly to God. They transported into the ethereal world and saw beauty and wonder beyond comprehension. They witnessed heavenly "Glyphs" and other phantoms before their eyes. They saw their names inscribed in the Book of Life among the names of the saints. And they warded off the temptations of the Evil One. Such visions became so common that some worshippers assumed a person had to enter a trance and see the workings of heaven before he or she could be fully converted to Christ.

Pastor Nicholas Gilman in Durham, New Hampshire, found so much power in the visions of his female parishioners that he reported them in detail during his sermons, and saw one woman, Mary Reed, as a veritable conduit to God. She became the church oracle, describing radiant images of heaven and the power of the Holy Ghost—sometimes for weeks on end. She wrestled with Satan and sung with angels and inspired her neighbors to follow her example. Soon others saw doves and angels and heavenly lights, too, and heard celestial voices and issued messages to Gilman sent from the spirit world, with themselves as the Lord's messengers. Indeed, some radical sects honored women as great mystics, and "rejoiced in women leaders who claimed to be incarnations of God."

Not surprisingly, the spectacle of homegrown prophets touting their visions and claiming to be messiahs terrified the Old Lights and the moderate revivalists. In *Seasonable Thoughts*, Charles Chauncy thundered against all such enthusiasts, especially women, whose "agitations and terrors" derived from "the weakness of their nerves, and from hence their greater liableness to be surprised and overcome with fear." He railed against them as an affront to decency and order, and demanded they desist from their actions.

He compared such women to the notorious figure of Anne Hutchinson, who a century before had led worship services at her house and encouraged her followers to turn away from orthodoxy and toward what the Puritan authorities called sedition and blasphemy. She even talked to God and heard the voices of the biblical prophets. For these and other transgressions, the Bay Colony excommunicated and exiled her to Rhode Island, where she later perished in an attack of Siwanoy warriors, who scalped her and left her for dead.

Chauncy had more examples at hand. He accused women exhorters and oracles of being little different from the French Prophets of thirty years before in England—just as Alexander Garden had when attacking George Whitefield. These radicals claimed to have special knowledge of Christ's return, and they asserted their power to raise people from the dead. They would writhe about, fall over, "foam at the mouth, roar, and swell in their bellies, and that some of them affirm themselves to be equal with God." Chauncy railed against such horrors in detail, filling page after page with examples of self-proclaimed prophets running amok as they channeled the Holy Spirit, including sacrificing animals, dancing naked, mouthing blasphemies, and otherwise behaving like lunatics.

As with so much of his work against the revival, Chauncy's writings bred anxiety in his readers and forced the revivalists to respond. Jonathan Edwards, for one, had long worried about the "spirit of delusion" that led the "wildest enthusiasts" to become "the objects of ridicule of all the rest of mankind." He and other traditional men of the cloth wished to see the women prophets and exhorters reined in, to prevent another demagogue from rising from their ranks as Davenport had, and to return to their old place of being quiet and submissive in church.

However, what men like Reverend Edwards didn't understand was that many evangelical women had not only seized the New Birth for themselves, they had thrown it back in the face of their former ministers. They openly questioned them, they split from them, they formed their own churches in spite of them—and they were no longer afraid of them. They would partake in beautiful visions of heaven and describe them with all the passion they could muster, and no old-fashioned preacher could stop them.

Enthusiasm had set thousands of Christian souls alight. It offered the same radiant power that had marked religious uprisings since the time of Martin Luther, but this time it had come to the American colonists and melted their hearts. One English Puritan had described it well, long before the revival, "Let your auditors be awed with your flaming zeal, as if they heard a voice from the burning mountain, or the dark cloud bursting with flashes of fire." For when preachers put the Holy Spirit in the hearts of sinners, "their words must be daggers and drawn swords."

Charles Chauncy remained undeterred by the passions of his foes. He saw that the rise of enthusiasm allowed a motley collection of clairvoyants, soothsayers, and fortune-tellers to upend society from its lowest ranks. This group of miscreants even included the enslaved—"yea, Negroes, have taken upon them to do the business of preachers." The rise of such exhorters was particularly loathsome to him, and the result was "certainly a very bad one, and portends evil to these churches" where the New Birth held sway.

Slavery was present everywhere in America, and not only in the South. In the Middle Colonies, Pennsylvania had dramatically increased its import of African slaves since the turn of the eighteenth century, and 10 percent of Philadelphia's population was black and unfree—and 40 percent of the dock workers were either slaves or indentured servants. While most Quaker merchants had turned against slavery by this time and proclaimed the practice to be immoral, businessmen of other sects defended and expanded their trade in human chattel. In New York, the enslaved made up one out of every five residents of the city, and half of all families may have owned at least one forced laborer. Boston, too, profited from the trade after the turn of the century, quadrupling the number of its citizens stripped of legal rights, justice, and freedom.

Most ministers defended slavery and excused it with elaborate references to the Bible and gospel verses cherry-picked to assuage their consciences that God approved of it. Jonathan Edwards owned slaves and tried to justify the practice, George Whitefield argued for leniency in the treatment of slaves but not for their freedom, and a full range of clerics from Charles Chauncy to Gilbert Tennent either openly supported slavery or gave it their tacit approval. The notable exceptions included the New Light radicals.

Roving preachers like Daniel Rogers, Andrew Croswell, James Davenport, and many others encouraged free and unfree colonists to give voice to the Holy Spirit in their meetings, and they found countless bondsmen willing to do so. They encouraged their exhortations and led services where people spoke with passion and energy, regardless of their color, sex, or age. Unlike Edwards and Tennent, these New Lights did not shrink from the implications of their preaching upon those held in bondage, and Croswell condemned slavery with the same towering rhetoric he used against unconverted ministers.

Through the teaching of the radicals, as well as their own interest and determination, many slaves learned to read—often to peruse the Bible for themselves and to find out that the Good Book included verses condemning slavery instead of upholding it. From their readings they learned to preach and to use lessons from scripture, and from preaching they came to influence others, until the entire project of black education and exhortation acquired momentum and threatened the power of the slave holders. New England ministers worried that "slaves in a state of grace thought themselves above the laws of their masters" as they "exhort[ed] their betters even in pulpit before large assemblies."

The threat of the enslaved becoming enlightened increased the number of white foes of the revival. At first the slave holders had been the most opposed to the edification of black men and women, but by 1743 the fear and anxiety spread to others who didn't own slaves. Old Lights and colonial authorities warned of the dangers of bondsmen *freely choosing* to follow the Holy Spirit wherever it led them, since "poor Negroes have not been vindicated into the glorious liberty of the children of God unless their manners have been altered by becoming better servants, more faithful, diligent, honest and obedient to their own masters."

In this view, the soul of a slave could only be uplifted if he became a better slave. And yet many slaves had come to learn that their salvation did not depend on their own dutiful imprisonment. It came through the grace that God delivered, through the visions and words they spoke in inspiration, and through the divine power that led them to speak and testify. But the more the passions of the revival increased, the more the opposers railed against it. They reminded their readers that slave liberty could lead to slave rebellion, recalling the spring and summer of 1741, when the so-called Negro Conspiracy erupted.

Though two years had passed, few in the northern colonies could forget the conspiracy. What it was exactly, they did not fully recall or understand, other than it had something to do with black people. The stories were too lurid and conflicting to form a coherent narrative. Nonetheless, royal officials and other authorities were only too happy to remind colonists of the event, and what they saw as the danger of giving the enslaved even the faintest hope of freedom.

The alleged conspiracy began when a series of robberies and fires in New York City put residents on edge. No immediate cause could be determined, and an official investigation uncovered stories of slaves being served rum in taverns, whites and blacks fraternizing in those establishments, and prostitutes plying their trade there. None of this was particularly new or surprising, but in the climate of anxiety that gripped the city at the height of the revival, it explained a great deal. Many assumed the arson and larcenies were surely the result of whoring and drinking among slaves, with a few white tavern owners and criminals also having a hand in it. And so, with only the thinnest of evidence, a few forced confessions and contradictory witness statements convinced many white New Yorkers that enslaved black men and women had not only tried to burn the town, they had plotted the robbery and murder of its white inhabitants.

Ninety blacks and a dozen whites came under suspicion, and in the dubious trial that followed, thirty-four people were sentenced to death by hanging and burning, almost all of them black. Two supposed leaders of the plot died on medieval-style gibbets, as a public warning to any current slaves and future conspirators of the consequences of rebellion in New York or any other colony in America.

George Whitefield also came under suspicion in the conspiracy, even though he had already sailed back to Britain. Although witnesses did not connect him to a direct role in the controversy, they charged that his ministrations to slaves, his encouragement of their conversions, and his attacks upon the slave holders had contributed to a climate of insurrection. If he didn't light the flames himself, he was at least responsible for gathering the tinder, and for providing the spark. Of course, the Grand Itinerant had no interest whatsoever in leading slave rebellions and, if anything, was even more frightened of black people than other revivalists. Yet in the Middle Colonies the charge of sedition adhered to his name and those of the other ministers of the New Birth.

◆

Two years later, suspicions of the revivalists continued to mount as many began to minister to Indians on the frontier. Missionaries had long attempted to convert the indigenous peoples of the colonies, but the spiritual awakening made the push to proselytize more urgent, with more preachers wandering into the hinterlands to spread the gospel to those unfamiliar with it. Radicals especially found success with proclaiming the power of the Christian God to tribes in the Middle Colonies and New England. Whitefield and Davenport had drawn many Indians to the New Birth, as did other preachers who followed in their wake, bringing their message to the Mohegan, Pequot, Montaukett, Shinnecock, and Narragansett peoples. In 1742 conversions spiked, as the radicals' freewheeling services attracted many who had avoided the staid ceremonies of conventional churches. Daniel Rogers wrote of how he ministered to penitents regardless of their race and encouraged anyone from black slaves to poor women to Indians to become "itinerants, exhorters, prophets, and visionaries, embracing their own radical awakening."

Standing at the vanguard of this movement was Andrew Croswell, who ministered to Indians as he did to others overlooked by conventional churches, and spurred his congregants to learn to read and study the Bible for themselves. As with his gospel to freedmen and slaves, he personally converted fifty Pequots and encouraged them to testify to their new faith. When the Indian converts decided to create a Christian school and hire a schoolmaster, they wrote a petition to the Connecticut General Assembly asking for financial support. Croswell delivered their petition to the Assembly himself.

Along with his other activities, the Groton minister continued to hold ecstatic, chaotic worship services unlike any known in the colonies. In his meetinghouse, parishioners were not divided by rank or race or class—they all gave praise to God in a great helter-skelter assembly where they "sang, prayed, hugged, and fainted" without regard to the rest of society or what anyone else thought of them. He shouted with delirious joy and "encouraged blacks and Indians along with women and children to exhort, pray, and testify publicly to God's free grace." He charged through the pews with fearsome energy to inspire passion in the worship of the Lord. He gave up his pulpit so anyone feeling the Holy Spirit could express it. He spoke in the rough, everyday language of his congregants. And he sometimes even preached without a shirt or clerical vestments—almost naked, his critics said.

The moderate revivalists and opponents of the New Birth still singled him out as an example of everything wrong with the radicals. Yale rector Thomas Clap linked Croswell to the raving excesses of James Davenport and cast him as partially responsible for Davenport's running amok in New London. Croswell in turn denounced Davenport for his behavior, but would not apologize for his own background role at New London or his encouragement of Davenport to go to Boston in 1741. In fact, Croswell refused to criticize his own actions or take back any of the scabrous things he had said about ministers who opposed him. He would never apologize for those things, because condemnations had become his stock in trade.

Croswell collected the grievances so many had about colonial life and incorporated them into his theology. He cursed the moderates who promoted proper behavior and fashionable ethics: "Curse be that charity, for it is fierce, and that moderation, for it is cruel." He envisioned nothing less than a second Reformation in the New World, casting himself as Martin Luther and his enemies as the Pope's legions, and announced that there could be no compromise in the titanic struggle.

He especially blasted Jonathan Edwards, who had tempered some of the most extreme aspects of the revival by calling them into question. Croswell thought this to be middling and absurd. He called Edwards a coward and defended the intense passions the revival had unleashed, writing of the moderates, "God's order differs vastly from their nice and delicate apprehensions of it." For the Lord often brought turmoil when he offered redemption to sinners, and he cared little for decorum when he melted their hearts in Christ. According to the gospel of Andrew Croswell, the Holy Spirit drove colonists toward God with a violent, irresistible force, and converts should never apologize for channeling his divine ferocity.

As the revival burned on, Croswell's rhetoric grew more vehement. He published tracts throughout the Middle Colonies and New England in which he eviscerated his enemies for their spurious beliefs and equivocations. In one lengthy reply to a book written by moderate Presbyterian Jonathan Dickinson, he claimed the author was leading his readers into hell with "Christ-despising and soul-murdering doctrines," and he called those who hadn't been converted Pharisees and "rotten-hearted hypocrites," among other choice words.

Croswell cast himself as the most savage warrior of the New Lights. He wrote that the power and success of Christianity often depended on "contention, persecution, and bloodshed. . . . and if it should please God still to pour out his spirit in a more glorious manner upon the Earth, there is reason to fear there would be scenes in blood in every country and colony; and many would be forced to die for the testimony of Jesus."

Whereas Jonathan Edwards had imagined terror in the afterlife as God judging and punishing sinners, now Croswell applied the same doctrine on earth, with himself as the judge. He wrote, "my soul has heard the alarm of war; and the question is, Who will arise on the Lord's side? Who? Who will come to the help of the Lord against the mighty?" It was a call to religious conflict, a crusade for holy war, and he knew such language would inspire fear in his enemies as much as it inspired faith in his followers. He felt he had no choice but to use such rhetoric to crush the philosophy of his enemies, for "if they will keep hugging this monster, while I am killing it; what can I do? For I breathe out nothing but slaughter against it: As far as GOD enables me, I will be the death of it. Killed it must be, because it kills the souls of men."

Such ideas made Croswell a bane to the governors and magistrates of the colonies, who not only assumed he had been part of the turmoil at New London, they feared he had other plans to upend more than a century of religious tradition and disrupt the social order. He did nothing to disabuse them of this notion, and even compared the current rulers of British North America to the sinful authorities who persecuted Christ, for their behavior resembled that of a witch possessed by demons. "The truth is, every persecutor is a madman."

He did not stand alone in attacking the colonial magistrates. Political dissent crept into the ministry of other New Lights as well. In one New Haven congregation, the parishioners separated from their minister and compared him to Pontius Pilate and Herod. The women of the church led the charge toward schism, seeing not only their reverend but the town councilors as a failure in God's eyes. They believed the Lord had given them license to denounce anyone who stood in the way of the Holy Spirit, regardless of whether his power derived from civil or canon law. The driving faith of such radicals allowed them to violate whatever rules they saw as sinful. For even Jesus broke the law when he overturned the money-changers' tables—proving that disobedience could be holy and just, and rebellion divinely inspired.

The bedlam of radical Christianity that Andrew Croswell championed had been four years in the making. Ever since George Whitefield had shaken the foundation of American institutions in 1740 with his attacks on the clergy and the established hierarchy, the revival had inspired waves of men and women to question everything they knew about God. From this arose a deeply personal understanding of how the Holy Spirit worked in their hearts, and a proud and rabid individuality that would continue to grow in American life. The radical ministers harnessed the fervent beliefs of their congregants and pushed them to defy the current religious hierarchy that was unresponsive to their needs. They disputed old traditions and values and left behind them a trail of divided congregations and disputed pulpits, and angry traditionalists whose power had been seized without warning.

Charles Chauncy, the revival's greatest critic, wrote that the legacy of recent events meant "the body of the ministers were never treated with more insult and contempt than by multitudes, and of those too, who once esteemed them the glory of New England." When people stopped deferring to established authority, any kind of anarchy was possible, including revolution. Only by smothering the fires of revival could the elite ministers once again regain control of their flocks and protect society from disintegration and madness. As Chauncy wrote, "The country was never in a more critical state, and how things will finally turn out, God only knows."

Pastors like Whitefield, Tennent, and Edwards may have lit the flames, but Croswell and the radicals now fed the blaze without restraint. And as it burned, it forged something new out of the ashes of the old order—the hazy outlines of an American populism. The Calvinists of the New World, with their unforgiving theology, had led a revolt of the spirit that undermined British customs and set faith in the individual above respect for civility and authority. As historian Alan Heimert saw it, Calvinism offered "a radical, even democratic, social and political ideology, and evangelical religion embodied, and inspired, a thrust toward American nationalism."

None of this radical change came without consequence, and the America at the peak of the revival little resembled the America of just four years before. Such a fundamental transformation affected everyone, and all the old relationships came into question. "Wives rebuked husbands for their lack of piety; children evangelized their parents; clergymen undermined one another by quarreling openly in public and in the press; laymen became exhorters; and even women refused to keep silence in the churches any longer."

The world had turned upside down and gave everyone a sense of vertigo. Yet regaining the balance and harmony of the former world would not be possible. Too much had changed and too many had been transformed. No one could return to the complacent peace of early America where Puritan divines and Anglican authorities held unquestioned power. British North America had become broken, its old ways shattered and replaced by strange forms that few could have imagined or expected. A new, feral, violent America was growing up from the ruins of English gentility and propriety, and "a psychological earthquake had reshaped the human landscape."

EIGHT

THE BOW OF JONATHAN

The governors, magistrates, and town councilors of British North America did not stand by and let New Light firebrands like Andrew Croswell wreak havoc. They passed a series of laws to turn back the tide of enthusiasm that had washed over the region, and to reestablish control over civil order. Connecticut led the charge, having already forbidden itinerants to ply their trade in the colony without permission, to undercut the power of ministers like James Davenport. Its leaders followed that legal maneuver with another that revoked the toleration of dissenters and cracked down on Separatist churches and ministers—effectively trying to silence religious freedom and speech.

New York followed suit. Alarmed by the Moravians' and other evangelists' attempts to Christianize Indians of the frontier, that colony's leaders outlawed missionaries who brought the gospel to so-called "ignorant savages." Other colonies prohibited the more extravagant behavior of the radicals, to fight the "perfect mess-medley of all kinds of disorder and error, enthusiastic wildness and extravagance." However, while these new laws and public campaigns were a clear exercise of raw power, they also displayed a great deal of wishful thinking. For nothing could undo the changes wrought in the previous five years, no matter how much the authorities tried.

The legal prohibitions prompted the New Lights to become more active in politics, and to make concerted attempts to remove their adversaries from political office, whether they were magistrates or justices of the peace. And as secular leaders increasingly meddled to control spiritual practices, clerics and laypeople became a force in lawmaking. In Connecticut they formed a party that eventually wrested control from their establishment foes, and other colonies saw nasty partisan battles break out in the pages of newspapers and in the public square. Matters of God and matters of state started to intertwine: royal authorities tried to clamp down on any practices they saw as aberrant or a threat to their power, while ministers made brazen attempts to outlaw ideas and practices they saw as depraved, and to give the sanction of law to their own theology over others. It was called "preaching politics" and it became common wherever the revival left its mark.

Amid all the tumult between the New and Old Lights, the denomination whose members actually controlled much of colonial government continued to advance in power. The Church of England made progress in turning weary parishioners, exhausted by the battles among revivalists, into good and proper Anglicans. They used the Society for the Propagation of the Gospel (SPG) to change the beliefs of many colonists and created much controversy in their wake. The Anglican Church had emerged as the foremost nemesis of the revival, and its clerics used whatever platforms they had to attack it. Most were paid by the church as missionaries for the SPG, so they could denounce the Calvinist uprising with little fear of popular backlash to their positions or salaries. And they did so with vigor.

For a long time they had seen dissenters plagued with "visions and delusions" that appealed to the "vanity and vapours of an empty skull." Now, with their claims of lunacy against their rivals borne out in the mad antics of the enthusiasts, they extended their critique. They decried the extemporaneous preaching of the New Lights as uncontrolled and dangerous. They saw the revivalists as obsessed with damnation, predestination, and other unpleasant notions, which only served to create a climate of "endless feuds, censoriousness, and uncharitableness." And they saw all dissenters as heirs to the Puritans who had murdered King Charles I a century before. Thus, not only were the Anglicans' adversaries touched with madness, they were outright traitors and a continuing threat to the British state.

Amid this spiritually unsettled landscape, a ship arrived from Britain in 1744 bearing an Anglican traveler who had much to do with the recent upheaval in America. George Whitefield returned to the colonies, to face the consequences of his actions and answer for them.

As with his previous trip to the colonies, Whitefield's arrival followed a flurry of newspaper reports of his travels: his recent doings in Britain, his fundraising for the Bethesda orphanage, and his plans for fresh soul-saving in America. However, he arrived gravely ill in York, Massachusetts (now part of Maine), and had scarcely begun his ministry before he faced a series of ugly accusations from enemies who had multiplied in his absence. One writer in a Boston paper demanded he apologize for all the harm he had caused to colonial pulpits, while others linked him to the radicals who greeted him in York as proof of his rebellious nature.

Whereas in 1740 he faced few critics in New England outside the Church of England, now many of the moderate dissenting churches he had once preached in shut their doors to him—and his old friends remained silent in response to attacks on him. The critics produced a lengthy list of transgressions for which they blamed Whitefield: inspiring wild enthusiasm in worship, encouraging armies of lay exhorters to degrade the word of God, mismanaging his orphanage and misusing its funds, offering maudlin and hollow sermons, abusing clergymen with differing views, and impugning the reputations of native colleges. In turn, eight associations of New England ministers denounced him; many Old Side Presbyterians condemned him; a series of pamphlets picked apart his ideas and tore apart his methods; and college leaders repudiated his itinerant ways. Almost all of his foes accused him of grievously harming the ministry and ruining the harmony of Christian worship.

Even the revivalists who had befriended him years before now seemed to turn their backs on him. With the specter of James Davenport still fresh in their minds, they worried Whitefield had been too eager a disruptor, too ready to divide congregations to conquer them. Harvard authorities spoke for many when they claimed he had caused "the detriment of religion, and the entire destruction of the order of [some] churches" and was nothing less than "an enthusiast, a censorious, uncharitable person, and a deluder of the people" whose mischief needed to be stopped, and soon.

By 1744 Whitefield had become used to being the target of abuse. In Britain, his Methodist movement to reform the Anglican Church had split into competing factions, with John and Charles Wesley espousing "free grace" and dismissing old-fashioned Calvinism like Whitefield's as cruel and fatalistic. Yet regardless of ideology, Methodists of all kinds came in for withering scorn from the priests and bishops of the state church, and that in turn inspired crowds to attack revivalists and those associated with them. Whitefield learned this in 1741, when he returned to England to discover that his press agent William Seward had been beaten to death at the hands of a mob. In other cases, his colleagues faced gunfire, beatings and (if female) rape and sexual abuse due to their beliefs, and the authorities often chose to look the other way as the mob held sway.

On more than a few occasions when he preached, miscreants climbed into trees to mock him and shout him down, also exposing themselves or trying to urinate on him. At Hampton, one unruly crowd hurled a fellow minister into a lime pit, as Whitefield narrowly escaped and a female follower had her arm broken. At Moorfields, Whitefield faced off with stage actors, puppeteers, and clowns, as the masses threw rocks, eggs, and chunks of dead cats at him, a clown tried to whip him, and a would-be assassin nicked him in the temple with a sword. But his luck ran out at Plymouth, just before his trip to America, when he was staying at an inn and an intruder burst into his room and nearly beat him to death with a cane. Whitefield finally escaped in his nightclothes screaming "Murder!" down the stairs.

Adding to the danger was the reality that, unlike in America, where critics merely accused Whitefield and his revivalists of damaging the church, in Britain the authorities considered them an active threat to the nation. The ongoing war with France fueled charges that he was disloyal to the Crown and defied the monarchy with his brash actions and seditious beliefs. Worse, he recalled the murderous habits of the 17th-century Puritan radicals who had committed regicide, and thus aroused "the body of the people into a national madness and frenzy in matters of religion." To avoid being further accused of treason or tossed into prison, Whitefield had to pen pamphlets and official statements attesting to his patriotism and support for the king, even to the point of slavish adoration—"May the Crown long flourish on his Royal Head, and a Popish Pretender never be permitted to sit upon the English throne!"

In York, Massachusetts, as Whitefield recovered from the beating he had endured in Plymouth, he found that the strong emotions he had provoked remained palpable. While his critics derided him in print, his remaining New Light supporters flocked to his bedside with words of encouragement, from radical clerics to Boston merchants to assorted laypeople. As he listened to the sermons of sympathetic ministers, he learned that York had recently experienced a fresh revival and, if he so chose, he could spark an even greater upheaval. He wrote that when he preached, "the invisible realities of another world lay open to my view. . . . I spoke with peculiar energy. Such effects followed the word, I thought it was worth dying for a thousand times." But Whitefield did not return to his old ways. Instead he chose to explain himself, and to control the passions of the masses instead of enflaming them.

With memories of the tumult in Britain still fresh in his mind, he began his latest New England tour chastened and humbled, and more than a bit wary. In Boston he met with a group of moderate ministers and announced that he had never meant to cause division or church separations, and only wanted to "preach the gospel of peace . . . and promote charity and love among all." He apologized if anyone had taken his earlier sermons the wrong way and said that he had no interest in the radical transformation of American religion. He even qualified his endorsement of Gilbert Tennent's attacks on unconverted ministers: "I told them that these words were not wrote to imply that it was absolutely impossible but that it was highly improbable that an unconverted man should be made instrumental to beget souls to Christ." Surprisingly, this hair-splitting legalism convinced several key ministers of his good intentions. Some like Benjamin Colman even opened their meetinghouses to him and his new, subdued version of the gospel.

From the pulpit he adopted a balanced tone that encouraged a sober and thoughtful faith, with much less preaching of terrors and fewer threats of damnation. He regretted being zealous and judgmental in his behavior and, having just turned thirty years of age, looked forward to having a more mature perspective. He even apologized to Harvard for his unfair criticisms of the school and resolved to preach nothing but old-fashioned Calvinism as the "pious ancestors and the founders of Harvard College preached long before I was born." At the same time, his remaining allies defended his conduct in pamphlets and newspapers, and they persuaded more clerics to open their church doors to his restrained, and much milder, orations.

Not all were convinced. One of the most aggressive of Whitefield's critics continued to be Thomas Clap, rector of Yale, who had seen his college consumed in enthusiastic wildness after the visits of Whitefield and, especially, James Davenport. With the Grand Itinerant once more making the rounds in the Northeast, Clap made the bold claim that Whitefield had secret plans to swap out the region's Old Light ministers with radicals of his choosing. Clap claimed he had gotten the news from Jonathan Edwards—which Edwards claimed was a lie, and which embroiled him in a public dispute for several months that embarrassed all parties involved.

Troubled that Whitefield had to endure such charges, Edwards took pity on him and defended him in print. He allowed the Itinerant to preach in Northampton, and hosted him for nearly a week, convinced that his rival for the affections of worshippers had set a more temperate course. In return, Whitefield criticized the "wild and extravagant people" in eastern Connecticut—where Davenport's revival had burned the hottest, and still continued to smolder—and praised Christ in a manner that would neither challenge dogma nor raise any eyebrows. He spent nine months in New England repairing the damage the moderates thought he had caused. In the end he won over men like Edwards, who saw that Whitefield had truly repented for his earlier behavior, and now bowed to the wisdom and stature of men like himself.

Whitefield made further strides, engaging once more with former radicals like Davenport, who offered apologies for his conduct. More importantly, he met Gilbert Tennent and appeased him with a long-overdue denunciation of the Moravians and began rebuilding his friendship with him.

He soon discovered Gilbert was no longer the agitator he had once known. Instead, Gilbert issued sermons on topics like "The Necessity of Studying to Be Quiet and Doing Your Own Business," in which he warned against "taking up evil reports against our brethren without sufficient evidence, and spreading of them with delight; both which are expressly forbidden by the Almighty." Whitefield realized that Gilbert had become a cautious and prudent man in recent years and had begun trying to repair the damage he had caused to his church. And once he learned more about Gilbert's struggles, he understood how much the revival fires had burned him.

THE SECOND REBIRTH OF GILBERT TENNENT

The frightening zenith, and spectacular collapse, of James Davenport affected Gilbert Tennent deeply. Not only did the Long Island minister defame the worthy aspects of the revival, he also brought disrepute on Gilbert directly. For Davenport's methods were just an extreme version of Gilbert's own. While he had vilified Davenport in the press as a monster whose various sins had led his "deluded votaries into the strangest absurdities in opinion, and most enormous evils in practice," he also feared the line between his own rhetoric and Davenport's was uncomfortably thin. He knew the consequences of his own actions had caught up to him and had trampled over his reputation.

In the summer of 1743, just after Davenport's implosion, the congregants of the New Building in Philadelphia had asked permission for Gilbert to become their minister. The meeting-house once built for Whitefield's evangelizing had since become the center of revivalism in the city, but as yet had no regular pastor—and the Moravians had begun to preach there more frequently. To have a minister of Gilbert's stature would be a spiritual and political coup for the Philadelphians, and would help counter the influence of the Moravians. It would also make him the only full-time revivalist pastor in town, though it would require the assent of Gilbert's own New Brunswick Presbytery, which he had led for seventeen years.

Gilbert's New Jersey flock readily agreed to let their preacher go. They had become used to his lengthy absences and high profile, but chafed under his pastoral care. What might work well in the pulpit—maligning his enemies with the wrath of God—did not help those who simply wanted spiritual advice, or blessings for a major life decision, or comfort in a time of crisis. Gilbert had outgrown his church, and its members had outgrown him. It was time to move on.

In late 1743, a wiser and warier Gilbert Tennent came to Philadelphia. As the leader of a parish of 140 souls, he continued to support the revival, but now took the role of a moderate cleric. He toned down his rhetoric, began preaching with notes, and even changed his attire, trading in his leather girdle and unkempt hair for a proper wig and robes. Emphasizing church doctrine became central to his ministry, and freewheeling evangelizing and judging others much less so. He had learned the hard way that merely firing people up into fits of terror was not enough to bring them closer to God. They had to understand their faith, to appreciate the rich theology and ideas of the Reformed Christian tradition, and to never assume they were any more righteous than their neighbors. For him, "experimental knowledge was not enough to create a steadfast faith," which was the very opposite of what Whitefield had preached in 1740 and what Gilbert had championed during the height of the revival.

He had come quite a way from his early days preaching hellfire in log houses and frontier meetinghouses; and his style in the pulpit wasn't the only thing that would change in Philadelphia. In a few years this son of Northern Ireland would hold formal services in an ornate, Anglican-style brick building with a steeple and glass chandeliers. The Second Presbyterian Church of Philadelphia would become one of most important in the colonies, its congregants among the wealthier and more influential in the city, and its minister a force for unity and reconciliation instead of mockery and damnation.

Still, peace and contentment would not find Gilbert any time soon. As he wrote upon departing New Brunswick, "I leave this place with no expectation of worldly comfort." He continued to face battles with the Moravians, with the enemies in the Synod, even within his new church, which split into schism once he became the minister. The specter of figures like Andrew Croswell also continued to vex him and other revivalists, and Gilbert would forever have to answer for The Danger of an Unconverted Ministry *and everything it had unleashed in the church and wider society. Even some of the successes of the revival he saw as ephemeral, and he noted how a number of converts "have lost their religious impressions and returned with the dog to his vomit, and some others have fallen into erroneous sentiments."*

He seemed to realize, too, that he had been both a champion and casualty of the forces he had released, and that his new ministry did not portend an improvement in his fortunes or make his sins any less onerous. As he wrote, "I am fully persuaded that change of place and outward circumstances is very often but a change of miseries, and little else is to be expected on this side of eternity."

◆

After several months in the colonies, and encounters with the likes of Gilbert Tennent and other repentant evangelists, George Whitefield had sufficiently ingratiated his listeners with his newfound moderation that some of the controversy that had attended his American tour began to subside. He even placated the Crown by offering his support for the upcoming military action against the French fort at Louisbourg (in Nova Scotia), in which an all-New England force of 3,600 soldiers and a thousand sailors would mount an attack against the stronghold that guarded the St. Lawrence River. The British government enlisted the aid of 450 preachers to stir up support among the public, and Whitefield proved to be one of the most eager to promote the expedition. He announced, "Christ leads! Never despair!"—which became an unofficial motto for the troops—and stood dockside in Boston exhorting mariners to fight as they entered their transports. Many of the soldiers faced mounting debts and desperate conditions, and Whitefield promised that war would bring them relief from their woes and glory in battle. His presence was an undoubted success in recruitment and helped bring spiritual sanction to a military campaign that was widely opposed by many New Englanders. It also won him much-needed favor from imperial authorities.

He had another opportunity to rally the troops the following year when British armies crushed the Jacobite rebellion of Bonnie Prince Charlie in Scotland. Although his role this time was to exhort victory from afar, Whitefield nonetheless made an impression on the colonists by summoning every bit of anti-Catholic invective he could muster. Recalling the fire-and-brimstone sermons of earlier years, this time the Itinerant warned against the wickedness of the Pope's legions—instead of unconverted Protestant ministers.

In his Philadelphia sermon, *Britain's Mercies and Britain's Duties*, he announced that the Scottish uprising was a "horrid plot, first hatched in hell" by the enemies of the government, with threats of monks and friars swarming over the landscape like locusts, Bibles ripped from innocent hands and liberty of conscience denied with "bigoted zeal." He described Catholicism as "a religion that turns plowshares into swords, and pruning hooks into spears, and makes it meritorious to shed Protestant blood," and asked, if not for the military campaign, "How soon would that mother of harlots have made herself once more drunk with the blood of the saints[?]" While Whitefield would no longer deploy such hateful rhetoric against the enemies of the revival, he found it convenient to use it against the Church of Rome. In Calvinist America, this helped him to further rebuild his reputation and restore his standing with clerical and civic leaders.

Moreover, Whitefield was now a married man, and this gave him a certain esteem that he had lacked while still a bachelor priest. A few years before he had wed a woman named Elizabeth James, who was a decade older than him and had initially resisted being married to the Itinerant—indeed, the prospect even kept her from eating or sleeping for a time. She had no desire to be his helpmate in a union that would be largely free of intimacy and romance. Whitefield's own words about her didn't help, writing in a letter to Gilbert Tennent that he found her neither wealthy nor attractive, but she was at least "a true child of God [who] would not, I think, attempt to hinder me in his work for the world."

Once he wore down her resistance and no better prospects seemed available for her, they married and he set her to work helping him manage his traveling ministry and, later, the Bethesda orphanage. He quickly became more interested in having her attend to his stateside affairs as a "ministry coordinator" than building a loving relationship, and often acted more as a work supervisor than a dutiful husband. On one occasion he was so intent on keeping her at Bethesda—despite her strong desire to return to England—that he sailed home without her, not even bothering to inform her of his departure. Such behavior bred frustration and anger in Elizabeth, but Whitefield seemed indifferent. Though he respected her faith in God, he often did not respect *her*, and would no more treat her as an equal than he would relieve her of her duties as his assistant. This made him all too typical for an orthodox preacher of the era. Unlike the radicals he had helped inspire, he remained callous and regressive in his views of women, and no one knew this better than Elizabeth.

In the autumn of 1745, the Whitefields headed south to South Carolina and Georgia, to inquire on the state of affairs at the orphanage. The revival had still not greatly affected the South, its residents either too wedded to Anglican ways or too uninterested to take part in the commotion that had upended the North. While a different movement, Separatist Baptism, was on the rise in the region, to Whitefield the South didn't look much different from its earlier appearance. Most of the people were still unchurched in the true faith, and what allies he had were either scattered or had defamed themselves.

The most notorious example was his old friend, Hugh Bryan, who had taken a wild turn at the height of the revival and had rivaled James Davenport in ferocity. When Whitefield was in Britain, Bryan had led passionate meetings of slaves that had enflamed the fears of their masters and the colony's racial hierarchy. The slave owners accused Bryan of ignoring the teaching of proper Christianity and instead inspiring their bondsmen with "a parcel of cant-phrases, trances, dreams, visions, and revelations," which took a turn for the apocalyptic when he began behaving like a sibyl preaching the end of the world. As one observer wrote, "he came to working miracles and lived for several days in the woods barefooted and alone and with his pen and ink to write down his prophecies." He foresaw the destruction of Charles Town for its wickedness, and promised that slaves would rise up from their bondage with sword and flames to avenge their captivity. Bryan was himself a slave owner, and the authorities realized how dangerous his threat was to the social order and tried to stop him before he caused another uprising like the Stono Rebellion.

But just as Bryan posed his greatest danger, he seemed to lose his mind. An "Angel of Light" ordered him to take a wooden rod and use it to "smite the waters of the river," dividing it like the Red Sea, until he reached dry land on the other side and proved himself to be a miracle worker. Bryan duly followed the angel's command, but instead of finding transcendence, he nearly drowned. His brother had to rescue him from the river current, and the incident turned Bryan from social rebel to public buffoon. His reputation destroyed, he lost his zeal for revival and—like so many others of his kind—apologized for his conduct, and "the dishonor I've done to God, as well as the disquiet which I may have occasioned to my country." He turned his back on justice for enslaved people and returned to his comforts as a plantation owner. The authorities and much of the public chalked up his temporary madness to "the workings of Whitefieldism in its native tendency."

When Whitefield came to Charles Town he had to answer for Hugh Bryan's behavior. Again he spoke against radicalism and accepted Bryan's apology, but still had to address lingering concerns that he cared too much for the welfare of slaves. Remembering his 1740 attacks on the vicious treatment Southern planters meted out to their captives, Whitefield's critics branded him a potential troublemaker and waited to see what fresh outrages he might have in store. But he was too distracted by his own affairs to answer them.

Upon his arrival at Bethesda, Whitefield saw the perilous state of his orphanage's finances, and it daunted him: "through the badness of the institution, and the trustees' obstinacy in not altering it, my load of debt and care was greatly increased, and, at times, almost overwhelmed me." He'd been soliciting funds for its improvement throughout his preaching tour, but couldn't seem to silence his opposers, who claimed he had squandered money raised to support the orphans, or abused those orphans with excessive moral instruction, or had left the place filthy and abandoned and the children starving.

Whitefield defended himself in print from such charges, provided an accounting of the orphanage's finances to Ben Franklin's *Pennsylvania*

Gazette, and gave Elizabeth a greater role in keeping track of the affairs of the institution. He also began to see the answer to the orphanage's problems in the ownership of human beings. First privately, then increasingly in public, Whitefield agitated for the legalization of slavery in Georgia. He spoke in favor of both Christianizing enslaved people and keeping them in chains, and even advocated for using forced labor to support the finances of his institution. Less than eighteen months later, he claimed it was "impossible for [Georgia's] inhabitants to subsist without the use of slaves. But God has put it into the hearts of my South Carolina friends, to contribute liberally toward purchasing, in this province, a plantation and slaves, which I propose to devote to the support of Bethesda." And so this once-fiery critic of the slaveholders, and all their attendant cruelties and barbarism, now looked forward to becoming one himself. As he wrote, "one Negro has been given me. Some more I propose to purchase this week."

Thus, on his third trip to America, Whitefield became something very different than the man who had left it blazing just a few years before. In that earlier visit, he had come as a whirlwind, inspiring passion in the New Birth and inciting a frenzy by his grand theatrics. He declaimed, he exhorted, he offended at will—and he left America reeling after spending only fifteen months there. But now, on his current visit, he would stay nearly four years, until 1748. The crowds would be smaller and less fervent, the issues more complicated, the politics harder to navigate. Whitefield had grown up and perhaps even outgrown his notoriety, to become an icon of orthodox Calvinism. No longer a threat to the Northern civil order or the Southern racial order or the British nation, he was now a bland and inoffensive supporter of Christ, a slaveholding preacher who no longer inspired ecstasy or fury or other dangerous emotions, but instead protected the colonial hierarchy and the primacy of the established churches . . . with one notable exception.

While Whitefield had cast himself as a champion of British arms, he remained no friend to the Church of England. In previous trips, he had condemned its priests as unregenerate and its idols like John Tillotson as villainous. He declared its leadership to be corrupt, and its practices suspect. He had defamed its commissaries and the church, in turn, had denigrated and ridiculed him. And he had twice been arrested for his actions by

Alexander Garden, who, upon Whitefield's latest trip to America, formally suspended him from the ministry, only to have the Itinerant disregard the edict and continue to preach however he liked.

Regardless of the Anglican clerics' actions against Whitefield, he still brought the legitimacy of the church into question throughout the colonies—while strengthening the hands of its adversaries. Many churchmen recognized this, none more so than Boston commissary Timothy Cutler: "Whitefield has plagued us with a witness, especially his friends and followers, who are like to be battered to pieces by that battering ram they had provided against our Church here." Although the SPG and Anglican ministers had made headway in converting dissenters while Whitefield was in Britain, they had no interest in seeing him undermine their progress now that he had returned to America.

Though Whitefield had been more benign in his recent orations, his very presence seemed to cause trouble. During his New England trip, a public debate broke out over the character of the Anglican church and the perils its missionaries presented to other churches. Inspired by Whitefield, dissenting preachers condemned the Church of England as a menace to the true worship of Christ; and one of them, Noah Hobart, created a firestorm in his *Sermon Delivered at the Ordination of the Reverend Mr. Noah Welles*, on the last day of the year in 1746. He questioned the primacy of the church and rejected the idea that Anglicanism was essential to the British state and defended dissent and disobedience against the church's practices. He claimed any good Christian knew better than to follow its questionable theology instead of the "serious religion and practical godliness" of old-fashioned Calvinism.

Yet another pamphlet battle broke out between Congregationalists and Anglicans, this one without the involvement of Whitefield. Still, his presence was felt in the slashing rhetoric issued from both sides, in the accusations of corruption, and in the conspiratorial claims that ran rampant. Hobart saw the Anglican Church as little better than the Roman Catholic Church, for just as the latter "has made herself drunken with the blood of the saints, and with the blood of the martyrs of Jesus," Protestant faiths with similar ideas "are to be esteemed and detested as relics of Popery." Opportunistic ministers took Whitefield's calumnies against the Catholic faith and certain

Anglican practices and blended them into one comprehensive slander, and Whitefield could no more control its spread than he could stop the revival that he had unleashed a half-decade before.

In their paranoid mindset, the warring sides now saw Whitefield's legacy through opposing lenses—whether as a truth teller who had exposed the moral rot in the Church of England, as a subversive who had undermined the strength of that church, or as a clever rogue who had driven dissenters away from each other and gave Anglicans "a providential opportunity to divide and triumph." In fact, the name of Whitefield could be invoked to make any kind of argument. He was both radical and conservative, divider and conciliator, demagogue and unifier, patriot and subversive, conformist and dissenter. The shadow of his reputation had long since escaped him, and he came to learn that the colonists didn't exalt or condemn only one Whitefield, but many versions of him—and took vastly different lessons from whatever phantom they imagined him to be.

Without question, recent college graduate Jonathan Mayhew looked at Whitefield and saw a menace—a person who preached to "enlightened idiots" and made "inspiration, and the spirit of truth and wisdom, the vehicle of nonsense and contradiction." To his father he wrote that Whitefield's adherents were "chiefly of the more illiterate sort" who followed a rascal that delivered "as low, confused, puerile, conceited, ill-natured, enthusiastic a performance, as I ever heard." This attitude marked a dramatic change, for just a few years before, Jonathan had been swept up in the evangelical fervor that had swept New England and had seen the workings of the Holy Spirit upon the hearts of sinners and found comfort in it. Since then, however, his views had become wary, even cynical, and his mentors had no small part in it.

His father, Experience Mayhew, for one, had proved to be a relentless critic of the New Birth. He saw ministers like Whitefield "under the power of Satanical delusions" and advised his son that preachers who offered such appeals to low emotions were opponents of God and threats to a reasonable, well-understood Christian faith. More importantly, Jonathan proved highly receptive to the arguments of Harvard's president and tutors that Whitefield was "an uncharitable, censorious and slanderous man" and "a deluder of the people," as they said in their official statement upon the Grand Itinerant's return to New England.

Jonathan was eager to read many of the "Bad Books" Whitefield had condemned, including those of John Tillotson. From them he came to appreciate that the rigors of faith meant nothing without rationality. He learned how Christian ethics and morality could reflect a devout faith in God and enable earthly happiness, and he came to trust his own judgment about salvation and redemption. In turn he crafted an innovative ideology that rejected the ideas of the New Light radicals, the moderate revivalists, and even the Old Light Calvinists. None of them seemed to reflect the truth of God as Jonathan understood it, which in its universal power went beyond Congregationalism, Presbyterianism, or classical Puritanism. It was his own handcrafted philosophy, and he not only believed it, he began to state it publicly—to some controversy. But this was no great matter, for Jonathan reveled in controversy, and his life was marked by it, even before he left Harvard.

He broke college rules and was fined. He spoke his mind freely and raised provocative points. He kept a circle of friends that included Samuel Cooper, John Brown, and Gad Hitchcock, whose irreverent ideas made them seem like "a pack of young heretics." And during his thesis, when Jonathan argued that faith and reason were compatible with Christianity, a questioner proposed that any religion that upheld an idea like original sin was not rational. He readily agreed.

His changing beliefs set him apart from his father, who continued to act as an Indian missionary and wrote books like *Grace Defended*, which offered his own view of Calvinism. Jonathan took his father's writings to one of his Harvard professors, Edward Wigglesworth, and asked for his opinion. The professor pointed out the contradictions of Experience's argument, and that the idea of free grace and divine election were actually in conflict. So Jonathan was forced to choose: either human free will provided the key to salvation, or God chose to save some people and doom others to hell. He chose the former idea and drifted further away from orthodoxy.

He graduated from Harvard with a master's degree in divinity in the summer of 1747 in search of a pulpit to preach in. Not only did he wish to expound on his ideas before a congregation, he also needed a steady income to reduce some of his college debt load. A parish in Worcester invited him to partake in a preaching competition with one Thaddeus McCarty, a vigorous young man with a booming voice and a "black penetrating eye." Over the course of a month, the two gave sermons to the parishioners who would ultimately decide the victor. In the end the revivalist beat him forty-four votes to two. This frustrated Jonathan and pushed him still farther away from evangelicalism and closer to a liberal pulpit in the city.

Although an isolated church in Cohasset pursued Jonathan as its minister, he was much more interested in an open position in West Boston. Here, at West Church, a growing population of affluent merchants and upstarts looked to find an open-minded minister as their leader—someone who rejected the fanaticism of the New Lights and could assure them of their salvation by their own good conduct on earth. They had just seen their beloved pastor William Hooper change faith to Anglicanism and become the pastor of Trinity Church, a troubling sign of the Church of England's continuing advance in New England in the chaotic aftermath of the revival.

In replacing Hooper, Jonathan couldn't have imagined a better opportunity: an urban pulpit, a wealthy congregation, and a competitive salary of 15 pounds per week, plus an allowance for rent and firewood. For the congregation, the choice was easy. After hearing him preach, they overwhelmingly chose Jonathan to be their minister. Then the trouble began.

Jonathan still had to be ordained. Typically, an ordination ceremony would confer the blessing of the area's churches on a proposed minister. Various pastors received invitations, most of them accepted, and the ceremony proceeded with much solemnity, followed by feasting on delicacies and choice liquors. But the West Church congregation was aggrieved. Because their church had been the most opposed to the revival in Boston, their new minister had only been invited to preach in two of the nine other Congregational pulpits in town, which they saw as an affront. Therefore, the congregation only offered invitations to ministers of those two churches. These included such figures as Benjamin Colman and Thomas Foxcroft, both old allies of George Whitefield, and Charles Chauncy, a new friend of Jonathan's.

This set the uninvited clerics astir. Such arrogance offended tradition and made Jonathan's ordination suspect. Not only was the lack of proper respect regrettable, but the new minister's ideas were so close to heterodoxy that they found it difficult to endorse his ministry at all. So none of the invited pastors chose to attend (Chauncy because he had to defer to senior authority in his church), and on the eve of the ceremony, it looked like Jonathan wouldn't find enough ministers to confirm his appointment. The leaders of West Church then postponed the ceremony, sent out letters to a fresh crop of ministers throughout Massachusetts, ignoring the Boston pastors entirely.

Eleven liberal country pastors accepted, and Jonathan's ordination proceeded smoothly. However, everyone now understood that West Church and its minister were at odds with most of the other pastors in town and had become outcasts. The *Boston Evening Post* accused establishment ministers of trying to undermine Jonathan before he even took the pulpit and blamed it on their secret New Light sympathies. In his sermon for Jonathan's elevation, Ebenezer Gay understood this, and instead of offering friendship and unity to their rivals, he delivered a bracing call to arms: "Be valiant for the truth against all opposition from the lusts of men. . . . So that from the blood of the uncircumcised slain, from the fat of the mighty, the bow of Jonathan turn not back empty!"

It was a fitting metaphor that recalled Reverend Edwards's claim that God's arrows would be drunk with the blood of sinners. But now, instead of God, Jonathan Mayhew would be firing them at men who preached such terrors.

Jonathan settled in quickly as minister of West Church. His parishioners appreciated that he spoke in a clear and forceful manner, and that he attended to his pastoral duties and gave lectures on critical issues. They saw him as "candid, sincere, diligent, amiable, publicity-conscious, supremely aware of his many powers and few limitations." However, to his enemies in Boston, he could also be cruel and merciless. One writer who opposed him in print came away from a battle with Jonathan feeling like "Old Nick had thrown acid in his face."

Most of the controversy Jonathan caused arose from his view of God. Ironically, his claim that the Divine Spirit was "a merciful and faithful creator, a compassionate parent, a gentle master" and a being who offered "immeasurable, immutable, universal and everlasting love" inspired some of the greatest venom in his foes. Calvinism had become so entrenched in the beliefs of New Englanders that any claim that God was not capricious and authoritarian could cause great upset, as did any doctrine that said people were not inherently wicked and destined to go to hell unless they were offered divine grace. Whether Old Lights or New Lights, most ministers in Boston still descended from Puritan stock, for whom the God of predestination and divine election and the covenant with his chosen people were matters of strict orthodoxy. But Jonathan—to an almost unprecedented degree—now claimed those things were untrue.

In his view, not only did such a theology have no basis in scripture, it was brutal and inhuman and could only drive Christians away from God, not toward him. By contrast, Jonathan's theology was humane and rational. He emphasized good works as much as faith, and exalted morality, virtue, and ethical behavior. In previous years, churchmen like Samuel Hemphill and John Tillotson had been denounced for such ideas, but in 1747 Jonathan boldly took those notions and pushed them even further into heterodoxy—and closer to the natural religion of Ben Franklin. But instead of being pilloried for his ideas, he prospered by them and convinced many other Bostonians to follow his lead.

He described a new, modern God worthy of love and adoration, one well suited to local pride and self-determination, who had no desire to make believers shrink in fear from his awesome power. This deity cared little for the finer points of dogma or tallying who was converted and who wasn't. He was infinite in his love and mercy and rose above the petty human squabbles that had lately defined America. Jonathan inspired his parishioners with these ideas and let them know that the good-hearted among them would be rewarded in the afterlife instead of punished. Because of this, he did not need to preach terrors to them or threaten them with damnation, as the evangelists did with such feral energy. Rather, his gospel was tolerant and accepting, and his God was kind and merciful to sinners—even if his own attitude toward his enemies was anything but.

In the face of opponents in his own Anglican church, George Whitefield once said, "the more I am opposed, the more joy I feel." In the face of opponents in his own Congregational church, Jonathan Mayhew said, "I live very happily and contented without them." Yet while Jonathan's attitude recalled Whitefield's, in many ways he was the braver figure, for while the Itinerant could always depart for the next meetinghouse or field to preach in, Jonathan had to live in the same town with his adversaries and face them constantly. In short order, once he began to preach, a slew of anonymous accusations in the local press questioned his doctrine, his unorthodox views, his contentious ordination, and his disreputable sermons. He and his ally Charles Chauncy responded in kind to their opponents, attacking them and the turbulent revival they had promoted.

Despite their differences, though, even the most ardent opposers of the revival and its most committed supporters had a bit more in common than they would admit. None of them seemed interested in returning to the more placid state of affairs that had character-ized American churches in the 1730s; too much hostility had been exchanged, and too many emotions released for anyone to go back to the old days. Jonathan Mayhew and Charles Chauncy and others had learned much from their foes: how to mount effective publicity campaigns and use controversy to their benefit; how to defame their rivals on the basis of thin evidence or imaginary conspiracies; how to develop a following in the countryside through handbills, pamphlets, public sermons, and other tools; and how to convey their message to other churches and, if necessary, in the streets.

Though much of the religious passion would subside, the conflicts in America would not end, and the energy of the combatants would only find new outlets. And with Jonathan in the pulpit of West Church, the antirevivalists would finally capture the power of the revival and turn it on its head. The great spiritual awakening may have led to schism among Christians and called into question firmly held beliefs about church and society. Yet in the end, the subversion of faith had an unexpected effect: the rise of what was once called heresy. The liberals, the rationalists, and even the unconverted now carried the force of God, and in Jonathan Mayhew they found their greatest champion.

NINE

THE REVOLT FROM WITHIN

B y the mid-1740s, the fire of the revival had begun to cool. The caustic writings of ministers like Charles Chauncy had damaged the movement by depicting it as a hotbed of fanatics, and key evangelists like Gilbert Tennent and George Whitefield had offered apologies for their conduct and the excesses of their followers. But in large part, the momentum of the movement slowed because it had achieved its goal—spreading a new idea of religion throughout the colonies and melting the hearts of congregants who had experienced the New Birth. Those with less passion fell away from the movement and returned to their old ways, and those who had been intrigued at first by the revival became its foes once the danger of the radicals became evident. However, even though it was no longer the focus of most news stories and pamphleteering, the revival did not end. Instead, it found new avenues to bring people to Jesus.

No fewer than one hundred Separatist churches opened their doors after the mid-1740s. They swept up restive parishioners who had become frustrated by their pastors' lack of evangelizing or colorless and tepid sermons and wanted fresh new preachers who could give voice to the Holy Spirit with all the intensity it deserved. Sometimes that meant hiring itinerants who could speak to people's hearts with strength and vitality; sometimes it meant choosing lay congregants who styled themselves as ministers despite having no training for it.

Amid the wreckage of the parishes that had foundered in the revival, the one denomination that prospered was Baptism. Luring thousands of New Lights who longed for both a stricter interpretation of the Bible and a looser expression of emotions, the Baptists seemed well suited to the new spiritual reality, with a series of rules designed to speed people's path to salvation. They forbade unconverted ministers to lead worship in their services; they rejected the "Halfway Covenant" that allowed unconverted parents to baptize their children into membership; and they refused to accept anyone other than adults to become members through immersion in water. Non-Baptists saw the standards as severe, but the rules gave the sect an aura of moral purity that appealed to countless Separatists, who sought a faith that reflected their values and rejected the compromises that many Protestant churches allowed. Even though this faith had been a small and declining sect before the 1740s, it grew quickly in the years after the revival's peak, and finally began to convert large parts of America that hadn't yet been touched by the movement.

Separatist Baptists in particular were famed for their fierce preaching and missionary zeal. Using their passion and will to convert sinners to Christ, they poured into the frontier of New England and the isolated settlements and wooded encampments of New Hampshire and northeastern Massachusetts. They kept the revival alive in these places well after it had dissipated in the major cities; and from there, many itinerant Separatists descended into the Southern backcountry of Virginia and North Carolina to lend their fire to country parishes and turn them into evangelical strongholds.

Tireless Baptist preachers like Isaac Backus rode the circuit over huge distances—in his case giving 2,400 sermons over nearly 15,000 miles—to bring countless people closer to Christ. In Virginia, Baptists denounced the dancing, horse racing, and gambling popular with the gentry, and quickly became notorious for their edicts. They renounced fine clothing and frivolities, spoke solemnly and called each other "Brother" and "Sister," and decried the inequities of plantation society. They promised their audiences

years into his ministry. His congregation included a motley selection of cast-offs and fragmented groups who had fled other Congregational churches due to their unredeemed ministers or differences over faith and doctrine. Even before his assumption of the pulpit, the church already had a reputation as a pariah in town, and his leadership only ensured its ostracism. No mainline ministers wanted anything to do with it or him; they shunned him from official functions and organizations, and either outright opposed him or pretended as if he didn't exist. For he stood as an embarrassment to the Boston ministers—of the grotesque behavior of New Light fanatics, of the extremism of the revival, and of the contempt for moderation that had poisoned the community. The ministers called Croswell a Separatist who intended to destroy the harmony of local religion. He saw it differently: He was the apostle of true Calvinist faith, and they were the real Separatists from the word of God.

Shortly after he arrived, he set about to elevate the spiritual quality of his parishioners by interrogating them about the condition of their souls—all to "publicly pull down the Kingdom of Satan, and build up the Kingdom of Christ." Warning that some of them were returning to their old unregenerate ways, he forbade drinking and gambling, chattering mindlessly on the Sabbath, gossiping about others and—with the greatest cheek—"disputing about words and things which edify not, but only [en]gender strife." It took some gall for Croswell to denounce the rebels and dividers in his flock, but he meant it: anyone violating his rules would be rebuked and or even censured, if "they appear to be incorrigible in their wickedness." At the same time, he stressed that he preached "the joyful religion of Jesus Christ" filled with light and song and beauty, and admonished those Congregationalists who seemed to revel in gloom and misery. Oddly, despite the severity of Croswell's behavior against his foes, his spiritual exhortations became ever more hopeful and triumphant—making him perhaps the angriest optimist ever to occupy a pulpit in America.

Throughout his time in Boston, and before that in Groton, Croswell's peculiar methods infuriated other clerics, just as they endeared him to his parishioners. But his fellow pastors weren't the only figures of authority to cast a wary eye on his ministry. He also vexed the colonial magistrates who claimed his gospel of ecstatic praising and clamorous singing was a danger to public order. Undaunted, Croswell attacked civic leaders as "more fit for Bedlam than the Bench"—implying a notorious asylum suited them better than a courtroom.

Other New Lights also railed against legislators and the laws they had passed to crush the revival and stifle dissent. Most notably, in Connecticut they had enacted statutes to stop itinerancy, uncontrolled worship, and dissent from the established church. They passed laws that forced Separatists to pay taxes to support religions that were not their own and threatened them with jail time if they attended unauthorized services. Labeled as "fraudulent dissenters," many New Lights trundled off to prison rather than compromise their faith, and their plight became so notorious that it influenced other colonists to turn against such taxes and laws that favored official religions.

Some Separatists went further and condemned any civil interference with religion whatsoever. They saw it as dangerous and corrupting and could recite any number of instances in which the authorities had favored one sect over another, to the detriment of both. Whether it was Anglicans earning favored status in Virginia or Congregationalists in Massachusetts, the Separatists became so incensed by such biased laws that they resolved, as Reverend Isaac Backus did, to resist "the illegal and discriminatory practices of government on behalf of the state Church." From these complaints arose new ideas of religious toleration and liberty of conscience—not because of a commitment to universal human values, but because people of faith wanted their own system of belief to be protected by colonial laws, not targeted by them. The only way to do that was for the British state to favor no sect over another. It was a powerful idea that took shape in the aftermath of the revival, though its ultimate consequences would take another forty years to emerge.

Unfortunately, the demand for religious freedom came at the wrong time. The Crown and the administrative weight of the British state had no interest in diminishing their own power. If anything they sought to enlarge it, and to find new avenues for securing control over the king's subjects in America and bringing the empire to other parts of the world. And the best way to achieve that kind of dominion was through the continued, and seemingly endless, pursuit of war.

What Americans called King George's War had been going on for several years as the North American theatre of the War of the Austrian Succession. The objectives were complex, but for the colonists fighting for Britain, it meant capturing the fortress of Louisbourg, which guarded the approach to the St. Lawrence River. This "Gibraltar of the New World" enabled France, Britain's current enemy, to control the cod fisheries off Newfoundland and launch attacks with its Indian allies against the northern frontier of America. It was a relatively straightforward mission, but proved to be controversial.

In Philadelphia, Benjamin Franklin, now clerk of the Pennsylvania Assembly, pleaded with lawmakers to assist the expedition and provide whatever troops and funding they could. Aside from a token bit of financial support, however, the Quaker-dominated legislature refused to endorse any campaign of foreign violence, just as it resisted creating an armed militia to protect the colony from domestic attack. Farther north in New England, the campaign roiled public feelings for different reasons—the difficulties in finding mariners to sail, the opposition from many quarters of society, and the constant need for the British state to draw its manpower from local citizens. Despite a recruitment campaign led by preachers like George Whitefield, many New Englanders feared a debacle like Cartagena would ensue, in which 80 percent of the men who fought in that ill-fated expedition against the Spanish power in Colombia were killed.

Surprisingly, the attack on the fortress at Louisbourg was a success, as the French capitulated after a six-week siege. Some 3,600 men from Boston and other towns in the region fought in the campaign and took considerable pride in their role in the victory, by capturing a strongpoint more than a few observers claimed was unconquerable. In light of their success, they hoped that their triumph would translate into better fortune for themselves and their economically beleaguered—and spiritually exhausted—home region. But that hope proved to be fleeting.

Boston alone lost 8 percent of its population of adult men, mostly to disease as the soldiers contracted illness on the field of battle and in their frigid camps, bereft of fuel and protection from the elements. Those troops who survived received a full year of garrison duty at the fort for their troubles—not the French booty and prizes they had been promised, which went into the coffers of the Royal Navy. And instead of thanks from their superior officers for their volunteer service, the New Englanders received a fair share of contempt. Commodore Charles Knowles, the new governor of Cape Breton Island, which included the fort, called the victorious American troops little better than outlaws, made up of "blacksmiths, tailors, barbers, shoemakers, and all the banditry them colonies affords." To the Duke of Newcastle, Knowles wrote of their filth and laziness, and their stubborn and wayward attitudes, which made them unfit for proper soldiery and an embarrassment to the Crown.

The soldiers returned their officers' contemptuous feelings. They saw them as petty martinets, hostile to common men recruited from the countryside, and cruel and abusive in their conduct. When they finally returned home, they brought well-nurtured hostility and resentment against their British comrades—bitter feelings that quickly spread to the rest of the population.

Upon their return, the New Englanders discovered that the war had not brought an end to the troubles in their region; if anything it had made things worse. While the soldiers had been suffering at Louisbourg, colonial elites had profited handsomely by their labors. War profiteers amassed fortunes through bribes and corruption, and they flaunted their wealth with expensive mansions and shameless displays of affluence. Meanwhile, more residents than ever became mired in debt, with the war fueling runaway inflation and the collapsing value of paper currency.

Amid such hardships, the character of public speech had also changed. The recent victory of the British armed forces over Bonnie Prince Charlie and the Jacobites in Scotland had enhanced the stature of the military—and provoked an unwelcome crackdown on dissent. In the House of Commons, lawmakers fearful of future rebellions demanded submission to the government under the excuse of the Divine Right of Kings, which cast the British monarch as the infallible vice-regent of God. They warned that any act of subversion against the Crown would be treated with the severity used against the Jacobite rebels, and that any questions over the legitimacy of the British throne would be treated as treason. In this creeping authoritarian atmosphere, royal governors demanded prayer and fasting in the name of King George II, and many colonists took pains to profess their loyalty to the monarchy, upon fear of imprisonment or worse.

One who did not cower was Charles Chauncy. Although he certainly had no interest in undermining the king, he had grown frustrated with the rule of local magistrates and their seeming disinterest in fixing the problems of Massachusetts and other provinces. His own financial condition was precarious, as he struggled on a meager salary amid the colony's high inflation. Thus, this member of the religious elite, who had held so much sway in public opinion in recent years, now felt reduced to the status of the common folk he occasionally belittled. Like them, he blamed the authorities for the colony's woes.

In May 1747, Chauncy gave an election sermon, a speech to the colony's legislature at the beginning of its session. Free from the fears many had about criticizing public officials, Chauncy used the sermon as an opportunity to scold the lawmakers for neglecting the needs of their constituents and implored them to do better. He told them religion was at a low state, riven by faction and blasphemy, and sin had crippled the unity and values of the community. College teachers, ministers, and other professionals were underpaid or lived in penury. The value of currency had plummeted, the economy had stagnated, and instead of fixing matters, the higher powers had waged fruitless battles against other countries. As he said, "Rulers also should endeavor to keep the state from being embroiled in foreign war, by contriving, in all prudent ways, to engage and continue the friendship of neighboring nations." He warned against the infringement on the rights of British subjects and questioned the excuses the colonial leaders had made when they did so. "Tis the just exercise of power that distinguishes right from might; authority that is to be revered and obeyed, from violence and tyranny, which are to be dreaded and deprecated."

Chauncy demanded that rulers be fair and impartial in executing the laws of the nation, and above reproach in their conduct—not mired in corruption, deceit and self-interest. They should not defraud or oppress the public, or use violence as a means of achieving political ends. Instead, they must "preserve and perpetuate to every member of the community, so far as may be, the full enjoyment of their liberties and privileges, whether of a civil or religious nature."

It was a bracing call to arms for both secular and spiritual freedom, and it echoed some of the things the Baptists and Separatists had been saying about the importance of dissent in a climate of repression. While Chauncy had fiercely battled the New Lights in the past over religion, his rhetoric in politics now began to parallel their own. Published throughout the region, Chauncy's sermon was simply titled, *Civil Magistrates Must Be Just, Ruling in the Fear of God.*

Although the speech drew Chauncy favorable attention, even among revivalists, one group to whom it did not appeal were clerics of the Church of England. Still reeling from being cast as villains during the revival, these churchmen attacked the works of dissenters and allied themselves closely with the government. In print and from the pulpit, they compared leading nonconformists to Jacobites, and argued for the complete marriage of church and state in one happy and unquestioned union. They drew new attention to the holiday of Fast Day in midwinter, offering prayers and lamentations for the martyred soul of King Charles I, who had been executed by Puritan rebels a century before. They warned of contemporary dissenters—heirs of those murderous Puritans—who demanded such things as religious liberty and freedom from the established church. And they claimed that colonial subjects who refused to submit to the Church of England put their allegiance to Britain into question. In short, the supremacy of the king was paramount, and submission to the state church essential, all of it adding up to "obedience to God, king, lords and bishops—and in that order."

Some Anglican churchmen went further and argued that a bishop should be elevated to govern America on its own soil. Such a bishop would have seemingly innocuous powers—to ordain ministers locally, instead of forcing them to sail back to Britain; to oversee priests and commissaries and other figures in the American church; and to provide a method of governance that would ensure adherence to church laws and cohesion with church policy. But what sounded benign to Anglican clerics sounded like nothing less than tyranny to American dissenters.

◆

Fired up by George Whitefield's attacks on the leaders of the Church of England, as well as Charles Chauncy's own condemnations, Reformed Protestants chafed against the primacy of that faith and its protected status. To them the church was a menace that threatened to crush native traditions while it forced compliance to a minority faith governed by an overseas monarch. Its leaders had been enemies of the revival from the beginning and had done all they could to thwart it, to shame its proponents, and to trumpet its failings. And now, with Anglicanism pressing farther into the heartland of New England, the threat arose that the British state and church might unite to crush any sects that didn't accept the king as the Lord's earthly emissary.

Accordingly, Anglican clergymen openly argued that more needed to be done to advance the Church of England's cause in the New World. Clerics in Connecticut sent a letter to the Bishop of London decrying the lack of an American bishop, which was "a very great obstruction to the propagation of religion." Their eagerness matched that of powerful figures like the Bishop of Oxford, Thomas Secker, who had been calling for the creation of such a bishop since 1741. Secker had been ascending the church hierarchy for more than a decade, and had emerged as a formidable opponent of dissenting faiths. He exhorted SPG missionaries to convert as many wayward Protestants as they could to the Church of England, and developed a strategy that, if enacted, would create an all-encompassing system of spiritual and secular belief. Even Secker's own colleagues feared his rising power, calling him "Leviathan."

By 1747 Secker's efforts and those of other Anglican high churchmen had had a galvanizing effect. One sympathetic writer in a Boston newspaper even claimed that "in a few years time Episcopacy will generally prevail in this part of the world." Slanted laws, SPG missionaries, ample funding, and a taste for revenge all motivated the churchmen to try converting New Englanders to the national religion, and to make inroads into places where few had dreamed it would ever penetrate. Their pride reached an apogee when the first Anglican church in Boston, King's Chapel, erected its foundation on a hallowed burial ground for Puritans from the previous century—literally building a church upon the bones of people's ancestors.

Congregational and Presbyterian ministers and laity reacted with horror to such developments. They had warned for years of such a dangerous moment, and now it had come to pass. However, they failed to admit that their own actions had let it happen. Namely, they had preached during the revival against the moderates and the unconverted in their own faiths, and sowed controversy with each new attack. As these battles over belief raged, the more tolerant parishioners drifted over to the Church of England, since they saw no place for themselves in Calvinist churches that demanded moral purity in exchange for salvation. Others were repelled by the spectacle of James Davenport and Andrew Croswell and the other radicals and wanted only to join a church that could offer quiet reassurance and support for their good works—instead of condemnations. And still others refused to believe that the New Birth or the rigid "five points of Calvinism" were the only means of finding God. If aligning themselves with the state church meant a closer connection to their creator, many northerners were happy to do so. Still, for a lot of wavering American Christians, this was a brutal choice: whether to support a British-oriented church headed by a secular monarch, with all of its threats of tyranny and subjugation, or to hold to their old dissenting faiths, which condemned them for being imperfect and which promoted a bleak and judgmental theology.

Put into ever more extreme camps by the evangelical revival, the Calvinists and the Anglicans could find little common ground. The members of each group saw the worst in the other, even if they shared many of the same traits—harsh judging, censorious behavior, divisive tactics, broken loyalties. And with each new religious or political controversy, the distance between the groups only grew, and the antagonism hardened. For many, the greatest test of faith occurred when Boston erupted in the worst riots in memory.

The roots of the trouble went back to the checkered victory at Louisbourg. After capturing the fort, the Royal Navy had plans to make it a juggernaut in the war against its maritime enemies. Manning and protecting the fort would be essential, and the most convenient sailors for the job were just down the coast in New England. However, many of them had returned home bitter at their treatment and wary of the prospect of ever serving in the armed forces again. Wages were higher with private shippers, and few wanted to endure the deprivation and cruelty of the British navy when they had the choice not to, so most chose to remain private citizens. However, the navy could not accept such intransigence. It faced huge rates of desertion when its ships entered port, and had countless difficulties finding mariners to enlist. So instead of trying to persuade these experienced sailors to join the ranks, it decided to force them instead.

The practice of impressment had become critical for running a modern global empire. Britain deployed the practice ruthlessly and repeatedly in the Americas, filling its fleet with men it either apprehended through offshore interceptions of private vessels, or through the onshore attacks of press gangs. Hunting down sailors known to have skills in operating a vessel, the gangs would seize these men in the streets, on the seas and sometimes in their homes, dragooning them for duty for months or years on a British warship. Often the friends and families of sailors would help them resist such kidnappings, but they had neither the force of law nor arms on their side. Impressment was legal under British legal codes, subject to the approval of royal governors, and resistance to it was forbidden. Despite this, reaction to the practice was common and sometimes violent.

Colonists saw impressment as a violation of their rights as British subjects, and an encroachment on their ability to decide their own affairs. Massachusetts governor William Shirley attempted to moderate the policy with intermittent success, but new outrages seemed to undercut any possibility of compromise between the sailors of coastal cities and the mounting needs of the Royal Navy. In 1745 two seamen lost their lives at the hands of a press-gang in a Boston boarding house, and the event incited protest and public anger. Two years later, a parliamentary act upheld the old "Sixth of Anne" policy that placed limits on impressment—but only in the West Indies. The lawmakers decided it had never applied in North America, and naval officials were free to nab any men they needed.

An anonymous pamphlet by "Quincius Cincinnatus" denounced the open infringement on colonists' liberties and wondered whether the people of the Northeast, despite all they did for the Crown, would be "the first victims destined to be sacrificed to a arbitrary and illegal power[.]" Conspiracy talk surfaced of the British government bargaining away the Louisbourg fort back to the French, and then handing over the whole of New England to the Catholic power. Such a prospect was unlikely, but it did heighten ill feeling against the government, and made people who had always considered themselves loyal subjects of the king wonder whether His Majesty's government cared at all to protect their rights and security. They soon found their answer, as the fleet of Commodore Charles Knowles appeared in the waters off New England, ready to round up sailors and press them into service against their will.

Knowles had already insulted colonial troops and thought them slovenly and drawn from the lowest quarters of society. He claimed they were exceptionally lazy and in camp they had used timber from the walls of their own living quarters for firewood, and buried the dead under their floorboards. He didn't necessarily want to kidnap such wretched New Englanders for naval service, but with manpower in the fleet running low, he had little choice but to secure maritime labor however he could.

Residents of Boston knew the fleet might have designs on its citizens and took steps to prepare themselves. Skilled sailors took the most precautions, refusing to man the private coasters that carried fuel and provisions into Boston, for fear of being abducted. But with the town dependent on the water trade for much of its supplies, the loss of such cargo threatened its livelihood. It was in this charged atmosphere that on November 16, 1747, Knowles mounted one of his boldest roundups yet.

In the late evening hours, his press-gang swept over the vessels in the harbor and snatched any men they could find, including shipbuilders' apprentices, shipwrights, and other unlucky souls who had the misfortune to be working on boats when the invaders arrived. From there, the gang stormed into town, accosting sailors as well as craftsmen, laborers, slaves, servants, and random civilians. They scoured the docks and the waterfront looking for any other able-bodied men who could man the fleet and then summarily hauled them back to captivity for service in the Royal Navy.

The press-gang hadn't completed its brutal work before a mob of Bostonians arose to stop them. Armed with sticks, cutlasses, clubs, and shipwrights' pitch mops, the hastily assembled crowd swarmed through the streets looking for members of the press-gang and, finding few of them, decided to seize naval officers instead. First a lieutenant, then about a dozen other men of rank found themselves shackled and led away by the mob—collateral to secure the release of the forty Americans who had been pressed into military service.

The masses then assaulted a sheriff and his deputies and surrounded the governor's house, with a few troublemakers lobbing rocks at it. The mob leaders blamed William Shirley for the roundup, but the governor claimed he had permitted no such action in the town or its waters. That part was true: Knowles had acted illegally. Hours later, as a legislative council discussed the matter with the governor, the mob surrounded its chambers, breaking windows and threatening to storm the building. Persuaded they should refrain from attacking the legislature, the crowds moved on to the waterfront, where they burned a barge they thought was part of Knowles's fleet, though it actually belonged to one of the rioters. Shirley used the distraction to flee the town and deliver any remaining British officers back to the protection of the navy offshore. He also called out the militia to suppress the crowds, which now numbered in the thousands, but few militiamen arrived to put down the violence. Many, in fact, were part of the mob itself.

Communicating with the commodore, Shirley argued for the release of the impressed sailors, since he had not approved such a move and it had to be reversed. Knowles refused and instead threatened to bombard the town with his cannons: "By God I'll now see if the king's government is not as good as a mob!" In the end, however, Shirley prevailed upon Knowles to refrain from firing on Boston and used his political skills to negotiate with the rioters, the navy, the legislature, and the General Court to bring matters to a conclusion without further violence. Although it took several days for the mob to disperse, for the militia to appear, and for order to be restored, the town did return to peace and the goals of the Boston rioters were achieved: the impressed men would be released in exchange for the return of the British officers to their vessels.

In the days to come, official reports would appear condemning the violence and blaming it on "foreign seamen, servants, Negroes, and other persons of mean and vile condition." Governor Shirley, however, knew better. In a letter, he wrote "the insurrection was secretly countenanced and encouraged by some ill-minded inhabitants and persons of influence in the town." Indeed, instead of the traditional "lower orders" alone rising up in protest, this time a broad swath of citizens contributed to the violence, from the elite who Shirley suspected had quietly encouraged the rioters, to merchants, craftsmen, farmers, and women—all of them enraged by the tactics of the British military and willing to risk their lives to stop it.

The governor realized something unusual had taken root in Boston. A restless, aggressive energy animated the town folk, and contributed to their peculiar hostility to colonial rulers. In the last decade, their bellicose nature had worsened considerably, and Shirley thought he knew the reason. As he saw it, "what I think may be esteemed the principal cause of the mobbish turn in this town is its constitution" and the town meetings that were controlled by "the meanest inhabitants." Instead of top-shelf gentlemen and wealthy merchants running things, Shirley feared the rabble had gained the upper hand, both in the streets and in the town caucuses. He could already see the dangers of democracy, even on a small scale, and it disturbed him. So in his letter to the Lords of Trade, he recommended changing the town's constitution to make it hospitable to the proper execution of British law—and stifling this new, potentially seditious, American disorder.

The Knowles Riot was the greatest revolt against the power of the British state since the Revolution of 1688. It drew most of the Boston populace into a tumult against the authorities, it lasted for several days, and it largely succeeded. Despite the overwhelming firepower that the Royal Navy could have directed against the town, the protestors did not retreat, and instead achieved their goal of curbing impressment, at least temporarily. It was both a warning of the threat of the masses to the ruling elite and a milestone in disobedience against a colonial system many had come to see as unfair, oppressive, and increasingly foreign to their interests.

Such a daring act could not have happened in the Boston, or the America, of a decade earlier. The previous seven years of battles over faith had hardened the town folk and made them resistant to calls for their submission. Through repeated bouts of conflict and near anarchy, they had gained courage and audacity, whether they were hurling insults against preachers or testifying to God in the streets. And now they had summoned that same energy to fight for their freedoms as royal subjects. As historian Gary Nash wrote, "Such bold defiance of the highest authorities, moreover, accorded well with the vision that the Awakeners had called forth," as common citizens rose up to demand an answer to their grievances from "power-hungry, morally bankrupt figures who misused their power."

Two weeks after the violence peaked, an anonymous pamphlet appeared that brought all the objections of New Englanders together in one brief, cogent argument. It carried the title *An Address to the Inhabitants of [Massachusetts and Boston]; Occasioned by the Late Illegal and Unwarrantable Attack upon Their Liberties, and the Unhappy Confusion and Disorder Consequent Thereon*. It was easy to see why the author of the pamphlet chose to hide his name, for the publication was a strike against the ruling powers—a warning that would "inspire in the minds of the people in this province, especially, in this town, with a proper sense of the imminent danger their lives, and liberties, are in."

The author denounced the barbarous system of impressment that had plagued the colony as well as "the arbitrary, and illegal conduct, of those who have been the authors of our late sufferings, and the confusion and disorders consequent upon them." He implicated the British navy, and all the men of power who licensed its actions, for much of the suffering, and vilified the press-gangs who did the dirty work. New Englanders had repeatedly made their grievances known about these issues, but their legislature had never delivered them to the Crown, and as a result, they continued to have their liberties violated and their rights abused. Although the recent mob activity was dreadful and regrettable, it was also inevitable under the present regime, as people labored under the yoke of such a system. The author signed the pamphlet as "your most humble servant, Amicus Patriae"—"a lover of his country," in Latin—but the signs pointed to Samuel Adams as the actual scribe.

The twenty-five-year-old Adams was a little-known market clerk whose family was in the business of making malt for beer. His father Samuel Sr. also worked as a church deacon, and had been popularly elected as a representative in the Boston Caucus by a town meeting—exactly the kind of institution Governor Shirley had found so threatening. Members of the caucus worked to protect the common people against abuses by the gentry and local magistrates, and Samuel Sr. became one of its most powerful and well-known members. Through watching his father's endeavors, Samuel Jr. came to have a flair for politics himself.

He graduated from Harvard College in 1743, part of the same class as Jonathan Mayhew, but did not pursue a course in divinity. Instead, his interest was in public affairs. In his thesis for the degree of *artium magister* (the modern Master of Arts) he answered the question, "Whether it be lawful to resist the Supreme Magistrate, if the Commonwealth cannot be otherwise preserved" with a bracing defense of the right to resist oppression. Such an argument was almost unheard of from a graduate student. Young Adams claimed that natural rights existed that allowed citizens to defend their liberties, even by force. The logic for the argument derived from John Locke—the same philosopher who had animated the writings of Jonathan Edwards, to a very different end—and it served as a defense of freedom against tyranny. Some authorities interpreted his thesis as "an unprecedented act of incipient 'treason,'" but Samuel Adams could have argued in no other way. For he had seen what the British state could do to ruin a person, and that person was his father.

At the beginning of the 1740s, Samuel Sr. had been instrumental in crafting an innovative idea called the Land Bank, in which Massachusetts land owners desperate for hard currency could mortgage their holdings in exchange for legal tender, with goods like hemp, flax, and iron also accepted in trade. The scheme became popular among the public, but it incurred the wrath of Parliament, which had repeatedly withdrawn issue of the colony's paper money and wanted only hard currency like gold or silver to be used as payment for debts. The Land Bank was an affront to their plan, and as an idea that derived from the colonists, it was doubly cursed. So Parliament made an ex post facto judgment declaring that the Land Bank had been illegal from the moment of its creation. Worse, any disgruntled holders of its currency could demand the full value of their money back in hard currency plus interest. If the directors of the Land Bank could not pay it, they would be held liable for triple damages in court or could forfeit their estate or be imprisoned.

Working class people saw the attack on the Land Bank as an attempt to enrich the wealthy, and they cursed them openly as "carnal wretches, hypocrites, fighters against God, children of the devil, cursed Pharisees" among other insults that tied together the villains of the evangelical revival with the villains of the economic system. Public outrage and protests ensued, and one observer wasn't alone in fearing anarchy and the outbreak of "mutiny, sedition, and riots" in response to the legislative action.

Parliament crushed the Land Bank and nearly destroyed the material wealth of Samuel Adams Sr., including much of his property holdings. This was the intended result, since men like current governor William Shirley and later governor Thomas Hutchinson thought the best way to cripple the town meetings was to undercut their leaders. If they could devastate the finances of Samuel Sr., it would serve as a potent example to other restive colonists of the danger of testing the will of the authorities.

For the next twenty years, Samuel Sr. and his successors would continue to be on the hook for old debts held by Land Bank customers. These obligations were even passed down to Samuel Jr., who had much less skill in business than his father and who would struggle to hold the family estate together. Ultimately, he learned a stern lesson in imperial politics from his dad's troubles and from the bank's failure: namely, the British government cared not a whit about fairness, and would take any arbitrary, unfair action it desired—even if that action ruined families and plunged citizens into debt—in order to achieve a political end. So Samuel Jr.'s Harvard thesis was no mere exercise; it was a profound statement of principles, just as his "Amicus Patriae" pamphlet was in fighting military oppression.

Samuel Jr.'s father died a few months after the Knowles Riots, and he became the sole Samuel Adams. Having imbibed much of his father's animosity against the government, he continued to express his feelings publicly—first by forming a political club devoted to debating the controversial matters of the day, then by creating a newspaper filled with essays by that club's members, called *The Independent Advertiser*. Although the paper had several authors, Adams controlled much of its editorial content and perspective, and often his views were designed to provoke a reaction.

By 1748 Adams's newspaper essays had gone well past the sentiments of Amicus Patriae. He now claimed the anti-impressment rioters not only had the right to fight the press-gangs, but should have resisted any bombardment from Commodore Knowles's fleet with outright insurrection—"if he offered to advance upon the town, he should advance at his peril." He compared Governor Shirley to King James II, who was widely seen as a tyrant who had been justly toppled by the Glorious Revolution. Not only did citizens have the "natural right" to resist such despots, but they had no other choice if their magistrates refused to protect them. In fact, riots and other violent actions could be considered natural rights.

Adams demanded the king curtail the power of Governor Shirley over Massachusetts, and that the acts of the colony's General Court be given the same weight as those of the British Parliament. As he saw it, only local institutions, and not overlords from overseas, could guarantee the protection of the colonists' rights. He had contempt for the esteemed gentlemen and country squires whose economic interests Parliament had taken pains to protect, and said they had "an itch for riding the beasts of the people" in order to subdue them. And he channeled the populism that was now rising in the streets of New England, condemning any elitist who "despises his neighbors' happiness because he wears a worsted cap or a leather apron," and any man of wealth who "struts immeasurably above the lower size of people, and pretends to adjust the rights of men by the distinction of fortune." This type of rhetoric had a strong effect in the heady atmosphere of Boston. And it had a familiar ring, too, in the voices of colonists just as passionate as he was.

Samuel Adams had grown up during the evangelical revival. He had witnessed Whitefield at his fiery peak, and the effects of the New Birth on his classmates at Harvard. This experience had a profound impact, even for a scholar studying public affairs and classical authors. For Adams became as much a student of the new revivalists as he was of the old philosophers, and he learned to unite the power of God with the power of civil action to battle inequity, tyranny, and greed. Indeed, "his first revolt was against materialism and his first hatreds were against those he believed hostile to the rebirth of the Puritan or 'old Roman' spirit in New England." Just like ministers such as Jonathan Edwards, he blamed sin as the primary cause of injustice and exalted people's return to faith.

He had come to God early in life, with his father encouraging him to become active in the Congregational church, or even to study for ordination as a minister. But while Adams found politics more to his liking, he never strayed far from the rugged old Calvinism he heard preached in the meetinghouses and at home. Mankind was depraved, wickedness was ubiquitous, and the only way to find redemption from misery was through God's grace. Didn't Boston's struggles prove the truth of that theology? And wasn't it a test of faith to stand up to despotic rulers, even under threat of death or imprisonment? He could only answer in the affirmative, and promise to fight the corruption in society as the revivalists had fought it in church.

He saw moral decay throughout New England, from the wealth of its merchants to the practices of its magistrates, and in the *Independent Advertiser* he inveighed against both. He lamented how Puritanism had declined and left "our morals, our constitution, and our liberties" in a degenerate state; and he called for a rebirth of the old virtues and new protections for the freedoms all people shared under God. Like Whitefield, he targeted Anglican high churchmen—not for their religious beliefs, but for being agents of oppression. He claimed the new King's Chapel in Boston, being constructed over the burial ground of Puritan forefathers, was just like those of "Popish countries," built and beautified at the expense of the poor. He attacked the mercantile trade with the French Catholic enemy, and was later aghast when the fort of Louisbourg was bargained away in a negotiation between the world powers—an insult to all the New Englanders who had fought to take it. And he raised the ominous issue of a colonial Anglican bishop, which was not only a danger to native dissenters, but "might be likely to disturb this people in the enjoyment of their inviolable liberties."

The *Independent Advertiser* folded after only a year. But as Samuel Adams rose to prominence in the coming decades, it served as a template for the rhetoric of rebellion he would pioneer. The grievances might have been secular, and the political theory taken from the European Enlightenment, but the incendiary style and piercing rhetoric came straight from the evangelical movement . . . and the flames of revival that still flickered on.

TEN

HOLY GROUND

B y the end of the 1740s, the reputation of Jonathan Edwards was secure. He had emerged as the revival's most original thinker and galvanizing spirit, and its greatest herald for the rebirth of Calvinism. Long before George Whitefield ever set foot in America, Edwards had enflamed entire regions with his evangelism. He had written influential justifications for his work, had battled foes like Charles Chauncy in print, and had witnessed some of the hottest spiritual fires of New England. He had even preached one of the most famous sermons in American history, *Sinners in the Hands of an Angry God*, which would ensure his name throughout posterity long after most other revivalists had been forgotten.

His work was not finished. Even as the energy of the revival began to flag, Edwards wrote his classic volume *A Treatise Concerning Religious Affections* to defend the power of the emotions to redeem the hearts of sinners, and to correct some of the errors he saw in the recent spiritual movement. One of the most notorious was the way enthusiasts became stirred into a frenzy under delusions of salvation. He knew that extreme passion could be dangerous, and its "effects on the animal spirits are more violent, and the mind more overpowered, and less in its own command."

Edwards didn't trust the radicals who unleashed those spirits because he remained an orthodox Puritan at heart. In *Religious Affections*, he established a rigorous test for deciphering the true signs of God's grace upon repentant sinners, the clues that would tell whether a conversion was real or illusory. He also questioned those who established "pure" independent churches outside the control of the major faiths, and who confused wild enthusiasm for genuine transformation.

But if Reverend Edwards thought that his latest work could enable him to channel the untamed energies of his followers, he was wrong: He had no more control over what they did than any of the other revivalists had. If anything, his books and sermons had proved to be so influential for the Separatists, they took his message and found their own truth in it.

For example: Edwards told them they could use their feelings and emotions to testify to God's grace; they took this to mean they could exhort in the streets and proclaim their own visions and revelations. Edwards told them a divinity degree did not guarantee a minister had been redeemed in Christ; they took from this they didn't need ordained pastors at all and could preach from their own pulpits. Separatists like Isaac Backus even claimed he understood Edwards's message better than the students at Yale, and he spread this gospel over thousands of miles in places Edwards had never been, in ways Edwards could not have imagined.

Edwards refused to accept these radical notions, because he could not contain them. American religion had become personal, pervasive, and populist, and the radicals had made it so without asking his permission or by following his edicts about proper conversion. Evangelists like Andrew Croswell even attacked Edwards personally, claiming he had been too timid in following the earth-shaking import of his ideas. He painted Edwards as a milquetoast who valued "ecclesiastical tranquility" over the wondrous disorder of being reborn in Christ, and he challenged Edwards to embrace the turmoil instead of running from it. But Edwards had no use for men like Croswell, who embodied everything base and fraudulent he saw in the extremists, who gloried in their own arrogance, and who perverted true faith in God.

◆

Edwards wearied of such battles, and found a dour pessimism creeping in. The revival had not turned out as he had expected, but had become "very sorrowful and dark," and not only because of the radicals. Declension from faith was apparent everywhere. Countless redeemed souls had returned to revel in their old sins. The energy of the New Birth had waned and those who had first fed the flames had long since given up. In fact, Edwards no longer saw much that was unique in the religious experience of America. In writing to Scottish ministers and revivalists, he discovered a greater growth in piety overseas than at home, and he helped to foster a transatlantic network of faith seekers who knew no bounds of nationhood or background or creed. While the rest of America was becoming ever more Anglophobic, Edwards continued to find new friends across the sea, and warm new avenues to express the message of Christ.

He kept writing works that he hoped would lead his readers away from sin and toward salvation. In 1749 he composed a biography of the late David Brainerd that showed the true path of a Christian soul. Brainerd had gone from fiery young zealot who had been expelled from Yale to a more thoughtful seeker of the Holy Spirit, a man who rejected fanaticism and instead undertook missions to convert the Delaware peoples to Christianity—and learned much about his own faith in so doing. He had died young, but Edwards intended to exhibit Brainerd's life as an example of how moderation in the pursuit of salvation could be a worthy goal, and radicalism a destructive temptation. The biography of his late friend became his most popular book, acclaimed as another fine volume to add to the shelf of devotional classics, but the praise it earned did not fully satisfy Edwards because it did not reignite the revival. It was yet another example of his readers enjoying his work, taking comfort that they were good Christians, then ignoring everything he had written.

Why had the revival faltered? Why had his message of rebirth and the promise of God's grace fallen on intentionally deaf ears? Edwards knew the depravity of man played a role. He knew people had succumbed to Satan's rich temptations. And he began to suspect the gospel of the colonies was not that of Jesus Christ, but the worship of money, power, and hedonism.

In response he denounced the "false scheme of religion" which "gave men both an undue sense of their own importance and an errant definition of the way to wealth." The message of Christ had been twisted by opportunists into a gospel of material success, in which the most prosperous members of the community lauded themselves as the most holy—because surely God showed his favor by showering his saints with economic benefits. The blasphemy of this idea sickened him.

He began to preach more openly about the wickedness of the burgeoning market economy, and all the ways that colonists' livelihoods could be destroyed by men of power. Inflation, currency depreciation, uncontrolled market forces all led to the ruin of society and the abuse of the poor, because "greed and selfishness flourished in an unfettered market." He saw how international trade and commerce could be tantamount to extortion, and how the profit motive could encourage sin and wastefulness. And while a few Enlightenment figures like John Locke provided valuable tools to understand human emotions, he spurned other thinkers from the same movement who trafficked in market theories that justified the accumulation of capital. Such theories emboldened the great men of Massachusetts and Connecticut to justify their shameless pursuit of wealth—and to ignore their duty of ensuring charity and justice for everyone else.

The elites of Northampton did not take kindly to Edwards' criticism of their economic prerogatives. Many of them openly disavowed the revival and tried to undercut the message of the reverend by depicting him as antiquated and out of touch. Moreover, Edwards had left himself open to charges of hypocrisy: while he pitied those who had been crushed by the market society, he also defended slavery and owned several humans himself.

Although was aware of the miseries of the slave trade and the abuses bondsmen suffered, he could never go as far as to reject it. Instead he put his faith in hopes that it might be abolished, in future "glorious times" well after his own slave-owning life ended. Many of his parishioners in Northampton, however, did not find his logic convincing. As early as 1744, they had demanded an accounting of his expensive taste for slaves as well as "jewelry, chocolate, Boston-made clothing, children's toys" and other luxuries. Edwards argued with them vehemently, and employed biblical examples to defend himself, but the charge of greed and hypocrisy still resonated as the years passed. And by the end of the decade, it would threaten his career.

The congregation of Reverend Edwards had been paying him handsomely, tripling his salary to 870 pounds by 1748. Yet Edwards continued to fret over the rising inflation in Massachusetts and the challenge of keeping up with the cost of goods and services. He asked for a fixed long-term contract that would rise with inflation, as a symbol of his parishioners' faith in him and his need to maintain a certain lifestyle. But instead of granting his request, they rejected it. His growing number of doubters aired their apprehension about whether he was truly spending his money on the Lord's work, or on mere frivolities. This charge shocked Edwards and damaged the relationship between the pastor and his flock. He became further estranged from them when he realized many were tossing worthless old currency into the collection plate, knowing it had no value. Such an act revealed a growing lack of respect for him.

He decided to put a stop to the wayward behavior of his congregants. In his *Humble Inquiry into the Rules of the Word of God*, he proposed new tests to determine the spiritual quality of the members of his church. Not all conversion experiences were valid simply because the sinner felt saved, Edwards argued, and external signs of redemption were critical to determining whether God's grace had been offered and accepted. Ministers like himself would judge such matters. He determined that "none ought to be admitted as members of the visible church of Christ but visible saints and professing saints." No backsliding sinners or self-proclaimed prophets or wild-eyed enthusiasts should participate in communion or the sacraments; only those whose lives and souls were spotless, for "visible saints or converts are those who are so in the eye of man."

Edwards's church members reacted with outrage to the proposal. Primed by a decade of revivalism, they had no interest in returning to the bad old days when ministers lorded over their parishes and judged the state of people's souls as worthy or corrupt. Edwards's plan threatened to restrict membership to a small fraction of people who met with his approval, and to condemn those who didn't as outcasts.

This did not sit well with his congregation. They didn't need "skillful guides" to lead them toward the New Birth, because as one critic said, "only God could see into the heart" and no one should step in the way of a deeply personal relationship between the convert and the Creator. And Reverend Edwards was proposing just that.

In 1750 Northampton church members took one of the boldest steps any laypeople had in seizing the power of the pulpit: they fired Jonathan Edwards as their minister. Citing him with betraying the word of God and exploiting his position in the community, they cast the most famous preacher in America out of the church he had led for more than two decades. His renowned sermons, his influential writings, his grand theories—none of it helped save his job. His congregation had no more use for him, and he would have to find a new role in the upturned world of Calvinist America. The creation had long since outgrown its creator.

With the fall of Edwards, the revival had swallowed up its last great evangelist. All the awakeners who had first promoted it to great success—Whitefield, Tennent, Davenport, and himself—had fallen victim to their own pride or foolishness or become victims of the forces they had unleashed. And those who prospered were the unexpected ones: the radicals like Andrew Croswell, who continued battling for the New Birth long after its original champions had left the fight; the Separatists and the Baptists, who grew most in the aftermath of the revival; women and slaves and Indian preachers, who found a new avenue for their expression; and heretics like Jonathan Mayhew, who had no use for Calvinism but was learning to be his own kind of evangelist.

Reverend Mayhew represented everything in religion that Jonathan Edwards opposed. While both were pastors of the same faith—Congregationalism—the young minister continued to attack the revival without mercy and detailed its compendium of errors in his popular sermons at Boston's West Church.

In just a few months since his ordination as pastor, Jonathan had been disowned by most of the rest of the clergy in town. In an open rebuke, they denied him admittance to the Boston Association of Ministers and kept him from participating in the Thursday Lecture, one of the town's religious traditions, in which a given pastor would offer a chosen homily on a pressing topic. Jonathan countered by offering his own lecture series, also on Thursdays, to compete with the sermons of his foes. He drew much bigger crowds, and more controversy, for these speeches, in which he questioned almost everything local preachers had been preaching, and believers had been believing, for the past decade . . . or even much further back.

Enjoying his status as an outcast, Jonathan made no effort to hedge his beliefs or moderate his rhetoric. For example, he took the core Calvinist doctrine of original sin and called it fanciful. His God was not a capricious tyrant; he was "a merciful and faithful creator" who had no interest in making people suffer for the sins of Adam and Eve. "We have sins enough of our own to bewail, without taking those of others upon ourselves." Moreover, this reasonable God made humans to be reasonable, too—to use their heads, not their emotions, to worship him and to embrace all the splendid faculties of the mind to find true religion, which had nothing to do with "vice, ignorance and superstition." He said people should not be "dragooned" into becoming orthodox Christians, and that following such absurd ideas was akin to getting knocked in the head—and they are "more readily embraced by a man after his brains are knocked out, than while he continues in his senses, and of a sound mind." The most extreme example of this lunacy was in the recent revival, in which enthusiasts enjoyed "frequent raptures, and strange transports of mechanical devotion" and went "from one degree of religious frenzy to another, till they run quite divinely mad."

He took special pleasure in rejecting the tenets of Calvinism that had guided the revival—from predestination and human depravity to the election of the saints—and showed them to be dubious and unbiblical. He exalted instead the "natural religion" that showed "beauty, order, harmony and design" to be hallmarks of God's creation, and said the natural world reflected the perfection of the ethereal.

The dichotomy between good and evil really came down to a conflict between happiness and misery, and humanity should simply pursue the former at the expense of the latter. The best way to accomplish this was to do good, to be wise, to behave well, and to have faith. As he saw it, "Christianity is principally an institution of life and manners; designed to teach

us how to be good men, and to show us the necessity of becoming so." Ben
Franklin couldn't have said it any better himself.

Jonathan published his controversial ideas in 1749 as *Seven Sermons Upon
the Following Subjects . . .* , which included measuring truth versus falsehood, honoring one's own judgment on spiritual matters, and loving God
and neighbors. In Boston, the publication met with stony indifference from
the clergy, but in Britain, the sermons attracted great attention among
nonconformists and those who followed more tolerant schools of thought.
Since Jonathan had based his sermons on the work of British theologians
he had read at Harvard, supporters from across the Atlantic quickly picked
up on his references to their own heroes, and he became "the toast of dissenting Britain."

Jonathan's British allies were surprised that such works had come from
the heart of Calvinist America—that land of widespread evangelism with its
legacy of Puritanism. He acknowledged that they had cause to be shocked,
and that it was akin to hearing "good things coming out of Nazareth."
Soon after, the University of Aberdeen made Jonathan an honorary doctor
of divinity, a rare award for an American, previously bestowed on such
worthies as Charles Chauncy, Joseph Sewall, and Jonathan's former teacher
at Harvard, Edward Wigglesworth, who had first steered him away from
his father's brand of Calvinism.

Among the recommendations Jonathan received for the degree was one
from Governor William Shirley of Massachusetts. This was no surprise:
royal officials often befriended pastors with liberal views, encouraging them
to drift over to Anglicanism. From Timothy Cutler to William Hooper, the
previous pastor of West Church, antirevivalists had fallen into the arms of
the state church. These ministers' ambition within the colonial hierarchy
made such a move logical, and their elitist philosophy seemed to accord
better with the ideas of aristocratic clerics than with the "low rabble" of
the revivalists. Governor Shirley had witnessed the ordination of Reverend
Hooper into the Church of England and no doubt hoped Jonathan would
follow his example.

Jonathan knew the British magistrates had high hopes for him. They saw
that his congregation—urban and urbane, posh and sophisticated—included

just the kind of top-shelf parishioners who could fill the pews at an Anglican church. And they assumed that his battles against the evangelists of the New Birth heralded his first step toward the embrace of His Majesty's own religion, because if the Anglicans were anything, they were against the revival, and few spoke against it as passionately as Jonathan. However, if they thought the enemy of their enemies was their friend, the Anglican clerics were mistaken. Because in the imperious power of the established church, Jonathan found something he despised even more than the Calvinists. And he let them know it.

Anyone who closely read the *Seven Sermons* understood this. For Jonathan spoke not only against the orthodoxy of religion; he also excoriated the tyranny of those in power. And to him they were often one in the same. In his work he described a series of "enemies" of liberty that deserved all the scorn he could muster. At the top of the list was the Roman Catholic Church, which he said had allowed the torture and murder of Christians and others during the Inquisition and similar campaigns of terror. He ripped the Church of England, denouncing those "who punish dissenters and nonsubscribers by fines and imprisonments" and other unjust actions. And he cut down the orthodox Calvinists, using the rhetoric described earlier.

The anti-Anglican invective may have been the most unexpected, but to Jonathan the issues went beyond theology; he despised the Anglican elite because they had made their alliance with the British state, and that state had brought corruption and abuse of power to the colonies. He asked, "whose authority then is to be regarded, that of the King, or that of the Monarch of the Universe, the King of Kings and the Lord of Lords?" He suggested that earthly kings had no business heading religions—as George II did over the Church of England—and inquired "how any civil magistrate came by any authority at all in religious matters; and *who gave him this authority?*"

He also claimed that no nation, however powerful it might be, had a right to control people's free thoughts and religious liberties. Radical revivalists had been making this argument for years, and now it found a central place in the rhetoric of Jonathan Mayhew, one of their committed opponents. But to him it made sense: untrammeled human liberty naturally followed from resistance to tyranny. He made it plain in one sermon, in which he said, "We have not only a right to think for ourselves in matters of religion, but to act for ourselves also. . . . Nor has any man whatever, whether of a *civil* or *sacred* character, any authority to control us, unless it be by the gentle methods of argument and persuasion."

Needless to say, these were dangerous statements to be making during the British government's campaign to extend its dominion over its territories and keep the colonists under its heel. But Jonathan had already taken a risk in antagonizing his fellow ministers in Boston, and it pained him little to extend the critique to royal authorities as well. Because he knew everything he said was true, and it became more apparent as the miseries of New England only seemed to worsen by the day.

In the fall of 1749 Boston threatened to erupt in riot once more. The issue this time was the retirement of the wartime debt of Massachusetts, which had reached ungodly proportions and created an economic drag in the form of massive inflation and the shrinking value of the currency in relation to the British pound. Under the influence of Governor Shirley, Parliament had designated 183,000 pounds in silver specie to retire the old currency and replace it with legal tender acceptable to the British government. The legislature thought this would be a kindly gesture to reimburse the colony for all its sacrifices at Louisbourg in King George's War. But instead of placating the colonists, it made them burst into fury.

When the ship carrying the silver arrived in Boston Harbor, people swarmed through the streets, looking to find imperial officials to assault or to engage in other violent acts. The speaker of the General Court, Thomas Hutchinson, became so frightened he fled the town for his country estate, no doubt remembering how the previous spring his house had briefly taken flame while an angry crowd surrounded it, shouting "Let it burn! Let it burn!"

The protestors were angry none of the shipment of British silver would find its way into their pockets. Rumors had circulated of wealthy individuals hoarding depreciated bank notes, hoping for a fat return on their investment, instead of that money going into the hands of the soldiers, their families, or other people who deserved it more. They felt it had been earned with "the blood of the lower classes on the Canadian expeditions" and saw it as yet another bald-faced insult to the pride and heroism of New Englanders. The comments of men like speaker Hutchinson didn't help either: he proudly took credit for the currency replacement act and its approval by the king, and demanded that the colonials obey it, or else.

His haughty attitude continued a disturbing trend. The British state and its organs like the Board of Trade had been increasingly interfering in colonial affairs, demanding compliance with their edicts and threatening those who resisted them. The people might disapprove, but without organized opposition or a powerful force of arms, they had little chance to overturn even the most unjust decisions of Parliament. Unpopular legislators like Hutchinson who championed widely hated policies might get voted out in local elections—and he was, in 1749—but that did little to stop those policies or bring relief from suffering. And in any case, even if agreeable legislation were enacted in America, it could always be defeated in London. The example of violent convicts being shipped to the New World proved this: despite the efforts of Ben Franklin and countless others to enact laws to forbid the practice or tax it heavily, Parliament rejected those laws and kept shipping criminals across the Atlantic, despite whatever harm they might inflict. Without true autonomy, local government was rendered toothless, and people took their only recourse in the streets.

The signs of increased imperial control became unavoidable, not only in the threats of royal officials, but in the symbols of the Crown's supremacy itself. The most obvious was King's Chapel, rising on a plot once home to a Puritan graveyard, and now vying to be one of the most imposing sights in Boston. An anonymous pamphlet claimed "the ashes of the dead were inhumanely disturbed" to create the bulky stone Georgian edifice, and the much-hated Commodore William Knowles—cause of the eponymous riot—had even pledged one hundred pounds toward its construction.

The site of the church was no accident. It had been intended by its founders to remind dissenters of the irresistible power of the state religion. As a later history put it, "the new church arose, to symbolize by the massive walls which made it a cathedral amid the simpler structures around it. . . . dominating the metropolis of New England as with a visible sign of the presence of the English Church and the supremacy of the British Crown."

In concord with the grand new church came increased calls for submission to Anglicanism. A pamphlet appeared, *A Calm and Dispassionate*

Vindication of the Professors of the Church of England, that celebrated the church's missionary work and expansion in New England. At the same time, Fast Day celebrations became more adulatory of Charles I, with churchmen describing him in near-saintly terms. A London cleric, Thomas Pickering, in a sermon at St. Paul's Cathedral, proclaimed the dead king to be "swifter than an eagle—stronger than a lion" but who was nonetheless murdered by "vermin." Anglican clerics reviled the century-old Parliamentarians who had fought the king's armies as "a disorderly rabble of enthusiasts scrambling for power in every part of the kingdom" and linked them to the nonconformists of the current era. A missionary in Boston, Thomas Brockwell, claimed the same kind of zealots who had lorded over Britain with such barbarity would likely do so again if they were ever given the chance.

All of this disgusted Jonathan Mayhew. He had already seen the British government acting with disregard for colonial liberties, and now added to that were the push to convert New Englanders to the state church and the fusillade of insults directed at those who refused. On the occasion of Fast Day, he resolved to provide a response. He didn't consider himself a political philosopher but knew that history and politics would be essential to his message. So he studied everything from John Locke—increasingly a favorite author for dissenters—to John Milton, Benjamin Hoadley, and *Cato's Letters.* And he made sure to delve into the circumstances of the English Civil War, that monumental conflict that had destroyed and rebuilt the bonds of church and state, whose shadow still loomed over America in the memory of Puritan revolutionaries and the Lord Protector Oliver Cromwell.

THE LEGACY OF
OLIVER CROMWELL IN AMERICA

In 1645, the English-speaking world balanced on a precipice. Royalist armies under King Charles had been fighting Parliamentarians in the English Civil War for nearly three years, with control of the home country and the colonies of the New World at stake. The power of the monarchy, the establishment of religion, the very nature of the English nation had all come into question, with the answer to be provided by force of arms and a brutal political struggle.

Twenty thousand dissenters from the state church awaited the outcome with special interest. During the previous twenty-five years, these Puritans had come to Plymouth and Massachusetts Bay colonies as the founders of what they planned to be a theocracy in the wilds of America, and as exiles from a hostile English government. But ever since reformers had gained control of Parliament in 1640, many had been returning home.

They had good reason. Economic conditions in New England were bleak and few jobs could be found amid the immigration surge of previous years. Ministers and Harvard graduates made up the bulk of returnees, hoping to complete the revolution in church governance set about by Henry VIII. To do so, they enlisted to fight with Parliamentarians in a conflict they believed was an "apocalyptic sign of a new world ruled by the saints." Some New Englanders fit in well among the revolutionary "Roundheads"—eight took positions in Parliament and ten held major roles in the New Model Army led by Oliver Cromwell, a legislative backbencher who had emerged as the army's foremost commander.

After several indecisive battles and stubborn royal resistance, Cromwell's forces won a decisive victory at Naseby, effectively crushing Charles's army. Word of the triumph of Parliament arrived in New England like a thunderbolt. Long hoped for and desperately imagined by Puritan exiles, the downfall of the king seemed like a sign of Providence. His most hated advisors had been deposed, others had been executed, and the foundation of the Church of England—its legal establishment and system of episcopacy—stood in ruin along with the monarch's autocratic power. Four years later, on January 30, 1649, the king himself faced ruin, as Cromwell signed his death warrant and he was executed at his own banqueting house.

Despite the controversy that ensued over the king's killing, dissenters at home and abroad supported Cromwell. They called him "friend and disciple," held fast days for him in Massachusetts, and one prominent New England minister, John Cotton, commended him for fighting the Lord's battles. Another minister from Salem, Hugh Peter, even preached sermons that had encouraged the king's execution and played a prominent role in seeing it through. For decades afterward, men who returned to New England after fighting in the New Model Army would be hailed for their service and treated as heroes.

Cromwell did all he could to return the affections of New Englanders. Under the advice of Puritan divines, he allowed the persecution of Anglicans in the New World, and when they complained, he ignored their protests. He conquered Ireland, subjugated native Catholics and stripped them of their land and gave it to Protestants. He encouraged the banishment of rebels like Anne Hutchinson from Massachusetts and forbade any formal inquiry into the governance of that colony. He imagined greater power for Puritans over the rest of the New World, approving an expedition to the Caribbean led by Admiral William Penn, later namesake of Pennsylvania, that laid claim to Jamaica. And he allowed open trade with the northeastern colonies by giving them "that extraordinary privilege of having their goods imported into England free from all custom," potentially a great boon to their economy.

But the Puritan Commonwealth and the later Protectorate—a military dictatorship led by Cromwell—did not last beyond the 1650s. Upon the Lord Protector's death and the misrule of his son, Puritan control of Parliament ended with defeat at the hands of resurgent royalists. Charles II took the throne and countermanded virtually every major Puritan policy, reestablishing the monarchy and the Church of England, and trying and executing those who had conspired to murder his father, including Hugh Peter, who was hanged, drawn, and quartered. Most importantly, the new royal government drove some two thousand nonconformist ministers from their offices and harassed and imprisoned scores of Presbyterians, Congregationalists, and Baptists, as well as Quakers and Roman Catholics. His campaign of reestablishing royal dominion became known as the Restoration.

For fear of being arrested or otherwise persecuted, many Puritans returned to the New World, where they attempted to rebuild their broken theocracy. Only now, dissenters and nonconformists were *severely hampered by law, and it would take decades before the Crown recognized their right to toleration—and they remained forbidden from public office. Accordingly, praise for Lord Protector Cromwell vanished from official circles, and any prominent Puritan had to carefully denounce his actions when speaking of him at all. But underground, among common people and in hushed tones among the upper classes, Cromwell's legacy endured as an "avenging savior."*

For those who cared to look, signs of reverence for the military chieftain were not hard to find. Parents in New England named their children "Oliver" in his honor, much more than they did in the South or the Middle Colonies, and librarians in Massachusetts added books to their shelves written by sympathizers of the Puritan Commonwealth. In Boston, Cromwell's Head Inn forced visitors to bow to a giant sign featuring the Lord Protector's titular head before they could enter the premises. In that town and others, commoners celebrated Pope's Day with tarring and feathering the effigies of the pontiff and the devil, dragging them along in violent processions before burning them in a great spectacle. As time passed, the event evolved into "a ritual of detestation of the Stuarts," with the torch-bearers playing the part of Puritan revolutionaries against the power of an oppressive monarchy.

As the mid-eighteenth century came, the colonists grew bolder. Ministers like John Dickinson openly defended the Puritan Revolution and claimed the Commonwealth had exterminated evil in the realm; and when it collapsed, wickedness had returned in a flood that threatened to drown the nation. Anonymous pamphlets called Charles I an "execrable tyrant" and dissenters said he deserved to lose his head, and in turn, "Christ's ambassadors were represented by Calvinists in the image of Cromwell."

Anglican ministers reacted scornfully to such claims. To them Cromwell was anything but divinely inspired. He would always be a cruel and merciless regicide who showed just how devious noncon-formists from the state church could be unless they were kept under the heel of a powerful monarchy. But as years passed, their warnings to keep quiet about the Puritan Revolution only encouraged its heirs to speak out more loudly.

The revival brought praise for the Lord Protector from New Light evangelists. Jonathan Edwards, especially, lauded the zeal and resolution he found in the English commander—"And how much were the great things that Oliver Cromwell did, owing to these things!" His hosannas allowed lesser clerics to express their own admiration, which "nearly every pietist in New England had secretly shared since the Great Awakening." Although many moderate pastors and laypeople still thought of Cromwell as a regressive dictator, to many revivalists, he was just the kind of benevolent strongman the country needed—someone who could summon God's armies to fight corruption and declension from faith, and who could not be bribed or bargained with, or otherwise bought off. They claimed Cromwell had been as stalwart in religion as he was on the battlefield. For he had accepted or at least tolerated all the sects of the Reformed Christian faith, whether they were theocrats who wanted to remake the government in God's image, or groups like the Levellers and Diggers who sought to destroy the social hierarchy and rebuild it from the ground up.

As time passed and crisis followed crisis in the colonies, young rebels like James Otis and Samuel Adams raised the name Cromwell as a rallying cry, and inspired others to do the same. On a later tour of the English countryside with Thomas Jefferson, John Adams visited one New Model Army battlefield and was struck with reverence. He asked of the local villagers, "[D]o Englishmen so soon forget the ground where liberty was fought for? Tell your neighbors and your children that this is holy ground, much holier than that on which your churches stand. All England should come in pilgrimage to this hill once a year."

However, even as New Englanders sought to elevate the Lord Protector's reputation in history, monarchists demanded ever more promises of loyalty to the Crown and praise for martyred kings, and they threatened colonists with greater subjugation for their loose talk.

Some ministers and laypeople cowered in the face of such threats, but those who didn't could achieve a strange sort of fame—a seditious celebrity that drew the affection of their countrymen, even as it put their lives and careers at great risk.

On January 30, 1750, Jonathan Mayhew delivered the third in a series of sermons based on the verse from Romans 13, "Let every soul be subject unto the higher powers." Anglican prelates had long taken this verse to defend unlimited submission to the monarchy—upholding the Divine Right of Kings, the primacy of the Church of England, and "the people's duty of passive obedience and nonresistance to tyrants." These clerics issued their message on the anniversary of Charles I's execution, and their message was rarely answered in kind. But fed up with hearing the same calumny repeated year after year, Jonathan resolved to do just that.

He began by offering his support for George II as a wise and just ruler, for "disobedience to civil rulers in the due exercise of their authority, is not merely a political sin, but an heinous offense against God and religion." A rightful ruler like the current king had nothing to fear from his colonial subjects, because he had done nothing wrong and was in no way a tyrant. But what of actual tyrants?

He revealed to his parishioners that throughout history, many despots had been banished or killed by their subjects for justifiable reasons. Tarquin faced expulsion from Rome; Julius Caesar faced daggers in the Senate; and, in the Glorious Revolution sixty years before, James II "was made to fly that country which he aimed at enslaving." Jonathan said that these banishments and executions were justifiable because these men were base and wicked rulers, and that "It is blasphemy to call tyrants and oppressors God's ministers. They are more properly the messengers of Satan to buffet us." He continued:

> For a nation thus abused to arise unanimously, and to resist their prince, even to the dethroning him, is not criminal; but a reasonable way of vindicating their liberties and just rights; it is making use of the means, and the only means, which God has put into their power, for mutual and self-defense. And it would

be highly criminal in them not to make use of this means. It would be stupid tameness, and unaccountable folly, for whole nations to suffer one unreasonable, ambitious and cruel man, to wanton and riot in their misery. And in such a case it would, of the two, be more rational to suppose that they [who] did NOT resist, than that they who did, would receive to themselves damnation.

With this in mind, he set about exorcising the ghost of Charles I.

He called him an agent of oppression, a wretch who had married a French Catholic and threatened to bring the Pope's legions to England. He said he governed in a "wild and arbitrary manner" that employed "illegal and despotic measures" to bring his subjects under his boot. He gave license to evil counselors and ministers to inflict harm on the populace, using unjust taxation, imprisonment, and "unheard-of barbarities" to do so. Worse, "he supported that more than fiend, archbishop Laud and the clergy of his stamp, in all their church tyranny and hellish cruelties," thus describing the head of the Church of England as an ogre. All in all, Charles used armed force to intimidate Parliament, ruled without legislative consent for decades, and used the state church to do his dirty work.

Jonathan summoned the fire of radical preachers, who had for years inveighed against the power of oppressive government and demanded liberty from it. He channeled their zeal with his own furious rhetoric, polishing his words into daggers, and held his listeners spellbound.

He asked them, who were the people who finally brought down such a menace to the English nation? They weren't any mere rebels, but "the LORDS and COMMONS of England." The people's own representatives—those legendary Puritans who had dissented from the Church of England and peopled the New World—had forced the end of Charles's reign, and had earned God's favor for it. So whatever flaws that Oliver Cromwell may have had, he and his allies "were not, properly speaking, guilty of rebellion; because he, whom they beheaded, was not, properly speaking, *their king*; but a *lawless tyrant*."

He said it was the civic duty of Parliamentarians to rid the nation of a royal scourge! For they had slain a devil, and rescued the nation from drowning in the corruption and dissolution in which the depraved monarch had engulfed them. He was no martyr—and certainly no saint! No, Jonathan announced, he was "a man black with guilt and laden with iniquity . . . and it was the oppression and violence of his reign that brought him to his untimely and violent end at last."

As a flourish to his oration, Jonathan offered a dramatic threat: *"Britons will not be slaves;* a warning to all corrupt councilors and ministers, not to go too far in advising to arbitrary, despotic measures. . . . Let us learn to be *free*, and to be *loyal*. Let us not profess ourselves vassals to the lawless pleasure of any man on earth. But let us remember, at the same time, government is *sacred*, and not to be *trifled* with."

Jonathan's sermon, *A Discourse Concerning Unlimited Submission and Non-Resistance to the Higher Powers,* was a bold political declaration, and as brazen a statement as any clergyman had ever made in New England. Though he wasn't yet thirty years of age, he gave voice to beliefs that had circulated for many decades in quiet tones and qualified comments, but this time using his own blunt, slashing rhetoric. While many in his congregation had heard him hint of such sentiments before, few had imagined he would knit his arguments into such a damning critique of the House of Stuart and the current churchmen who held up Charles I as a role model. And those churchmen were quick to anger once they took notice.

They called the sermon a justification for murder and anarchy, a scandalous and scurrilous tract that lacked decency or merit. They accused Jonathan of sedition, and of encouraging disobedience to the current king or even of being in league with secret Jacobites, or Catholics, or other such enemies. They said his attack on Archbishop Laud was tantamount to attacking the entire Church of England. Jonathan's longtime nemesis Charles Brockwell even called the sermon a work of treason and urged the Bishop of London to have him arrested and shipped back to Britain to meet his fate.

Luckily for Jonathan, attacking a century-old dead king did not meet the legal definition of treason, and he had taken great pain not to impugn the name of George II in his sermon, but rather praised him effusively. This gave him some protection from his critics, whose attacks were almost all anonymous. Jonathan challenged his foes to put a name to any single criticism so he could answer it, whether in print or in court, but none would.

He faced a greater challenge in defending himself from charges of plagiarism. He had knowingly lifted many of his ideas from the work of British authors like Benjamin Hoadley, who had argued for the protection of liberty in the face of oppression. The nameless critics said Jonathan was a mere mouthpiece for such opinions and that his literary merits were as dubious as his loyalty to the British nation. But Jonathan did not apologize for borrowing such ideas. Rather, he sent Hoadley a copy of the sermon along with a note thanking him for his influence.

Fueled by all the controversy, the sermon had a huge impact: it set off a six-month battle in the press over the idea of citizens rebelling against their government—with Anglicans and Congregationalists on warring sides—and sections of the speech found their way into the papers of the Middle Colonies and the South. Many colonists immediately recognized it as a groundbreaking work: a statement of past and perhaps future resistance against unjust rulers, and a political manifesto that became "the most famous sermon preached in pre-revolutionary America." To New Englanders it was also a long-awaited salvo in their battles against royal magistrates, after years of political crackdowns, war, impressment, riots, currency chaos, and economic misery that did not seem to end. And for Americans beyond the Northeast it had a powerful meaning too, and one rich with irony.

Namely, Jonathan Mayhew was to evangelists the arch villain of liberal theology, who rejected original sin, predestination, the New Birth, and all the Calvinist principles of the revival that they proudly believed and promoted. But this enemy heretic had also delivered an oration that, in its aggressive tone, its open mockery, and its uncompromising rhetoric, outdid anything their own preachers, including George Whitefield, had ever said against the ruling elite. Jonathan took all the force of the revival, all the anger and passion and piercing accusations, and directed it against British magistrates and the Church of England—the sworn enemy of the New Lights. In so doing he fed the American populist rage and became "a pre-eminent spokesman in the colonies for everything that was new, bold, and radically nonconformist in matters of church and state."

One young man paying particular attention to the minister and his speech was a fourteen-year-old John Adams. He had attended West Church at various times to watch Reverend Mayhew preach, and even decades later, remained struck by the impact of his words. In a letter to Thomas Jefferson that accompanied a copy of the tract, he wrote that he had pored over the sermon, "till the substance of it was incorporated into my nature and indelibly engraved on my memory." And he knew others had too, for the sermon "was read by everybody; celebrated by friends, and abused by enemies." He called it his own "catechism" of revolution.

Thus, at the dawn of the 1750s, the collective attacks of Jonathan Mayhew, along with those of Charles Chauncy, Sam Adams, and legions of Separatist dissenters and frontier Baptist preachers, put at risk the system of governance that had guided British North America since the early 17th century. And the change came both in the hearts and minds of Americans, through their transformation into vehement protestors, subversive preachers, spellbound enthusiasts, and potential revolutionaries. The outcome of the great revival, then, was to make America both more devout and irreverent, fearless and reckless, pious and uncivil. Driven by the religion of Jonathan Edwards and the politics of Jonathan Mayhew—a volatile mix that offered an explosive promise.

SPIRITS

ELEVEN

THE AWAKENERS

After his dismissal from the pulpit in Northampton, Jonathan Edwards lingered in town with his family for a year. As the months passed, the locals became ever more suspicious of him. Rumors circulated of his alleged schemes to manipulate his parishioners to his own ends, and the town folk claimed he had "sinister views" and a "tyrannical spirit" that made him a menace. They even voted to revoke a grant of pastureland they had previously given him, which damaged his finances and made it all the more essential that he find a new job. Adding to his worries: he and his wife Sarah had ten surviving children, some of whom they still had to support.

His former parish's unfair treatment of him, coupled with his role as a target for critics of the revival, drove him to write *Misrepresentations Corrected, and Truth Vindicated*, in which he laid out a careful defense of his actions at Northampton and rebutted the charges made against him. He said his enemies had caricatured his ideas for determining the spiritual state of church members and had attacked him with specious logic and false claims. He said they meant to "exhibit my scheme to the world in a ridiculous light" and defame whatever reputation he had left.

Although some wags claimed he was a man out of step with the times and a clumsy master of his parish, Reverend Edwards's real problem was that he was a perfectionist. He had expected great things from the people of Northampton in the 1730s and again in the next decade, and he could never accept that they would fail to live up to his high standards. They would backslide, return to their wretched ways, and glory in greed and hedonism and everything else he despised, and he chastised them for it. They would make excuses for their wickedness, speak with forked tongues, and engage in the most blatant hypocrisies, and he condemned them for it and compared them to heathens and apostates. He had done all he could to persuade them, and finally resorted to judging their souls himself. As a result, he had to look for new work.

He found it on the frontier of far western Massachusetts in Stockbridge—as an Indian missionary. It was a surprising turn for him, to seek a position in the sparsely settled hinterlands, but after the mission's previous pastor died, Edwards consulted with his family and a ministerial council and accepted the role.

He planned to educate the children of the Mohawk people in Christianity and oversee a boarding school where they would be fed and clothed and taught vocational skills. Although he viewed the Mohawk as degenerate in their ignorance of Christ, he saw many of his white peers as worse for having heard the gospel and rejecting it. And after his recent struggles, Edwards had such a negative opinion of his fellow Britons, as well as the French and Dutch, that he told his Indian audiences that Europeans had willfully prevented their education, "for as long as they keep you in ignorance . . . 'tis more easy to cheat you in trading with you." He knew how notoriously western traders had behaved—defrauding the Natives and abusing their trust—and called Anglican missionaries in particular "great bigots" for their actions. All of this gave rise to understandable fears among the Mohawk and other tribes in the Iroquois Confederacy that "if they sent their children to English schools, the English would enslave them." Trust was hard to come by in relations between the peoples, but Edwards was willing to try.

Edwards oversaw a small group of Mohawk boys and girls, and their instruction in reading, spelling, math, and sacred music, as well as scripture. His six-year-old son, Jonathan Jr., took an even greater interest in the mission than his father, and had several young Indian friends and was better versed in Mahican and Mohawk than English. The reverend even considered grooming him to be a missionary. As for the rest of his family, though, several older Edwards children did not move to Stockbridge, and stayed behind in Northampton, since the cost and stress of uprooting them from their home would be considerable. Through all these changes, the Edwardses lacked for money: his wife Sarah and their daughter had to make silk-paper fans for extra cash, and the reverend so lacked for writing paper that he was reduced to scrawling on their discarded scraps.

Other problems developed. While Edwards found some success as an overseer of the Indian school, many Mohawk parents took their children back to the land for sugaring season, making attendance erratic at the mission. Worse, the behavior of some British colonial officials was nothing less than barbaric to Native peoples, making them even more distrustful of white interlopers. These factors, along with the meager pay and difficulties of living on the frontier, made Edwards's work as a missionary challenging enough. But what made it unsustainable was the drumbeat of another round of imperial warfare with France.

In the coming conflict, the question of Indian allegiance was paramount. Britons outnumbered the French in frontier settlements, but for years the French had worked at securing the alliance of Native peoples against the spread of British settlement. Edwards recognized how essential the Indians in Stockbridge (as well as the larger and more dominant groups of Iroquois) would be in battling the king's enemies in the war to come, but he also knew how miserably British leaders had failed them. He wrote that the Indians would surely become "a sore scourge to use as a just punishment of our cruelty to their souls and bodies, by our withholding the Gospel from 'em, defrauding them of their goods, prejudicing them against Christianity by our wickedness; and killing of multitudes of them, and easily diminishing their numbers with strong drink." For good reason, Edwards worried his family would be on the edge of the war zone.

In the mid-1750s his fears were realized, as the conflict erupted into violence in multiple places along the frontier, and one of them was near Edwards's own house: soldiers built a stockade surrounding it and prepared for an onslaught of enemy warriors. With troops lodged in their own home,

Jonathan and Sarah sent some of their children to live with relatives in Bethlehem, Connecticut, and Jonathan found himself pressed between the need to mission to the remaining Mohawk and to protect and provide for his family. The stress of it all gave rise to illness, and the reverend became gravely sick for seven months, plagued by weakness and fever, and lost so much weight he resembled a skeleton.

Terror gripped the community as fears of an Indian uprising led to talk of conspiracies and even outright panic, fed by rumors of town folk being tomahawked and murdered. Stockbridge Indians became targets for the rumors, even though other Natives were to blame for the attacks that had occurred; and this only encouraged them to distrust the European colonists even more and to flee the area. Meanwhile, the "friendly" British soldiers devoured the Edwards family's food and supplies and forced the reverend to petition the General Court to reimburse him for the nearly one thousand meals, fodder for 150 horses, and seven gallons of rum the soldiers had consumed.

In July 1755 the news from the front took a darker turn, as General Edward Braddock met defeat and death near Fort Duquesne and the British army suffered a devastating loss—which not only damaged the war effort against the French, but imperiled the survival of the settled towns of the frontier, including Stockbridge. Many Native troops, aside from the Mohawk, had already deserted to fight with the French, and the entire war effort threatened to become a grand imperial debacle. Edwards blamed the disaster on the sins of his own people: "God is indeed frowning upon us everywhere; our enemies get up above us very high, and we are brought down very low. . . . God is making us, with all our superiority in numbers, to become the object of our enemies' almost continual triumphs and insults."

It did seem like a cruel cosmic joke, that Edwards had been forced to leave his longtime home because of the distrust of his parishioners; and when he found a position in which he gained the trust of the locals, war intervened to destroy whatever goodwill he had earned. But he did not feel pity for himself and kept trying to do his duty. He remained resolute in putting his faith in God's hands.

Luckily, God had other plans for Jonathan Edwards than killing him on the front lines of a war zone. Though the conflict with the French would escalate, and draw ever closer to Stockbridge, the death that took him away from the frontier was not his own, but that of Aaron Burr Sr. (father of the future vice president). Burr had been the president of the recently chartered College of New Jersey, but more importantly, he was Edwards's own son-in-law and the husband of his daughter Esther. When Burr expired at only forty-one years of age, the news shocked the Edwards family and the community, and drove the college trustees to offer the vacant presidency to Edwards himself.

It seemed like an easy choice to offer the job to Edwards, but the reverend agonized over it. In a lengthy letter, he offered the trustees a long list of his flaws. He informed them of his sickly nature, and his "childish weakness and contemptibleness of speech, presence and demeanor; with a disagreeable dullness and stiffness, much unfitting me for conversation, but more especially for the government of a college"—among other regrettable traits like his poor education in algebra, higher math, and the Greek classics. In fact, Edwards wondered why the trustees were even considering him for such a job, given his many failings. He was honored by the offer but couldn't immediately accept it. Instead he put the choice in the hands of a council of ministers. They in turn deliberated over whether the first major evangelist of the revival should lead the first major American college founded by dissenters.

The College of New Jersey at Princeton was a bastion of New Light philosophy and scholarship. Its first president had been the moderate Presbyterian Jonathan Dickinson and its second, Burr, had learned divinity under the influence of Edwards himself. A local revival had recently broken out at the college—one of the few hot spots for religion in the northern colonies in the 1750s—and many felt that no better figure could keep the revival burning than the great evangelist himself. So whatever weaknesses Edwards may have thought he had paled in comparison to the monumental presence he would have at the school, and the opportunity he could afford to future ministers who wanted to learn at his knee. The council recommended he leave Stockbridge and take the position.

Samuel Hopkins, who had studied under Edwards during the revival, described his mentor's reaction to the decision: "he appeared uncommonly moved and affected with it, and fell into tears on the occasion; which was very unusual for him." Hopkins would carry the torch for Edwards's gospel for the next generation, but for now he was pleased to see him so justly rewarded for his life's service, and to take the next step in his career: "He girded up his loins, and set off from Stockbridge for Prince-Town in January."

The presidency of the College of New Jersey held great promise: it would allow him once again to fully provide for his family, and to redeem his reputation from recent struggles. He had great plans for his new role, too, and an array of treatises and sermons to write on some of his favorite topics. Among these were proud defenses of old-fashioned faith and pointed criticisms of new heresies.

In a recent letter to Edward Wigglesworth at Harvard, Edwards had warned of the liberalism of men like Jonathan Mayhew, whose work he saw as a danger to the survival of Calvinism. He published defenses of Congregational doctrines against the criticism of Mayhew and others, including *The Great Christian Doctrine of Original Sin Defended*, nearly 400 pages of theology that updated and reinforced Protestant orthodoxy. He wrote important works like *The Freedom of Will*, laying out his view of predestination and explaining how true human freedom was an illusion, since no one could be independent of God's will. And he had great plans to show the unity of Christian ideas in *The Harmony of the Old and New Testament*, and to sum up his career as a revivalist with his magnum opus, *History of the Work of Redemption*. But before he could finish any of those things, he died.

No sooner had he settled in as the president of the College of New Jersey in winter 1758, than he became aware of a smallpox outbreak at Princeton. Knowing the devastating toll the disease could take, Edwards chose to have his family inoculated against the disease. His daughter Lucy had recently contracted smallpox and survived, and Edwards didn't wish any of his other children to suffer the same fate, or worse. However, while the vaccinations turned out well for other family members, for Edwards the cure became the disease. He contracted smallpox soon after receiving the treatment and realized he would be dead very soon. He settled his estate and asked that any money that would have been spent on a lavish funeral instead be given to the poor. A few weeks later he met his end—without regret or anger and with full acceptance of the Lord's will. He had only been the college's president for a month when he expired.

A short time after, his daughter Esther caught a fever and died, and by the end of the year, his wife Sarah had died of dysentery. It was a grim conclusion to the family's struggles, but it did not diminish their legend. Even in death, they remained one of the best-known families in American religion. Edwards in his writings had lauded them as examples of piety and grace and, in Sarah's case, holiness in her conversion to Christ. In the coming years, his son Jonathan Jr. would continue his father's ministry and ensure that the family name would live on. And the deceased pastor's own writings would do the rest, providing thousands of pages of ardent and complex defenses, justifications, exhortations, and explanations of the greatest religious revival America had yet known, and building the intellectual foundation for upheavals yet to come.

Reverend Edwards might have become the most renowned college president in America had he lived. As it was, he briefly led an institution that would grow into a citadel of dissent, a seminary for New Light ministers, and a breeding ground of future troublemakers against royal officials. And this wasn't surprising, for the College of New Jersey had its roots in a small but controversial wooden structure in Neshaminy, Pennsylvania: the original Log College of William Tennent Sr.

The elder Tennent had died in 1746, and his influential college foundered with him, but its ideals lived on in the College of New Jersey, which was chartered only six months after his death. Many graduates and associates of the Log College became trustees of the new college, and like the little wooden school, the new one's mission was to train ministers with "experimental knowledge" in the Christian faith. It was to be nondenominational, and to draw students throughout the colonies from dissenting ranks. But that feature also made it a threat to the Church of England, which tried to prevent it from being chartered and, failing that, pushed the governor of New Jersey to give it control of its governance. Such overt attempts to meddle led to outrage among school authorities.

The Anglicans had good cause to worry, for the College of New Jersey became a rock of nonconformity and a thorn in the side of Anglicanism.

And one of its greatest champions was no friend to the Church of England, but a confirmed opponent: Gilbert Tennent, the original Son of Thunder.

Although Gilbert still carried the nickname among revivalists, he had long since ceased to be a source of thunder in the pulpit: He had adopted a measured tone and an appearance of moderation. However, even if he no longer marshaled the thunder, he could not avoid it. In 1745 he became its literal target when lightning struck him inside his home. The bolt sheared bricks off the chimney, tore through the house, melted his belt buckle, and ripped his shoes. Though he survived his injuries, his enemies pointed to his electrocution as evidence of divine disfavor. But Gilbert saw it differently, and wrote a sermon, *All Things Come Alike to All*, that attempted to examine why the Lord had nearly killed him.

He explained the event by not explaining it. He had no answers for why God did what he did. It was all part of a mysterious plan of which humans were ignorant, and at some point one had to stop demanding answers to unanswerable riddles. "God's paths are in the great deep, and his footsteps are not known. The Almighty sometimes hides the face of his Throne, and makes darkness his pavilion." Gilbert's life had gone in strange directions after the revival, and he could do little but follow them, no matter where they led.

After his embarrassment at the hands of radicals like James Davenport, and relocation to Philadelphia from his longtime home in New Brunswick, Gilbert's rhetoric had changed with the times. He quenched much of his hellfire, and he no longer spoke of people's bones being torn apart at the Lord's whim, and their hearts ripped out like carrion, and other horrific images. He even subdued his talk of the damnation awaiting the unconverted, not because he no longer believed it, but because he thought it came perilously close to substituting his judgment for God's. In fact, he had learned that too much zeal could be destructive, and could endanger the cause he loved: promoting experimental religion and rebirth in Christ.

Over twenty years until the mid-1760s, Gilbert preached to a congregation that included the governor of Pennsylvania and other important officials. He spoke in a somber fashion, without browbeating his listeners, and wore a proper pulpit gown and wig. He spoke with extensive notes and reused many of his old sermons, to avoid the risk of any errant phrases littering his message.

He once again attracted the attention of Ben Franklin, who had printed the famous works that had gained him a fearsome reputation throughout the colonies. Now, Franklin had his eye on the New Building where Gilbert preached. He offered to assume control of the building for use as a proposed nondenominational college, in exchange for freeing Gilbert's congregation of the substantial debts they had accrued while operating it as a church. Gilbert accepted the offer, knowing he would have to quickly raise funds to build a new church—and one of the first people he asked to donate was Franklin.

Franklin was too canny to put his own money into supporting the Presbyterian cause that he had rejected in his youth. But he did provide Gilbert with some good advice for fundraising—asking everyone from close allies to sworn enemies to drum up the money—and within a few years the minister had succeeded in creating a fancy new home for the Second Presbyterian Church, complete with glittering chandeliers and an elegant steeple. To those who felt the creation of the building undercut the low-church piety and hardscrabble faith Gilbert had once preached, he offered an answer that could have come straight from a high-born Anglican cleric: "in cities where there is a greater resort of persons of honor, distinction, and polite taste, the structures of a religious kind should be adorned with greater beauty and exactness, than in obscurer places." The contrast with the humble log house where he had found his faith couldn't have been clearer.

He also reconciled part of the church he had once helped divide. He created an alliance with other moderate revivalists to form the New York Synod, which became a rival to the Philadelphia Synod that was dominated by Old Siders. This added another contradiction to Gilbert's life, which was increasingly full of them: He preached in Philadelphia for a synod based in New York, to a congregation made up of elites he had once belittled, in a church rich with ornaments he once decried as fripperies. His transformation was thereby complete, and anyone ignorant of recent history could have scarcely imagined him as a Son of Thunder, aside from his lightning scars.

Still, however much he embraced moderation, it did not free him from the attacks of his Old Side foes. Despite his efforts to become an honored gentleman of the cloth, he preached in a city dominated by those who had battled him over matters of faith. He could not break free of this entanglement, and he knew that to advance the mission of his church, he had to reconcile the bonds he had once casually severed.

In his 1749 sermon *Irenicum Ecclesiasticum*, or "The Church of Peace," Gilbert offered a gesture of reconciliation to the warring Presbyterians. He minimized their theological differences, and claimed it was "absurd and blasphemous" to accept divisions between people of faith. "Schisms and divisions, my brethren, do not only expose the church to contempt and scorn, but likewise to a total dissolution, to entire ruin, and destruction." The new Gilbert had no use for dissension and wished only to unite people once more in a spirit of "humility, weakness and love." However, while the old holy warrior now seemed to put down his sword, he still needed an enemy. He praised how "the visible church strikes a dread, a panic, into the hearts of all her foes, like an army with banners . . . and drawn up in battalia." Gilbert might have proclaimed the value of love, but his heart remained militant.

He began to preach of battle outside the pulpit, too, exhorting all Presbyterians to support the creation of a colonial militia, and proclaiming the value of defensive war. When the conflict with France resumed in the mid-1750s, Gilbert joined with his foes in calling for military preparation against the Catholic enemy. While he no longer wanted to wage battles against those of his own faith, he embraced the call to arms against the Pope's legions. He knew that warfare could affirm the shared beliefs of all Presbyterians, and make their differences seem small in comparison.

Ultimately, however, Gilbert's attempt to reconcile with his foes did not succeed with martial rhetoric alone. He could only reunite the church with the power of numbers—in the form of ordained ministers and British pounds.

In 1753 Gilbert Tennent and Samuel Davies embarked on a fateful trip to the old country, to raise money for the endowment of the College of New Jersey. The trustees had tried to use public lotteries and domestic donations to fund the institution, but the New Jersey legislature banned the former and the latter proved insufficient. Only donors in Britain could contribute enough money to support the New Light institution, and the evangelists would have to woo them to part with their pounds in person.

It would be an arduous trip. Gilbert's wife and mother had recently died, and he was overcome with grief and in a foul mood. Moreover, he remembered how the Tennent family had once fled Great Britain to avoid its all-powerful bishops and magistrates, and with the visit he would be back in their rationalist, decadent lair. Even the character of Presbyterianism seemed foreign to him—divided by liberal churchmen influenced by natural religion and fiery enthusiasts who thought Gilbert had gone soft in his middle age. Nonetheless, when he and Davies arrived at Christmas, they went to work.

Over the next year they scoured the islands from England and Scotland to the Tennent homeland of Ireland. They sought audiences with local synod leaders, legislators, royal officials, and anyone with money who might be interested in promoting colonial piety from a distance of 3,500 miles. They split up and toured the places where each was more popular and knocked on countless doors and met with people of both substantial and middling wealth, through tireless and numbing efforts. As Davies put it, "I never engaged in such a series of wasting fatigues and dangers as our present mission is attended with. . . . I have walked in the tedious, crowded streets of London from morning to evening, till my nature has been quite exhausted; and I have been hardly able to move a limb." And then they returned home, exhausted from the kind of monotonous money-begging that only George Whitefield seemed to enjoy.

They succeeded beyond expectation. Their original goal had been to collect 300 pounds for the college, but within the first three months they had already tripled that amount, and in the end may have raised as much as 3,000 pounds in the mission. It was a great sum to fund a college for reborn pastors, and it paid off in ways that multiplied as the years passed.

With such ample funding, the College of New Jersey could now afford to educate more ministers in its seminary and train more men to spread the New Birth throughout America. And because each new divinity degree meant filling a new pulpit, the ranks of revival men quickly grew: In 1745 the divided ranks of Presbyterian pastors were roughly equal, but by 1758 there were three times as many New Siders as Old Siders. The success of the College of New Jersey in handing the power to the revivalists was invaluable, and the traditionalists had no choice but to capitulate.

The terms of the long-awaited Presbyterian reunion were charitable to the losing side, on the surface. With Gilbert as moderator overseeing the terms of unification, the church committees decreed that convulsions in worship, divine revelations, and enthusiastic madness were to be condemned; arguments over doctrine were minimized and papered over; and "all former differences and disputes are laid aside and buried." But despite these good words, there was no doubt the New Side pastors had triumphed. The unified sides confirmed the value of an experimental faith in Christ and approved of revivals as "a blessed work of the Holy Spirit." William Tennent's long-held goal of reforming the church on his terms had found success, and his son had accomplished it with grit, legwork, passion, and money.

Gilbert Tennent died five years after the reunion. His legacy as a reborn Christian turned zealous minister, turned fearsome demagogue, turned moderate evangelist would remain controversial for decades afterward. But beyond his role in the revival, much more lasting was his influence as an educational trustee and fundraiser. For his College of New Jersey did not lose its influence after it led the New Side to victory in the figurative Presbyterian war; it also played a prominent role in the actual war to come.

In the first twenty years of the school's existence, it graduated ninety-seven "highly articulate and unusually vocal" Presbyterian ministers who took public stands on matters spiritual and, increasingly, political. It gave degrees to dozens of important lawyers and doctors of prominence, and many key legislators and governors of the future American nation. Indeed, ninety-four of its graduates would ultimately take arms against Britain (against only eight loyalists), and more than one hundred would serve in political office for the new republic, with five becoming members of the Constitutional Convention. Of course, it was never Gilbert Tennent's goal to create a cradle of sedition against the British government; he only wanted to train reborn men of the cloth to fill pulpits. But as with everything in the revival, the result was unexpected—the rise of the first major dissenting college in America, a bulwark of nonconformity against the Church of England, and a breeding ground for future revolutionaries.

◆

The College of New Jersey was not alone as a groundbreaking school. It had a rival in an institution called the Academy of Philadelphia, based in the very New Building where Gilbert Tennent and George Whitefield had once preached. Its founder had an independent view of religion and had designed the Academy as a nonsectarian refuge for students of a variety of beliefs, and a bastion of free thought. Once again, Ben Franklin had put an innovative idea into practice.

By this time, Franklin had moved on from promoting religious revivals. Doing so in the previous decade had benefited him handsomely, enabled him to eclipse his rival Andrew Bradford, retire from his print operation, and put it in the hands of his business partner. He had cultivated many other interests at the time—developing an early hospital and insurance company, acting as alderman and colonial assemblyman, trying to create a militia to protect Pennsylvania, and most famously, conducting electrical experiments and inventing the lightning rod, for which he earned a Copley Medal from the Royal Society. And increasingly, he began to argue for the alliance of the colonies in a defensive union, against frontier Indians or whomever else his countrymen feared might have designs on them.

Franklin also set about undermining the control of the colony by the Penn family—the "proprietary party." No longer sympathetic to common Quakers, the party had mismanaged the affairs of Pennsylvania, and Franklin tried to strip them of their power to spend money and appoint magistrates, and to defend citizens from their taxation. In response the proprietors called Franklin "the chief author and grand abettor" of sedition, and an anarchist and republican who threatened the power of the elite. Of course, Franklin was none of these things, but that didn't prevent the party from exacting its revenge: through the influence of Anglican clerics, they heaped scorn upon him as a public menace and forced him out as president of the Academy of Philadelphia.

Yet the days of the proprietors were numbered, as were those of other colonial aristocrats. The Penn family and their allies in the Church of England lost important elections and saw their forces divided in the assembly, and the cleric who had become provost of the Academy, William Smith, so offended Quaker assemblymen that they had him arrested and jailed for libel. Franklin had a quiet hand in many of these actions, demonstrating his skill for both diplomacy and coercion.

Franklin also maintained a friendly correspondence with leading writers, scientists, and statesmen of the time, while keeping up with his longtime friends and associates—including one who returned to America in the 1750s to preach a bit of old-fashioned Calvinism. The man's reputation had preceded him, and he held great appeal among dissenters, so Franklin didn't have to publicize his return. America knew George Whitefield well, and was happy to welcome him back.

Even though his and Franklin's business dealings were now largely in the past, the two men remained friends and correspondents. Whitefield lauded Franklin for his scientific experiments and, now that he had mastered the physical world, encouraged him to explore the spiritual world through the New Birth. Franklin evaded his attempts at conversion, but still appreciated conversing with someone who genuinely believed what he preached. He even proposed they settle a new colony on the Ohio River, with the prospect of business and evangelical opportunities for both. Franklin wrote, "What a glorious thing it would be, to settle in that fine country a large strong body of religious and industrious people! . . . In such an enterprise I could spend the remainder of life with pleasure; and I firmly believe God would bless us with success."

In an era when divisions of faith and politics had separated many friends into opposing camps, these two oddly matched men had proved to be reliable stalwarts for each other. Whitefield and Franklin may not have found common cause in orthodox religion, but they did in their distrust of institutions and hierarchies. They despised privilege divorced from merit, and the way the colonies were often run by toadies for the Crown and their corrupt apprentices. Whether in matters of God or country, they had resolved to undermine the aristocracy, and for more than a decade, through revival and upheaval, they had done just that.

Regarding those times of turmoil, Whitefield had been rewriting his past and selling it in a new form to the public through the work of John Gillies, a historian and minister in the Church of Scotland. Gillies wrote sympathetically of the Grand Itinerant, and in his book *Historical Collections Relating to Remarkable Periods of the Success of the Gospel*, he linked Whitefield's revivals with the spiritual upheavals of the past, including the Acts of the Apostles in the Bible. Gillies also accumulated Whitefield's writings in preparation for a biography—carefully removing the parts of his *Journals* that had infuriated his foes and sowed controversy. In so doing, Gillies gave Whitefield a more moderate image as a figure of peace and unity; this expurgated version of his life would have a profound influence over the way he would be seen by coming generations.

The affirmations of Ben Franklin, the writings of John Gillies, the support of dissenters, all of it shaped Whitefield's reputation, along with the successful conversion of thousands of Americans whom he had enflamed during the revival. His reinvigorated popularity was especially apparent on one of his recent trips, in a broadside that celebrated him with fulsome praise:

> Is blessed Whitefield come again?
> Our heart does now rejoice,
> We pray good people all attend
> And hear his lovely voice.
> For fourteen years he has been tried
> By enemies and friends;
> And now upon this new return
> The heavenly sound it rings.

Yet even as Whitefield cleaned up his image in America as a figure of grace and piety, he still felt the need to remove his mask on occasion and speak bitter words against his enemies. Like Gilbert Tennent, he couldn't resist war rhetoric, and when the French and Indian War broke out, he tried to rally the colonists with every ounce of venom he could summon. He railed against "an insulting, enraged and perfidious enemy" that had been responsible for "horrid butcheries and cruel murders" using Indians to fight the battles of priests. He wrote of martyrs slaughtered, innocents devastated, and enemies in league with the devil—all to fuel the hatred of French Catholics as he had once fueled the hatred of Jacobites. Some of his rhetoric was even more scalding than it had ever been, to unite Americans of all Protestant sects against a common foe and cast himself as an icon of patriotism to the Crown.

With their stark imagery, his exhortations also recalled the fury he had aimed at Anglican clerics fifteen years before. This was classic Whitefield—feeding the fire anew, condemning his enemies to hell, renouncing sin and reveling in the New Birth. He may no longer have condemned the unconverted with the same vigor, but what did it matter now that he rallied Americans against another foe, the Pope's armies? He was a Calvinist among Calvinists, and spoke to his thousands of followers with a simple ecumenical appeal that was equal parts sweetness and terror—an irresistible combination to dissenting Christians with an axe to grind.

However, what worked brilliantly in the New World proved to be controversial at home. He discovered this hard lesson whenever he returned to Britain, where far from a figure of piety and devotion, he was the subject of ridicule.

Thanks to a popular play, *The Minor*, which described a scheming charlatan named Dr. Squintum, the many British foes of Whitefield now applied that nickname to him. Whitefield's lazy eye made him seem to fit the character's name, and his hellfire preaching made him seem like a relic in the rationalist, materialist world of Britain. As one character described Dr. Squintum, "this here doctor is capable of seeing two sides of a thing at once, and keeps one eye upon earth and the other upon heaven." Other characters described a leering hypocrite who prattled about the New Birth while groping at prostitutes, and who pummeled audiences with his stern words while violating all the scruples he preached. Crude pamphlets and low poems followed, including this bit of doggerel describing his antics:

> Of all the knaves and all the fools
> That ever left the public schools
> To make the honest poor their tools
> The worst is Dr. Squintum. . . .
> "Do nothing and be saved," he cries

His stupid audience close their eyes
And groan in concert to the lies
Of the canting Dr. Squintum.

As this tune, "Friendly Advice for Dr. Squintum," became popular among the working class as a broadside against his dignity, Whitefield reacted with pained sarcasm, writing, "I am now mimicked and burlesqued upon the public stage. . . . All hail such contempt!" The attacks seemed particularly hurtful since Whitefield was raised in the company of actors and had proved to be a brilliant dramatic performer himself in the pulpit. But now those who might have been his allies in a different life showered him with disdain. Even artists like William Hogarth joined in, offering engravings like *Credulity, Superstition, and Fanaticism: A Medley,* in which enthusiastic madness holds sway as a mad preacher reigns over the turmoil, with actual lines from Whitefield's poetry providing ironic commentary. Thus, the passage of years had been unkind to the Itinerant in the land of his birth. Whereas in his early days he had inspired fear and awe in his enemies, now he brought forth mirth and mockery. It wasn't surprising he spent so much time across the Atlantic as an honorary American.

By the 1760s, Franklin, too, was facing trouble in his home country. He was ensnared in the increasingly nasty business of Pennsylvania politics, working with the Quaker party in the Assembly against the no-longer-Quaker proprietors of the colony and their high church allies. Adding to the animosity, Franklin tried to strip the proprietors of their control over the colony and put it in the hands of royal governors—even as violence erupted on the Pennsylvania frontier.

Some of these problems derived from the end of the war against the French in 1763, when an uprising of Indians against British policies led to Pontiac's Rebellion, followed by violent encounters between white settlers and Natives in the Ohio country and western Pennsylvania. In the most notorious case, a group of vigilantes called the Paxton Boys slaughtered a group of Christian Indians and began marching toward Philadelphia, with an eye toward killing the 140 Indians who had fled to the city for safety. Franklin took the lead against those he called

"Christian White Savages" and hastily organized a militia to keep the Boys from ransacking the city.

Philadelphia filled with dread. Not only did the threat of mob rule raise the locals' anxiety, but an economic recession and desperate living conditions increased the possibility of anarchy. Although British troops quashed the Paxton Boys, their threat became another point of contention between Quakers, who saw them as zealous fanatics, and Presbyterians, who defended their right to self-defense, since many of the Boys shared their faith. Franklin interpreted the melee as a disaster for civilized behavior and warned of "violent parties and cruel animosities" that might cause bloodshed between the factions. He was drawn into another round of verbal warfare, with his high church enemies calling him a lecher and a corrupt tool of the Quakers, and his allies spreading bile against their opposers, calling them reptiles and toads, liars and schemers. The Presbyterians especially came in for abuse, labeled as "Piss-brute-arians" in one pamphlet.

By this time the incitement and division of the revivalists and their foes had been fully incorporated into politics, as "religious groups split among political lines and clergymen became parapolitical leaders." Such battles gave the impression that the conflicts of the 1740s had never ended, just resumed with new factions. Internal dissension could be held at bay as long as there was a foreign enemy to fight—from the Spanish to the French to frontier Indians—but when such wars abated, domestic rivals turned on each other with pent-up aggression. And when they weren't fighting each other, they battled the policies of the British government, and its seemingly endless demand for money.

The most pressing need after the French and Indian War had been to address the massive imperial debt that had accrued, and to pay for the presence of ten thousand soldiers to guard British North America. Franklin had proposed a clever scheme to Parliament creating a loan office that would offer paper-money credit at a 6 percent annual interest rate. Such a plan could raise money from colonists without unnecessarily provoking them, and reduce some of the red ink that threatened to overwhelm colonial government. But Parliament ignored Franklin's thoughtful idea and passed the Stamp Act instead.

LEFT: George Whitefield. *From* Sermons on Important Subjects by the Rev. George Whitefield, A.M. CENTER: *The Sleeping Congregation* (William Hogarth). *Courtesy of the Metropolitan Museum of Art.* BOTTOM: *Whitefield Preaching in Moorfields, A.D. 1742* (Eyre Crowe). *Courtesy of the New York Public Library.*

ABOVE: Benjamin Franklin (Robert Feke). *From the Harvard University Portrait Collection.* BOTTOM LEFT: Portable field pulpit. *From the Library of Congress Prints and Photographs Division.* BOTTOM RIGHT: Whitefield Preaching from the Old State House Steps, Philadelphia. *From A.S. Billingsley,* The Life of the Great Preacher, Reverend George Whitefield, "Prince of Pulpit Orators."

ABOVE LEFT: *Danger of an Unconverted Ministry* sermon by Gilbert Tennent. *From the Library of Congress Prints and Photographs Division.* ABOVE RIGHT: Gilbert Tennent. *From Joseph Tracy,* The Great Awakening: A History of the Revival of Religion in the Time of Edwards and Whitefield. BELOW: View of Boston, 1744. *From the Boston Public Library.*

Ketoohomaonk. XII.	*Pſalm.* XII.
2 Newutche kuſſeh, matcheetoowog onchepunahteaog: quaſhinumwog ukkounkquodtou, ut wutahtumannoowout, onk woh keme pumwaog ſampwutteahonutcheh.	2 For lo, the wicked bend their bow, they make ready their arrow upon he ſtring; that they may privily ſhoot at the upright in heart.
3 Ohpohteaſhikiſh woskehteomuk toh woh wutuſſeneau ſampweuſſeaenuog?	3 If the foundations be deſtroyed, what can the righteous do?
4 Jehovah appu wunnetupanatamwe wut-templeut, Jehovah wutappuonk ohteau keſukqut : wuskeſukquaſh namoomooaſh, wanadteaskeſukquaſh qutcheheau wunnaumonauh wosketompaog.	4 The Lord is in his holy temple, the Lord's throne is in heaven: his eyes behold, his eyelids try the children of men.
5 Jehovah qutcheheau ſampweuſſeanuh, qut ukketeahogkounoh ſekeneauau matchetoowoh, kah noh womontog chekeenehhuwaonk.	5 The Lord trieth the righteous: but the wicked, and him that loveth violence his ſoul hateth.
6 Matchetowoh piſh wuſſokanummauoh ahpehhanoh,	6 Upon the wicked he ſhall rain ſnares, fire and

ABOVE: Massachusett (Wampanoag) Psalter, translation of Psalms by Experience Mayhew. *From John Carter Brown Library, Brown University.* BELOW: *Enthusiasm Display'd: or, the Moor Fields Congregation. From the Library of Congress Prints and Photographs Division.*

/// THE
WHOLE DUTY
OF A
WOMAN:
OR, A
Guide to the FEMALE SEX,

From the A G E of *Sixteen,* to *Sixty,* &c

Being Directions, How Women of all Qualities and Conditions, ought to Behave themselves in the various Circumstances of this LIFE, for their obtaining not only Present, but Future Happiness.

I Directions how to obtain the Divine and Moral VERTUES of *Piety, Meekness, Modesty, Chastity, Humility, Compassion, Temperance, and Affability,* with their Advantages; and how to avoid the opposite VICES.

II. The Duty of *VIRGINS,* directing them what they ought to do, and what to avoid, for gaining all the Accomplishments required in that State. With the whole ART of LOVE.

III. The Whole Duty of a WIFE.

IV. The Whole Duty of a WIDOW, &c.

Also Choice Receipts in Physick and Chirurgery: With the whole ART of Cookery, Preserving, Candying, Beautifying, &c.

Written by a LADY.

THE EIGHTH EDITION.

LONDON: Printed for *A. Betterworth* and C. *Hitch,* at the *Red-Lyon* in *Pater-Noster-Row;* R. *Ware,* at the *Sun* and *Bible,* in *Amen Corner;* and *James Hedges,* at the *Looking-Glass* on *London Bridge.* 1735.

The Nature, Certainty and Evidence
of True Christianity :

IN A

LETTER

FROM A

GENTLEWOMAN

In Rhode-Island.

To ANOTHER, her dear Friend, in
great Darkness, Doubt and Concern, of a
Religious Nature.

1 Cor. i. 26—31.

☞ Though this Letter was written in great
Privacy from one Friend to another; yet on
reprefenting that by allowing it to be printed, it
would probably reach to many others in the
like afflicted Cafe, and by the Grace of God be
very helpful to them; the Writer was at length
prevailed on to fuffer it—provided her Name
and Place of Abode remain concealed.

PROVIDENCE: Re-printed by J. CARTER.

ABOVE: Publication by Sarah Osborn. *From the Library of Congress Prints and Photographs Division.*
BELOW: Andrew Croswell. *Courtesy of Historic New England.*

CREDULITY, SUPERSTITION and FANATICISM.
A MEDLEY.

Believe not every Spirit, but try the Spirits whether they are of God: because many false Prophets are gone out into the World.

1 John. Ch. 4. V. 1.

Design'd and Engrav'd by Wm Hogarth.

Publish'd as the Act directs March y^e 15th 1762.

Credulity, Superstition and Fanaticism (William Hogarth). *From the Boston Public Library.*

Charles Chauncy (Henry W. Smith). *From William Chauncey Fowler,* Memorials of the Chaunceys.

TOP: Detail on Whitefield from *The Scheming Triumvirate. From the The British Museum.* CENTER: Whitefield Assaulted in Bed. *From A.S. Billingsley,* The Life of the Great Preacher, Reverend George Whitefield, "Prince of Pulpit Orators." BOTTOM: Whitefield Mobbed. *From A.S. Billingsley,* The Life of the Great Preacher, Reverend George Whitefield, "Prince of Pulpit Orators."

ABOVE: Commodore Charles Knowles. *From Portsmouth Athenaeum.* BOTTOM LEFT: The Press Gang, or English Liberty Display'd (naval impressment protests). *From the Library of Congress Prints and Photographs Division.* BOTTOM RIGHT: Samuel Adams. *From the Library of Congress Prints and Photographs Division.*

LEFT: Jonathan Mayhew. BELOW: Attempt to Land a Bishop in America (episcopacy controversy). *Both images from John Wingate Thornton,* The Pulpit of the American Revolution.

ABOVE: "Wicked Statesman" Thomas Hutchinson (Paul Revere). *From the American Antiquarian Society.* BELOW: Flight of Hutchinson Before the Rioters. *From Edmund Ollier,* Cassell's History of the United States, *vol. 2.*

RIGHT: Earthenware bust of George Whitefield. *Courtesy of the Metropolitan Museum of Art.* BELOW: *A Elegiac Poem, on the Death of the Celebrated Divine . . . George Whitefield* (Phillis Wheatley). *Courtesy of the Beinecke Rare Book and Manuscript Library, Yale University.*

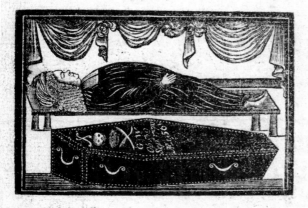

A
POEM,
By PHILLIS, a *Negro* Girl, in BOSTON.

ON THE DEATH OF THE REVEREND
GEORGE WHITEFIELD,

RIGHT: Phillis Wheatley (Scipio Moorhead, engraver). *From the Library of Congress Prints and Photographs Division.* BELOW: *Newport Mercury* advertisement for slave commerce. *Courtesy of the Rhode Island Historical Society.*

LEFT: *A Dialogue Concerning the Slavery of the Africans* sermon by Samuel Hopkins. *From the New York Public Library.* BELOW: Wood engraving of Samuel Hopkins by John Orr, 1870. *Courtesy of the New York Public Library.*

A

DIALOGUE

CONCERNING THE

SLAVERY

OF THE

AFRICANS;

Shewing it to be the *Duty* and *Interest* of the *American* States to emancipate all their *African* Slaves.

WITH AN

ADDRESS to the owners of such SLAVES.

DEDICATED TO THE HONOURABLE THE

CONTINENTAL CONGRESS.

To which is prefixed, the Institution of the Society, in NEW-YORK, *for promoting the Manumission of Slaves, and protecting such of them as have been, or may be, liberated.*

Open thy mouth, judge righteously, and plead the cause of the poor and needy.   PROV. XXXI. 9.
And as ye would that men should do to you, do ye also to them likewise.   LUKE vi. 31.

NORWICH : Printed by JUDAH P. SPOONER, 1776.

NEW - YORK:
Re-printed for ROBERT HODGE.
M,DCC,LXXXV.

SAMUEL HOPKINS, D. D.

ABOVE: Stamp Act Riots at Boston. *From* Cassell's Illustrated History of England, *vol. 5.* BELOW: *The Prayer in the First Congress, A.D. 1774* (Harrison Tompkins Matteson). *From the Library of Congress Prints and Photographs Division.*

This disastrous plan was designed to raise money by requiring revenue stamps to be purchased for a huge quantity of printed materials—everything from newspapers and pamphlets to legal contracts, college diplomas, and playing cards. Franklin knew the plan would be politically unpalatable and an obstacle for reestablishing peace between the rulers and the ruled. He was right: riots broke out in many cities and towns, and colonies like Virginia passed resolutions calling the Act unfair and illegal. Many colonists resolved to fight the official action in the streets if necessary.

To try to limit the damage, Parliament called on Franklin to explain and clarify the grievances of his countrymen. It was a logical choice, for while he had sometimes thwarted the will of royal officials in Pennsylvania, he managed to strike an even-tempered pose that gave his opinions a veneer of respectability—and he knew a good number of legislators who could help undo the act. But when Ben Franklin came to London to state his case, he did not come alone. George Whitefield came too, ready to provide moral support.

In many ways it was the highlight of their relationship. No longer bound by simple monetary interests, the two men had shared a great deal in their twenty-five-year friendship. They had faced off against their adversaries, been buffeted in political and religious conflicts, and witnessed great social changes that they themselves had helped engineer. And now they shared a stage at the center of the British imperial world.

Franklin did not miss his opportunity. He defended Americans' popular sovereignty to the Parliamentarians and described how they remained loyal subjects of the king, even if they had no interest in paying unjust taxes. The legislators interrogated him about the violence in the colonies and the threat of mob rule. He did not justify such behavior, but he told them Americans had the right to resist their mistreatment. The legislators asked, if the Stamp Act were repealed, would the colonists then acknowledge Parliament's right to tax them? Franklin said, "No, never . . . they will never do it, unless compelled by force of arms." And he added, "No power, how great soever, can force men to change their opinions."

Whitefield sat in awe of Franklin's performance. He credited his friend with playing a major part in getting the Stamp Act repealed, and said, "Dr. Franklin has gained immortal honor by his behavior at the bar of the

House. His answer was always found equal to the questioner. He stood unappalled, gave pleasure to his friends, and did honor to his country." But while Franklin may have impressed his English friends in London, he faced much more contention when he returned to America.

Franklin had made sure to have his notes and a transcript of his questioning published in Philadelphia, which made his answers widely known and his words subject to close inspection. Soon enough, Franklin's adversaries noticed that he had suggested Parliament might be able to tax the foreign trade of Americans, and had played down their feelings of revolt and seemed to hedge against their independent spirit. Word even got out that he had recommended a friend to be a revenue agent before the Stamp Act was repealed—a sure mark of hypocrisy. Thus, more than a few colonists figured that, if Franklin wasn't quite a traitor, he had at least done his fellow Pennsylvanians a disservice and deserved censure for his actions. But as he came under fire, the one person who had the most power to defend him, and stood willing to do it, was Whitefield.

The Grand Itinerant doubtless remembered how, at the nadir of his own reputation in America in the mid-1740s, Franklin had testified to his honor, lauding his integrity and character in the pages of the *Pennsylvania Gazette*. Now, Whitefield returned the favor by offering rousing praise for his friend—saying he "spoke very heartily and judiciously in his country's behalf"—and offering a firsthand testament to the thrilling words he had spoken to Parliament. And since the Englishman Whitefield was more popular in America than the native son Franklin (just as their roles were reversed in Britain), the preacher's defense had a salutary effect, preventing the name of Franklin from being further sullied and reinforcing his own reputation for truth and integrity. As one critic wrote, "[W]ho would dare deny Mr. Whitefield's authority—will the Church? Will the Presbyterians?"

In his later life, Franklin would fully recover his reputation and grow more comfortable in Europe, first as a colonial emissary in London, then, after the outbreak of war, as a minister to France. His countless achievements and accomplishments would become known to every schoolchild in America, his face and name adorning cities, roads, buildings, and currency. But his role in promoting the great evangelical revival would be largely forgotten by posterity, even though that accomplishment—long before most of his others—would be the first that set Americans down an independent course. It imbued in them a spirit of dispute and contention, and a flair for violence and schism, that proved essential to stirring feelings of revolution. Thus, unlike almost any other Founding Father, Ben Franklin played a role at every stage in creating a new America, from planting the seeds of revolt in the 1740s to seizing the fruit of independence thirty years later.

Unlike Franklin, who lived for decades after his testimony against the Stamp Act, Whitefield lasted only a few years. In Britain, he reconciled with fellow Methodists like John Wesley, though they disputed many questions of faith, and grew ever more committed to the reform of the Church of England even as its likelihood grew ever more distant. He knew that the high churchmen's domineering ways would eventually get the better of them in America, where they had continually pushed for the appointment of a bishop with broad powers. Whitefield now echoed the feelings of his dissenting friends, knowing Anglican policies would continue to breed resistance and feelings of revolt. It was one subject even he and his theological foe Jonathan Mayhew could agree on: The Church of England had no business creating an episcopacy to oversee the colonies, and doing so would only encourage further resistance from American Protestants.

In 1769 Whitefield left Britain for the last time. He arrived in Charleston and began preaching to wide acclaim. His longtime nemesis, Alexander Garden, had died a dozen years earlier, so there was no one with the authority or the will to drag him before an ecclesiastical court or otherwise impugn his reputation. He visited his orphanage at Bethesda and oversaw the creation of a related academy. Here, young slaves would be taught to read and learn artisan skills while also receiving the catechism of Christianity.

However, the reason there were slaves at all at Bethesda owed much to Whitefield himself—his constant demands for forced labor resulted in the legalization of Georgia slavery at the turn of the 1750s, and Whitefield's operation had greatly profited by it. Forty percent of Savannah's population now included enslaved laborers, and Whitefield included himself among the ranks of the slave owners he had once condemned. The irony was bitter and invited a certain heavenly comeuppance, though Whitefield would not be alive to witness it. The orphanage took flame in 1773 after being hit by a lightning bolt and burned to the ground.

By this time, his wife Elizabeth had long ceased to administer the orphanage directly—and in fact did not even visit America after 1749. She and Whitefield thus spent months or even years apart, he traveling and preaching in Scotland, England, and the colonies, and she running the ministry operations from London. He called her his "yoke-fellow," which largely summed up how he viewed her, or in one critic's words as a "treasured but distant ally." She had suffered far more as his wife than even she could have expected, enduring not only her husband's cold and decorous demeanor, but no fewer than four miscarriages and the death of an infant son. Yet she persisted through these trials, and never lost her faith in a heavenly reward for her struggles. Indeed, through the 27 years of their marriage, she grew to have much more affection for Whitefield's ministry than for the man himself—and others knew it, too. In 1754, the reformed James Davenport wrote to her, asking, "Shall I now sympathize with you, under the frequent and sometimes long absence of your dear husband? Or shall I not rather?" Given the indifference the Whitefields had for each other, it may have been better the Grand Itinerant spent much of his time overseas.

Elizabeth died in 1768 of complications of a fever, and Whitefield mourned her loss publicly. He grieved over the loss of his "right hand" in the ministry and the valuable role she played in spreading the gospel. But to one intimate observer, Cornelius Winter, who traveled with him, Whitefield did not seem overly troubled: "Her death set his mind much at liberty." In the end he could offer her his loyalty and decorum as a public figure; his spiritual advice as a man of God; his zeal for revival as a fellow Christian. But he could never offer her love and devotion, or the semblance of a real marriage. He had given his heart to God, and left none to share with anyone else.

In the spring of 1770 Whitefield set out for the North, long the place of his greatest appeal. As he traveled up the coast, the mood of the colonies about the mother country changed, from toasts to the health of the king in Georgia to conspicuous silence or even outright hostility past the Chesapeake. He preached to packed congregations in Philadelphia thick with mixed crowds of dissenters, and received thanks from locals who remembered how he had defended the name of Ben Franklin from charges of disloyalty.

Also in the Middle Colonies, he dined with his old friend William Tennent Jr. Many decades before, young Tennent had died and been brought back to life in a mysterious resurrection. Now Whitefield, with mortality on his mind, inquired if Tennent was ready to meet the Lord again, since he had reached old age. But instead of a gentle agreement, Whitefield received a surprising rebuke: "I have no wish about it," Tennent said. "No, sir, it is no pleasure to me at all; and if you knew your duty, it would be none to you. I have nothing to do with death. My business is to live as *long* as I can, and as *well* as I can." This was not the answer the Itinerant expected, and it brought him to silence. Whitefield realized he had to work as hard as he could with the time he had left, and dreaming of his heavenly reward wasn't only presumptuous, it verged on pride and blasphemy.

He continued on to Boston and the Puritan homeland, which were astir in violence and reaction against the policies of the British government. He wrote in a letter, "Poor New England is much to be pitied; Boston people most of all. How grossly misrepresented!" He saw the British army occupying the town and the common folk suffering at its hands, and decried "the great mischiefs the poor pious people suffered lately through the town's being disturbed by the soldiers." He admired Bostonians for the fortitude and the way they kept the Sabbath holy better than any other town folk he knew, and it disgusted him that such people of God could be abused by the imposition of brute force.

Yet despite the intimidating atmosphere, he preached well and received huzzahs for his ministry, enjoying the company he kept and touring the region at a breakneck pace—which may have done severe damage to his health. He sweated in the pulpit and took ill with colds and fever. He traveled on horseback through rough and dismal conditions, and still managed to proclaim the gospel to anyone who wanted to hear it. He woke up in the night with "a violent lax, attended with retching and shivering" and still pushed on, preaching in small towns and waysides and spreading the word of God to anyone who wasn't already well acquainted with it. He drove himself to exhaustion repeatedly, became fatigued and breathed with difficulty, and still kept up his testimony to the New Birth. He met with overwhelming

popularity as an honorary son of America and friend to dissenters everywhere, and the support he received pushed him through the summer even
as his health collapsed. And when the summer ended, so did he.

In a little town called Newburyport, George Whitefield died on the last
day of September 1770. He met his end in the parsonage of a Presbyterian
church, where in his final days he had asked to be buried in a crypt under the
altar. Unlike Jonathan Edwards, however, Whitefield did not donate money
for his funeral to the poor, but instead spent it on an elaborate ceremony complete with cortege and mile-long procession. Six thousand people attended, a
considerable turnout for an 18th-century funeral, and the clerics and common
folk lionized the Grand Itinerant as an evangelist beyond compare and a
sanctified man who had earned the right to sit at the Lord's Table. Thus,
a priest of the state religion of Britain died in an occupied colony in America,
and was buried not in a grand church of his own faith in London, but among
dissenters in an obscure church in a little-known hamlet. The contradictions
of Whitefield were many and complex, even after his death.

The same held true for the honors he received at his passing. Ben
Franklin, despite being a foe of Calvinism, did not equivocate in lauding
its foremost defender as a man whose "integrity, disinterestedness, and indefatigable zeal in prosecuting every good work, I have never seen equaled,
I shall never see exceeded." More curiously, Whitefield's passing brought
forth elegies from a number of black and African writers, preachers and
activists, many of whom had been enslaved. Prominent figures like John
Marrant, Olaudah Equiano, and Phillis Wheatley offered hearty praise of
Whitefield. Wheatley composed a famous poem in which she gave hosannas
to her fellow Methodist:

> Thy lessons in unequal'd accents flow'd
> While emulation in each bosom glow'd
> Thou didst, in strains of eloquence refin'd
> Inflame the soul, and captivate the mind. . . .
> Towards America—couldst thou do more
> Than leave thy native home, the British shore,
> To cross the great Atlantic's wat'ry road,
> To see America's distress'd abode?

Like others who praised the Itinerant, Wheatley became an abolitionist—even though Whitefield's record on slavery was checkered at best, and depraved at worst, and he had been instrumental in the legalization of slavery in Georgia and owned human beings himself. However, to those black Americans who offered their good words, the honors were not strictly for Whitefield but rather for the revival he had unleashed. For even though Whitefield was an enemy of liberation, his evangelism had altered countless aspects of American life and transformed them in ways he could not have expected. Groups like enslaved people who had once been excluded from Christianity now partook in it, studied it, and drew their own lessons from it, often contrary to the views of those who claimed to own them. And it was this version of the gospel—the New Birth and its radical effect on those who experienced it—that shook social bonds and threatened the hierarchy of the wealthy and powerful. And in the years before the revolution, the people seizing on those transformative effects and giving them new momentum were none of the original awakeners like Whitefield. They were the New Lights who took his gospel and did something else with it entirely.

TWELVE

THE NEW DIVINES

After the revival ended, Sarah Osborn rose up through her own enterprise. Rarely stopping to pity herself or her troubles, she followed several important pursuits and elevated her profile in Newport. She gathered a growing number of women for Bible study at her home, she taught school to children in the community, and more than anything, she wrote. In the 1750s she was well on her way toward writing, by the end of her life, thousands of pages of devotional text in some fifty volumes, and countless letters and poems and fragments that expressed her understanding of God and her relation to him.

She led a crusade against theatrical entertainment in Newport, calling it a "temple of wickedness," and for her efforts and those of other evangelicals, Rhode Island later banned such performances. She made her opinions known throughout the town and felt emboldened that God had given her the passion to denounce evil and to uphold righteousness—and she even saw his design in catastrophe. When an earthquake struck New England in 1755, she didn't ascribe it to his wrath, as Whitefield and other preachers might have, but to his wondrous power. Such an awesome event was a sign of his "adorable perfections" and she felt he was personally offering her "a pledge of his love and faithfulness." But if God showed his favor by bestowing shock and tragedy on people, then he favored Sarah very much indeed.

More than a decade before, her only son Samuel died at the age of eleven. Stricken as he was with jaundice, scurvy, and tuberculosis, she watched him wither away, rattling and choking to breathe and writhing in pain. What crushed her hopes, however, was not the fear that he would die, but that he would die unredeemed. Misery overwhelmed her as "I could discern no evidence of a work of grace wrought on his soul" even though she prayed that his spirit might ascend in the afterlife. As he lingered for days in agony, Sarah felt her heart sink at the prospect that the boy might be consigned to hell for lack of conversion: "My heart even almost died with fear of what would become of him." Letters from her friend Susanna Anthony helped revive her spirit a bit, but Sarah couldn't avoid thinking of the doom that would befall Samuel. In the end she had to no other choice but to assign the tragedy to God's mysterious and sometimes cruel plan for her. As Anthony instructed her, "Kiss the hand, though it have a rod in it—it is the hand of *your* God still."

Many years had passed since that loss, but Sarah had not forgotten the terrible scar it had left. The death left her without children of her own. Instead of God rewarding her in some way for her persistence and faith, he just seemed to put more obstacles in her path. Her husband Henry could not work a regular job because of his lingering injuries, which forced her to cobble together enough task work to keep the family going, anything from baking and sewing to teaching and spinning flax. She also had to support Henry's son John (from another marriage), and his wife and their four children—and all this in poverty. When the war with France came, prices accelerated in Newport and made food and household goods, from flour to firewood, expensive for poor families. Reduced to eating pigeons and pudding, she finally resorted to raising the price of her tuition for teaching. Many of her students then left her tutelage, which did nothing to improve her finances. Added to this were her physical ailments that made it hard to walk or even see, and she could not perform common tasks without jolts of pain.

She and Henry were forced to take in boarders to make ends meet, which made her feel like "a poor overloaded weak animal crouching and trembling under its burden." God kept the tragedies coming: John Osborn died fighting in the war, and left his father saddled with grief, especially since his brother Edward had died two years earlier. Sarah and Henry also had to take in, and somehow care for, another grandchild after its parents had been negligent in their duties. Thus, the impoverished Osborn household had to rely on Sarah's meager income, and whatever Henry could earn from odd jobs, to support themselves and a bevy of stepchildren and grandchildren, while also living with boarders, a few students, and one slave.

The slave was a child named Bobey, and it was surprising that a poor woman like Sarah could claim title to any human being given her own impoverished condition. But she had owned him nearly all his life, from the time he was an infant after her own son had died (when friends purchased him for her) into the late 1750s when he became a teen. Never far away, Bobey's mother Phillis was a member of Sarah's church, as well as her women's study group. Throughout her son's life she had maintained intermittent contact with him in Sarah's household, and doubtless joined the study group to maintain a relationship with him. However, Phillis herself was a slave to another member of the church, and her legal right to care for her son was nil. She could only ask Sarah for leniency in how she treated the boy. Thus she saw it as a great affront when Sarah, desperate for money for her own family, considered selling Bobey for cash.

Phillis didn't let her lack of rights hold her back. She reacted angrily, telling Sarah she was "vexed" that she could even consider taking the boy away. She wanted her son to remain near her in town, and she could only imagine what horrors might await him after Sarah packed him off to the highest bidder. Phillis's reaction shocked Sarah, who scolded her for privileging sentiment and anger over reason—but she had no choice but to consider what she said. For ten days Sarah prayed about what to do. She hid in a closet and wrote searching notes to herself. She beseeched God for an answer and found it difficult to reconcile her feelings. Was she not a good and virtuous person, as all her suffering proved? How could Phillis suggest she would be harming the boy, when she had schooled him in God's grace—despite owning him, despite renting him out for work, despite profiting from his labors. The questions proved vexing indeed to Sarah, because the things Phillis told her went against what she knew from the Puritan divines and Jonathan Edwards: slavery was part of God's plan, they said, and good Christians could both approve of it and own those of other races without guilt or remorse. But for once, something about the argument rang hollow. Sarah did not sell Phillis's son.

Phillis and Bobey gradually disappeared from Sarah's journals and little is known of them beyond her words. However, the young man's fate and his mother's brave and desperate protection of him resounded in the years that followed. Because in the 1760s a new Sarah Osborn slowly emerged, one who created her own ministry that respected no boundaries of color, and one who embraced all the controversy that followed.

In the spring of 1765 a group of free black residents of Newport asked if they could use Sarah's house as a place of prayer and Bible study on Sunday nights. Sarah had already received a letter from a slave named Quaum asking for religious guidance. He likely knew Phillis and learned of Sarah's evangelical work through her. With little hesitation, Sarah agreed to provide whatever instruction she could to him and the other individuals who had solicited her.

She arranged a series of meetings in her home, and they quickly became popular with a variety of worshippers. Expanding to Tuesday nights as well as Sundays, some forty-two slaves, a smaller number of freedmen and women, and a handful of white children began filling her kitchen to praise God and discuss his role in their lives. Sarah encouraged the gatherings of up to seventy people over the months that followed, acting as a sort of spiritual guide to the groups and drawing even more of them to hear what she said about the meaning of the Bible and God's great plan for them. In many ways, she became their personal preacher, though she would never admit to such a prideful claim.

Sarah's gatherings proved to be so popular that by the next year she began a new revival. Word quickly got out that men like Quaum and others had converted to Christ, and other local residents, both black and white, flocked to her house to discover what Sarah could do to elevate their spirits, too. Her life and home were now fully given over to religion: Sunday nights for young men, Mondays and Tuesdays for teenage girls and boys, respectively;

Wednesdays for her women's study group; Thursdays and Saturdays for children; and Fridays for the heads of families. Among these groups she also taught Christianity to the enslaved and to an "Ethiopian Society" of free blacks. While she did not preach liberation, something about her handcrafted ministry nonetheless appealed to them; she offered a place for communion with others of similar background, people who faced cruelty and violence in their own ways. This made the gatherings as much about community building as religious uplift.

Many were Akan, a West African people from the Gold Coast (now Ghana), who had been kidnapped by white slavers, or otherwise sold in interethnic resource wars, and shipped across the Atlantic via the deadly and horrific Middle Passage. On boats known as rum vessels, the captives were tightly shackled and bound in a hold of three-and-a-half-feet high in a voyage of six to ten weeks. Most ended up in the West Indies, but enough were shipped on to Newport that it made the city home to more slaves than any other place in New England. Once the ships arrived, they anchored off the coast, often among 100 other such vessels, until the captives were transferred to white owners who would shave their heads and brand their hips or other body parts with hot irons as a chattel mark.

Most were beaten and abused into compliance; others manifested "turbulent and unruly tempers" that led to their punishment with thumb screws and other devices. The great majority were stripped of their own traditions, names, and religions and given Anglo-American replacements. Thus, Quaum became John Quamino, and Okyerema Mireku became Newport Gardner. As slaves they lived closely among whites in the city as forced laborers, mostly for child rearing and manual labor, though some were sent out to work on local plantations for raising dairy cows and brewery grains. Those who were free had gained freedom from white Quakers in previous decades. The Quaker annual meeting in 1761 had officially forbidden the practice of owning other humans.

Despite the Quakers' efforts, the trade in human flesh continued in Newport without restraint. Along the town's main street, the minister of the Second Congregational Church, Ezra Stiles, counted numerous warehouses and businesses for spirits distillation, transatlantic shipping, and slave trading—all part of the triangle trade that connected the export of African slaves, West Indies molasses, and New England rum. From 1763 to 1774, Newport's trade with Africa in liquor and slaves peaked, with new shippers and investors entering the field, and the rice plantations of South Carolina emerging as an alternative destination for many bondsmen. Almost one in seven residents of Newport was a slave, equating to more than 1,200 people deprived of freedom. Profiting by their suffering, the slave traders and merchants of Rhode Island brazenly showcased their financial success by building great estates and displaying their wealth conspicuously. Although such blatant greed was the very thing that the revivalists of earlier years had denounced, they continued to turn a blind eye to the much greater sin of turning humans into chattel.

This made it appear strange that so many slaves in Newport, who so often resisted the demands of their owners at the cost of violence and trauma, should embrace the Christianity preached to them, the faith of the oppressing class. However, the Newport revival wasn't just about their acceptance of the religion of the slave owners. In fact, many converts maintained their spiritual beliefs and traditions from Africa, or combined them with Christian theology to form a new syncretist belief system, or solely became Christians but put the Old and New Testaments in a much different light than the slave lords—emphasizing the liberation they saw in its stories instead of the labored justifications for their captivity.

Unlike most of the ordained ministers who preached the gospel, Sarah Osborn spoke to the pain and trauma of what colonial society could do to a person. Although she could never possibly understand the horrors of slavery, her poverty and illnesses made her a sympathetic figure. She also had a magnetic personality, and a compelling gift for words that made her appear divinely inspired—a strange, holy woman whom God had cursed with infirmities and yet blessed with the gift of inspiration. The black residents of Newport had recognized it first, and once they drew attention to her ministry, many others followed until the numbers of worshippers became huge, even shocking. In the summer of 1766 Sarah hosted 500 people a week at her house, and 140 alone on Sunday evenings. The house obviously wasn't suited for such great numbers of worshippers, yet they kept coming—filling her kitchen and overflowing into other rooms and other people's houses. She attracted Baptists and Anglicans as well as Congregationalists—almost all the Protestant sects except Quakers. It made for a stunning homemade revival, and to her it was proof of the creator's glorious ways. She asked, "Who would ever have thought that God by such a mean, despicable worm would have gathered such a number as now steadily resorts to this house every week?"

By the winter of 1767 the revival showed no signs of abating. Some 525 people now crowded her house every week, and she "greatly feared that it would be as the river Jordan overflowing all the banks." But more worrisome was the sharp counter-reaction to her ministry from the town elite. Since the Ethiopian Society remained at the center of the movement, increasingly vocal critics accused her of "keeping of a Negro House" and violating the social codes that kept the races apart and fearful of each other. They raised the issue of miscegenation—the dangerous intermixing of white and black—and the slave owners claimed that large groups of free and unfree black people would incite rebellion or otherwise threaten the town and, presumably, their profits.

Sarah acknowledged the criticism but would not end her ministry. To those who said she had no business praying in public in front of black men, she said the approval of God was all that mattered, and that "Man can't determine me . . . Man's opinion alone shant content me for or against." She also defended her actions to her spiritual advisor, Reverend Joseph Fish, and said that she had asked male authority figures to guide the revival and they had no interest in it, and that the presence of other Christians regardless of color gave her life meaning and purpose. She said she would starve without her regular religious practice, and that "sweet refreshing evenings [were] my resting reaping times." And she became disgusted with Fish for even questioning her leadership, asking, "Would you advise me to shut up my mouth and creep into obscurity?"

Comparing herself to a warrior who wore "the whole armor of God" and wielded a "shield of faith" to fight Satan and all his wickedness, Sarah was not alone as a woman fighting for her ideas in this tumultuous age. During the years preceding the Revolution, Americans argued about women's role in society, especially the need for education and their contributions to the culture. No longer accepting the demand to be silent and submissive, many women like Sarah found their creative outlet in religion. In Sarah's First Congregational Church of Newport, more than 70 percent of the members were women, and that number was not unusual for the time. Thanks to the revival and the growing power of parishioners, they influenced the course of worship; they formed their own study groups; and they sometimes even chose the minister himself. Sarah had a role in all these things.

Taking such a prominent position in her community meant getting embroiled in church politics. And in the late 1760s at First Church, the main subject of contention was the minister, William Vinal. Though he would never admit it, the reverend was clearly an alcoholic, and it affected the way he led the church. When questioned about his behavior, he frequently lapsed into paranoia and anger against his parishioners and accused them of undermining him behind his back and scheming at Sarah's own house. She tried to assuage his concerns and explain the congregants' feelings and said that if he was unable to perform his duties, visiting ministers could be brought in to help with services. He responded by telling her she was the wrong kind of Christian and a near fanatic: "Your zeal for God if you are not on your guard will carry you astray."

Sarah kept trying to encourage him not to drink, but his illness became worse and he lashed out at anyone who raised the subject. Eventually the governing committee of the church, doubtless under her influence, fired Vinal from the pulpit after twenty-two years, for "bad habit of body" and other euphemisms. He went down fighting, blaming church members for being "odious, malicious, cruel, unmerciful," and singled Sarah out as a saboteur. She was shocked by the charge and mounted a forceful defense. But as much as she wanted to clear her name, she also knew most of her energies needed to be spent finding a new minister.

In the months after, the people of First Church auditioned a series of pastors by inviting them to demonstrate their skills at Sarah's house, which became the temporary, de facto home of the church itself. The members saw a number of good and worthy men with a flair for explaining the gospel, but the one that appealed most to Sarah and Susanna Anthony was an unexpected choice.

◆

Sarah had been reading the works of contemporary theologians like Joseph Bellamy, who had taken the ideas of Jonathan Edwards and altered them with a greater call for "communalism, social responsibility, and moral reform"—all things Edwards had preached, but that his followers now gave greater importance to due to the torn fabric of American society, rent by inequality and economic malaise. Bellamy, along with Edwards's own minister son, was labeled as part of the New Divinity movement, whose proponents updated ideas of original sin, free will, and divine providence to underscore the importance of human responsibility and moral virtue. In so doing, they also gained a reputation for being judgmental and censorious and for lording over churches racked with schism and plagued by controversy—almost as if it were 1740 again. One of the other prime figures of this movement was Samuel Hopkins.

Hopkins was a middle-aged preacher known in theological circles, but otherwise obscure to much of the Newport public, as a former minister to a frontier congregation in far western Massachusetts. He had learned Calvinism from Jonathan Edwards himself, arriving at his doorstep as a stranger in 1741, inspired by the revival aflame in New England and eager to learn more about it. He spent two years intermittently studying the Bible with the theologian, often doubting his purpose and whether God intended any good use for him. However, thanks to his studies, the residents of the hamlet of Housatonic, later called Great Barrington, gave him the opportunity to be their minister in a unanimous vote in 1743, and he accepted. Although there were only thirty families in the congregation, and life in the hinterlands was difficult, he persisted in his role for twenty-six years.

During that time the Boston commissioners of a frontier Indian mission offered him the role of pastor of Stockbridge. He turned them down and instead recommended his mentor Edwards, recently fired by his congregation in Northampton. Edwards of course accepted the role and for the next six years lived only seven miles from his former student, the two of them regularly sharing thoughts on religion and faith and the difficulty of life on the frontier. After the trustees of the College of New Jersey offered Edwards the presidency of the school, Hopkins regretted that he "should lose the future benefit of his company and instructions. But I considered him as so eminently qualified for the presidency of a college" that he offered his highest recommendation. A year later, Edwards was dead, and Hopkins had to find his own way in matters of God.

He admired Edwards but came to differ from him in several key ways. For one, unlike the preacher of *Sinners in the Hands of an Angry God*, Hopkins was a rough and blundering orator; he drawled and mumbled and had a difficult time pronouncing common words. Moreover, he preached a severe strain of Calvinism that emphasized human depravity and God's absolute power, and adopted peculiar ideas that departed from Edwards's own: eager converts were worse than heathens because they were selfish, sin had a noble purpose in contrasting with goodness, and a "true Christian should be willing to be damned for the glory of God." Despite these curious notions, he did establish one key parallel with his mentor: his congregants eventually became sick of him and fired him from his job.

Hopkins's church members harbored a number of complaints about him. Not only did they chafe at his bland orations in the pulpit, they warred with him over his Calvinist rigidity, his strict limitations on who could receive the sacraments, and his fierce anti-imperial politics. Disgusted with his intransigence, they refused to pay him and forced him to seek a position in another town. With his dismissal, Hopkins became dejected and considered becoming a farmer instead of persisting as a preacher.

The parishioners of First Church in Newport rescued him from that fate, at least temporarily. With Sarah's strong encouragement, they offered him a chance to preach to them and possibly to become their leader. He accepted the offer and preached for more than a month of Sundays, impressing enough of the all-male voters on the governing committee that he survived a narrow vote to become their minister. He was pleased with the outcome, for he enjoyed the local atmosphere and found among the church members "a number who appeared to be excellent Christians, and the best regulated church that I had seen." But as he began to settle in and contemplate life as a pastor in Rhode Island, the trouble began.

Second Congregational Church's minister Ezra Stiles let it be known that he dreaded the arrival of Hopkins in Newport as his colleague. The man's fusty Calvinism was an embarrassment, and a reminder of First Church's backward and lower-class congregation, so different from Stiles's own wealthy and enterprising church members. Charles Chauncy wrote to Stiles to take pity on him, recounting all of Hopkins's drawbacks, and claiming he was such a bad preacher, he drove his flock in Great Barrington toward Anglicanism. "He will preach away all his congregation at Newport, or make them tenfold worse than they are at present." The threat carried some weight in the town, where the Quaker and Congregationalist faiths were declining at the hands of a revived Church of England, which found success in converting members of the upper class along with many slave merchants.

Things got worse for Hopkins when an anonymous pamphlet mocked his tedious style in the pulpit. The tract was crude but had some merit: Hopkins seemed to have little interest in adopting the theatrical style of preachers like George Whitefield and could only offer his plodding praise of the Lord. The pamphlet had a baleful effect on the minds of church members, and Hopkins discovered many of the congregants "had appeared dissatisfied with my doctrines, and pains had been taken to promote prejudices against me." Soon the church leaders rescinded their endorsement of him. Embarrassed by the debacle, Hopkins withdrew from consideration to be their minister. He preached a farewell sermon and prepared for a life of agriculture.

Surprisingly, his last sermon had a greater effect than he expected. Many parishioners cried and let his words affect them deeply. The next morning, "there appeared to be a revolution in the congregation" as his opposers repented their actions and "said that their consciences accused them so severely of their wickedness in what they had done, that they had little or no sleep during the night." Others were struck by the power of his homilies and asked him to forgive their rude treatment of him. His farewell preaching affected his allies the most: Sarah Osborn and Susanna Anthony planned to use their influence to get him his job back.

Hopkins had befriended many in the women's society ever since he had come to town. He had discussed God with Sarah and had assisted with her home ministry and found a number of friends in the group who were willing to fight to ensure he would be their pastor—even in the face of resistance from the small number of men who voted. But while women like Sarah fully endorsed him, Hopkins himself had fears over whether the position suited him, and knowing how abruptly he had been chucked out of the pulpit in Great Barrington, he worried that it would happen again.

Unlike Reverend Vinal, he opened up to Sarah about his anxieties and weaknesses, and he told her "I have been much dejected and sunk in my own mind" and hesitant to accept the job even if it were offered to him a second time. He knew his limitations in the pulpit, and later reflected that his strongest sense of God's grace came in his private devotions, while in public "my preaching has always appeared to me as poor, low and miserable, compared with what it ought to be; and frequently a sense of my deficiencies in this has been very painful and discouraging." Even with his own considerable doubts, though, Sarah and Susanna saw something in this preacher—a spark of the Holy Spirit, perhaps—that made them even more determined to put him in the pulpit. They prayed fervently to God for his success, and they lobbied the voters to grant Hopkins the job once more.

They won. With a near-unanimous vote, Hopkins again secured the pulpit and became the minister of First Church. Even Ezra Stiles couldn't help but be impressed with the astounding coup Sarah and her allies had pulled off, twisting enough arms to make her church's governing committee admit their error and do the right thing: "Mrs. Osborn and the sorority of her meeting are violently engaged and had great influence." Stiles was impressed enough that he even preached at Hopkins's installment as minister and published the honorific tract throughout New England.

Once Hopkins assumed the role of pastor, he continued his strong bond with Sarah and Susanna. With the former he met regularly, sharing tea and prayer on Saturdays and receiving her advice on his sermons. His relationship with Susanna, though, was much more intense, and the two enjoyed sublime and wide-ranging conversations on God and faith. They both corresponded with leading Calvinist ministers in New England, shared their thoughts on theology, and drew so close together that some town folk made cutting insinuations there was more to their relationship than just friendship. But like Sarah, they had learned to ignore the jibes of others, regardless of how low and spiteful they might be.

Much more unexpectedly, Hopkins found a friend in Ezra Stiles, his theological adversary. While neither man could agree with the other's ideas of the gospel truth, they found each other's company congenial and could regularly be spotted walking together in Newport, the lumbering Hopkins towering over the small, sprightly Stiles. They even exchanged pulpits on occasion and cooperated in each other's missionary work, and one project in particular.

With Sarah continuing to decline in body, Hopkins assisted her by ministering to the still-numerous black students and congregants who came to her house every week for study and worship. She continued her women's society, but desperately needed assistance with other groups to keep the meetings going. Soon, a growing number of slaves and freedmen paid visits to Hopkins's house to hear the preacher speak, and they also visited the quarters of Reverend Stiles.

Hosting ninety black visitors every week, Stiles preached his own, more liberal version of the gospel, as both he and Hopkins continued the revival Sarah had begun more than a half-decade before. This cooperation was unusual, the Old Light and New Light ministers working in tandem instead of denouncing each other as they might have in years past. Stiles and Hopkins made for an odd pair, differing in theology but coming to agree on many social and political subjects. Stiles learned that, for all his Calvinist bluster, Reverend Hopkins possessed one critical virtue that so many other men of the cloth lacked: the ability to listen and change his mind.

Hopkins began to change his views about one critically important subject almost as soon as he arrived in Newport. He heard his black congregants' stories of their cruel and despicable treatment, and their desire for freedom, and he started to inquire more about the slave system that brought them there. He witnessed the horror of the auction block in Newport and saw the slave markets at Mill Street and at North Baptist Street where human beings were bought and sold as commodities, the marks on their bodies proving how their captors viewed them as animals. Most white Newport residents consciously ignored such sights, but Hopkins knew he couldn't. He had to accept the truth that he witnessed. He remembered how he had once owned a slave in Great Barrington as part of his ministerial salary, but now felt shame and guilt for it.

He continued to study and learn: he met Obour Tanner, an enslaved woman active in women's gospel work who acted as mentor and friend to the poet Phillis Wheatley; and he corresponded with Wheatley herself and other black evangelicals, and learned a new perspective on faith in light of the desire for freedom. He befriended artists like Newport Gardner, who learned to read and write in English and several African languages, and then taught himself to sing and compose music until he was one of the city's best musicians—giving the lie to those who claimed enslaved people were inferior to whites in any way. He saw the dedication of John Quamino and Bristol Yamma to higher education, and with Ezra Stiles did all he could to raise funds for their education at the College of New Jersey as the first black students at the school. He may have even seen the elaborate, joyous funerals of former slaves, which proved the boundless capacity of the human soul in the face of the greatest terrors; and may have paused at their grave-stones, carved by master stone mason Zingo Stevens. And thus through the accumulated, indisputable weight of the evidence, and the friendship and testimony of black residents of the city, he came to a conclusion that no other prominent minister of a mainline faith had ever preached in America: Slavery was a sin against God, an abomination to which he had closed his eyes throughout his life, and yet now those eyes were open, and he became inspirited with truth. He would speak against the brutal practice in the pulpit and denounce those who gained by it.

He knew this would set much of the white town folk against him, and would "procure me many enemies." With few exceptions, no minister of any sect spoke against slavery; only the Quakers, whose numbers were small and whose theology was atypical. Hopkins was alone, but he felt imbued with faith in his own judgment. He called out other ministers for defending and upholding slavery, and said there were "many established falsehoods, as well as many vulgar errors wherein multitudes of men have followed one another for whole ages almost blindfold."

He first spoke against slavery from the altar in 1771. No record exists as to what he said, but he likely had a resounding effect on his flock. Only one family resigned its membership in response to his exhortation, and the other members listened in silence to his dramatic condemnation: "The majority of his hearers were astounded that they, of themselves, had not long before seen and felt the truths which he disclosed to them." Many of the First Church members were common workers or poor and did not have the same vested interest in slavery that some of the parishioners at Second Church did. Still, even that church's pastor, Ezra Stiles, cooperated with Hopkins and tried to raise funds for a missionary society that would work to discourage slavery in Africa.

As the years passed, more and more of Hopkins's words were devoted to raising the specter of God's wrath against slavery and those who gained from it, and he banned slave holders from becoming members of First Church. His actions and stirring rhetoric convinced others in the New Divinity school to follow him. Figures like Levi Hart and Ebenezer Baldwin also renounced the practice, demanding the "opening of the prison to the bound . . . [for] slavery or bondage is terrible and to be avoided." Like Hopkins, they took the ideas of Jonathan Edwards and innovated them and reconciled their contradictions, and asserted that people could not be liberated in Christ if they denied liberation to others. And joining them in revising the elder Edwards's ideas was his son Jonathan Jr., who raised the specter of hypocrisy against white American colonists for demanding liberty when they withheld it from those of a different race. And he posed the provocative question, "If it be lawful and right for us to reduce the Africans to a state of slavery, why is it not as right for Great Britain, France, or Spain, not merely to exact duties on us; but to reduce us to the same state of slavery, to which we have reduced them?"

Hopkins seized on the ideas of the younger Edwards and expanded them with the most conspicuous statement he could muster, *A Dialogue Concerning the Slavery of the Africans*. Just weeks after the signing of the Declaration of Independence, he dedicated an address to the Continental Congress and spoke of the true meaning of virtue, faith, and freedom. He demanded that they, as revolutionaries, put an end to the vile trade and to release "thousands of blacks in slavery, who have an equal right to freedom with ourselves" as the colonists battled for their own independence. He called for immediate abolition and asked them to deliver bondsmen "out of the hands of the oppressor; and be the happy instruments of procuring and establishing universal LIBERTY to white and black, to be transmitted down to the latest posterity!" It disgusted him that Europeans and Americans claimed to possess high-minded ideals and Christian beliefs, but "by the murdering or enslaving of millions of millions, they have brought a curse upon themselves," through trafficking in terror and barbarity. "Who can realize all this, and not feel a mixture of grief, pity, indignation and horror, truly ineffable! And must he not be filled with zeal to do his utmost to put a speedy stop to this seven-headed monster of iniquity, with all the horrid train of evils with which it is attended."

In an accompanying dialogue, he broke down the excuses for slavery that had been made over the centuries and recounted the horror stories of Africans kidnapped from their land, abused, enchained, and otherwise denied their freedom before God. For it was "inexpressible unjust, inhuman and cruel [and] glaringly contrary to the whole tenor of divine revelation." He said the promoters of slavery had twisted and misrepresented passages from the Bible to make money on human misery, and that God was not indifferent to slavery but outright condemned it—and he offered chapter and verse to prove his point. Ultimately, he told all slave owners that their actions risked the wrath of the Almighty unless the practice was ended immediately. He told them God would punish oppression, and asked, "Are you willing to be the instruments of bringing judgments and ruin on this land, and on yourselves and families, rather than let the oppressed go out free?"

Perhaps only an extreme Calvinist could have been brave enough in 1776 to aim an antislavery sermon to a group of revolutionaries that included many slave owners. But Hopkins did just that, and his fearless words inspired both praise and derision in the years that followed, along with a growing interest in abolition among other preachers of his stripe. He knew ministers of all kinds for far too long had winked at slavery, had allowed it, had made excuses for it, had even indulged in the practice themselves—he had been one of them. But now, motivated by penance as much as virtue, Hopkins seized the mantle of abolition and inspired others to do the same.

In Newport, his ministry continued with an elevated profile, as he discussed plans for abolition with the slaves and freedmen who had inspired the revival of the 1760s, and who had first directed his attention to the cruelties of slavery. Some did a great deal to promote liberation and alleviate suffering: Newport Gardner and Zingo Stevens founded the African Union Society, a mutual aid society that provided assistance for the poor and financial resources for loans and property purchases to aid black people in Newport, as well as an apprentice program to help the enslaved. Obour

Tanner launched the Free African Female Benevolent Society to clothe and educate black children in poverty, support the widows of slaves, and provide for their children. John Quamino and Bristol Yamma worked as missionaries to abolish slavery. Though Quamino died at sea, Yamma returned to help lead the African Union Society. Along with these figures, countless other lesser-known members of First and Second Church would take action in Rhode Island and throughout New England to change the heart of its people and outlaw the import, trade, and persistence of any form of human bondage.

In years to come dozens of New Divines would join them in the campaign and would create organizations like the Society for the Promotion of Freedom and the Relief of Persons Unlawfully Holden in Bondage. And the Rhode Island legislature enacted gradual prohibitions against the practice—first banning the internal trade in human cargo to the colony in 1774, then establishing gradual emancipation a decade later. Unfortunately, such measures had a limited effect at first, because many of the powerful merchants were as much investors in the wider business of North American slavery as they were participants in the rum and slave trade. Newport remained a center of human oppression in one form or another for years to come.

Though it would take decades longer to convince the people of New England to support abolition, and still longer to change the minds of other Northerners, the antislavery ministry that Samuel Hopkins championed at the dawn of independence would eventually reach its goal. He knew this monumental struggle would continue after his death, and might well involve bloodshed, as it eventually did. But he had faith it would succeed, just as he had faith he could change an individual soul as much as he could an entire society. For him, the most important belonged to the person that first drew him to First Church.

At some point during the 1770s, Hopkins's jeremiads against slavery had a moving effect on Sarah Osborn. She was infirm by then and scarcely able to leave her house due to her mounting ailments, and Hopkins often gave Sunday services in her home so she could participate in them. He had done well in her eyes and fulfilled all the hopes that she and Susanna had put in him. In return she opened her eyes to the truth as he preached it: The Bible did not uphold slavery but condemned it, and any good Christian knew better than to risk the wrath of God by arguing otherwise. During this time she composed a poem that expressed her new feelings, describing a view of heaven for slaves released from their chains: "Those we see here who once have been / Made slaves to man by horrid sin / Now through rich grace in Christ are free / Forever set at liberty."

Sarah's release from her own suffering came in 1796, at the age of eighty-three. She had accomplished much in her years, from battling grief and debt and poverty, to supporting her extended families, to founding religious societies and enflaming revivals, to seeking out Samuel Hopkins as the minister of First Church. Her body collapsed long before her spirit, and from her example, Hopkins gained much of his own inspiration. At Sarah's funeral, a surprising number of people came to honor her memory. Fitting with her life, the funeral sermon preached was a plea to God: "I therefore, the prisoner of the Lord, beseech you, that you walk worthy of the vocation, wherewith you are called." Hopkins would live for another seven years after her, as the first major white abolitionist of the new republic, and the author and editor of memoirs on Jonathan Edwards, Susanna Anthony, and Sarah herself. Moreover, he would become widely known for his new, muscular version of Calvinism, which took Edwards's theology and stripped it of its contradictions, until it became a real moral force of reform well into the nineteenth century.

Ultimately, though, the most important participants in the struggle were lesser-known to posterity: Phillis the enslaved Christian, who first demanded protection for her son from Sarah. The black religious seekers who created a color-blind revival. The free and unfree congregants of First Church who convinced Hopkins of the need for abolition. And the many freedmen and bondsmen who led their own revivals in Newport, worshipping with whites and telling their stories of violence and hardship to anyone who would listen. For it was they who knew slavery firsthand who struck the first blow against it and began to alter the terrible system of human oppression, with Osborn and Hopkins the willing agents of their crusade.

THIRTEEN

THE BLACK REGIMENT

By the turn of the mid-18th century any hesitation American divines might have had about crossing the boundary between church and state had long since disappeared. Elections became fraught contests between the forces of the established order—often Anglican and Old Light Congregational—against the upsurge of neo-Calvinist, evangelical, New Light disruptors. Barefaced attempts to manipulate the electorate resulted in the passage of laws like Connecticut's 1756 ordinance against "the artful applications of designing men," i.e., corruption and bribery. But at a time when even esteemed figures like Yale's president Thomas Clap were caught scheming to sway elections, such laws had little power to keep religion and politics from becoming more entangled and encumbered.

It wasn't always so. Up until the mid-18th century, most ministers considered the spiritual and the secular to be too volatile a compound to be mixed. One observer asked "how ridiculous is the sight and sound" of clergymen ignorant of the affairs of state to offer their observations on politics from the pulpit. But when the revival came, such distinctions between the sacred and profane vanished in many places. The arrival of self-styled preachers and exhorters drew even more Americans into battles over religion in civic life, as the poor and working classes became energized in the pews and took their newfound power into the streets.

The militancy of parishioners had not ebbed much in the years after the revival's peak. A provocative sermon here, or an angry pamphlet there, might be enough to send a restive congregation up in arms. Such feelings became even more combustible when colonial assemblies passed laws that congregants saw as hostile to them, favored one religion over another, or tried to outlaw practices like itinerancy. In response many American Christians demanded liberty to pursue their own sense of faith, and for civil powers to let them practice it without restraint. And when they didn't get their way, they either protested more vehemently or tried to escape their rulers' authority.

Many Separatists left the cities and decamped into the frontier, where they could experiment with their beliefs however they pleased. In time many drifted toward New Light evangelism, and still others toward Separatist Baptism. After having broken from Regular Baptism to light the fires of revival in the hinterlands of New England, the Separatist Baptists had, over thirty years, expanded their numbers and worshipped in two-and-a-half times more churches than they had at the beginning of the revival. They conquered the frontier and built meetinghouses and communities led by the figure of the "farmer-preacher" who could till the land and save souls, and didn't need a divinity degree or any kind of training to do it.

By the 1760s the Separatist Baptists had perfected a system for seeding the countryside with their religion. It started with itinerant preachers, who would go from town to town spreading the gospel and setting up meetings in which they would exhort their listeners to confess their sins and accept God's grace and be reborn in Christ. From these locations, "mother churches" would form, and once they were established, laymen with a flair for ministry carried the word to new towns and formed "daughter churches." So the process went until the frontier from New England down into the South erupted in evangelical fervor. Hundreds of Baptist ministers seeded the faith, especially in Virginia, where they battled mobs and hostile authorities to do the Lord's work as they saw fit. Some were horse-whipped, imprisoned, beaten, urinated upon, almost blown up, and "smoke[d] with brimstone and

Indian pepper," yet still they persisted. In the Carolinas and Georgia they found particular success converting rural folk, even when threatened with assaults and fistfights by local ruffians.

The Baptists' greatest enemies continued to be the Anglican gentry, who charged them with being "ignorant enthusiasts" ruled by delusion and claimed they presented a monstrous threat to the social order. They also frightened Regular Baptists and mainstream sects with their radical means of worship. In some Separatist Baptist churches, women became "deaconesses" who took leadership positions, while in most others, women prayed and exhorted openly and without censure. Black and Indian preachers, too, served as deacons and exhorters, and sometimes became church elders and shared pulpits with white pastors. This activity helped define the Separatist Baptists as a trailblazing sect—far more than any other in colonial America.

Separatist Baptists reveled in the enthusiasm of their faith, which included everything from extensive feet-washing and laying on of hands to "kisses of charity" to ceremonies that involved, as one observer wrote, "some roaring on the ground, some wringing their hands, some in ecstasies, some praying, some weeping; and others so outrageously cursing and swearing that it was thought they were really possessed of the Devil." Although such reports were overstated, they nonetheless showed how emotional a Baptist service could be, and how it appealed to rural Christians who had little interest in formal sermonizing or tedious church rituals.

For their efforts they met with the seemingly bottomless scorn and mockery of the higher classes, who still didn't know what to make of these fervent rustics and perceived them as a threat to their way of life. They did not duel, cockfight, race horses, gamble, drink, dance, or subscribe to any of the other rituals that Southern society esteemed. Instead, they lived simply and prayed constantly and never stopped trying to advance their cause at the expense of their adversaries. It made a difference, too: The Separatist Baptists captured the minds and hearts of many Southerners and started to push the Anglicans into eclipse.

Aided by New Side Presbyterians and New Light Congregationalists—the charter members of the old revival—the radical Baptists demanded the Church of England be disestablished over the colonies. It was a bold move against the Crown, for such colonies owed their existence to royal charters, with the understanding that the Church of England would be favored by law there. But the evangelicals did not yield; they pushed for greater toleration, greater liberty, and greater respect for their faith. In response, royal officials either ignored or suppressed them, or enforced new laws designed to counter their advance. This made the dissenters' demands for tolerance even more aggressive and unyielding.

The contrast was striking: Whereas in previous years, New Light ministers took pains to excuse their parishioners' enthusiastic "wildness" or apologize for it, they now exalted in it. Some pastors saw the conflicts with royal officials through the lens of apocalyptic Millenarianism and warned of God's vengeance upon those who impeded their faith. Others encouraged behavior that critics called insane—crying and screaming, yelling and convulsing, writhing and speaking in tongues, and revealing spectacular visions of heaven and hell.

To prominent dissenters, such enthusiasm became a hallmark of God's grace; to the new American nationalists, it was a sign of homegrown religion. The rising thirty-year-old lawyer John Adams supported it fully: "I believe it will be found universally true, that no great enterprise for the honor or happiness of mankind was ever achieved without a large mixture of that noble infirmity." The Puritans, too, had been derided as extremists; yet they had founded a nation in the wilderness and built the fountain from which all current radicalism flowed.

Amid these striking shifts in belief, one figure remained proud, unrestrained and hostile to anyone who opposed him—Andrew Croswell. Several decades had passed since he had torched New England with his spiritual fire, inspiring thousands of New Lights and singing, marching, hollering and stripping down to praise God with every bit of ferocity he had in him. After midcentury, he continued to lead Boston's Eleventh Church, and to "champion a radical, experiential faith . . . defiantly outside the religious mainstream." He had few allies in town, and regularly heard "the ministers are all against you," even from his friends. He stood outside most of the factions of New England religion—the Old Light Calvinists, the New Divinity preachers, and the growing number of liberals. None of them had room for Croswell, a man who praised the love and joy to be found in rebirth in Christ but who spit bile at anyone who challenged him.

For the most part, he was more a relic than a pariah. His condemnations of salvation through works, his attacks on the liberalism of colleges like Harvard, his rearguard defense of the old extremism—it all gave him an antique quality. This was unfortunate, for many of Croswell's critiques still resonated, or should have to anyone paying attention. He continued to renounce slavery and the trade in human flesh as an abomination. He practiced an open-minded spirituality that encouraged exhortation from women, blacks, and Indians, who remained sidelined and silenced in other Boston churches. He promoted prison reform and attacked the cruelties of the penal system. And he even declaimed against military whippings and other forms of corporal punishment that were so widespread to be seen as unremarkable to everyone else but him.

Until the end of his long life, he would remain a champion for justice and fairness, a proponent of humane laws and honest government, and a proclaimer of the power of a loving God. For these and other reasons, established ministers treated him dismissively when they noticed him at all. Despite his diminished stature, a spark inside kept him aflame. Perhaps it was divine inspiration, perhaps simple human emotion. But whatever it was, it gave him voice to channel his fury and target those who promoted sin and blasphemy as he saw it. One particular minister who vexed him, and became the target of his invective, was Jonathan Mayhew.

The minister of West Church, Jonathan continued to provoke the orthodox by challenging long-held dogma. He had already undercut the notion of original sin and various other Calvinist truisms, and had tied his own theology to the rationalism of Isaac Newton and Enlightenment philosophers John Locke and Samuel Clarke. In the 1750s he angered even more of his adversaries by questioning the truth of the Trinity, and claiming Christ acted as a mediator between humans and God, and was his subordinate instead of his coequal. These heresies offended countless Calvinists—Croswell most of all.

In a piercing rebuttal, the paleo-Calvinist took aim at Jonathan and accused him and other liberals of "daring attempts to confute and ridicule the doctrines once delivered to the saints." He said, "My heart burned within me, while I read" Jonathan's recent sermons, for his "horrible talk about the Trinity" was as "wretched nonsense as ever was printed." Croswell promised to employ "all proper means to destroy his [theology] from under the whole heavens." But Croswell could no more destroy Jonathan's ideas than he could get people to accept his own, and in any case Jonathan didn't even bother to respond to him. Yet strangely enough, aside from theology, the two men shared more in common than either might have cared to admit—namely, politics.

Croswell had been a committed opponent of British authority and Anglican high churchmen ever since he had defended George Whitefield from Alexander Garden's attacks in 1741. Jonathan had echoed many of the same sentiments in his *Discourse on Unlimited Submission*, and in his risk-taking sermons that followed it. He had even delivered an election sermon in 1754 to Governor Shirley and the Massachusetts legislature that exceeded Croswell's polemics for its fiery demands to protect the hard-won freedoms of colonists from the threat of tyranny. He invoked God as the highest power over the "divine right of monarchy [and] . . . the despotic, unlimited power of kings" and the "learned parasites, or other graceless politicians."

Speaking boldly before royal officials, Jonathan denounced those who claimed "loyalty and slavery mean the same thing. . . . to prepare us for the dutiful reception of an hereditary tyrant." He did not levy criticism only at British politicians. He also channeled Whitefield in his attacks on Catholic France. If anything, Jonathan's rhetoric was even more manic than Whitefield's ever was, in imagining the outcome of a French victory over Britain:

> Do I see Christianity banished for Popery! The Bible, for the Mass book! The oracles of truth, for fabulous legends! . . . Do I see all liberty, property, religion, happiness, changed, or rather transubstantiated, into slavery, poverty, superstition, wretchedness! . . . O dishonest! profane! execrable sight! O piercing sound! that entereth into the ears of the Lord of Sabbath! Where in what region! in what world am I! Is this imagination? (its own busy tormentor) or is it something more divine? I will not, I cannot believe 'tis prophetic vision; or that God has so far abandoned us!

The speech proved Jonathan had learned much from his orthodox enemies in fifteen years. He had captured the tones, cadences, and rhetoric of the most ardent revivalists, and now funneled them into attacking that favorite enemy of colonial Protestants: the pope and Catholicism. Jonathan depicted the conflict between Britain and France as an apocalyptic struggle with control of the civilized world at stake. In so doing he imbued his audience with a sense of their own righteousness against adversaries who were Satanic, insidious, and somehow less than human. It was a masterpiece of inflammatory rhetoric, with more than a touch of demagoguery, and it made his name even more famous than it already was. As one historian wrote, Jonathan deployed "an enraged language that patriot ministers would later imitate in fomenting revolution against England." Along with the *Discourse on Unlimited Submission*, "these sermons would stand as the apotheosis of revolutionary preaching in New England."

Jonathan continued to channel the spirit of the revivalists when an earthquake struck New England in 1755. Like the Grand Itinerant, Jonathan blamed the tragedy on the moral failings of the colonists and the sins of the mother country, calling it "a nation where infidelity, irreligion, corruption and venality, and almost every kind of vice, seems to have been increasing all the time!—Will not almighty God, who 'only is holy,' sooner or later visit us for things? And will not his soul be avenged on SUCH A NATION AS THIS!" He said only faith in God could stave off destruction, and those who rejected him "are dogs, and sorcerers, and whoremongers, and murderers, and IDOLATERS, and whosoever loveth and maketh a LIE."

These were peculiar words coming from someone who praised natural religion and civic virtue over human depravity and divine punishment. But Jonathan employed these fire-and-brimstone tropes not only because he believed them, but because they managed to increase his appeal to the many Calvinists of America who would otherwise be his foes. While his theology might appall them, his political harangues and jeremiads appealed to them—and forming such alliances would prove to be crucial as the conflicts with Britain only worsened.

As the years passed, Jonathan's reputation increased with each new blast he directed at the authorities. In his personal life, his conflicts in the public arena had dour consequences for his health—in the 1750s he became stricken with smallpox and survived, then faced painful kidney stones and pleurisy to add to the misery. He grieved the loss of his father and sometimes mentor Experience Mayhew (who died at the age of eighty-five), knowing he could never reconcile his own liberal ideas with his father's Calvinism. He did find some comfort when he married Elizabeth Clarke, with whom he started a family, but few beyond his family and friends would ever come to know the relaxed, personable side of Jonathan Mayhew. His stern public image proved to be a strength as well as a burden to maintain.

He spoke repeatedly in his sermons against despotic monarchs and lamented the demise of one of the good ones in his *Discourse Occasioned by the Death of King George II*. He saw the late king as a constitutional monarch, a protector of colonial freedoms despite the nefarious designs of some of his counselors, and he could only hope his son would emerge as a worthy successor. Such hopes proved fleeting when George III took the crown, and let himself be influenced by Tories like the Earl of Bute, who persuaded him that royal power over the colonies must be strengthened with greater taxation and commercial regulation, and dissenters must be brought to heel. Jonathan suspected such policies would lead to disaster, and that recent events "confirm the apprehensions which I have all along had concerning the [king], and make me almost tremble for the consequences."

In this new, increasingly repressive atmosphere of the 1760s, Jonathan courted more trouble with royal officials. In one episode, he overheard a rumor of Governor Francis Bernard accepting a small bribe from a petitioner and spread the story to a few friends, who spread the rumor to others until it made its way back to the governor. Infuriated, Bernard called the pastor to his residence at Province House and interrogated and insulted him, calling him a liar who "did not understand, but abused British liberty" and represented "the diabolical spirits of slander and defamation." As a final touch, Bernard demanded satisfaction, which Jonathan thought referred to the law, but may have just as well referred to a duel. In the face of such hostility from the colony's highest ranking official, Jonathan had no choice but to privately back down and blame a misunderstanding for the allegation. But Bernard's furious reaction showed that his sermons and rhetoric had a powerful effect—while Jonathan might be a hero to many of his peers, he had also become an enemy to those in control.

Bernard's sharp rebuttal was not unique. Anglican high churchmen followed the lead of their magistrates and became ever bolder in confronting dissenters like Jonathan and showcasing their power. In Boston, the grand King's Chapel had opened a few years before to great controversy. In Cambridge, within sight of Harvard College, Anglicans founded Christ Church, which dissenters called a "dagger aimed at the heart of Puritan tradition in America." They claimed it would act as a garrison for missionaries to convert Congregationalists to Anglicanism, and to pressure other nonconformists to abandon their religion. They assigned much of the blame for these offenses to the Archbishop of Canterbury, Thomas Secker, whom they saw as an archenemy for his long-held desire to install a colonial bishop and create an American episcopate.

Jonathan took a special interest in checking the advance of the Anglicans. Not only did he stir up anxieties about the state religion of Britain, but he had been working with Charles Chauncy to establish a rival to the Society for the Propagation of the Gospel, which had plans to spread the gospel into the interior of New England. Jonathan's family background included a long line of missionaries who operated on the frontier, and now that the frontier was once again pacified after the war with the French, he saw a great opportunity to proselytize to Indians who lived there. Of course, the experience of the late Jonathan Edwards and other missionaries had shown that, once converted, groups like the Mohawk and Stockbridge Indians provided little interest to colonial rulers. They were openly mistreated and abused, their earnest conversions offering little protection from the machinations of corrupt British rulers and local swindlers. Nonetheless, despite its often tragic outcome, the push to convert Native peoples to Christianity became something of an obsession for both Anglicans and Congregationalists, and Jonathan used the controversy to arouse even greater anger against his foes in the Church of England.

East Apthorp made his work easy. The ambitious young cleric was an Anglican missionary and heir to a family fortune who had a knack for offending people with his garish taste and opinions. He lived in a mansion that inspired envy and disgust among Bostonians, and regularly penned tracts for the press "equating New England nonconformity not only with superstition, fanaticism, hypocrisy and persecution" but with Roman Catholicism and Islam. Apthorp upheld the SPG as blameless in its conduct and pure in its motives, and dared to challenge anyone to say otherwise. Jonathan could not resist the opportunity.

In response to Apthorp, he wrote a lengthy tract, *Observations on the Charter and Conduct of the Society for the Propagation of the Gospel in Foreign Parts*, claiming the Society used subterfuge to effect its aims, which were not those of conversion, but a conspiracy to deprive Americans of their freedom. He warned that its missionaries had sinister aims, and attacked the "narrow, censorious and bitter spirit that prevails in too many of the Episcopalians among us." He raised the prospect of bishops installed in America, overseeing forced conversions of dissenters, and recalled how "furious episcopal zealots" had done the same thing in the previous century. The threat was dire, and he asked "the people of New England to stand fast in the liberty wherewith CHRIST hath made them free; and not to return under that yoke of episcopal bondage, which so miserably galled the necks of our forefathers."

Line by line, Jonathan so eviscerated the hapless East Apthorp that a greater response was called for than one from an immature cleric. Adherents to the Church of England denounced Jonathan's attacks, one writing "this blind bigot is for setting up an Inquisition against the religion of the nation" just as Oliver Cromwell had done in the 17th century with his "forty-thousand cutthroats." Still, most of these responses were anonymous, and with Jonathan's work gaining praise among Congregationalists and Presbyterians of all stripes—and being printed in the newspapers of Britain—the church knew it had to respond with a better defense of its missionary conduct. The task was left to Archbishop Secker.

Secker thought little of Jonathan, and in private referred to him as "a most foul-mouthed bespatterer of our church and our missionaries in print." He still championed episcopacy, but knew the violent reaction that might ensue if he tried to force Americans to accept it. Privately, many other clerics in Britain saw the struggle as futile, and compared trying to organize Anglicans in the New World as akin to hanging from a "rope of sand; there is no union, no authority among us; we cannot even summon a convention for united counsel and advice." So Secker proceeded cautiously, and in his anonymous response to Jonathan's *Observations*, he promised that if bishops ever came to America, they would act tactfully and respect the native traditions and faiths of the king's subjects. He granted a number of points in the *Observations*, and adopted a tolerant tone and support for a wide range of faiths and promised harmonious coexistence between Anglicans and dissenters.

With Secker retreating from the controversy, many observers thought Jonathan had triumphed over his adversaries. His *Observations* were printed and reprinted in London, his British allies lauded his efforts, and high churchmen compared his work to "the devil's thunderbolt." Not only did the minister of West Church provoke a response by the top cleric of Great Britain, according to one writer, he "won for himself a transatlantic reputation as the champion of British Nonconformity, and it is doubtful if Benjamin Franklin had as many readers." East Apthorp humbly retired to England, and Jonathan received praise from the city's orthodox ministers who had once treated him as a pariah.

His words unified the warring sects of Protestantism in a way they had not been in a quarter century. These united clergymen now formed a "Black Regiment"—named for the color of their robes—that aimed to further undermine the authority of Anglican clerics and royal officials. Just as the Baptists of the South had been doing recently, the Black Regiment threatened the colonial hierarchy and shifted the battle lines of American religion and politics. No longer was the conflict principally between revivalists and their foes; instead, it was between dissenters and their enemies within Britain's state religion—and soon after that, within its very government. As John Adams wrote, Jonathan Mayhew's controversies "spread an universal alarm against the authority of Parliament . . . and if Parliament could tax us, they could establish the Church of England with all its creeds, articles, tests, ceremonies, and tithes." Fear of British imperial power became further inflamed the next year, when the legislature passed the Stamp Act.

Parliament's latest attempt to demonstrate its supremacy over the wayward colonists had followed its Sugar Act of 1764, which levied taxes on molasses and limited the export of some colonial products only to Britain. That act was unpopular, but it did not encourage the same defiance as the Stamp Act. Passed at the beginning of spring 1765, the Act had an implementation date of November 1. As it came closer, elites like Ben Franklin became alarmed at the consequences (and later did something about it, as noted earlier), when public anger swelled and threatened to send the colonies into revolt. By the summer boycotts against British-made products became widespread, merchants of the Middle Colonies and New England vowed not to import British goods, and various groups, from college students to fire companies, singled out particular imported products to boycott—anything from beer to clothing.

The New Lights were especially hostile to the Act, and some threatened violence against those who tried to enforce the law. In mid-August turmoil erupted when a mob of Bostonians hung effigies of the colony's stamp collector Andrew Oliver and the king's counselors from an elm tree and proceeded to destroy the local stamp office and set a bonfire outside Oliver's luxurious home. Though the sheriff and Lieutenant Governor Thomas Hutchinson tried to stop the rioters, they broke into Oliver's house and demolished it, spiriting away bottles from the wine cellar as they ransacked the garden and pulverized the furniture. The stamp collector quit his job soon after.

Many in West Church and throughout Boston awaited Jonathan Mayhew's verdict on the mayhem, and eleven days later he delivered it. In his bracing sermon, he did not condone the violence, but did use passages from the Bible to tell his congregation that in any nation, people should not be governed contrary to their desires. They should not be abused by their magistrates and should retain their full rights as subjects loyal to a king, or as citizens loyal to a republic. If their rights were abrogated, they became slaves. Of course, Jonathan did not mean the ruinous and inhuman slavery that Andrew Croswell called an abomination to God; he meant the metaphorical kind, applied to free citizens alone.

Jonathan said, "slaves are bound to labor for the pleasure and profit of others; and to subsist merely on what their masters are pleased to allow them." For colonists to be stripped of their rights by the imperial overlords or distant legislature of another country was nothing more than cruel servitude—"this is really slavery, not civil liberty." He mentioned the Stamp Act by name and urged his listeners to do all they could to fight "the execution of unrighteous and oppressive laws," not through brute force of arms, but through concentrated civil action. He added this careful warning because he knew how enflamed his audience could get after listening to his words. But what may have seemed to him like a plea for nonviolent resistance translated into something very different on the streets of Boston.

The following evening, another riot broke out. This time the angry masses broke into the homes of several royal officials and ransacked them and seized their valuables before moving on to the residence of Thomas Hutchinson. The lieutenant governor was inside dining with his family when the mob approached, and he scarcely had time to escape before the rioters smashed inside with axes and obliterated the walls and gardens. They drank the wine, they stole the coin, and they scattered the official papers. They even began pulling apart the brickwork before the structure finally gave way and collapsed under their assault. The damage came to 25,000 pounds sterling.

Many Bostonians blamed the policies of the British government for causing the riot, and claimed that without representation in Parliament, people would resort to violence to achieve their ends. The crowd included numerous artisans and laborers aggrieved not only by the acts of taxation, but by the years of abuse they had endured at the hands of elite bankers and royal officials, who called them a "herd of fools, tools and sycophants." Hutchinson's own rhetoric had contributed to their grievances, as had his support for noxious policies dating back to the 1740s. As for Hutchinson himself, he blamed Jonathan Mayhew.

In his official history of Massachusetts Bay, Hutchinson claimed Jonathan's sermon had a galvanizing effect on some of the rioters, and cited an accused mob member as saying "he was excited to [violence] by this sermon, and that he thought he was doing God service." Those in the Anglican elite also targeted Jonathan for encouraging defiance, saying he had preached "one of the most seditious sermons ever delivered, advising the people to stand up for their rights to the last drop of their blood." They painted Jonathan as an anarchist and seditionist and stopped just short of calling his words criminal.

Jonathan felt unjustly accused. Had he not warned his listeners against rash and violent action? Did he not call for civil and peaceful protest against unjust policies? He had no desire to see anarchy bloody the land, or for rightful rulers to be dispatched at the hands of street criminals. Besides, he had written to Hutchinson after the mayhem offering his sympathies, saying, "I had rather lose my hand, than be an encourager of such outrages." Still, he knew he had elevated his profile to such a degree that one spark of his rhetoric could ignite a firestorm of trouble. And so for once, he had to publicly back down.

He delivered a sermon the following Sunday in which he expressed his love for liberty as well as his apprehensions of violence in protecting it. He warned against "abusing liberty to licentiousness" and condemned those who would sully a noble cause through their own selfish or barbaric ends. Jonathan was earnest in his thoughts and measured it his tone, but his words made little difference. His supporters continued to interpret his homilies as a justification for forceful resistance to the Crown, and his enemies continued to see him as a figure of rebellion against civil authority. The lesson only proved one thing, which revivalists like George Whitefield had learned twenty years before: a man of the cloth could stir people up and drive them toward acts of strength and resolve, but controlling their behavior once unleashed was impossible. They would take his words and act on them however they pleased. And once that man had developed a reputation as a firebrand or demagogue, it would take great effort to convince them otherwise.

Less than a year later Jonathan Mayhew was dead. A stroke felled him in July 1766 and his demise followed a few days after. The tributes came in from prominent clergymen and citizens throughout New England, the liberals praising his daring theology, the Calvinists lauding his commitment to liberty. A line of fifty-seven carriages and coaches led his body to the grave, with Charles Chauncy offering a eulogy that Jonathan might have appreciated: "[I]f his zeal, at any time, betrayed him into too great a severity of expression, it was against the attempts of those who would make slaves either of men's souls or bodies." A more unexpected honor came later from Andrew Croswell, who lionized his adversary's virtue and integrity, and said despite his faults, "he was a shining example for his brethren in the ministry to follow." But the most important honor came from John Adams.

Himself a prominent opponent of the Stamp Act and Parliament's other taxation attempts, Adams had followed Jonathan's career since he was a teen, relishing his attacks on historical tyrants and current officials. He called him "a Whig of the first magnitude, a clergyman equaled by very few of any denomination in piety, virtue, genius, or learning, whose works will maintain his character as long as New England shall be free." And he wrote, "to draw the character of Mayhew would be to transcribe a dozen Volumes. . . . [he] threw all the weight of his great fame into the scale of his country in 1761, and maintained it there with zeal and ardor." Adams would later claim that there were five critical figures who drove America toward revolution, and Jonathan Mayhew was the only minister among them.

Another man on that list was Samuel Adams—John's cousin. Since the Knowles Riot of 1747, he had made his name as a prominent figure in the Boston town meetings and more recently as a legislator in the Massachusetts assembly. He was also active in the Caucus Club, the Masonic Lodge, and the fire companies—all organs of rebellion in the eyes of colonial officials—and penned articles and pamphlets that denounced cruel British policies and instructed his readers how to fight them. For his many efforts of resistance, many in the royal government saw him as nothing less than "the most dangerous man in America."

This wasn't entirely true. Though many of his artisan and shipyard worker allies in the Sons of Liberty had rioted in recent months, he was hardly their puppet master, and was careful not to call for outright violence. Rather, he was a masterful exhorter and agitator of the people who worked closely with the Loyal Nine, a group of upper-middle-class merchants who helped arrange many of the protests that shook the city.

Like Jonathan Mayhew, Sam Adams wove spiritual ideas in with the struggle against Britain, writing, "the religion and public liberty of a people are so intimately connected, their interests are interwoven, and cannot exist separately." Unlike Mayhew, however, he saw the protection of liberty through the eyes of an orthodox Calvinist. He demanded a return to moral virtue and a rejection of wickedness, and praised the rustic simplicity of 17th-century America, when Puritan rectitude held sway and traditional values were protected by force of law. He aimed his message at the commoners of Boston, praising their struggle for liberty against the selfish designs of their betters, and identified himself an enthusiast in religion and politics. Like a revivalist of old, he said, "mankind is governed more by their feelings than by reason" and used this idea to incite his followers against those he claimed oppressed them. Thus, in his methods, Adams was both radical and reactionary, an aggressive herald of the republic to come, and crusader for the values of the antique past.

He was not alone in this feeling. Americans from a variety of backgrounds and beliefs invested the age-old Puritans with a radiant sense of virtue they tried to recapture. Esteeming New England's distant history, some ministers resurrected the idea that modern dissenters were the heirs of the saints who had built their proud "city on a hill" in America. They claimed the colonists resisted Satan by standing on their holy traditions while the mother country stood awash in corruption and turpitude, which threatened its damnation: "there is no truth, no mercy, nor knowledge of God in the land. . . . As they have increased, so have they sinned, therefore God is changing their glory into shame."

Sam Adams took these ideas and innovated them. While he venerated the past as much as any Calvinist, he also employed modern communications and mass-market rhetoric that preachers like George Whitefield had pioneered. With his ally James Otis, Adams spread information via the press and organized his campaigns against imperial policy through private societies and secret clubs. He did not act heedlessly, however. He knew the patriot clubs had to legitimize their actions with the sanction of church authority. The Black Regiment served this role, until "scarcely a patriot club was without a divine who lent an odor of sanctity to what conservatives believed would otherwise have been rank treason." One of the staunchest members of this regiment was Charles Chauncy.

Now sixty years old, Chauncy had emerged from the battles of the revival scarred but still standing, a citadel of Whig values—namely the primacy of popular elected representation over the privileges of the Crown and nobility—and opponent of British policy. He knew and worked with many of the men in the patriot clubs, among them Adams and Otis as well as Benjamin Edes, a leader of the Loyal Nine who printed many of his tracts and published the *Boston Gazette*. Chauncy delivered regular sermons and jeremiads against the laws of Parliament, stating that colonists' privileges were actually "RIGHTS that had been dearly paid for by a vast expense of blood, treasure and labor, without which this continent must have still remained in a wilderness state." He challenged even the most ardent New Lights in supporting religious liberty against tyranny, and acquired a reputation as a source of trouble for the Crown, despite being a senior citizen. A notable piece of doggerel mocked him:

> That fine preacher, called a teacher
> Of Old Brick Church the First,
> Regards no grace to men in place,
> And is by Tories cursed.
> At young and old he'll rave and scold,
> And is in things of state
> A zealous Whig than [John] Wilkes more big,
> In church a tyrant great.

Curiously, while his anti-British rhetoric grew more aggressive, his theology went in the other direction. He dabbled with heresy in works like *The Benevolence of the Deity,* in which he stressed the generous spirit of God and diminished such dogma as original sin and the damnation of unbaptized infants. He exalted "the power and wisdom of the infinitely benevolent Creator" whose grace allowed the ultimate salvation of all people after the expiation of their sins. Along with *Benevolence,* his other major work, *The Mystery Hid from Ages and Generations, Made Manifest by the Gospel Revelation,* wouldn't be published until 1784—three years before his death—and then only anonymously. But by then many ministers in Boston knew who the author of this controversial tract was, along with Chauncy's code word for it: "the pudding."

The pudding was either sweet or bitter depending on one's taste for Calvinism. For the revivalists it was unpalatable, since Chauncy emphasized human free will and associated sin with sickness and pain, instead of endless damnation. Moreover, his idea of salvation was universal, available to anyone beyond just the Calvinist elect, and required good works as well as faith to achieve it. Ultimately, Chauncy argued that salvation meant reconciling with God, for "all of life and part of life after death is a process of trial and discipline, by which sin is conquered and virtue triumphs in the soul."

Human perfectibility meant loving God and becoming his ally, not running in terror from him and fearing his wrath. Oddly, these straightforward ideas still carried the taint of heresy, and threatened to alienate Chauncy from his New Light colleagues in the struggle against Britain. So he kept them quiet, and only revealed the pudding once the cause of independence was secured. Eventually Chauncy's Universalism become one of the roots of the religion of New England liberals, taking his and Jonathan Mayhew's ideas and developing a new, spiritually tolerant movement from them.

In the run-up to the war, however, Chauncy appeared anything but tolerant. After the repeal of the Stamp Act, the minister of First Church kept tempers simmering with public statements against whatever colonial laws issued from the legislature. Parliament soon passed the Quartering Act, which required the billeting of redcoated troops in public buildings, and followed it with the Townsend Acts, which validated its right to control the trade and taxation of the colonies. These measures predictably enflamed anger against the British government, but while Chauncy made sure to criticize these laws, he reserved much of his scorn for the potential installment of an American bishop for the Anglican church.

Like Mayhew, he warned against a sinister plot to bring episcopacy to the New World and said such a measure would threaten the rights of dissenters everywhere. He charged the agents of the church with "an occasion of pride, haughtiness, tampering with princes, and advising and helping forward oppressive tyranny over conscience." One of his tracts, *The Appeal to the Public Answered*, sold 400 copies in a week and fed the Boston press's appetite for controversy, reminding readers of the growing threat to their liberties and calling for resistance to the Church of England and its clerics' underhanded ways.

The church and state of Britain came under greater fire in the 1770s, as relations with the king's American subjects reached new lows. In the most notorious event, scuffles between Boston rope makers and the occupying British army led to crowds hurling taunts and snowballs and ice at the troops, who were under orders not to fire on civilians without authorization. When the crowds pressed in, some of the soldiers fired and left five citizens dead. Figures at the highest levels of the British government blamed Sam Adams for the Boston Massacre, calling the crowd members "Sam Adams's regiments"—though his involvement was hard to prove. To ensure a fair trial for the soldiers involved in the shooting, his cousin John surprisingly acted as counsel for the accused and provided a successful defense in court. Sam Adams, however, tried the soldiers in the *Boston Gazette* under the name "Vindex," declaring them guilty of murder regardless of the actual jury's verdict.

The verdict of Charles Chancy was just as damning. Instead of preaching God's abundant mercy as he did in his theology, he raised the specter of the Lord's judgment upon the wicked and demanded convictions for the accused. He announced that "if I was to be one of the jury upon [a soldier's] trial, I would bring him in guilty, *evidence or no evidence*." British critics reacted with shock, and accused the minister of equating "divinity, zeal, rancor and revenge. . . . He was always for calling down fire from heaven to destroy his opposers."

Chauncy confirmed their fears in the sermon that followed, *Trust in God, The Duty of a People in a Day of Trouble*, in which he inveighed against "the streaming blood of many slaughtered, and wounded innocents. So shocking a tragedy was never before acted in this part of the world; and GOD forbid it should ever be again!" Like an old-fashioned Calvinist, Chauncy threatened that God "would not suffer the town and land to lie under the defilement of blood! Surely, he would not make himself a partaker in the guilt of murder, by putting a stop to the shedding of their blood, who have murderously spilt the blood of others!"

By 1773 the memory of the Massacre had not been forgotten, even as most of the Townsend Acts (except on tea) had been repealed and Archbishop Secker had died, stifling the push for episcopacy in America. Despite these victories, the radicalism of Charles Chauncy continued unabated. He continued to preach incendiary sermons and worked ever closer with many of the militants in Boston like Sam Adams and the Sons of Liberty. They called on Chauncy to "advise, persuade, propagandize, comment on the times, and lend the influence of his position to the cause"—including the creation of the committees of correspondence.

Adams and his allies had created the committees to disseminate information via letters and pamphlets over hundreds of miles, organize resistance to imperial policy, and act as an ad hoc government in some areas. This appealed to an increasing number of Americans who no longer saw themselves as colonists dependent on the will of Parliament; instead they claimed they were citizens in independent states, still loyal to the king but free to rule themselves. British officials like Governor Thomas Hutchinson fiercely resisted such arguments, yet the rebellious Americans had plenty of supporters—including John Adams, who wrote favorably of colonial self-government.

His cousin Sam, however, did not wish to simply argue with the governor. He actively sought to undermine him. First, he publicized a series of letters Ben Franklin had given to him that revealed Hutchinson's private thoughts on matters of state. Most were innocuous, but Adams excerpted the most controversial parts and had them read before the Massachusetts assembly. This embarrassed the governor, and Adams created more problems for him when he plotted against the new British tea policy. The idea was to thwart the smuggling of illicit, untaxed tea from Holland by offering colonists cheap East India Company tea at reduced duties, thereby encouraging the purchase and taxation of the beverage and breaking their ongoing boycott against it. This plan was meant as a subtle means of raising revenue and gaining a monopoly over American commerce, and many rebels realized it immediately, calling it "parliamentary despotism." Sam Adams was among them.

Goaded by Adams and other figures in the resistance movement, on December 16, 1773, some sixty or more Bostonians dressed as Indians clambered aboard ships carrying East India Company tea and dumped 342 chests into the water—a loss of 9,000 pounds. Delighted with the vandalism, Adams said the act brought joy to everyone except the British officials it embarrassed. Those officials quickly petitioned Parliament for redress, and within months the legislators delivered it with the Coercive Acts, which Americans called the Intolerable Acts. These measures closed the port of Boston until its residents paid for the cargo loss; they allowed the quartering of royal soldiers throughout British North America; and they stripped Massachusetts of its charter and gave the royal governor the power to appoint local magistrates, instead of the people electing them.

Outrage ensued, as Sam Adams expected. Boston's committee of correspondence acted quickly to arrange resistance to these measures, calling itself the Solemn League and Covenant after a Puritan alliance formed against Charles I during the English Civil War. Charles Chauncy remarked on how well the committee operated to provide relief for embattled New England communities, as "bountiful donations from one part of the country and another are daily flowing in upon us." Such donations were needed since he and other committee men called for an economic boycott of British goods "to frustrate the designs of those who would rule [Americans] with a rod of iron, instead of the laws of constitutional government."

Chauncy didn't only argue for this rebellious course in his letters; he preached it from the altar at First Church. He had become militant, invested with the desire for revolt, and now fully aligned his mission with that of the Sons of Liberty. Like so may others in the Black Regiment, he stood willing to provide sanction in the house of God for the actions of revolutionaries in the streets.

So much had changed in three decades. In 1743, when he was entering middle age, Chauncy had battled ferociously against enthusiasm and threats to the public order. He had called the New Lights lunatics and wildmen, and argued they posed a peril to civility as well as sanity. The revivalists and their opponents spent years calling each other tools of the devil, unconverted heathens, or enthusiastic madmen, and destroyers of the unity of Protestantism. They issued threats and received them, fired off angry pamphlets and were forced to answer them, and passed laws to secure their own version of the gospel above all others. In the end, the New Lights may have triumphed in numbers, but the Old Lights more than held their own, and the conflict made both sides better combatants. They had warred for many years and kept the edges of their rhetoric sharp and the design of their strategy current. And when they finally found a common enemy that they perceived as a greater threat to their liberties than each other, it was not hard for them to unite.

By 1774 they formed a fearsome, battle-tested front against their British adversaries, who like East Apthorp could not answer their charges, or like Thomas Secker withdrew from the conflict or died before it could be fought out. The American pastors out-preached, out-organized, and outfought their Anglican-Loyalist-British foes; and once these foes realized they had no other options, and that persuasion and incremental legislation had failed, they resorted to armed force.

Events followed rapidly and dramatically. The Continental Congress arranged for the nonimportation and nonconsumption of British goods, with social pressure and the threat of violence hanging over those merchants who continued to trade with the mother country. Loyalists came under threat from angry mobs, and responded with demands for further punitive action against the disloyal masses. George III opted to use military power to bring the colonists into line, and Paul Revere and William Dawes rode to announce the march of the redcoats. War broke out at Lexington and Concord in April 1775, and the Second Continental Congress met the following month. The next year it passed the Declaration of Independence, which severed bonds with Great Britain and renounced the authority of the king.

In August 1776, in an address to his congregation, the now seventy-one-year-old Charles Chauncy offered the most radical sermon of his career. He read not from the Bible, but from the declaration itself, and many of his parishioners heard these passages recited in full for the first time. Abigail Adams sat in a pew and was struck by the power of the words. The minister told his flock how the document offered them the prospect of new "free and independent states" that rejected the dominion of the British Crown; how God had endowed them with unalienable rights to life, liberty and the pursuit of happiness; how the king had oppressed them with tyrannical ministers and unjust policies that trampled upon their rights; and how citizens had the prerogative to abolish their old government and enshrine a new one that honored their principles and protected their freedoms. He said, "with a firm reliance on the protection of divine Providence, we mutually pledge to each other our lives, our fortunes, and our sacred honor."

Abigail watched, as Chauncy concluded the reading and "lifted his eyes and hands to heaven," invoking the protection of the deity for the battles yet to come.

"God bless the United States of America, and let all the people say Amen." The crowd answered him, *"Amen."*

POSTSCRIPT

NOTES ON LIBERTY AND DEATH

The Revolution had no shortage of heroes. Some had proved their valor in politics, others on the battlefield. But some heroes were yet to be created. One Founding Father whose legend only grew over time was Patrick Henry—a man whose dynamic rhetoric and divine invocations borrowed much from the evangelists of the Great Awakening, and a leader who showed just how enduring the hallmarks of the Christian revival could be.

As a child of the Anglican faith, Henry grew up in a climate of New Light fervor. He witnessed the ministry of George Whitefield but was most taken with the passion and zeal of Samuel Davies. Davies, a Presbyterian minister, had brought the revival to Virginia as a missionary, saving thousands of souls for Christ. He later raised money for the College of New Jersey with Gilbert Tennent and served as its president. Henry saw Davies as "the greatest orator he ever heard" and learned from him a style of oratory that could provoke listeners to a state of excitement and uproar, and unite them in a cause blessed by God himself. By the mid-1770s, that cause was no longer evangelical rebirth, but revolution against Britain.

Henry became a well-known planter and lawyer, and an agitator for war with the mother country. His most famous oration was, of course, delivered to the Second Virginia Convention on March 23, 1775, forever known as the "Give me liberty or give me death!" speech. Yet before Henry finished his speech with that famous line, he invoked the Deity to bless the coming struggle for independence, with all the flair of a country revivalist: "There is a just God who presides over the destinies of nations; and who will raise up friends to fight our battles for us. . . . There is no retreat but in submission and slavery! Our chains are forged! Their clanking may be heard on the plains of Boston! The war is inevitable and let it come!"

The speech was calculated to be incendiary and went well beyond the style of Samuel Davies into rhetoric that was more familiar in the pulpits of Charles Chauncy and Jonathan Mayhew. As one historian wrote, "With its effective mixing of Revolutionary and biblical themes, the 'Liberty or Death' speech resembles the sermons of New England's 'Black Regiment.'" However, though Henry was without a doubt a stirring orator and a key figure in pushing Virginia toward war, no one knows what he actually said on that day in 1775.

None of Henry's revolutionary orations survive in print, and "Liberty or Death" was no different. Although the speech conveyed much of his renegade spirit—if anything he may have used language that was even more slashing against the Crown—it wasn't published until forty years after the revolution. And its author was William Wirt.

The enterprising lawyer Wirt was about to become attorney general in the James Monroe administration when he penned Sketches of the Life and Character of Patrick Henry in 1817. It had been a lengthy undertaking to cobble together the words of the famous Virginian from a variety of accounts, memories and anecdotes. For "Liberty or Death," Wirt relied heavily on the recollections of a lawyer named St. George Tucker, who claimed to have witnessed Henry in action and provided a report that detailed Henry's verbal flourishes and wizardry—almost four decades after the fact. Tucker doubtless invented many passages he attributed to Henry, and the speech became an object of contention among scholars in the years after Wirt published it. Nonetheless, the Sketches . . . of Patrick Henry had a singular effect on the Virginian's reputation, vaulting him from being one of several notable revolutionaries in Virginia to the preeminent orator of the new republic.

Patrick Henry became a totem of the evangelical style adapted to American politics. His jeremiad against the British—thick with Biblical allusion and threats against transgressors of native liberties—served to influence countless public figures in the nineteenth century. Thus, even in a distant echo, the firebrand populism of the Great Awakening electrified listeners once more, this time with God as part of the packaging instead of the core message. Politicians of the era invoked the Deity for purposes both noble and base, whether asking him to bless their public endeavors or issuing divine threats against their enemies or declaiming against conspiracies real and imagined.

This budding populism gave rise to one of the first third parties in U.S. history, and the first of any kind to hold a nominating convention. It was known as the Anti-Masonic Party, and in 1831, its presidential candidate was none other than William Wirt. The party was founded in reaction to the disappearance of a Freemason named William Morgan, who had threatened to expose the society's many secrets. With countless politicians and gentry linked to Masonry, the Anti-Masonic Party peddled fantastic tales of conspiracies and threats to American liberties at the hands of the organization, with a message that nakedly trafficked in fear and demagoguery. Wirt joined the fray in his letter to the nominating convention, writing that Masonry was "at war with the fundamental principles of the social compact, as treason against society, and a wicked conspiracy against the laws of God and of man which ought to be put down." However, despite his calumny against Masonry, Wirt was himself a former member, and later tried unsuccessfully to withdraw his name as a presidential candidate. In the election of 1832, he secured around 8% of the vote and won a single state—Vermont.

Though the Anti-Masons soon disappeared, their style of demagoguery endured. Ironically, the man who best showcased it was their enemy "Old Hickory" Andrew Jackson. The American general had parlayed military fame at the Battle of New Orleans and the Seminole War to national celebrity by the 1820s, and his defeat in the election of 1824—despite receiving a plurality of the vote—allowed him to chastise the victor John Quincy Adams as the recipient of a "corrupt bargain" that undermined democracy itself. Riding high on fears of political malfeasance, Jackson won the presidency four years later, and presented himself as a tribune of popular will who took on scheming elites and scoundrel politicians even as he showed many of the same flaws he denounced in others.

For two terms he infuriated his political opponents by dissolving the national banking system, creating a spoils system that rewarded friends with plum government jobs, and pushing the limits of presidential power beyond what law and tradition allowed. Jackson was a slaveholder who entrenched slavery in the U.S. economy, and tried to thwart the rise of abolition however he could. He was thin-skinned and bellicose, and his body carried bullets that had been fired into him from duelists he had faced. He used blunt and fearsome rhetoric against his opposers, arrogated authority to the executive branch, and even occasionally dismissed the power of federal courts to stop him. His critics said he behaved like a despotic monarch—"King Andrew I." Others were even less kind, and called him everything from a "roaring demagogue" to a "pocket-sized Paul Bunyan" to "a frontier bully." His actions against native peoples especially made him notorious, as he broke treaties protecting Native American land rights and oversaw "the forced relocation of the eastern Indians. . . . on a massive scale," resulting in atrocities like the Trail of Tears. Yet despite all the criticism, Old Hickory remained undaunted, and with each brash step he took to dominate the national agenda and crush his adversaries, he became only more popular—and he was reelected in 1832 in a landslide.

Future demagogues of the left and right would take Jackson's brand of populism and recast it for their own purposes: the Know-Nothings deploying it against immigrants and Catholics; the prairie populists against bankers, robber barons, and Wall Street; McCarthyites against liberal New Dealers; and Donald Trump and his supporters against immigrants and racial minorities. This style of politics proved to be remarkably elastic and adaptable for different eras and conditions, and it continues to surface whenever class inequality or status anxiety boils over, and opportunistic politicians feel secure that attacking economic and cultural elites will bring them popular notoriety, and ultimate success at the ballot box.

Beyond politics, the Great Awakening established a model for the growth of future evangelical movements. One such revival—the Second Great Awakening—borrowed from the original an emphasis on religion of the heart, enthusiasm in worship, and emotional transcendence over legalistic doctrine and ritual. It hit its peak from the 1820s to the 1840s and spread widely across the country, from upstate New York to the pioneer country of the West to the camp meetings of the South. Some compared it to a prairie fire; others called it "an expansion of religious feeling unknown in American history."

Like the first movement a century before, it drew on people's dissatisfaction with contemporary life, and their dislocation in a rapidly industrializing economy. With canals, steamboats and mercantile trade gradually turning America into a world power, many citizens saw the rural country of their youth disappearing in the shadow of great cities connected by train tracks and telegraph wires. Protestant revivalists answered their fears with a call to piety and devotion, and told them God could ease their worries and solve their problems. This time, however, strict theology and Calvinist dogma would play little role in the revival. Instead, evangelists told people they had the free will to accept Jesus Christ as their savior and be reborn in him—instead of the old, depressing idea that God might damn them no matter what they did.

What arose, then, was a unique form of homegrown American religion, inspired by the Great Awakening but departing from it in important ways. The Church of England was no longer a target—it had been reinvented as the Episcopal Church of America and now ordained its own homegrown bishops, without controversy. And instead of provoking chaos in the pews, this revival bolstered the power of ministers and grew evangelical churches by the tens of thousands, especially the Methodists and Baptists. Professional organizers and formal literature helped drive conversions, and the leaders of the revival understood that modern planning and organization would be as important to saving souls as melting hearts in Christ.

The greatest proponent of the Second Great Awakening was Charles Grandison Finney, who, for all his fervent evangelizing and Christian exhortations, might be called the era's own George Whitefield—except he was a Presbyterian, he encouraged the education of both black and women worshippers, he was president of what would become one of the most liberal schools in America, Oberlin College, and he fought vigorously against slavery. He even dismissed hoary Calvinism with his book on free will, *Sinners Bound to Change Their Own Hearts.*

The churches of professional ministers like Finney became bulwarks of the new faith, but the flames of revival could not be so easily contained within them. Through the tumult and economic trials of the 1830s, public dissatisfaction grew and spread, and new, more radical sects emerged like

Joseph Smith's Mormons and the Millerites of New York. The Mormons faced ridicule and violence in trying to establish their communities, while the Millerites embraced "chaos as the birthpangs of a new and perfect era" in predicting the end of the world—which their leader, William Miller, announced would occur in October 1844. The failure of his prophecy led to a "Great Disappointment," but it also inspired new apocalyptic sects that took advantage of the freedom of American religion to welcome God's inevitable destruction of the earth. (The Millerites also led to the growth of new denominations like the Seventh-Day Adventists.) At the same time, a counter-reaction to apocalyptic Christianity arose in utopian communities in the Northeast and Midwest, from New Harmony and Brook Farm to Hopedale and Oneida, with the promise of creating an ideal community under God with its own rules, beliefs and best practices for living.

Whether worshippers expected worldly doom or moral perfection, eventually the fracturing of faith inspired even smaller splinter sects, and consumed many of the established churches of the Second Great Awakening—just as it had the First. By the mid-1840s, the Presbyterian church once again split over the practices of revivalism, and then fractured again over slavery, as did the Methodists and Baptists. Other evangelical sects followed them in breaking into Northern and Southern branches.

As in so many aspects of American life, slavery became the touchstone for conflict in religion. But while most ministers of the original Awakening either apologized for or embraced human bondage, now the majority of those in the North condemned it as an affront to God and a stain upon the national character. They took their ideas not from slaveholders like George Whitefield and Jonathan Edwards, but from the radicals who had resisted slavery—the likes of Edwards's son Jonathan Jr. and Samuel Hopkins. In the eighteenth century, those ministers and their followers had taken proud and perilous stands against slavery, and often found themselves chastised for it. Yet over the decades their work, and those of black men and women who had experienced slavery like Obour Tanner, Bristol Yamma, and Phillis Wheatley, eventually triumphed in the Northern Christian revival.

Thus, the impact of the Great Awakening resonated well into the nineteenth century, though in strikingly different ways. On one hand, it created a model for populist upheaval, and a way for politicians to undermine and transform society on their own terms. On the other, it shaped religion as a powerful force of social change, in which radicals called for moral reform even if it led to turmoil.

The reformers had the most lasting impact. For them, "liberty or death" was not an either/or proposition. They knew that both often went hand in hand, and there could be no true human liberty as long as slavery degraded the ideal. They realized that demanding it could lead to the deaths of hundreds of thousands of their countrymen, in a harrowing new conflict fought on American soil. Yet when the Civil War came, they embraced it, as battlefield chaplains and missionaries. One of them, Indiana minister John Hight, even wrote of how *the flames and smoke surged amongst the burning buildings, like ocean waves, and struggled upward like a thousand banners in the sky. . . . How wondrous the judgments of an avenging God against the crime of slavery.* He and other evangelicals brought the fire of belief to the fire of the cannon, and gave holy sanction to the unholy practice of war, just as their predecessors had done nearly a century before at the violent birth of the new republic.

NOTES

INTRODUCTION

Note that 18th-century spelling, grammar, capitalization, and punctuation vary widely, and in quotations from primary sources, the author has harmonized discrepancies with modern usage. For example, George Whitefield's original line, "Young Men's Heads are ſtuff'd with Heathen Mythology, Chriſt or Chriſtianity is ſcarce ſo much as named amonſt them" is here rendered as "Young men's heads are stuffed with heathen mythology. Christ or Christianity is scarce so much as named amongst them." [Whitefield, *Fifth Journal*, 65] The intent is to provide greater readability at some expense of the antique flavor of the original text. All such sources are cited in the notes that follow.

p. xiv   "as the term has been used as an 'attack word' for hundreds of years"—J. Justin Gustainis, "Demagoguery and Political Rhetoric: A Review of the Literature" (*Rhetoric Society Quarterly* 20:2 (1990), 155). The author also provides an extensive list of examples of historical demagogues.

p. xvi   "In the Middle Colonies like Pennsylvania, New Jersey, and New York, there were too few clergymen"—Martin Lodge, "The Crisis of the Churches in the Middle Colonies, 1720–1750" (*The Pennsylvania Magazine of History and Biography* 95:2 (1971), 199–200).

p. xvi   "churches had become insular and hidebound, and delayed or denied admission to those"—Stephen Grossbart, "Seeking the Divine Favor: Conversion and Church Admission in Eastern Connecticut, 1711–1832" (*The William and Mary Quarterly*, 46:4 (1989), 731).

p. xvi   "American pastors had to fight and scrape for their income from skinflint congregations"—Lodge, "The Crisis of the Churches," 203, 204, 218; Richard

Bushman, *From Puritan to Yankee: Character and the Social Order in Connecticut, 1690–1765* (Cambridge, MA: Harvard Univ. Press, 1967), 155–158.

p. xvi   "Pastors were paid so little, they couldn't even provide for their families"—James Schmotter, "Ministerial Careers in Eighteenth-Century New England: The Social Context, 1700–1760" (*Journal of Social History* 9:2 (1975), 261).

p. xvii   "the pastors they did encounter typically delivered dry, airless sermons that argued the finer points of theology"—Lodge, "The Crisis of the Churches," 215–216.

p. xvii   "Organized religion seemed on the verge of collapse when the Great Awakening . . . rescued the floundering churches"—ibid., 198.

p. xvii   "Historian Joseph Tracy invented this term for the movement in 1842"—Jon Butler, "Enthusiasm Described and Decried: The Great Awakening as Interpretive Fiction" (*The Journal of American History* 69:2 (1982), 307).

p. xix   "he can rightly be labeled Anglo-America's first modern celebrity"—Harry Stout, "George Whitefield and Benjamin Franklin: Thoughts on a Peculiar Friendship" (*Proceedings of the Massachusetts Historical Society*, 3rd Series, 103 (1991), 10.

p. xxii   "'psychological earthquake' of the Great Awakening"—Bushman, *From Puritan to Yankee*, 187.

p. xxiii   "the Revolution was effected before the war commenced" to "This radical change in the principles, opinions, sentiments and affection of the people"—John Adams, Letter to Hezekiah Niles, February 13, 1818 (National Archives, Founders Online, accessed at founders.archives.gov/documents/Adams/99-02-02-6854).

CHAPTER 1: DISSECTING THE HEART

The starting point for any research on Benjamin Franklin is bound to be his *Autobiography* (reprinted for the Library of America; New York: Vintage, 1987), which not only covers this period in his late youth, but is an excellent source for his thoughts on George Whitefield, the printing business, and views of religion generally. Most other biographical sources minimize his relation to Whitefield, so good secondary sources include articles written by John R. Williams, "The Strange Case of Dr. Franklin and Mr. Whitefield" (*The Pennsylvania Magazine of History and Biography* 102:4 (1978), 399–421); and David T. Morgan, "A Most Unlikely Friendship—Benjamin Franklin and George Whitefield" (*The Historian*, 47:2 (1985), 208–218). Frank Lambert's excellent "Subscribing for Profits and Piety: The Friendship of Benjamin Franklin and George Whitefield" (*The William and Mary Quarterly* 50:3 (1993), 529–554) describes the mutual business interests of the two men in promoting the latter's revival tours; and Harry Stout's "George Whitefield and Benjamin Franklin: Thoughts on a Peculiar Friendship" (*Proceedings of the Massachusetts Historical Society*, 3rd Series, 103 (1991), 9–23) reviews their overlapping personal interests in the context of their respective faiths and public personas. Additional historical context is offered in Peter Charles Hoffer, *When Benjamin Franklin Met the Reverend Whitefield: Enlightenment, Revival, and the Power of the Printed Word* (Baltimore, MD: Johns Hopkins Univ. Press, 2011); and Leonard Labaree, ed., *The Papers of Benjamin Franklin, vol. 2, 1735–1744* (New Haven: Yale Univ. Press, 1960).

George Whitefield's *Journals* are essential to understanding the man and his ministry, though they exist in several forms. The most comprehensive is the complete set from 1738–1741 republished by Banner of Truth Trust (Carlisle, PA, 1960), in a handy single reference guide. However, these collected volumes are based on editions Whitefield "corrected" and bowdlerized more than a decade after they were written, largely to downplay his zeal and, critics would argue, arrogance in some of the entries. For a more accurate edition, the original seven journals in pamphlet form must be consulted. For this chapter, the crucial one is the fifth volume, titled *A Continuation of the Reverend Mr. Whitefield's Journal, from His Embarking After the Embargo, to His Arrival at Savannah in Georgia* (London: W. Strahan, 1740), which presents the minister's voyage to and initial travels in the New World in a full, unexpurgated narrative.

The Sermons of George Whitefield (Peabody, MA: Hendrickson Publishing, 2009) further illuminate his dramatic oratory on the stump, in this case "Abraham Offering Up His Son Isaac" (pp. 15–25). Contemporary interpretations of Whitefield range from adulatory to mildly dubious. In the former category, Arnold Dallmore, a Baptist preacher, devoted many years of his life to honoring Whitefield with the extensive, often uncritical *George Whitefield: The Life and Times of the Great Evangelist of the Eighteenth-Century Revival* (Carlisle, PA: Banner of Truth Trust, 1970). A more critical, though still laudatory, modern view is Thomas Kidd's *George Whitefield: America's Spiritual Founding Father* (New Haven: Yale Univ. Press, 2014), following on his excellent *The Great Awakening: The Roots of Evangelical Christianity in Colonial America* (New Haven: Yale Univ. Press, 2007). A shorter treatment of similar ideas is Jerome Dean Mahaffey's *The Accidental Revolutionary: George Whitefield and the Creation of America* (Waco, TX: Baylor Univ. Press, 2011).

Some of the most important research on Whitefield in recent decades has come from Harry Stout, who provides a comprehensive look at his performative aspects in *The Divine Dramatist: George Whitefield and the Rise of Modern Evangelicalism* (Grand Rapids, Mich.: Eerdmans Publishing, 1991), while in *The New England Soul: Preaching and Religious Culture in Colonial New England* (New York: Oxford Univ. Press, 1986), Stout offers a broad historical view of Whitefield and other itinerants in 18th-century society. Another scholar, Frank Lambert, depicts Whitefield's role in mass communications and popular culture in the colonial era, in *Inventing the "Great Awakening"* (Princeton, NJ: Princeton Univ. Press, 1999) and *"Pedlar in Divinity": George Whitefield and the Transatlantic Revivals, 1737–1770* (Princeton, NJ: Princeton Univ. Press, 1994), as well as his article, "'Pedlar in Divinity': George Whitefield and the Great Awakening, 1737–1745" (*The Journal of American History* 77:3 (1990), 812–837).

Other key studies that focus on related aspects of Whitefield include Jessica Parr, *Inventing George Whitefield: Race, Revivalism, and the Making of an American Icon* (Jackson, MI: Univ. Press of Mississippi, 2015); Nancy Ruttenburg, "George Whitefield, Spectacular Conversion, and the Rise of Democratic Personality" (*American Literary History* 5:3 (1993), 429–458); and Susan O'Brien, "A Transatlantic Community of Saints: The Great Awakening and the First Evangelical Network, 1735–1755" (*American Historical Review* 91:4 (1986), 811–832). For an incisive look at the Anglican counterreaction to Whitefield, see Gerald Goodwin, "The Anglican Reaction to the Great Awakening" (*Historical Magazine of the Protestant Episcopal Church* 35:4 (1966), 343–371).

For perspective on the difficulties facing ministers in colonial America, and the often antagonistic attitudes of their parishioners, see James Schmotter, "Ministerial Careers in Eighteenth-Century New England: The Social Context, 1700–1760" (*Journal of Social History* 9:2 (1975), 249–267); and Martin Lodge, "The Crisis of the Churches in the Middle Colonies, 1720–1750" in *Colonial America: Essays in Politics and Social Development*, 4th edition, ed. by Stanley Katz, et al. (New York: McGraw-Hill (1993), 581–604). The crises caused by ministerial itinerancy, which Whitefield exemplified, are explained in Timothy Hall, *Contested Boundaries: Itinerancy and the Reshaping of the Colonial American Religious World* (Durham, NC: Duke Univ. Press, 1994); and T. H. Breen and

Timothy Hall, "Structuring Provincial Imagination: The Rhetoric and Experience of Social Change in Eighteenth-Century New England" (*American Historical Review* 103:5 (1998), 1411–1439). A wider perspective on American religion is offered in Sydney Ahlstrom's magisterial *A Religious History of the American People* (New Haven: Yale Univ. Press, 1972), especially "Part III: A Century of Awakening and Revolution," pp. 261–384.

CHAPTER 1 REFERENCES:

p. 3   "20,000 people near Bristol"—Lambert, "Subscribing for Profits," 532.

p. 3   "80,000 in Hyde Park"—Stout, *Divine Dramatist*, 84.

p. 3   "table tops, open windows, courtyards, hills, wagons, and marketplaces"—Lambert, "Subscribing for Profits," 532.

p. 4   "He called his approach 'preaching without doors'"—Kidd, *America's Spiritual*, 65.

p. 4   "preached to upwards of a million Britons"—Stout, *Divine Dramatist*, 85.

p. 5   "Creator of the Universe" to "peculiar Doctrines"—Franklin, *Autobiography*, 78–79.

p. 5   "This was his 'bold and arduous project of arriving at moral Perfection'"—ibid., 79–81.

p. 5   "helped found one of the colonies' first subscription libraries and volunteer fire companies"—Daniel Gifford, "Was Benjamin Franklin the Father of American Philanthropy?" National Museum of American History, accessed at americanhistory .si.edu/blog/benjamin-franklin-philanthropy.

p. 5   "he faced real competition from Andrew Bradford"—Lambert, "Subscribing for Profits," 544.

p. 6   "He had also created a juggernaut with *Poor Richard's Almanack*"—Hoffer, *When Benjamin Franklin*, 35.

p. 7   "Whitefield had recently arranged for the publication of his sermons in serial form"—Lambert, "Subscribing for Profits," 534.

p. 7   "the evangelical publisher James Hutton had achieved a signal success"—Kidd, *America's Spiritual*, 52, 78.

p. 7   "transnational publicity network to advertise"—Hoffer, *When Benjamin Franklin*, 50–51.

p. 7   "Franklin had also put his hard-earned cash into ventures"—Lambert, "Subscribing for Profits," 536.

p. 8   "He would also be the primary publisher of Whitefield's journals, at prices five times that of the sermons"—ibid., 533–534.

p. 8   "delivered the sacrament to the ship's crew, and shared with them the spirit of Christ in a great 'love-feast'"—Whitefield, *Journal (Fifth)*, 16.

p. 8   "polluted, proud, and treacherous heart" to "at the remembrance of my sins"—ibid., 15–17.

p. 8   "remembrance of my humiliations" to "Amazing that the High and Lofty One"—ibid., 24–26.

p. 9   "Anglican churchmen called them 'young quacks' and fanatics"—Kidd, *America's Spiritual*, 63, 66.

p. 10   "Some parishioners might argue with their ministers over matters of long-held doctrine"—Schmotter, "Ministerial Careers," 257.

p. 10   "heaven for farmers, paradise for artisans"—quoted in Lodge, "Crisis of the Churches," 593n.

p. 10   "His friend William Seward had spread the word of his journey, writing hundreds, perhaps thousands of letters"—Lambert, "Pedlar in Divinity," 814–817.

p. 11   "As he climbed the steps of the courthouse on Market Street, he looked out on a crowd of 6,000 people"—Kidd, *America's Spiritual*, 89.

pp. 11–12   "Take now thy son" to "Adieu, adieu, my son"—Whitefield, *Sermons*, 17–21; Stout, *Divine Dramatist*, 93–94.

p. 12   "The angel of the Lord called unto him from heaven and said, 'Abraham, Abraham'" —Whitefield, *Sermons*, 21–22.

p. 13   "Faith and salvation were paramount, and no amount of questioning or equivocation could change that"—ibid., 24–25.

p. 13   "I computed that he might well be heard by more than thirty-thousand"—Franklin, *Autobiography*, 105.

p. 13   "it meant that Whitefield might well have drawn upwards of 25,000 people or more to his British sermons"—ibid.

p. 13   "Franklin made plans to publish twenty-four volumes of Whitefield's sermons in two volumes"—Williams, "The Strange Case," 404.

p. 14   "They claimed that with his soft features, effusive tears, and 'clear and musical voice,'"—Stout, *Divine Dramatist*, 95.

p. 14   "Hark! He talks of a sensible New Birth—then belike he is in labour"—Mahaffey, *Accidental Revolutionary*, 51.

p. 14   "the extraordinary influence of his oratory on his hearers"—Franklin, *Autobiography*, 102.

p. 15   "I esteemed the essentials of every religion, and being to be found in all the religions" —ibid., 78.

p. 15   "You know my house, if you can make shift with its scanty accommodations"—ibid., 104.

p. 15   "[T]he only people fit for such an enterprise, it was with families of broken shopkeepers"—ibid., 103.

p. 16   "his fellow Methodists John and Charles Wesley, who had come to Georgia several years before"—Kidd, *America's Spiritual*, 42–45.

p. 16   "everything from brass candlesticks, nails, duck and goose shot, to rugs and blankets, buttons and silk"—*Pennsylvania Gazette*, November 8, 1739, quoted in Franklin, *Papers* v.2, 241–242.

pp. 16–17   "I silently resolved he should get nothing from me" to "At any other time, Friend Hopkinson"—Franklin, *Autobiography*, 103–104.

p. 17   "old, grey-headed disciple and soldier of Jesus Christ"—Whitefield, *Journal (Fifth)*, 31.

p. 17   "the established Presbyterian Synod was as much an adversary to Tennent as the established Church of England"—Stout, *Divine Dramatist*, 102–103.

p. 18   "Though we are but few, and stand alone"—Whitefield, *Journal (Fifth)*, 31.

p. 18   "what God had done for our souls" to "The devil and carnal secure ministers"—ibid., 34–35.

pp. 18–19   "railing against the regular clergy" to "enthusiastically mad"—Goodwin, "Anglican Reaction," 358.

p. 19   "So when he came to ask Commissary William Vesey"—Parr, *Inventing George Whitefield*, 46–48.

p. 19   "He was nothing less than 'an open enemy to religion'"—Goodwin, "Anglican Reaction," 359.

p. 19   "What manner of spirit are the generality of the clergy possessed with?"—Whitefield, *Journal (Fifth)*, 37.

p. 20   "Itinerancy held bad stock with the authorities"—Hall, *Contested Boundaries*, 6–7.

p. 20   "he would tell the kids to 'go to Heaven without them!'"—Breen and Hall, "Structuring," 1428.

p. 20   "He spoke in a range of settings, from the grand Wall Street Presbyterian Church in New York"—Kidd, *America's Spiritual*, 91–94.

p. 21   "never before heard such a searching sermon" to "my soul was humbled"—Whitefield, *Journal (Fifth)*, 35.

CHAPTER 2: THE WAY TO IMPERIAL HEAVEN

George Whitefield has attracted much more scholarly interest in recent decades than Gilbert Tennent, perhaps unfairly. Tennent's contributions to the revival movements in colonial America are extensive, and still under-researched. One of the better attempts to explain Tennent, within the context of the European evangelical tradition, is Milton Coalter, Jr., *Gilbert Tennent: Son of Thunder: A Case Study of Continental Pietism's Impact on the First Great Awakening in the Middle Colonies* (Westport, CT: Presbyterian Historical Society, 1986). Coalter's book is one of the few book-length treatments of the New Brunswick preacher, but other valuable research can be found in Archibald Alexander, ed., *Biographical Sketches of the Founder, and Principal Alumni of the Log College* (Princeton, NJ: J. T. Robinson, 1845), which is the rare book to detail the lives and ministry of the father William Tennent and his sons; as well as articles by James Bennett, "'Love to Christ': Gilbert Tennent, Presbyterian Reunion, and a Sacramental Sermon" (*American Presbyterians* 71:2 (1993), 77–89), focusing on his later conciliatory approach; and Kristen Fischer, "'Religion Governed by Terror': A Deist Critique of Fearful Christianity in the Early American Republic" (*Revue Française d'Etudes Américaines* 125:3 (2010), 13–26), a look at the general theological style of preaching terror.

Many of Gilbert Tennent's sermons are extant, and through these we can get the best picture of him as a revivalist. Some of the most bracing imagery of sin and redemption can be found in *The Necessity of Religious Violence in Order to Obtain Durable Happiness* (New York: William Bradford, 1735) and especially *A Solemn Warning to the Secure World, from the God of Terrible Majesty, or, the Presumptuous Sinner Detected, His Pleas Considered, and His Doom Displayed* (Boston, 1735), whose title alone provides a capsule view of his theology.

For more on the Tennent family's relationship with, and conflicts within, the Presbyterian church—and the complex factions arrayed in that church—see Janet Fishburn, "Gilbert Tennent, Established Dissenter" (*Church History* 63:1 (1994), 31–49), covering his status as fomenter of trouble and later reconciler in the sect; Elizabeth Nybakken, "New Light on the Old Side: Irish Influences on Colonial Presbyterianism" (*Journal of American History* 68:4 (1982), 813–832), a comprehensive discussion on the alliances and conflicts within the factions; and Leonard Trinterud, *The Reforming of an American Tradition: A Reexamination of Colonial Presbyterianism* (Philadelphia: Westminster Press, 1949), still the best overall look at the subject.

George Whitefield's exploration of the South is detailed in the fifth of his journals, titled *A Continuation of the Reverend Mr. Whitefield's Journal . . .* (London: W. Strahan, 1740), which offers the clearest view of his checkered perspective on the region and the construction of his orphanage, as well as his growing number of conflicts with Anglican officials. A small portion of this chapter also includes reference to the sixth journal, *A Continuation of the Reverend Mr. Whitefield's Journal, After His Arrival at Georgia . . .* (London: W. Strahan, 1741). For a view on the content of Whitefield's preaching at the time, see *Sermons on Important Subjects* (London: Thomas Tegg, 1841), of which Sermon XLVII is the most important for this chapter.

Whitefield's feelings about his ministry in the context of the South are also detailed in *George Whitefield's Letters, 1734 to 1742*, republished by Banner of Truth Trust (Chatham, UK: 1976), from which the December 15, 1739, letter to Gilbert Tennent is excerpted. A separately published, and greatly controversial, letter was his anti-Tillotson missive, *A Letter from the Reverend Mr. Whitefield in Georgia, to a Friend in London, Showing the Fundamental Error of a Book Entitled, The Whole Duty of Man* (Charles Town, SC: Peter Timothy, 1740), later printed in London, New York, and Philadelphia.

David Morgan Jr. looks critically at this period in the minister's life in "The Consequences of George Whitefield's Ministry in the Carolinas and Georgia, 1739–1740" (*The Georgia Historical Quarterly* 55:1 (1971), 62–82) and in "George Whitefield and the Great Awakening in the Carolinas and Georgia, 1739–1740" (*The Georgia Historical Quarterly* 54:4 (1970), 517–539), while Richard Cox, in "Stephen Bordley, George Whitefield, and the Great Awakening in Maryland" (*Historical Magazine of the Protestant Episcopal Church* 46:3 (1977), 297–307), shows how provocative, and infuriating, the Grand Itinerant could be to those who didn't support his ministry.

Frank Lambert is the essential scholar for analyzing the communications and marketing strategies of Whitefield, as well as his press agent William Seward, in several key works: "The Great Awakening as Artifact: George Whitefield and the Construction of Intercolonial Revival, 1739–1745" (*Church History* 60:2 (1991), 223–246), and the books *Inventing the "Great Awakening"* and *"Pedlar in Divinity": George Whitefield and the Transatlantic Revivals, 1737–1770*. Similarly, Harry Stout discusses the theater of Whitefield's sermons, along with the theater of his conflicts with the church, in *The Divine Dramatist: George Whitefield and the Rise of Modern Evangelicalism*. Supplementary sources include Arnold Dallimore, *George Whitefield: The Life and Times of the Great Evangelist of the Eighteenth-Century Revival* and Thomas Kidd, *George Whitefield: America's Spiritual Founding Father*. Also valuable, especially for uncovering long-forgotten letters and esoterica about the preacher, is the classic by Luke Tyerman, *The Life of the Reverend George Whitefield* (London: Hodder and Stoughton, 1876).

Whitefield's complex relationship to slavery is laid out in Stephen Stein, "George Whitefield on Slavery: Some New Evidence" (*Church History* 42:2 (1973), 243–256), in which he acts as both proponent and antagonist of the inhuman practice, and in Jessica Parr, *Inventing George Whitefield: Race, Revivalism, and the Making of an American Icon*, which looks at his ministry through the lens of racial conflict in colonial America.

Ben Franklin's *Autobiography* is an essential source for the Founding Father, but is less helpful in detailing his business affairs and his contributions to the spread of evangelical Christianity. More information is available in Leonard Labaree, ed., *The Papers of Benjamin Franklin, vol. 2, 1735–1744*, though the best sources—aside from Franklin's own testimony—are in the earlier-mentioned John R. Williams, "The Strange Case of Dr. Franklin and Mr. Whitefield"; Frank Lambert, "Subscribing for Profits and Piety: The Friendship of Benjamin Franklin and George Whitefield"; and Harry Stout, "George Whitefield and Benjamin Franklin: Thoughts on a Peculiar Friendship."

Additional background information for this chapter is drawn from Timothy Hall, *Contested Boundaries: Itinerancy and the Reshaping of the Colonial American Religious World*, describing just how divisive the practice of itinerancy could be; Michael Crawford, *Seasons of Grace: Colonial New*

England's Revival Tradition in Its British Context (London: Oxford Univ. Press, 1991), comparing the American and British versions of Christian revival; and Bernard Bailyn, *The Ideological Origins of the American Revolution* (Cambridge, MA: Belknap Press, 1967), which describes the roots of the rebellious temperament reaching back into this era.

CHAPTER 2 REFERENCES:

p. 22   "a rousing sermon that left people weeping for nearly two hours"—Parr, *Inventing George Whitefield*, 48.

p. 22   "Members of some fifteen different sects watched him orate"—Kidd, *America's Spiritual*, 94.

p. 23   "In 1718 his father had brought him and his three brothers"—Coalter, *Son of Thunder*, 2–3.

p. 23   "Presbyterians and other nonconformists could not hold public office"—Nybakken, "New Light," 818.

p. 23   "the establishment of the Church of England was weak in the Middle Colonies" —Bailyn, *Ideological*, 248–249.

p. 24   "The leaders who vexed him came from the 'Old Side,' comprising Scottish and Irish immigrants"—Fishburn, "Established Dissenter," 34; Nybakken, "New Light," 821.

p. 24   "Built in the woods of Neshaminy, Pennsylvania"—Lambert, *Inventing the "Great Awakening,"* 59.

p. 24   "and to me it seemed to resemble the school of the old prophets"—Alexander, *Biographical Sketches*, 15.

p. 25   "His conviction of his sin, danger, and misery"—ibid., 129.

p. 25   "He had seen how the Old Siders repeatedly attacked and undermined the Log College"—Coalter, *Son of Thunder*, 48–52.

p. 25   "He had watched them try to thwart the ordination of his brother, Charles"—Fishburn, "Established Dissenter," 43.

p. 26   "no person became a true believer without first experiencing the terror"—Bennett, "Love to Christ," 78.

p. 26   "From the Dutch Reformed minister Theodorus Frelinghuysen"—ibid., 77.

p. 26   "Sluggish souls are overgrown with corruptions"—Tennent, *Necessity of Religious Violence*.

p. 26   "Would it not cause intolerable pain"—Tennent, *Solemn Warning*, 230.

p. 26   "But is it not still more dreadful"—ibid.

p. 27   "ignorance, negligence, self-love, inconsideration, pride"—Coalter, *Son of Thunder*, 44.

p. 27   "Men must be frightened out of hell with the law"—Crawford, *Seasons of Grace*, 86.

p. 27   "terrors first, comfort second"—Coalter, *Son of Thunder*, 45.

p. 28   "We have a description of the way to the Imperial Heaven"—Tennent, *Necessity of Religious Violence*.

p. 28   "They were important members of the Synod whom Gilbert was trying to convert" —Coalter, *Son of Thunder*, 62–64.

p. 29   "your sermons have much confirmed the truths of Christ"—Letter from Gilbert Tennent to George Whitefield, Dec. 1, 1739, quoted in Lambert, *Pedlar in Divinity*, 156.

p. 29   "I love and honor you in the bowels of Jesus Christ. You are seldom out of my thoughts"—George Whitefield to Gilbert Tennent, *Letters*, 138.

p. 30   "[H]is language is mean and groveling" to "he is a very wretched divine"—Cox, "Stephen Bordley," 304–307.

p. 30   "in these parts Satan seems to lead people captive at his will"—George Whitefield to Gilbert Tennent, *Letters*, 138.

p. 30   "Here there are no great towns"—ibid.

p. 30   "what an indifferent manner everything was carried on" to "I cried mightily to the Lord"—Whitefield, *Journal (Fifth)*, 72.

p. 30   "virtually no local or private life"—Stout, "Peculiar Friendship," 12.

p. 30   "And like other Methodist reformers, Whitefield felt uncomfortable"—Stout, *Divine Dramatist*, 157–158.

p. 31   "she would oversee the Georgia orphanage in his absence"—Kidd, *America's Spiritual*, 104.

p. 31   "how well pleased the devil was with every step she took" to "suffer them not to go on in such a carnal security"—Whitefield, *Journal (Fifth)*, 77.

p. 31   "Masters reigned over their bondsmen with depraved cruelty"—Parr, *Inventing George Whitefield*, 67.

p. 31   "Even worse in Whitefield's view was the lack of spiritual instruction"—Stein, "Whitefield on Slavery," 244.

p. 31   "he had argued slavery should be made legal"—Stout, *Divine Dramatist*, 61.

p. 32   "their other 'false and unscriptural' beliefs, which he criticized in his letters" —Whitefield, *Letters*, 140.

p. 32   "hut full of negroes" to "in great peril of our lives"—Whitefield, *Journal (Fifth)*, 78.

p. 32   "completing a journey on foot, on horseback, and by canoe over 1,200 miles"—Stout, *Divine Dramatist*, 99.

p. 32   "destitute and abandoned children could receive shelter and nourishment"—Kidd, *America's Spiritual*, 101–102.

p. 33   "He threatened to denounce the trustees publicly"—ibid.

p. 33   "In response, he provided a full list of contributors, but failed to break down" —Lambert, *Pedlar in Divinity*, 177–178.

p. 33   "They claimed he was little more than a merchandiser of religion, a 'retailer of trifles' and a 'pedlar of divinity'"—ibid., 179–180.

p. 33   "It often pleases me to reflect how Christ's kingdom is securely carried on in spite of men and devils"—Whitefield, *Letters*, 151.

p. 33   "I have not had much enlargement in preaching, since I have been here"—ibid., 150.

p. 34   "Our great men had much rather spend their money in a playhouse"—Whitefield, *The Great Duty of Charity Recommended*, quoted in *Sermons on Important Subjects*, 527.

p. 34   "Go on now, you rich men, weep and howl for your miseries that shall come upon you"—ibid., 528.

p. 34   "the planter Hugh Bryan had even told him the writings of the theologian John Tillotson"—Williams, "Strange Case," 408.

p. 34   "The local church in Charles Town, St. Philip's, had barred him from speaking" —Morgan, "George Whitefield and the Great Awakening," 525.

p. 35   "Dissent had begun openly breaking out in nonconforming pulpits"—ibid., 524.

p. 35   "killed twenty whites, and met defeat at the hands of the colonial militia"—Kidd, *America's Spiritual*, 98.

p. 35   "a good soldier of Jesus Christ"—Whitefield, *Journal (Second)*, 14.

p. 35   "conservative as Dr. Johnston [sic], as vehement as Swift"—Andrew T. Nelson, quoted in Morgan, "Consequences," 70.

p. 36   "an arrant jumble of contradiction" to "a warm, frantic, enthusiastic brain"—Morgan, "Consequences," 69.

p. 36   "his dismissal of Anglican protocol like following the Book of Common Prayer"—ibid., 67.

p. 36   "Garden threatened him with violations of canon law"—Whitefield, *Journal (Sixth)*, 11.

p. 36   "Get you out of my house"—ibid.

p. 37   "he devoted one-quarter of the column text to him"—Lambert, "Subscribing for Profits," 538.

p. 37   "with 2,500 volumes ordered in the colonies"—ibid., 541.

p. 38   "when his bias became too obvious, he was forced to deny the charges"—Williams, "Strange Case," 408.

p. 38   "he had rented the troupe's ballroom in advance and locked it"—Lambert, "Artifact," 236.

p. 38   "the performers' season had actually ended"—Williams, "Strange Case," 409.

p. 38   "the article is allowed to be literally true, yet by the manner of expression" —*Pennsylvania Gazette*, May 8, 1740, quoted in Franklin, *Papers* v.2, 258.

p. 38   "'books of piety and devotion' over secular tomes"—Lambert, "Subscribing for Profits," 539.

p. 39   "be willing to do the divine will, and you shall know it"—George Whitefield to Benjamin Franklin, *Letters*, 226.

p. 39   "pray for my conversion, but never had the satisfaction"—Franklin, *Autobiography*, 104.

p. 39   "Upon Whitefield's visits to Philadelphia, he would be a guest in Franklin's own home"—Stout, "Peculiar Friendship," 21.

p. 39   "Instead they applied to everyone, including many people so often ignored in holy discourses"—ibid., 20.

p. 40   "He owned several slaves in his early life and advertised them for sale in the *Gazette*" —"Benjamin Franklin Petitions Congress," Center for Legislative Archives, National Archives, accessed at www.archives.gov/legislative/features/franklin.

p. 40   "[Some slaves] have been, upon the most trifling provocation"—Tyerman, *Life of the Reverend*, 354.

p. 40   "slothful shepherds and dumb dogs"—ibid.

p. 40   "sold more copies to missionaries than any other volumes"—Lambert, "Artifact," 231.

p. 41   "have built their hopes of salvation on a false bottom" to "false divinity and fundamental errors"—Whitefield, *A Letter from the Reverend Mr. Whitefield*, 3–10.

p. 41   "knew no more of true Christianity than Mahomet"—*Pennsylvania Gazette*, April 10, 1740, quoted in Lambert, "Subscribing for Profits," 542–543.

p. 41   "no real Christian at heart"—Whitefield, *A Letter from the Reverend Mr. Whitefield*, 10.

p. 41   "I never knew any good to come from the meetings of priests"—Lambert, "Subscribing for Profits," 542–543.

p. 41   "admired Tillotson more than any other theologian"—Williams, "Strange Case," 408.

p. 41   "You may make what use you will of it"—Whitefield, *A Letter from the Reverend Mr. Whitefield*, 10.

p. 42   "Franklin gave the entire front page of the *Gazette* to the Tillotson attack"—Lambert, "Subscribing for Profits," 543.

CHAPTER 3: INCREDIBLE RHAPSODIES

Though literary scholars regard Jonathan Edwards's sermons as the prime examples of homiletic art in colonial America, the sermons of Gilbert Tennent were arguably more influential in inspiring what we now call the Great Awakening. Foremost among these is doubtless *The Danger of an Unconverted Ministry* (Philadelphia: Benjamin Franklin, 1740), a rhetorical blast that helped trigger the revival, along with Whitefield's ministry. Providing context for this event is Milton Coalter, Jr., *Gilbert Tennent: Son of Thunder: A Case Study of Continental Pietism's Impact on the First Great Awakening in the Middle Colonies*, and Charles Maxson, *The Great Awakening in the Middle Colonies* (Gloucester, MA.: Peter Smith, 1958). For additional material on the ministry of Gilbert Tennent, see *A Historical Sketch of the First Presbyterian Church in the City of New Brunswick* (New Brunswick, NJ: J. Terhune & Son, 1852). A rundown on the struggle between rival Presbyterian factions can be found in Elizabeth Nybakken, "New Light on the Old Side: Irish Influences on Colonial Presbyterianism."

For an overview of the mystical side of the Tennent family's beliefs, see Jon Butler, *Awash in a Sea of Faith: Christianizing the American People* (Cambridge, MA: Harvard Univ. Press, 1990), which provides a compelling take on the role of the supernatural in native religions; as does Douglas Winiarski, "Souls Filled with Ravishing Transport: Heavenly Visions and the Radical Awakening in New England" (*The William and Mary Quarterly* 61:1 (2004) 3–46). A more detailed view of the family's spirituality and cosmology is in Archibald Alexander, ed., *Biographical Sketches of the Founder, and Principal Alumni of the Log College*. Major sources for the narrative of William Tennent Jr. include Elias Boudinot, *Life of the Reverend William Tennent, Formerly Pastor of the Presbyterian Church at Freehold, New Jersey* (New York: Robert Carter, 1847), and Boudinot's complementary text, *Memoirs of the Life of the Reverend William Tennent* (Philadelphia: Freeman Scott, 1827). Archibald Alexander, in *Biographical Sketches*, also provides an overlapping account of William Tennent's deathly experience, though qualifies it as a product of rational science instead of supernatural faith. For more on the Tennent ally, James Davenport, see Harry Stout and Peter Onuf, "James Davenport and the Great Awakening in New London" (*Journal of American History* 70:3 (1983), 556–578), or Chapter 4 references for additional material.

The first major historical treatment of the Great Awakening, and one that still has value for its myriad anecdotes, letters, and observations, is Joseph Tracy's *The Great Awakening: A History of the Revival of Religion in the Time of Edwards and Whitefield* (Boston: Charles Tappan, 1845). Whitefield figures prominently in that volume, and even more so in Luke Tyerman's excellent *The Life of the Reverend George Whitefield*. Other previously mentioned treatments of the minister's life that provide a good overview of his period in his life include Frank Lambert, *"Pedlar in Divinity": George Whitefield and the Transatlantic Revivals, 1737–1770*; Harry Stout, *The Divine Dramatist: George Whitefield and the Rise of Modern Evangelicalism*; and Thomas Kidd, in both *George Whitefield: America's Spiritual Founding Father* and *The Great Awakening: The Roots of Evangelical Christianity in Colonial America*.

Still, the best way to understand Whitefield's ministry is to read his own, original views of it in the early editions of his *Journals*. For this chapter, the key volumes are the sixth journal, *A Continuation of the Reverend Mr. Whitefield's Journal, After His Arrival at Georgia . . .* , and the seventh, *A Continuation of the Reverend Mr. Whitefield's Journal, from a Few Days After His Return to Georgia to His Arrival in Falmouth* (London: W. Strahan, 1741). Both contain Whitefield's strong initial feelings about his experiences, before he revised such feelings to make them more hospitable in later editions. A good supplementary source is *George Whitefield's Letters, 1734 to 1742*, from Banner of Truth Trust. One key letter, from May 24, 1740, is his response to John Wesley's own Arminian leanings, which are well summarized in the groundbreaking sermon, *Free Grace* (London, 1740).

The Grand Itinerant's ongoing struggles with Anglican authorities are recounted in Gerald Goodwin, "The Anglican Reaction to the Great Awakening," and in the words of the commissaries themselves who excoriated him from the pulpit. One of the first such scoldings is Archibald Cummings's *Faith Absolutely Necessary but Not Sufficient to Salvation Without Good Works* (Philadelphia: Andrew Bradford, 1740). A more famous reproach is Alexander Garden's influential *Take Heed How Ye Hear* (Charles Town, 1740). A larger volume expressing the weight of the Commissary Garden's denunciation is *Six Letters to the Rev. Mr. George Whitefield, etc.* (Boston: T. Fleet, 1740), containing pamphlets, letters, and assorted missives obsessively deriding him.

Whitefield's Georgia orphanage was a controversial topic at the time he built it, and it inspired much debate in the Southern low-country. Some of these disputes are covered in David Morgan Jr., "The Consequences of George Whitefield's Ministry in the Carolinas and Georgia, 1739–1740," and in Neil O'Connell, "George Whitefield and the Bethesda Orphan-House" (*Georgia Historical Quarterly* 54:1 (1970), 41–62). Other perspectives on Whitefield's activities in the South include Frank Lambert, "'I Saw the Book Talk': Slave Readings of the First Great Awakening" (*Journal of Negro History* 77:4 (1992), 185–198), and Leigh Eric Schmidt, "'The Grand Prophet,' Hugh Bryan: Early Evangelicalism's Challenge to the Establishment and Slavery in the Colonial South" (*South Carolina Historical Magazine* 87:4 (1986), 238–250).

Supplemental and background sources for this period in the early Awakening include Sydney Ahlstrom, *A Religious History of the American People*, as well as Patricia Bonomi, *Under the Cope of Heaven: Religion, Society, and Politics in Colonial America* (New York: Oxford Univ. Press, 1986), and Edwin Gaustad and Leigh Eric Schmidt, *The Religious History of America: The Heart of the American Story from Colonial Times to Today* (New York: HarperCollins, 2002).

CHAPTER 3 REFERENCES:

p. 43   "fits of weeping and fainting, and experiencing 'unusual bodily motions'"—Maxson, *Great Awakening*, 55.

p. 43   "Nottingham was a test case . . . lacking a minister after the previous one had died" —Coalter, *Son of Thunder*, 64.

p. 44   "'New Testament prophet of Christ's coming,' not unlike John the Baptist."—Coalter, *Son of Thunder*, 121.

p. 44   "grief for the injuries that have been done to the Church of God"—Tennent, *Danger* sermon, 2.

p. 44   "An ungodly ministry is a great curse and judgment" to "heaps of Pharisee-teachers" —ibid., 3.

p. 44   " they might hold powerful offices, but 'they had no experience of the New Birth. O sad!'"—ibid., 6.

p. 44   "polished with wit and rhetoric" to "zeal, fidelity, peace, good order, and unity"—ibid., 9.

p. 45   "are cold and sapless, and as it were freeze between their lips"—ibid., 9–10.

p. 45   "our blessed Lord informs us that he came not to send peace on earth"—ibid., 25.

p. 45   "doubtlessly damnably wicked in their manner of performance"—ibid., 10.

p. 45   "While some are sincere servants of God, are not many servants of Satan"—ibid., 25.

p. 45   "Does not the spiritual man judge all things?" to "let those who live under the ministry of dead men"—ibid., 30–31.

p. 46   "But more damaging they thought was how he goaded parishioners to cause trouble in the pews"—Coalter, *Son of Thunder*, 66–67.

p. 46   "He had already adapted the style of George Whitefield"—Bonomi, *Under the Cope*, 144.

p. 46   "when Ben Franklin published it throughout the colonies"—ibid., 258, note 32.

p. 47   "Some of his allies had even erected for him a stage upon Society Hill"—Tyerman, *Life of the Reverend*, 372–373.

p. 47   "Depending on the day, 15,000 or even 20,000 worshippers came to hear him orate"—Kidd, *America's Spiritual*, 115; Whitefield, *Journal (Sixth)*, 20.

p. 47   "he looked to erect a school and housing for slaves"—Kidd, *America's Spiritual*, 110.

p. 47   "Through Andrew Bradford, he published a pamphlet"—Lambert, *Pedlar*, 174–175.

p. 47   "What wild, distracted notions are these?"—Cummings, *Faith* sermon, 10.

p. 48   "Such vile and slanderous invectives are crimes doubtless"—ibid., 13.

p. 48   "Some they have made stark mad"—ibid., 25–26.

p. 48   "Little do my enemies think what service they do me"—Whitefield, *Journal (Sixth)*, 26.

p. 48   "I do not despair of seeing people bring his works"—Whitefield, *Journal (Sixth)*, 19.

p. 48   "to whom the Philadelphia Synod had denied ordination"—Coalter, *Son of Thunder*, 57.

p. 49   "all of this emotional labor had done foul things to his health"—Whitefield, *Journal (Sixth)*, 27.

p. 49   "[c]ovetous, proud boasters, self-willed blasphemers"—Tyerman, *Life of the Reverend*, 381.

p. 49   "I abhor controversy and disputation" to "the more I am opposed, the more joy I feel"—ibid.

p. 50   "They saw divine intervention in their ministries"—Butler, *Awash*, 184.

p. 50   "imagined themselves as direct participants in an unfolding cosmic drama that was rapidly drawing to its apocalyptic close"—Winiarski, "Souls Filled," 39.

p. 50   "Critics called such behavior a sign of madness or, worse to Protestants, akin to the miracles"—Kidd, *America's Spiritual*, 73.

p. 50   "this Tennent was a more relaxed soul, quieter and more hospitable"—Boudinot, *William Tennent*, 113.

p. 50   "mellowed by a sense of the divine pity"—Maxson, *Great Awakening*, 32.

p. 50   "Whitefield took to him immediately, when William 'refreshed my heart'"—Whitefield, *Journal (Sixth)*, 30.

p. 50   "our hearts burn within us when we opened the Scriptures"—Whitefield, *Journal (Sixth)*, 34.

p. 51   "a pain in his breast, and a slight hectic" to "a walking skeleton"—Boudinot, *William Tennent*, 20.

p. 51   "the eyes being sunk, the lips discolored, and the whole body cold and stiff"—ibid., 22.

p. 51   "It is shameful to be feeding a lifeless corpse" to "who had been ridiculing the idea of restoring to life a dead body"—ibid., 23–24.

p. 51 "I saw an innumerable host of happy beings" to "This seemed like a sword through my heart"—ibid., 29–30.

p. 52 "a Pennsylvania couple had a dream he was endangered"—Butler, *Awash*, 184.

p. 52 "the injury was done by the prince of darkness"—Alexander, *Biographical Sketches*, 233–234.

p. 52 "the power of God was much manifested"—Whitefield, *Journal (Sixth)*, 34.

p. 53 "God has lately highly honored [him]"—ibid., 32.

p. 53 "Davenport spoke with a style few had ever seen: he shouted with abandon"—Stout and Onuf, "James Davenport," 568–570.

p. 53 "[He] is looked upon as an enthusiast and a madman"—Whitefield, *Journal (Sixth)*, 32.

p. 53 "I abhor the thoughts of it"—ibid., 37.

p. 54 "some worshippers 'seemed affected as those that are in fits'" to "most worthy preachers of our dear Lord Jesus"—ibid., 38–39.

p. 55 "thousands cried out, so that they almost drowned my voice" to "they seemed like persons awakened by the last trump"—ibid., 43–44.

p. 55 "A certain Reverend Francis Alison rose to challenge Whitefield"—Kidd, *America's Spiritual*, 117.

pp. 55–56 "I believe he was an enemy to God" to "asked God to grant him a humble heart" —Whitefield, *Journal (Sixth)*, 45–46.

p. 56 "Sometimes I think it best to stay here" to "I dread your coming over to America" —George Whitefield to John Wesley, *Letters*, 182.

p. 56 "The children are industrious. We have now in the house near one hundred yards of cloth"—Whitefield, *Journal (Sixth)*, 55.

p. 56 "weight of their sins" to "they are even now in frequent agonies"—ibid., 53–54.

p. 57 "not a moment of innocent recreation, though necessary to the health"—Morgan, "Consequences," 76.

p. 57 "he would neither give an account of his finances nor consult with the trustees' secretary"—O'Connell, "Bethesda Orphan-House," 51.

p. 57 "the orphanage was in the hands of a 'parcel of wild enthusiasts.'"—Schmidt, "Grand Prophet," 240.

p. 57 "Whitefield relied on him to aid the financing of Bethesda"—Lambert, "I Saw the Book Talk," 186.

p. 57 "raptures of joy from the rays of divine light and love"—Kidd, *Great Awakening*, 217.

p. 58 "had some infernal spirit been sent to draw my picture"—Whitefield, *Journal (Seventh)*, 6–7.

p. 58 "he compared him to social radicals like the Ranters"—Whitefield, *Journal (Seventh)*, 7; Garden, *Take Heed* sermon.

p. 58 "the reformation and correction of his manners and excesses"—court writ to Whitefield, quoted in Tracy, *Great Awakening*, 78.

p. 58 "Whitefield and his attorney duly appeared in court"—Morgan, "Consequences," 67–68.

p. 59 "an unregenerate man, an enemy to God, and of a like spirit"—Goodwin, "Anglican Reaction," 364.

p. 59 "since the gospel was not preached in the church"—Whitefield, *Journal (Seventh)*, 8.

p. 59   "Whitefield had respectfully written to him and another important cleric"—George Whitefield to Jonathan Edwards, *Letters*, 121; George Whitefield to Benjamin Colman, ibid., 120.

p. 60   "weeklies carried extensive coverage of the revival"—Lambert, "Pedlar in Divinity," 814.

p. 60   "fertile soil of heresy and schism"—Gaustad and Schmidt, *Religious History of America*, 70.

p. 60   "old-fashioned Congregationalists denounced as 'the sewer of New England'" —Ahlstrom, *Religious History*, 154.

p. 60   "looked like a good old Puritan, and gave me an idea"—Whitefield, *Journal (Seventh)*, 18.

p. 60   "as he 'perceived fresh emanations of divine light'"—ibid., 23.

p. 60   "Whitefield replied, 'I believed they were'"—ibid., 24–25.

p. 61   "4,000 people in Colman's own meetinghouse," etc.—ibid., 26.

p. 61   "roamed around the portable field pulpit at will"—Stout, *Divine Dramatist*, 119.

p. 61   "I felt much of the divine presence in my own soul" to "There was more of the presence of God through the whole visitation"—Whitefield, *Journal (Seventh)*, 26–27.

p. 62   "The Spirit of the Lord was upon them all" to "ragged and becoming extremely ill" —Kidd, *America's Spiritual*, 125.

p. 62   "many (especially women) were thrown down and trod upon"—Stout, *Divine Dramatist*, 1z19.

p. 62   "God was pleased to give me presence of mind" to "I gave notice I would immediately preach upon the Common"—Whitefield, *Journal (Seventh)*, 27.

CHAPTER 4: THE BURNING AND SHINING LIGHTS

Studies on Jonathan Mayhew have been infrequent in the literature, but several authors have endeavored to give the minister his proper respect in reference to his later importance in prerevolutionary America. Among them are Charles Akers, in *Called Unto Liberty* (Cambridge, MA: Harvard Univ. Press, 1964), which provides a thoughtful look at Mayhew's background, education and early interest in the New Birth, along with the more recent J. Patrick Mullins, *Father of Liberty: Jonathan Mayhew and the Principles of the American Revolution* (Lawrence, KS: Univ. of Kansas Press, 2017), a fine introduction to the minister that puts his accomplishments in historical context. Additional works mentioned in this chapter that relate to him include Clinton Rossiter, "The Life and Mind of Jonathan Mayhew" (*William and Mary Quarterly* 7:4 (1950), 531–558), a broad overview of his career, and Conrad Wright, *The Beginnings of Unitarianism in America* (Boston: Beacon Press, 1955), in which the author puts the theologian as a forerunner to that liberal denomination, which would see notable growth closer to the end of the eighteenth century.

The works of Jonathan Edwards are the best introduction to the reverend's thoughts on Calvinism, free will, predestination, and myriad other subjects. The list of his critiques, analyses, and sermons is lengthy, but for this chapter, two works are paramount. His *Faithful Narrative of the Surprising Work of God in the Conversion of Many Hundred Souls in Northampton* (London: John Oswald, 1737) is still the quintessential guide to the nature of revivals in the early Great Awakening. His direct and penetrating writing makes the volume much more worthwhile than similar accounts of the time. Also key are the *Copies of the Two Letters Cited by the Rev. Mr. Clap* (Boston: S. Kneeland and T. Green, 1745), which are valuable for his post-Awakening perspective on events that later proved to be controversial; Edwin Gaustad's "The Theological Effects of the Great Awakening in New England" (*Mississippi Valley Historical Review* 40:4 (1954), 681–706) places the Northampton revival in the context of the wider movement toward revival in the region, especially as it related to the religious philosophy of the time. The template for "preaching terrors"—for which Edwards would become particularly notable—was set early on by Edwards's grandfather, Solomon Stoddard. His sermon *The Efficacy of the Fear of Hell, to Restrain Men from Sin* codifies the importance of terrifying potential converts into a state of fear and despair, only after which they can accept God's grace.

For a look at Edwards's criticism of the economics and social inequality of New England, Mark Valeri's "The Economic Thought of Jonathan Edwards" (*Church History* 60:1 (1991), 37–54) is a penetrating overview that details his concerns over community welfare in an age of burgeoning capitalism. His jaded early view of George Whitefield appears in Ava Chamberlain, "The Grand Sower of the Seed: Jonathan Edwards's Critique of George Whitefield" (*New England Quarterly* 70:3 (1997), 368–385), a breakdown of his sermon that castigated Whitefield's ministry through metaphor, even as he offered full-throated support to the revival movement in general.

Alexander Garden did not need to use metaphor to condemn Whitefield, and his *Six Letters to the Rev. Mr. George Whitefield* is a bracing and nasty series of public missives that assign his nemesis to the lowest level of sinners. Not quite as vicious, *The Querists* was the Old Line Presbyterian faction's anonymous attempt to deride the Grand Itinerant's preaching. Whitefield's defenses along with those of his other allies are included in the comprehensive volume *Extract of Sundry Passages Taken Out of Mr. Whitefield's Printed Sermons, Journals and Letters*, etc. (Philadelphia: J. Oswald, 1741). Unfortunately, unlike the New Side Presbyterians, many Old Siders did not have a flair for drama or incisive writing, and these interrogations devolve into a ponderous lecture about Calvinist dogma and nitpicking about clerical vestments and the proper role of attorneys. For a full and detailed explanation of how Whitefield became enmeshed in such inter-Presbyterian conflicts, see Leonard Trinterud's excellent *The Forming of an American Tradition: A Re-Examination of Colonial Presbyterianism* (Philadelphia: Westminster Press, 1949).

George Whitefield's own *Journals*, of course, provide a good look at the last phase of his second trip to America. The seventh volume, *A Continuation of the Reverend Mr. Whitefield's Journal, from a Few Days After His Return to Georgia to His Arrival in Falmouth*, is most useful here, as are his various *Letters* in the Banner of Truth Trust edition mentioned earlier. Other, modern perspectives on the Itinerant include Harry Stout's *Divine Dramatist*, for its lively narrative about his travels and sermonizing; Thomas Kidd's *George Whitefield: America's Spiritual Founding Father*, for its diligent research into its subject's tumultuous history; and Arnold Dallmore's *George Whitefield: The Life and Times of the Great Evangelist of the Eighteenth-Century Revival*, for its comprehensive, if occasionally too reverent, perspective on his ministry. David Morgan Jr. focuses on Whitefield's orphanage work and conflicts with Alexander Garden in both "The Consequences of George Whitefield's Ministry in the Carolinas and Georgia, 1739–1740" and "George Whitefield and the Great Awakening in the Carolinas and Georgia, 1739–1740."

George Whitefield attracted numerous up-and-coming revivalists toward his entourage, and the most notable of these turned up in Basking Ridge, New Jersey. The rise of Daniel Rogers, the former tutor who became a popular revivalist, is described in Thomas Kidd's "Daniel Rogers' Egalitarian Great Awakening" (*Journal of the Historical Society* 7:1 (2007), 111–135), a good introduction to the young minister's life. Studies of the much more controversial James Davenport are perhaps fewer than there should be, but among the most relevant are Harry Stout and Peter Onuf, "James Davenport and the Great Awakening in New London," which details the troubled rise of the Long Island preacher, and Robert Cray, Jr., "James Davenport's Post-Bonfire Ministry, 1743–1757" (*The Historian* 59:1 (1996), 59–73), which provides reference to his early career as well. In South Carolina, Hugh Bryan became quite notable after Whitefield led his conversion, and some of his exploits are discussed in Harvey Jackson, "Hugh Bryan and the Evangelical Movement in Colonial South Carolina" (*William and Mary Quarterly* 43:4 (1986), 594–614). A good complementary work, already cited, is Leigh Eric Schmidt, "'The Grand Prophet,' Hugh Bryan: Early Evangelicalism's Challenge to the Establishment and Slavery in the Colonial South." The last rising evangelist mentioned in the chapter is Andrew Croswell, whose *Answer to the Rev. Mr. Garden's First Three Letters to the Rev. Mr. Whitefield* (Boston: S. Kneeland and T. Green, 1741) helped to promote him as a defender of Whitefield and established an early marker for growing anti-Anglican sentiment in America.

General overviews of the early Great Awakening also inform the narrative of this chapter. The most important of these are the previously cited Nancy Ruttenburg, "George Whitefield, Spectacular Conversion, and the Rise of Democratic Personality"; Edwin Gaustad, "The Theological Effects of the Great Awakening in New England"; Thomas Kidd, *The Great Awakening: The Roots of Evangelical Christianity in Colonial America*; Frank Lambert, *Inventing the "Great Awakening"*; and Sydney Ahlstrom, *A Religious History of the American People*. Other key works include Erik Seeman, *Pious Persuasions: Laity and Clergy in Eighteenth-Century New England* (Baltimore, MD: Johns Hopkins Univ. Press, 1999), a useful study for analyzing that often-fraught relationship at the time; Edmund Morgan, *The Gentle Puritan: A Life of Ezra Stiles, 1727–1795* (New York: W. W. Norton, 1962), which provides a contrasting view of the Great Awakening from a traditionalist minister; and Alan Heimert, *Religion and the American Mind: From the Great Awakening to the Revolution* (Cambridge, MA: Harvard Univ. Press, 1966), the signature volume that began the debate over whether the Great Awakening led to the American Revolution. Heimert attests that it did, and provides compelling evidence for it, though that evidence is also selective, which makes his book as controversial today as when it came out more than a half-century ago.

CHAPTER 4 REFERENCES:

p. 63   "the chief college for training up the sons of the prophets in all New England" —Whitefield, *Journal (Seventh)*, 28.

pp. 63–64 "The Holy Spirit melted many hearts" to "its library contained numerous 'Bad Books'"—ibid., 29.

p. 64   "the great majority had been penned by authors whose orthodoxy was above reproach"—Wright, *Unitarianism*, 57.

p. 64   "they only enhanced his popularity on the revival circuit"—Stout, *Divine Dramatist*, 121.

p. 65   "he had to ask the General Court to grant him title to unappropriated lands"—Akers, *Liberty*, 21.

p. 65   "their ancestor Thomas Mayhew had used his business and political acumen to secure title to an obscure island"—ibid., 5–6.

p. 65   "He even composed a psalter that translated books of the Bible into Native languages"—ibid., 9–10.

p. 65   "Harvard granted him a Master of Arts—one of the first honorary degrees it ever awarded"—Rossiter, "Life and Mind," 533.

p. 66   "Jonathan had to ask for grants and jobs from the college to make ends meet"—Akers, *Liberty*, 26.

p. 66   "The same sons of the elite who wanted to use their Harvard education as a stepping stone"—ibid., 31.

p. 66   "extravagances and errors of a weak and warm imagination"—ibid., 32.

p. 66   "As for the universities . . . I believe it may be said, their light is become darkness" —Whitefield, *Journal (Seventh)*, 55.

p. 67   "he contracted a high fever from a dangerous illness"—Mullins, *Father of Liberty*, 25.

p. 67   "Comfort me with apples, slay me with flagons, for I am sick of love" to "May our souls be more and more enflamed with the love of Christ"—Akers, *Liberty*, 33–34.

p. 67   "He tried to convert his brother Zachariah to the cause, but found little success" —Mullins, *Father of Liberty*, 25.

p. 67   "'miserable enthusiast' laboring 'under the power of Satanical delusions'"—Akers, *Liberty*, 35–37.

p. 67   "The tutors and faculty and president of Harvard, too, became bitter"—Wright, *Unitarianism*, 64.

p. 67   "young, poorly educated, heedless of ecclesiastical order, intolerant"—Akers, *Liberty*, 37.

p. 68   "with an irresistible power bearing down all opposition!"—Ruttenburg, "Spectacular Conversion," 454.

p. 68   "Religion had become rigid and institutional"—Gaustad, "Theological Effects," 682.

p. 68   "no cause for anxiety nor any hindrance to social respectability"—ibid.

p. 69   "Under his grandfather's tutelage, he had graduated from Yale College at seventeen" —Lambert, *Inventing the "Great Awakening,"* 62.

p. 69   "The appearance of every thing was altered"—Ahlstrom, *Religious History*, 299.

p. 69   "farmers and merchants who had found material success reveled in their decadence" —Heimert, *American Mind*, 33.

p. 69   "a 'commercial frenzy' caused men to lust after wealth and consumer goods"—ibid.

p. 70   "Edwards saw Britain, in particular, as the root of 'wickedness of almost every kind'" —ibid., 34.

p. 70   "cease to any way be beneficial members to human society"—Valeri, "Economic Thought," 42.

p. 70   "behave 'like wolves one to another,' for "beastly lusts"—ibid.

p. 70   "Edwards used the skill he had acquired from his grandfather to speak vividly to his congregants"—Morgan, *Gentle Puritan*, 24.

p. 70   "seemed almost like a flash of lightning, upon the hearts of young people"—Edwards, *Faithful Narrative*, 21.

p. 71   "estimated that three hundred souls had been saved through God's mercy"—ibid., 32.

p. 71   "Later in the year, the revival traveled through the Connecticut River Valley" —Ahlstrom, *Religious History*, 283.

p. 71   "especially the Rev. William Tennent [Jr.]" to "very considerable revival of religion in another place"—Edwards, *Faithful Narrative*, 30–31.

p. 71   "It touched men and women equally, young and old, white and black, poor and rich" —Kidd, *Great Awakening*, 19.

p. 71   "Hell exploded in terror and sinners burned in everlasting torture"—Edwards, *Faithful Narrative*, 82.

p. 71   "They seemed like the work of the Holy Spirit, but their extravagance troubled him" to "teach persons the difference between what is spiritual and what is merely imaginary" —ibid., 81–82.

p. 72   "Some readers thought the events he described would lead to a new reformation" —Lambert, *Inventing the "Great Awakening,"* 11.

p. 72   "it is a great damp to that joy to consider how we decline"—ibid., 80.

p. 72   "rather go to Sodom and preach to the men of Sodom, than preach to you" —Chamberlain, "Grand Sower," 374.

p. 72   "people of God have complained of deadness and losing their first love" to "were filled, as it were, with new wine"—Whitefield, *Journal (Seventh)*, 45–46.

p. 73   "become fervent, as a flame of fire in my work"—Kidd, *America's Spiritual*, 128.

p. 73   "seeing him initially as 'weak in body' but later appreciating the reverend's full heart" —Whitefield, *Journal (Seventh)*, 45.

p. 73   "he would be pleased to send me a daughter of Abraham as my wife"—ibid., 46.

p. 73   "the bane of the Christian church" to "I think he is much to be blamed for endeavoring to prove"—ibid., 48.

p. 74   "I thought Mr. Whitefield liked me not so well, for my opposing these things" —Edwards, *Two Letters*, 2–3.

p. 74   "Some people with pious reputations claimed they were divinely guided"—Edwards, *Faithful Narrative*, 110–111.

pp. 74–75 "Satan seemed to be more let loose, and raged in a dreadful manner" to "as if somebody had spoken to them, *Cut your own throat*"—ibid., 109.

p. 75   "he decided to slash his throat and perish, rather than face any more agonizing fears" —Seeman, *Pious Persuasions*, 156.

p. 75   "the Spirit of God not long after this time, appeared very sensibly withdrawing" —Edwards, *Faithful Narrative*, 110–111.

p. 75   "produce not genuine convictions of conscience but greater hardness of heart" —Chamberlain, "Grand Sower," 374–75.

p. 75   "leaving it up to others (like Edwards) to carry the revival forward"—ibid., 381–82.

p. 75   "may shed a great many tears and yet be wholly ignorant" to "air of sincerity and fervency"—ibid., 378–379.

p. 75   "almost ready to follow the preacher to the ends of the earth"—ibid., 380.

p. 76   "he managed to deliver 175 sermons—nearly four a day"—Stout, *Divine Dramatist*, 132.

p. 76   "exceeds all other provinces in America, and, for the establishment of religion" —Whitefield, *Journal (Seventh)*, 54.

p. 76   "Garden called him a poor theologian and a rabid enthusiast"—Parr, *Inventing George Whitefield*, 54–57.

p. 76   "In your mountebank way you have David-like, as you fancy, slain your Goliath" —Dallmore, *Life and Times*, 84.

p. 76   "a medley of truth and falsehood, sense and nonsense"—Morgan, "Consequences," 68–69.

p. 76   "looked upon Whitefield no longer as an Anglican cleric, but as a cohort of the Log College men"—Trinterud, *American Tradition*, 94.

p. 76   "They picked apart his *Journals* for every error and deviation from orthodoxy they could find"—*Querists*, 23–34.

p. 77   "I think it no dishonor to retract some expressions"—Whitefield, quoted in *Querists*, 38.

p. 77   "like a mighty rushing wind, and carried all before it"—Whitefield, *Journal (Seventh)*, 57.

pp. 77–78 "divine manifestations flowed in so fast" to "God has remarkably revealed himself to my soul"—ibid.

p. 78   "with such joy in the Holy Ghost as I never experienced before"—Kidd, "Daniel Rogers," 114.

p. 78   "my dear brother [James] Davenport from Long Island"—Whitefield, *Journal (Seventh)*, 56.

p. 78   "gesticulating aggressively and distorting his body wildly"—Cray, "Post-Bonfire Ministry," 62.

p. 78   "Another of his techniques was to split his parishioners into groups"—Stout and Onuf, "James Davenport," 566.

p. 78   "Gilbert Tennent thought highly of Davenport"—Cray, "Post-Bonfire Ministry," 62.

p. 79   "people cried out in the crowd and broke down in tears"—Whitefield, *Journal (Seventh)*, 60.

p. 79   "as though his little heart would break"—ibid.

p. 79   "He is come! He is come!" and "I have found him!" to "weeping, sighing, groaning, sobbing, screeching, crying out"—Kidd, "Daniel Rogers," 115.

p. 79   "May I follow him as he does Christ. . . . [He is] our Mouth to God"—Whitefield, *Journal (Seventh)*, 60, 63.

p. 79   "he will be a burning and a shining light"—Whitefield, *Journal (Seventh)*, 63.

p. 80   "to blow up the divine fire" to "the welfare of dear Boston people, especially the welfare of your own soul"—Whitefield, *Letters*, 221.

p. 80   "Whitefield encountered several people who had accepted Christ into their hearts after hearing his preaching"—Whitefield, *Journal (Seventh)*, 68.

p. 80   "there the devil would fain have persuaded her to cut the child's throat with a pair of scissors"—ibid., 69.

p. 80   "in a very declining and piteous state" to " in the midst of life we are in death"—ibid., 77–78.

p. 80   "a fire on November 18 had wiped out three hundred houses and a fair amount of the town's material infrastructure"—Morgan, "George Whitefield and the Great Awakening," 531; Jackson, "Hugh Bryan," 601.

p. 81   "I endeavored to show what were the sins which provoked God"—Whitefield, *Journal (Seventh)*, 76.

p. 81   "Dissenting minister Josiah Smith preached a sermon"—Morgan, "Consequences," 72.

p. 81   "with more severe strokes of his displeasure"—Jackson, "Hugh Bryan," 62.

p. 81   "Alexander Garden condemned it as a 'scurrilous libel'"—Schmidt, "Grand Prophet," 240.

p. 81   "a false, malicious, scandalous, and infamous libel against the clergy"—Jackson, "Hugh Bryan," 603.

p. 82   "He charged the 'men in authority' with 'the heinous sin of abusing the power'"—Whitefield, *Journal (Seventh)*, 81.

p. 82   "God of the sea and the dry land [to] be with us on our voyage"—ibid., 83.

p. 82   "accused the commissary of being a 'meritmonger' and a liar"—Croswell, *Answer to the Rev. Mr. Garden*, 50–53.

p. 82   "[T]he AMERICANS live in a freer air, more generally taste the sweets of liberty"—ibid., 58.

CHAPTER 5: THE CREATURE IN THE EGG

The subject of the first section of this chapter, Sarah Haggar, became Sarah Wheaten upon marriage to her first husband, and under her remarried name wrote *Memoirs of the Life of Sarah Osborn*, later edited by Rev. Samuel Hopkins (Worcester, MA: Leonard Worcester, 1799). It's an engrossing statement of faith and perseverance in difficult times, of which there were many for her during the Great Awakening. A recent modern analysis of Osborn's life and writings comes to us by way of Catherine Brekus, whose *Sarah Osborn's World: The Rise of Evangelical Christianity in Early America* (New Haven, CT: Yale Univ. Press, 2013) provides context for the fervent revivalism that she and her peers experienced. It's also one of the better discussions of what the Great Awakening meant for poor and working-class women of the era. For additional research on women's struggles and opportunities in Osborn's hometown in mid-18th century America, see Christina Hodge, "Widow Pratt's World of Goods: Implications of Consumer Choice in Colonial Newport, Rhode Island" (*Early American Studies* 8:2 (2010), 217–234). Gary Nash offers further context on the economic and social crises of New England in the same era, which would later have an explosive effect, in *The Urban Crucible: Social Change, Political Consciousness, and the Origins of the American Revolution* (Cambridge, MA: Harvard Univ. Press, 1979).

Gilbert Tennent's tour of Boston and New England is one of the signature moments of the revival movement. However, he left very little in the way of written documentation of his travels, and most of what we know about them comes from letters, journals, and reports from those who witnessed him (as noted in the sources that follow). His core message is reflected in the sermon *The Righteousness of the Scribes and Pharisees Considered* (Boston: J. Draper, 1741), in which he drew from the Book of Matthew to excoriate New Englanders for their sins; also see his earlier *A Solemn Warning to the Secure World, from the God of Terrible Majesty*. Subsequent research and perspective on his preaching derive from Leonard Trinterud, *The Forming of an American Tradition: A Re-Examination of Colonial Presbyterianism* (Philadelphia: Westminster Press, 1949), still the best and most authoritative examination of the trials of the Presbyterian Church during the revival era. Supplementary sources include those previously mentioned, including Milton Coalter, Jr., *Gilbert Tennent: Son of Thunder: A Case Study of Continental Pietism's Impact on the First Great Awakening in the Middle Colonies*, one of the few monographs on Tennent's ministry; Charles Maxson, *The Great Awakening in the Middle Colonies*, an excellent overview of the tumult in the church; and Patricia Bonomi, *Under the Cope of Heaven: Religion, Society, and Politics in Colonial America*, discussing the nexus of those three combustible elements.

The schism in the Presbyterian Church, of which Gilbert Tennent was both cause and object, is detailed in the works above, but primary sources are also critical to understanding the legislative schemes and machinations of both sides. Much of this can be found in the Synod and presbytery annals from *The Records of the Presbyterian Church of the United States of America* (Philadelphia: Presbyterian Board of Publication, 1904), which despite its name mostly covers the colonial era from 1706–1788, in voluminous pages of reports, minutes, and embedded documents. The most important of these found in that source is the Protestation of Robert Cross (entered June 1, 1741), which forced the revivalists out of the church on shaky theological and legal grounds. For additional data on the breach, see the *Donegal Presbytery Minutes*, vol. 1 (Presbyterian Historical Society (1930), 253-258), and for biographical information on the putative cause of the rupture, Alexander Craighead, see his family's autobiography, written by Rev. James Craighead, *The Craighead Family: A Genealogical Memoir* . . . (Philadelphia: [privately printed], 1876).

The radical period of the Great Awakening begins in earnest in mid-1741 after Gilbert Tennent's tour of New England and intensifies through the following two years. Some of the better sources that describe the "enthusiasm" and frenzy the revival unleashed at the time include David Lovejoy, *Religious Enthusiasm in the New World: Heresy to Revolution* (Cambridge, MA: Harvard Univ. Press, 1985), which puts such behavior in the context of related Protestant uprisings from 17th-century Puritans to later Quakers; Douglas Winiarski, *Darkness Falls on the Land of Light: Experiencing Religious Awakenings in Eighteenth-Century New England* (Chapel Hill, NC: Univ. of North Carolina Press, 2017), a compendium of personal testaments of religious revival and social upheaval, and the best grassroots look at the Great Awakening; the previously noted Timothy Hall, *Contested Boundaries: Itinerancy and the Reshaping of the Colonial American Religious World*, a look at the threat to the social hierarchy itinerant evangelizing presented to the colonies; and Eugene White, "Decline of the Great Awakening in New England" (*New England Quarterly* 24:1 (1951), 35–52), depicting how the more extreme elements of the revival ended up coopting it and undercutting its reputation among more moderate elements of society. For a look at nascent ideas of abolition, and the rigid defenses of slavery within the church, see Kenneth Minkema and Harry Stout, "The Edwardsean Tradition and the Anti-Slavery Debate, 1740–1865" (*Journal of American History* 92:1 (2005), 47–74).

Most of the aforementioned sources also include information on the radical ministry of Andrew Croswell, but for a more detailed monograph on the pastor's doings, see Leigh Eric Schmidt, "'A Second and Glorious Reformation': The New Light Extremism of Andrew Croswell" (*William and Mary Quarterly* 43:2 (1986), 214–244), or any of his writings of the era, of which *Answer to the Rev. Mr. Garden's First Three Letters to the Rev. Mr. Whitefield* (Boston: S. Kneeland and T. Green, 1741) is the most colorful in its invective. Croswell's close ally, James Davenport, is only mentioned incidentally in this chapter, but for an overview see the earlier cited "James Davenport and the Great Awakening in New London" by Harry Stout and Peter Onuf. For a look at Tennent, Davenport, and Croswell's radical ideas of education in a revival ministry, see Richard Warch, "The Shepherd's Tent: Education and Enthusiasm in the Great Awakening" (*American Quarterly* 30:2 (1978), 177–198).

Other research on the period derives from sources that examine the structural, ecclesiastical, and social underpinnings of the Great Awakening. The most important of these are W. R. Ward, *The Protestant Evangelical Awakening* (Cambridge, UK: Cambridge Univ. Press, 1992), which also examines the parallel to British and European revival movements; Sydney Ahlstrom, *A Religious History of the American People*, and Edwin Gaustad and Leigh Eric Schmidt, *The Religious History of America: The Heart of the American Story from Colonial Times to Today*, two comprehensive perspectives on the spiritual changes that marked the era; and Thomas Kidd, *The Great Awakening: The Roots of Evangelical Christianity in Colonial America*, one of the most well-researched volumes on that epoch.

CHAPTER 5 REFERENCES:

p. 87 "some times revived, and sometimes sunk, and dejected"—Osborn, *Memoirs*, 43.

p. 87 "Rheumatism made her hands ache terribly"—Brekus, *Sarah Osborn's World*, 91.

p. 88 "She worked as a schoolteacher and housekeeper, but the money was always meager"—Brekus, *Sarah Osborn's World*, 1–4, 89.

p. 88 "a busy harbor, prosperous merchants, and prodigious wealth built on the shipbuilding industry and the transatlantic slave trade"—Minkema and Stout, "Edwardsean Tradition," 26; Nash, *Urban Crucible*, 182.

p. 88 "Although some women became clerks and shopkeepers"—Hodge, "Widow Pratt," 221.

p. 88 "She described her simple pleasures of playing cards with friends"—Brekus, *Sarah Osborn's World*, 120.

p. 88 "She knew friends who had been raised as Quakers"—ibid., 24.

p. 89 "God in mercy sent his dear servant Whitefield here"—Osborn, *Memoirs*, 43.

p. 89 "He delivered his sermons with blunt and angry words"—White, "Decline of the Great Awakening," 36.

p. 89 "I questioned the truth of all I had experienced"—Osborn, *Memoirs*, 43.

p. 89 "whom Whitefield had called 'a good old Puritan'"—Whitefield, *Journal (Seventh)*, 18.

p. 89 "My sins, from my cradle, were ranked in order before my eyes"—Osborn, *Memoirs*, 21.

p. 89 "singing songs, dancing, and foolish jesting"—ibid., 45.

p. 90 "very dark and melancholy circumstances"—ibid., 47.

p. 90 "I like your experiences well. They seem to me to be scriptural and encouraging"—Letter from Gilbert Tennent to Sarah Wheaten, quoted in Osborn, *Memoirs*, 48.

p. 90 "though they have played the harlot with many lovers"—ibid., 48.

p. 90 "After this my business failed" to "was persuaded God would point out some way for me"—ibid., 50.

p. 90 "The price of wheat reached an all-time high"—Nash, *Urban Crucible*, 112–114, 174.

p. 90 "If they ended up in penury, they might be put to labor in a workhouse"—ibid., 125–26.

p. 91 "Native New Englanders worried over the waves of Scots-Irish and Germans"—ibid., 103–4.

p. 91 "epidemics of diphtheria and malaria raged"—Lockwood, "Birth, Illness and Death," 112, 124 n5.

p. 91 "the death rate recently exceeded the birth rate in Boston"—Nash, *Urban Crucible*, 104.

p. 91 "most of the 3,500 men recruited from Massachusetts to fight for the Crown"—ibid., 169–172.

p. 91 "He spent three months in the region traveling from major cities like Boston"—Trinterud, *Forming*, 101.

p. 91 "He arrived at dissenting meetinghouses with little advance notice"—Coalter, *Son of Thunder*, 74.

p. 92 "You needn't boast of your dead hypocritical faith"—Tennent, *Righteousness*, 15.

p. 92 "the simplicity and power of the religion of Christ"—ibid., 4.

p. 92 "but he claimed that this was really a sign of God's anger—not his favor"—Tennent, *Solemn Warning*, 34–35.

p. 92 "their prosperity lifts them up" to "Are ye rich? Cursed are ye in the city and in the field"—ibid., 176, 190.

p. 92 "What will your good parentage avail you, unless you walk in the steps"—Tennent, *Righteousness*, 7.

p. 92 "the most awful awakening sermon I think I ever heard"—Kidd, *Great Awakening*, 96.

p. 92 "Many parishioners felt the same or greater agony of body and spirit"—White, "Decline of the Great Awakening," 37.

p. 93 "his words found special appeal at Yale"—Trinterud, *Forming*, 101.

p. 93 "a self-righteous, self-ruined wretch . . . who deserved hell"—Kidd, *Great Awakening*, 96–97.

p. 93 "he saw more converts in a week than he had in a career's worth of preaching"—Tyerman, *Life of the Reverend*, 424–25.

p. 93 "boys and girls, young men and women, Indians and Negroes"—ibid.

p. 93 "a monster! Impudent and noisy, and told them all they were *damned, damned, damned!*"—White, "Decline of the Great Awakening," 37.

p. 93 "his groundbreaking *Danger of an Unconverted Ministry* sermon appeared in print for the first time in New England"—Warch, "Shepherd's Tent," 179.

p. 94 "stone-blind and stone-dead" to "plain evidences of experimental religion"—Tennent, *Danger* sermon, 13, 16.

p. 94 "150 New England towns including Boston became swept up in his revival"—Ahlstrom, *Religious History*, 286.

p. 94 "observers noticing outbreaks of piety in the streets"—Tyerman, *Life of the Reverend*, 425.

p. 94 "spelled doom for the Congregational monopoly in New England"—Gaustad and Schmidt, *Religious History*, 61.

p. 94 "[m]ultitudes were awakened, and several had received great consolation"—Kidd, *Great Awakening*, 99.

p. 94 "the first clergyman who preached west of the Susquehanna [River]"—Craighead, *Craighead Family*, 42.

p. 95 "they made the woods ring, most sweetly singing and praising God"—ibid.

p. 95 "throngs of listeners heard him declaim against his enemies on the court"—Trinterud, *Forming*, 100.

p. 95 "accusing them by name of whoremongering, drinking excessively, lying and breaking the Sabbath"—Bonomi, *Under the Cope*, 148.

p. 95 "in the most scurrilous and opprobrious terms"—ibid.

p. 95 "The judges now accused Craighead of slander and incitement"—Trinterud, *Forming*, 100.

p. 95 "The mayhem then spread throughout the area"—Bonomi, *Under the Cope*, 149.

p. 95 "The Synod had already struck a blow the year before"—Trinterud, *Forming*, 97.

p. 96 "wounded and grieved at our very hearts, at the dreadful divisions"—Protestation, quoted in *Records of the Presbyterian Church*, 157.

p. 96 "the doctrines of the New Side men were heretical"—Maxson, *Great Awakening*, 79.

p. 96 "They pronounced them 'guilty of schism'"—Protestation, quoted in *Records of the Presbyterian Church*, 158.

p. 96 "The Old Side had taken a controversial, possibly illegal action"—Trinterud, *Forming*, 107.

p. 96   "It was an act of 'supreme disorder'"—Maxson, *Great Awakening*, 74.

p. 96   "He quickly organized two new, independent presbyteries"—Coalter, *Son of Thunder*, 84–85.

p. 96   "It was a misfit bunch upon which to build a new sect"—Trinterud, *Forming*, 110–12.

p. 97   "Others facing more resistance jettisoned their parish entirely"—Maxson, *Great Awakening*, 78–79.

p. 97   "The revivalists also surged into regions where no ministers had been ordained"—ibid., 76–77.

p. 98   "turbulence, shattered and divided congregations, and a rash of slanderous reports" —Bonomi, *Under the Cope*, 147–48.

p. 98   "wild rabble" to "'social leveling' threatened to collapse the hierarchy"—ibid.

p. 99   "But who were the *best men* now that so many in this new church were women"—Hall, *Contested Boundaries*, 56–59.

p. 99   "multitudes in the gospel net"—ibid., 73.

p. 99   "filled their converts with 'contempt of their betters' and pitted 'husbands against wives . . .'"—Lovejoy, *Religious Enthusiasm*, 196.

p. 99   "Every low-bred, illiterate person can resolve cases of conscience"—Nash, *Urban Crucible*, 215–216.

p. 99   "demanding that the New Side adopt the Solemn League and Covenant" to "independent Covenanters movement"—Coalter, *Son of Thunder*, 93.

p. 100   "encouraged New Side parishioners to leave their pastors"—Ward, *Protestant Evangelical*, 273.

p. 100   "he claimed sin could be expiated by 'the body's fermentation in the grave'" —Trinterud, *Forming*, 115.

p. 100   "Jesus Christ fights for the Moravian brethren"—Kidd, *America's Spiritual*, 161.

p. 100   "Whereupon the holy man, in the fear of the Lord, deflowered her"—Kidd, *Great Awakening*, 92.

p. 101   "In some meetinghouses they popped up and occupied the deacon's seat"—Hall, *Contested Boundaries*, 53.

p. 101   "Frequently these 'guests' interrupted the proceedings"—White, "Decline of the Great Awakening," 37.

p. 102   "for ignorant young converts to take upon them authoritatively" to "rise up and crush the enthusiastic creature in the egg"—Coalter, *Son of Thunder*, 94.

p. 102   "His first acquaintance with the New Birth came in the mid-1730s"—Schmidt, "New Light Extremism," 217.

p. 103   "enemies to the work of God"—Warch, "Shepherd's Tent," 180.

p. 103   "an education aboard a British warship was better than that of a New England college"—ibid.

p. 103   "He compared him to a 'zealous lady' overcome with the Holy Spirit" to "a harvest indeed for Romish missionaries!"—Kidd, *Great Awakening*, 121.

p. 103   "Over a little more than a week, the brash and unbridled evangelizer converted thirty-eight people"—Schmidt, "New Light Extremism," 218.

p. 104   "my former objections against singing were presently sung away"—ibid.

p. 104   "the great city Nineveh" to "breeding up exhorters"—ibid., 218–219.

p. 104   "I doubt not, but if you were to die tonight, three-quarters of you would be damned to Hell"—Winiarski, *Darkness Falls*, 148.

p. 104   "a man may live in all the commandments and ordinances" to "old, grey-headed sinners"—ibid., 149.

p. 104   "the fervors and frenzies of this teacher had answerable effects"—Kidd, *Great Awakening*, 139.

p. 105   "everyone delivering the yell he was particularly inspired with"—ibid.

p. 105   "God hates every one of you, as he does the devils and damned spirits in Hell"—Winiarski, *Darkness Falls*, 149.

p. 105   "Some of them followed Croswell to Charlestown, Massachusetts"—Kidd, *Great Awakening*, 139.

p. 105   "he condemned the abusive treatment of prisoners and the horrors of slavery"—Nash, *Urban Crucible*, 211.

p. 105   "Croswell repeated his performance with the added touch of stripping off his shirt"—Hall, *Contested Boundaries*, 53.

p. 105   "by the quart or tankard" to "red-hot comets"—Schmidt, "New Light Extremism," 221.

CHAPTER 6: ANIMAL SPIRITS

The most important volume for the study of Ben Franklin's life and business at the climax of the Great Awakening is undoubtedly Leonard Labaree, ed., *The Papers of Benjamin Franklin, vol. 2, 1735–1744*, which details his letters, transactions, proposals, and selections from *Poor Richard's Almanack*, as well as valuable excerpts from the *Pennsylvania Gazette*. Related first-person testimony from Franklin is available in his *Autobiography*, though it was published well after the events described in the chapter. Useful secondary sources include Frank Lambert, "Subscribing for Profits and Piety: The Friendship of Benjamin Franklin and George Whitefield"; David T. Morgan, "A Most Unlikely Friendship—Benjamin Franklin and George Whitefield" (*The Historian* 47:2 (1985)); and Edmund Morgan, *Benjamin Franklin* (New Haven, CT: Yale Univ. Press, 2002), the best short biography of the man and more insightful than many of the longer, more contemporary volumes.

Franklin's dealings with the Presbyterian Church, especially its established ministers, were often fraught, and some of this history is revealed in Leonard Labaree, "Franklin and the Presbyterians," (*Journal of the Presbyterian Historical Society* 35:4 (1957) 217–227). Valuable primary sources that offer a look into Franklin's frustrations with the church leadership, and underscore his freethinking views, include his "Dialogue Between Two Presbyterians," April 10, 1735 (in Leonard Labaree, ed., *The Papers of Benjamin Franklin, vol. 2*), and *A Defense of the Rev. Mr. Hemphill's Observations: or, an Answer to the Vindication of the Reverend Commission* (Philadelphia: B. Franklin, 1735). For useful background information on the trial of Rev. Hemphill and the lingering fallout of the episode, see Merton A. Christensen, "Franklin on the Hemphill Trial: Deism Versus Presbyterian Orthodoxy" (*The William and Mary Quarterly*, 10:3 (1953) 422–440), and William Barker, "The Hemphill Case, Benjamin Franklin and Subscription to the Westminster Confession" (*American Presbyterians* 69:4 (1991) 243–256). Jacquelyn C. Miller illuminates Franklin's ambivalent but often supportive relation to the Society of Friends in "Franklin and Friends: Benjamin Franklin's Ties to Quakers and Quakerism" (*Pennsylvania History: A Journal of Mid-Atlantic Studies* 57:4 (1990) 318–336).

The thoughts and philosophy of Jonathan Edwards are best analyzed from the reverend's own pen, and his voluminous works provide ample opportunity to study him from a variety of angles.

The requisite starting point for many is his sermon *Sinners in the Hands of an Angry God* (Boston: S. Kneeland and T. Green, 1741), which continues to draw significant commentary and interpretation nearly three centuries later. Some of the better analysis includes Christopher Lukasik, "Feeling the Force of Certainty: The Divine Science, Newtonianism, and Jonathan Edwards's 'Sinners in the Hands of an Angry God'" (*The New England Quarterly* 73:2 (2000) 222–245), and Edward J. Gallagher, "'Sinners in the Hands of an Angry God': Some Unfinished Business" (*The New England Quarterly*, 73:2 (2000) 202–221). Edwards's explanation of the revival, and apology for some of its excesses, is the centerpiece of his *Distinguishing Marks of a Work of the Spirit of God* (Boston: S. Kneeland and T. Green, 1741), which anticipates some of the criticism his adversaries would later launch against religious enthusiasm and his qualified defense of it.

An even more influential work, though written several years after the events in the chapter, is *A Treatise Concerning Religious Affections, in Three Parts* (Philadelphia: James Crissy, 1821), originally published in 1746. It lays out many of the arguments Edwards used to draw an emotional response from his listeners and is still greatly influential among some evangelical communities in the U.S. Helpful background material on the reverend and this essential period in the history of his ministry include Mark Valeri, "The Economic Thought of Jonathan Edwards"; and the biographies by George Marsden, *Jonathan Edwards: A Life* (New Haven, CT: Yale Univ. Press, 2003), and Philip Gura, *Jonathan Edwards: America's Evangelical* (New York: Hill and Wang, 2005).

In contrast to Edwards, Gilbert Tennent begins to fade from public attention and controversy after the peak of the revival. His tumultuous history, both among his fellow New Side evangelicals and the factions in the Presbyterian Church, is laid out in Milton Coalter, Jr., *Gilbert Tennent: Son of Thunder: A Case Study of Continental Pietism's Impact on the First Great Awakening in the Middle Colonies*, as well as the previously mentioned Janet Fishburn, "Gilbert Tennent, Established Dissenter," which reveals some of the paradoxes in his character and his ultimate refuge among the moderates after his days as a radical came to an end. One key sermon that illustrates Tennent's turn to a more conservative approach is *The Necessity of Holding Fast the Truth* (Boston: S. Kneeland and T. Green, 1743), which contains some of his most damning criticism against the Moravian sect and others who incurred his displeasure. For a look at the back-and-forth controversy over Tennent's contradictory statements, see the anonymously scribed *The Examiner; or, Gilbert Against Tennent* (Boston: John Hancock, 1743). In response, Tennent lays out a somewhat unconvincing defense in *The Examiner, Examined; or, Gilbert Tennent, Harmonious* (Philadelphia: William Bradford, 1743). Worthwhile supplementary material on the minister can be found in Frederick Brink, "Gilbert Tennent, Dynamic Preacher" (*Journal of the Presbyterian Historical Society* 32:2 (1954) 91–107).

Other research on Gilbert Tennent that illustrates his challenges after the revival met firm opposition in 1742 includes Eugene White, "Decline of the Great Awakening in New England"; and Richard Webster, *A History of the Presbyterian Church in America, from Its Origin Until the Year 1760* (Philadelphia: Joseph Wilson, 1857). Perhaps the most aggressive attack on Tennent, Whitefield, and the other revivalists during the Great Awakening is Charles Chauncy, *Seasonable Thoughts on the State of Religion in New-England* (Boston: Rogers and Fowle, 1743), which figures more prominently in Chapter 7.

The ministry of James Davenport was and continues to be one of the most contentious aspects of the revival. Since the reverend has relatively few modern defenders—and scant support even among writers of the 1740s whose work has survived—readers should examine stories of his frenzied performances with a critical eye. Still, even with extra attention to the veracity of source material, there's little doubt Davenport at his height was either mentally disturbed or a reckless agitator or both. Some of the best sources on his ministry include the previously mentioned Harry Stout and Peter Onuf, "James Davenport and the Great Awakening in New London"; Robert Cray, Jr., "James Davenport's Post-Bonfire Ministry, 1743–1757"; and Richard Warch, "The Shepherd's Tent: Education and Enthusiasm in the Great Awakening." The turmoil at Yale College, which he exacerbated and profited from, is further detailed in Norman Pettit, "Prelude to Mission: Brainerd's Expulsion from Yale" (*The New England Quarterly* 59:1 (1986) 28–50), and Franklin Bowditch Dexter, *Biographical Sketches of the Graduates of Yale College, with Annals of the College History, October, 1701–May, 1745* (New York: Henry Holt & Co., 1885).

Davenport's role in the wider social and religious changes of the era has attracted much scholarship, both as a harbinger of sectarian individualism and a sign of coming political revolution. For various perspectives on these subjects, see C. C. Goen, *Revivalism and Separatism in New England, 1740–1800: Strict Congregationalists and Separate Baptists in the Great Awakening* (New Haven, CT: Yale Univ. Press, 1962), an excellent source for the rising Separatist sects following the revival; Richard Bushman, *From Puritan to Yankee: Character and the Social Order in Connecticut, 1690–1765* (Cambridge, MA: Harvard Univ. Press, 1967), examining such changes in the rural landscape of Connecticut; and Joseph Tracy, *The Great Awakening: A History of the Revival of Religion in the Time of Edwards and Whitefield*, which contains numerous excerpts from personal testimonies and reactions to Davenport during the era. Authors Patricia Bonomi, in *Under the Cope of Heaven: Religion, Society, and Politics in Colonial America*, and Gary Nash, in *The Urban Crucible: Social Change, Political Consciousness, and the Origins of the American Revolution*, provide a contemporary view of how the Great Awakening's effects echoed among social classes and threatened the hierarchy of colonial order.

Finally, for valuable background information on the changes brought to America at the height of the revival, see Edmund Morgan, *The Gentle Puritan: A Life of Ezra Stiles, 1727–1795*, a biography of a strong critic of the New Lights; as well as Frank Lambert, *Inventing the "Great Awakening"* and Thomas Kidd, *The Great Awakening: The Roots of Evangelical Christianity in Colonial America*.

CHAPTER 6 REFERENCES:

p. 108   "the alteration in the face of religion here is altogether surprising"—*Pennsylvania Gazette*, quoted in Franklin, *Papers* v.2, 287.

p. 108   "His printing house now sold volumes on the life of Whitefield"—Lambert, "Subscribing for Profits," 542.

p. 108   "great variety of Bibles, Testaments, Psalters, spelling books, primers, hornbooks. . . ." —Advertisement in *Pennsylvania Gazette*, May 20, 1742, quoted in Franklin, *Papers* v.2, 361.

p. 108   "One third of everything he printed in the early 1740s concerned the evangelical revival."—Labaree, "Franklin and the Presbyterians," 224.

p. 108   "He printed a *Querists III* pamphlet attacking Gilbert Tennent"—Franklin, *Papers* v.2, 314n.

p. 108   "Gilbert passed on the offer because the pamphlet was 'stuffed with satire and burlesque.'"—Letter from Gilbert Tennent to Benjamin Franklin, September 22, 1741, quoted in Franklin, *Papers* v.2, 314.

p. 108   "In 1741 alone he published forty-six books and pamphlets on the revival"—Lambert, "Subscribing for Profits," 544.

p. 109   "payback for earlier years when Bradford had been postmaster"—Franklin, *Papers* v.2, 275n.

p. 109   "rules of honor and the laws of humanity"—ibid., 275–281.

p. 109   "Among the divines there has been much debate"—*Poor Richard's Almanack*, quoted in Franklin, *Papers* v.2, 338.

p. 110   "in his younger days in Boston, he had ceased going to services on Sunday"—Labaree, "Franklin and the Presbyterians," 219.

p. 110   "became skeptical of organized religion and instead embraced teachings that would later be labeled 'Deist.'"—D. Morgan, "A Most Unlikely Friendship," 213.

p. 110   "he would make public charity the guiding principle of his life"—E. Morgan, *Benjamin Franklin*, 24.

p. 110   "served principally to divide us and make us unfriendly to one another"—Stout, "Peculiar Friendship," 16.

p. 110   "morality or virtue is the end, faith only a means to obtain that end"—Franklin, "Dialogue," in *Papers* v.2, 33.

p. 110   "delivered with a good voice, and apparently extempore, most excellent discourses"—Franklin, *Autobiography*, 95–96.

p. 111   "unqualified for any future exercise of his ministry within our bounds"—Barker, "Hemphill Case," 248.

p. 111   "teaching of a religion based on the law of nature"—ibid., 250.

p. 111   "a virtuous heretic shall be saved before a wicked Christian"—Franklin, "Dialogue," in *Papers* v.2, 33.

p. 111   "Asses are grave and dull Animals"—Franklin, "Defense of Rev. Mr. Hemphill."

p. 112   "even became a trustee in charge of the New Building, since he belonged to no sect"—E. Morgan, *Benjamin Franklin*, 59.

p. 112   "Many of Franklin's closest friends were Quakers"—Miller, "Franklin and Friends," 320.

p. 112   "While he was not a subscriber to their doctrine of the 'inner light'"—ibid., 322.

p. 112   "Franklin found it difficult to accept that such a divine figure could ever be actively involved in his life"—Stout, "Peculiar Friendship," 20.

p. 112   "though the general government of the universe is well administered"—ibid., 21.

p. 113   "proportion of mankind consists of weak and ignorant men and women"—Miller, "Franklin and Friends," 321.

p. 113   "In the winter the failure of the local currency exchange caused economic panic"—*Pennsylvania Gazette*, January 8, 1741, quoted in Franklin, *Papers* v.2, 316.

p. 113   "In May a biblical-style plague of 'black worms or caterpillars' emerged from the earth"—*Pennsylvania Gazette*, May 27, 1742, quoted in Franklin, *Papers* v.2, 361.

p. 113   "During an October election, a crowd of up to eighty sailors attacked magistrates and constables"—*Pennsylvania Gazette*, October 7, 1742, quoted in Franklin, *Papers* v.2, 363–364.

p. 114   "he repeatedly denounced the practice of theft—not only simple larceny and fraud"—Valeri, "Economic Thought," 48–49.

p. 114   "creating 'national calamities' that fed injustice and 'threatens us with ruin'"—ibid., 47, 49.

p. 114   "God oftentimes gives those men that he hates great outward prosperity"—ibid., 52.

p. 115   "Edwards felt some resentment at the effect he achieved: his theatrics, his impromptu passions"—Lukasik, "Feeling the Force," 232–233.

p. 115   "employing a rhythmic structure that repeated and reinforced his points"—Gallagher, "Unfinished Business," 219–220.

p. 115   "Newtonian physical gravity could reflect God's own emphasis on moral gravity" —Lukasik, "Feeling the Force," 223, 228.

p. 115   "any lively and vigorous exercise of the will or inclination of the soul"—Edwards, *Religious Affections*, pt.1, 4.

p. 115   "the pit is prepared, the fire is made ready, the furnace is now hot"—Edwards, *Sinners* sermon, 7.

p. 116   "Your wickedness makes you as it were heavy as lead"—ibid., 12.

p. 116   "mere pleasure . . . keeps the arrow one moment from being made drunk with your blood"—ibid., 14.

p. 116   "he held the sinner in his hands like one might hold a spider—dangling by a thin thread over the chasm of hell"—ibid., 15–16.

p. 116   "greatest earthly potentates" to "bear the dreadful wrath of that God that is now angry with you every day"—ibid., 19, 24.

p. 116   "The wrath of the almighty GOD is now undoubtedly hanging over [a] great part of this congregation"—ibid., 25.

p. 116   "The congregants did not literally run for their lives, but they did fill the church with great weeping and moaning"—Kidd, *Great Awakening*, 104–105; Gallagher, "Unfinished Business," 219.

p. 116   "It also considerably advanced his name, as America's leading theologian"—Lukasik, "Feeling the Force," 234.

p. 117   "In recent months the college had become a battleground between New and Old Light students"—Pettit, "Prelude to Mission," 34.

p. 117   "roaring that thousands of persons roasting in the devil's kitchen"—White, "Decline of the Great Awakening," 40.

p. 117   "some praying, some exhorting and terrifying. Some singing, some screaming, some crying, some laughing"—Stout and Onuf, "James Davenport," 569.

p. 117   "His ancestor John Davenport was the town's cofounder and its first pastor"—Tracy, *Great Awakening*, 237.

p. 117   "James himself had graduated from Yale at the top of his class"—Dexter, *Biographical Sketches*, 447.

p. 118   "dead of heart, a blind leader of the blind" and a "wolf in sheep's clothing" —E. Morgan, *Gentle Puritan*, 32; Kidd, *Great Awakening*, 118.

p. 118   "no student could say 'the rector, either of the trustees or tutors are hypocrites, carnal or unconverted men'"—Pettit, "Prelude to Mission," 34–35.

p. 118   "He called the outbreaks of untamed emotion strange and unusual"—Edwards, *Distinguishing Marks*, 5.

p. 118   "tears, trembling, groans, loud outcries, agonies of body, or the failing of bodily strength"—ibid., 9.

p. 118   "'extraordinary effects on persons' bodies' occurred in the midst of spiritual conversions"—ibid., 14–15.

p. 119   "Grace dwells with so much corruption, and the new man and the old man subsist together"—ibid., 33.

p. 119   "during the reign of Oliver Cromwell in England when 'vital religion' held sway"—ibid., 37.

p. 119   "For it was an extraordinary event 'from the Spirit of God'"—ibid., 62.

p. 119   "more striking than what occurred six years before at Northampton"—ibid., 78.

p. 119   "Davenport's antics and Edwards's sermons empowered the radical students"—Pettit, "Prelude to Mission," 35–36.

p. 120   "In this atmosphere, the authorities found it impossible to contain the disruptions"—Warch, "Shepherd's Tent," 184.

p. 120   "They called it the Shepherd's Tent, and Allen set up classes on the second story of a convert's house"—ibid., 183.

p. 120   "Davenport brought his donations back to New London and funneled them into his 'Nursery of True Converts'"—ibid., 185–86.

p. 120   "All the applicants had to do was to pass a rigorous screening process to weed out the unconverted"—Stout and Onuf, "James Davenport," 571.

p. 120   "Young male and female revivalists prayed together"—Warch, "Shepherd's Tent," 187–188.

p. 120   "Critics decried New Light schools like Davenport's as 'castles or colleges in the air'"—Stout and Onuf, "James Davenport," 571–572.

p. 120   "The Shepherd's Tent represented a real threat to the legitimacy of classical education"—Warch, "Shepherd's Tent," 187.

p. 120   "Davenport already encouraged black and white, men and women, poor and rich, Indian and colonist"—Cray, "Post-Bonfire Ministry," 62.

p. 121   "By the fall of 1742, it had moved on to Rhode Island and attracted ever more attention"—Warch, "Shepherd's Tent," 187–88.

p. 121   "With Davenport he could only watch helplessly as the Long Island minister committed acts"—Coalter, *Son of Thunder*, 95.

p. 121   "I cannot justify the excessive heat of temper which has sometime appeared in my conduct" to "Alas for it! My soul is sick for these things"—Webster, *History of the Presbyterian Church*, 189.

p. 121   "damnable errors and confusions"—ibid., 190–91.

p. 121   "So instead of keeping the letter to himself, he sent it to Thomas Clap"—White, "Decline of the Great Awakening," 41.

p. 122   "Old Light critics delighted in Gilbert's his admission of the faults of the revival"—ibid.

p. 122   "They created a caricature of him as a merciless sadist"—Chauncy, *Seasonable Thoughts*, 127.

p. 122   "promoted schism with his ugly rhetoric"—ibid., 148.

p. 122   "One anonymous New Englander published a pamphlet titled *The Examiner; or Gilbert Against Tennent*"—Coalter, *Son of Thunder*, 113–15.

p.122   "Tennent has been severely censured in Boston where someone took all the arrows"—ibid., 113.

p. 122   "Gilbert responded with *The Examiner, Examined; or Gilbert Tennent, Harmonious*"—ibid., 119.

p. 122   "Gilbert had already rebuked him and his group for antinomianism"—Lambert, *Inventing the "Great Awakening,"* 243.

p. 122   "nonsense and contradiction" to "detestable doctrine"—Tennent, *The Necessity of Holding Fast the Truth*, second sermon, 32, 36.

p. 123   "God's children who strove to be 'nearest the mind of Jesus Christ'"—Coalter, *Son of Thunder*, 111.

p. 123   "Your high opinion of the Moravians and attempts to join with them shocks me exceedingly"—Kidd, *America's Spiritual*, 197.

p. 124   "In May a new law outlawed itinerant preaching in the colony"—Bushman, *From Puritan to Yankee*, 186.

p. 124   "If found guilty of breaking the law, transgressors were subject to fines, arrest and exile"—Bonomi, *Under the Cope*, 163.

p. 124   "Soon, the authorities forbade New Light separatist congregations from legal protection"—ibid.

p. 124   "The press followed his actions closely" to "shocking scenes of horror and confusion" —*Boston News-Letter*, July 1, 1742.

p. 124   "strange and unaccountable manner"—Goen, *Revivalism and Separatism*, 22.

p. 125   "After the first day's hearing, the reverend and his associates left the meetinghouse" —ibid., 22–23.

p. 125   "disturbed in the rational faculties of his mind, and therefore to be pitied and compassionated"—ibid., 23.

p. 125   "an association of ministers decided to bar him from their pulpits"—Bonomi, *Under the Cope*, 150.

p. 125   "where any congregation is in peace, the devil is their ruler"—Stout and Onuf, "James Davenport," 566.

p. 125   "were murdering souls by thousands and by millions"—ibid., 573.

p. 125   "hands extended, his head thrown back, and his eyes staring up to heaven"—Nash, *Urban Crucible*, 210.

p. 126   "so red hot, that I verily believe they would make nothing to kill opposers"—Bonomi, *Under the Cope*, 150.

p. 126   "it is impossible to relate the convulsions into which the whole country is thrown" —Nash, *Urban Crucible*, 212.

p. 126   "strong attempts to destroy all property, to make all things common, wives as well as goods"—ibid., 210.

p. 126   "Instead, his congregation censured him for spending so much time outside his parish"—Goen, *Revivalism and Separatism*, 24.

p. 126   "By this time, Davenport suffered from inflammatory ulcers and bodily weakness" —Tracy, *Great Awakening*, 252–53.

p. 127   "some extraordinary discovery and assurance of the very near approach of the end of the world"—Stout and Onuf, "James Davenport," 574.

p. 127   "one such mission was to purge his followers of their wicked possessions"—Tracy, *Great Awakening*, 249.

p. 127   "shouted and sang 'Hallelujah!' and 'Glory to God!' and imagined their authors being tortured in hell"—*Boston Evening-Post*, April 11, 1743.

p. 127   "scarlet cloaks, velvet hoods, fine laces, and every thing that had two colors"—Warch, "Shepherd's Tent," 191.

p. 127   "the calf you have made is too big"—*Boston Evening-Post*, April 11, 1743.

p. 127   "under the influence of an evil spirit, and that God had left him"—Stout and Onuf, "James Davenport," 575.

p. 128   "Appalled by the spectacle, most of his local acolytes deserted him"—ibid., 578.

p. 128   "drive learning out of the world, and to sow it thick with the dreadful errors"—Warch, "Shepherd's Tent," 195.

CHAPTER 7: DAGGERS AND DRAWN SWORDS

One of the few monographs available on Charles Chauncy is Edward Griffin, *Old Brick: Charles Chauncy of Boston, 1705–1787* (Minneapolis: Univ. of Minnesota Press, 1980), which is a good short overview of the Old Light minister's career, but far from comprehensive enough to analyze his wide-ranging, often critical perspective. For greater detail on this, see his published sermons: *Enthusiasm Described and Cautioned Against* (Boston: J. Draper, 1742), which also includes a letter condemning James Davenport after the radical's intemperate appearance at Chauncy's house; *Seasonable Thoughts on the State of Religion in New-England* (Boston: Rogers and Fowle, 1743), the most important primary work that undercut the revival; *Ministers Cautioned Against the Occasions of Contempt* (Boston: Rogers and Fowle, 1744), which Chauncy delivered at a ministerial convention and which fed the fears of his peers that the colonial world seemed to be going mad from unchecked enthusiasm; and *The Wonderful Narrative: Or, a Faithful Account of the French Prophets, Their Agitations, Extasies, and Inspirations* (Glasgow: Robert Foulis, 1742), a pointed comparison between the excesses of the revival and another spiritual uprising earlier in the eighteenth century.

Other key works that touch on topics related to the Old Lights include Jonathan Edwards, *Some Thoughts Concerning the Present Revival of Religion in New-England* (Boston: S. Kneeland and T. Green, 1742), which provided the impetus for Chauncy to write *Seasonable Thoughts* in response; Conrad Wright, *The Beginnings of Unitarianism in America*, in which Chauncy is an early figure who shaped the rhetoric and theology of what would become an important liberal movement; Timothy Hall, *Contested Boundaries: Itinerancy and the Reshaping of the Colonial American Religious World*, an overview of why the traditionalists were so frightened by the specter of itinerant preachers and lay exhorters; David Lovejoy, *Religious Enthusiasm in the New World: Heresy to Revolution*, a classic text covering similar ground on a longer time scale; and Alan Heimert, *Religion and the American Mind: From the Great Awakening to the Revolution*, the foremost modern defense of the revival and still a key text for those historians who see the New Lights as protorevolutionaries and the Old Lights as hidebound elitists.

Women in colonial America have been underrepresented in the historical literature, a condition that has only started to change over the last several decades. Sarah Osborn (née Wheaten) became one of the key female authors whose works have survived, and her saga is revealed in her own *Memoirs of the Life of Sarah Osborn*, as noted in Chapter 5. A more comprehensive, contemporary edition of those memoirs is available in Catherine Brekus, ed., *Sarah Osborn's Collected Writings* (New Haven: Yale Univ. Press, 2017), an excellent introduction to her view of Christianity. Brekus provides an excellent biographical look at Osborn, putting her in the context of her time and the tumultuous colonial world she lived in, with *Sarah Osborn's World: The Rise of Evangelical Christianity in Early America*.

Most of what historians know about Susanna Anthony is seen through the lens of minister Samuel Hopkins, who, as with Sarah Osborn's biography, redacted parts of her life story to make it more palatable for contemporary readers. His version of *The Life and Character of Miss Susanna Anthony* (Portland, ME: Lyman, Hall & Co., 1810) is a worthy place to begin research about her, keeping his own bias in mind. For a closer look at the intimate relationship of Sarah and Susa, see *Familiar Letters Written by Mrs. Sarah Osborn and Miss Susanna Anthony* (Newport, RI: Newport Mercury, 1807), which provides a compelling window into ecstatic Christianity, despite nearly all the letters being undated and hard to place in time.

Modern views of the struggles and achievements of women in early America have shed light on their role in enthusiastic forms of worship. Some of the better volumes include Susan Juster, *Disorderly Women: Sexual Politics and Evangelicalism in Revolutionary New England* (Ithaca, NY: Cornell Univ. Press, 1994), and Catherine Brekus, *Strangers and Pilgrims: Female Preaching America, 1740–1845* (Chapel Hill, NC: Univ. of North Carolina Press, 1998). For detailed perspectives on the economic and social position of women during the era, see Mary Beth Norton, "The Evolution of White Women's Experience in Early America" (*The American Historical Review* 89:3 (1984), 593–619), and Barbara Lacey, "Gender, Piety, and Secularization in Connecticut Religion, 1720–1775" (*Journal of Social History* 24:4 (1991), 799–821). Many similar themes also appear in the story of a Puritan woman from a century earlier, in Eve LaPlante, *American Jezebel: The Uncommon Life of Anne Hutchinson, the Woman Who Defied the Puritans* (New York: HarperCollins, 2004), a biography of the spiritual trailblazer who became a legend and target for later generations of Congregationalists.

Douglas Winiarski is one of the best current historians of the grassroots revival in Christianity. Through countless case studies, he has created a compendium of eighteenth-century enthusiastic worshippers and their ministers. His two key works for this chapter include "Souls Filled with Ravishing Transport: Heavenly Visions and the Radical Awakening in New England" and the monumental *Darkness Falls on the Land of Light: Experiencing Religious Awakenings in Eighteenth-Century New England*. Other authors have also written of the outbreak of passion and ecstasy at the height of the Great Awakening, among them Jon Butler in *Awash in a Sea of Faith: Christianizing the American People*, and Michael Crawford in *Seasons of Grace: Colonial New England's Revival Tradition in Its British Context*. For the measured perspective of Jonathan Edwards about what does and does not constitute legitimate emotion in church services (as well as those phenomena that are beyond judgment) see his *Faithful Narrative of the Surprising Work of God in the Conversion of Many Hundred Souls in Northampton*, which predates the events in this book, and his contemporary *Distinguishing Marks of a Work of the Spirit of God* and the later *Some Thoughts Concerning the Present Revival of Religion in New-England*.

The curse of slavery in the colonies has attracted increasing attention from scholars in recent decades, with research showing just how fundamental the practice was to the economy and hierarchy of prerevolutionary America. Dozens of critical volumes examine human bondage during the era; those which are the most relevant to the context of this book include Gary Nash, *The Urban Crucible: Social Change, Political Consciousness, and the Origins of the American Revolution*, a broad perspective on key urban issues including enslavement, and the same author's "Slaves and Slave Owners in Colonial Philadelphia" (*The William and Mary Quarterly* 30:2 (1973), 223–256). Also valuable is Frank Lambert's "'I Saw the Book Talk': Slave Readings of the First Great Awakening," for its discussion of what the evangelical movement meant to black men and women held in bondage; Thomas Kidd, "Daniel Rogers' Egalitarian Great Awakening," a short biography of the New Light preacher who crossed racial boundaries; and Kenneth Minkema's "Jonathan Edwards's Defense of Slavery" (*Massachusetts Historical Review* 4 (2002), 23–59), an overview of the lengths to which preachers like Edwards went to justify their own use of forced labor. For a look at one of the most violent and unfair manifestations of colonial racism, see Serena Zabin, ed., *The New York Conspiracy Trials of 1741: Daniel Horsmanden's Journal of the Proceedings, with Related Documents* (New York: St. Martin's Press, 2004).

Comparatively less scholarship has examined the role of Indians and indigenous people in the Great Awakening, but for now the most essential volume remains Linford Fisher, *The Indian Great Awakening: Religion and the Shaping of Native Cultures in Early America* (New York: Oxford Univ. Press, 2012). This book also covers Andrew Croswell's role in missionary activities to Native tribes, and for a broader look at his radical form the gospel, see Leigh Eric Schmidt, "'A Second and Glorious Reformation': The New Light Extremism of Andrew Croswell." The reverend's own incendiary, sometimes crazed, writing provides another avenue to view his ministry, and the key volumes include *Mr. Croswell's Reply to a Book Lately Published, Entitled, A Display of God's Special Grace* (Boston: Rogers and Fowles, 1742), a rather venomous attack on Jonathan Dickinson's moderate stance on the revival; *The Apostle's Advice to the Jaylor Improved: Being a Solemn Warning Against the Awful Sin of Soul Murder* (Boston: Rogers and Fowles, 1744), Croswell at his most garrulous, summoning martial imagery against those who opposed him; *A Second Defence of the Old Protestant Doctrine of Justifying Faith . . .* (Boston: Rogers and Fowles, 1747), summarizing the importance of faith as the key to salvation; and *The Heavenly Doctrine of Man's Justification Only by the Obedience of Jesus Christ* (Boston: Green and Russell, 1758), his post-Awakening analysis of the role of faith in Christianity. Several critical contemporary comments about the reverend appear in Richard Webster, *A History of the Presbyterian Church in America, from Its Origin Until the Year 1760.*

Lastly, for previously cited discussions of the changes wrought by the Great Awakening on the colonies and the nascent growth of American populism, see Patricia Bonomi, *Under the Cope of Heaven: Religion, Society, and Politics in Colonial America*; and Richard Bushman, *From Puritan to Yankee: Character and the Social Order in Connecticut, 1690–1765.*

CHAPTER 7 REFERENCES:

p. 129 "James Davenport decided to pay a visit to the Reverend Charles Chauncy"—Griffin, *Old Brick*, 67–69.

p. 130 "if God ever gives you a sound mind, you will cry to him from the deeps"—Chauncy, "A Letter to the Reverend Mr. James Davenport," quoted in *Enthusiasm Described*, iv.

p. 130 "To his own First Church congregation, he delivered a sermon, *Enthusiasm Described and Cautioned Against*"—Griffin, *Old Brick*, 69.

p. 130 "Chauncy undertook an exhausting 300-mile circuit from New England to the Middle Colonies"—Wright, *Unitarianism*, 37.

p. 131 "Chauncy accused them and other, more radical figures of sowing division in the churches"—Chauncy, *Seasonable Thoughts*, 40–45, 51–55, 114–115.

p. 131 "'I am sorry to hear it,' Chauncy said. Whitefield replied, 'So is the devil!'"—Griffin, *Old Brick*, 91.

p. 131 "Jonathan Edwards had anticipated many of the Old Light arguments and admitted some aspects of revival"—Edwards, *Some Thoughts*, 5–9.

p. 131 "strange effects upon the body, such as swooning away and falling to the ground"—Chauncy, *Seasonable Thoughts*, 77.

p. 132 "the plain truth is, an enlightened mind, and not raised affections, ought always to be the guide"—ibid., 327.

p. 132   "Such enthusiasm threw the whole system of pastoral education"—Griffin, *Old Brick*, 60.

p. 132   "they saw the evangelical churches as a magnet for 'the lower sort'"—Heimert, *American Mind*, 51.

p. 132   "It is a shame for WOMEN to speak in the church . . . 'Tis a plain case, these FEMALE EXHORTERS are condemned by the apostle [Paul]"—Chauncy, *Enthusiasm Described*, 13.

p. 133   "With her friends she discussed God, prayed and sang hymns to him"—Osborn, *Memoirs*, 51–53.

p. 133   "She dressed modestly and cast aside the old Sarah who enjoyed fun and frivolity" —Brekus, *Sarah Osborn's World*, 20.

p. 133   "With her 'steady, prudent zeal and activity' she tried to inspire her group members" —Osborn, *Memoirs*, 74.

p. 133   "If there was no divine providence in the world, but only fate or luck, then human life was sheer chaos"—Brekus, *Sarah Osborn's World*, 59.

p. 134   "It pleased him to remove a dear friend by death, with whom I was very intimate" —Osborn, *Memoirs*, 51.

p. 134   "She took comfort that he 'appeared to be a good Christian'"—ibid., 51–52.

p. 134   "Months later the newly married couple were bankrupt"—Brekus, *Sarah Osborn's World*, 130–132.

p. 134   "Worse, Henry was suddenly struck with physical infirmities and could not hold a job"—Osborn, *Memoirs*, 59.

p. 134   "I have often thought God has so ordered it throughout my days hitherto" —ibid., 55.

p. 135   "I have always reaped much benefit myself, by reading the lives and experiences of others"—ibid., 56.

p. 135   "They could not study for the ministry, they could not go to college"—Brekus, *Sarah Osborn's World*, 1.

p. 135   "They had fewer rights than their eldest sons to their estate"—Norton, "Evolution," 603–604.

p. 135   "women dramatically outnumbered men in the pews"—Bonomi, *Under the Cope*, 111–115.

p. 135   "there were nearly three times as many women as men"—Lacey, "Gender, Piety, and Secularization," 810.

p. 135   "Some parishes showed greater parity at the height of the revival"—ibid., 803.

p. 136   "as the world grew in years, so women grew in wickedness"—Brekus, *Sarah Osborn's World*, 55.

p. 136   "the Spirit of God came down in an astonishing manner—two or three screamed out"—Kidd, "Daniel Rogers," 116.

p. 136   "evangelical religion offered women a faith that explicitly embraced feminine qualities"—Juster, *Disorderly Women*, 44.

p. 136   "other ministers worried women would fall prey to lusty itinerants"—Hall, *Contested*, 57–58.

p. 136 "Such critics warned that if this happened, women would subject their husbands"—Brekus, *Strangers and Pilgrims*, 59.

p. 136 "women and children might feel themselves inclined to break forth and scream aloud"—Edwards, *Faithful Narrative*, 325.

p. 137 "Should I altogether hold my peace? . . . It appeared to me such a monstrous piece of ingratitude"—Brekus, *Sarah Osborn's World*, 128–129.

p. 137 "God must cease to be God if he damned me"—Osborn, *Collected Writings*, 57.

p. 137 "One such example was Sarah's friend Susanna Anthony"—Brekus, *Sarah Osborn's World*, 123.

p. 138 "she experienced a great spiritual uplift, only to come crashing back down"—Hopkins, *Life of Susanna Anthony*, 18.

p. 138 "I believe a bloody inhuman butcher would have been more welcome to my tortured breast"—ibid., 19.

p. 138 "one of the worst of monsters; and often wished that I might be annihilated"—ibid., 20.

p. 138 "through the violence of my distress, I wrung my hands, twisted every joint"—ibid., 24.

p. 139 "They witnessed heavenly 'Glyphs' and other phantoms before their eyes"—Winiarski, "Souls Filled," 17–19.

p. 139 "Soon others saw doves and angels and heavenly lights, too, and heard celestial voices"—Winiarski, "Souls Filled," 15; Brekus, *Strangers and Pilgrims*, 54–55.

p. 139 "rejoiced in women leaders who claimed to be incarnations of God"—Lacey, "Gender, Piety, and Secularization," 811.

p. 139 "'agitations and terrors' derived from 'the weakness of their nerves'"—Chauncy, *Seasonable Thoughts*, 105.

p. 139 "He railed against them as an affront to decency and order"—Brekus, *Strangers and Pilgrims*, 58.

p. 140 "For these and other transgressions the Bay Colony excommunicated and exiled her"—LaPlante, *American Jezebel*, 236–237.

p. 140 "These radicals claimed to have special knowledge of Christ's return"—Butler, *Awash*, 178.

p. 140 "foam at the mouth, roar, and swell in their bellies"—Chauncy, *French Prophets*, 77.

p. 140 "examples of self-proclaimed prophets running amok as they channeled the Holy Spirit"—ibid., 83.

p. 140 "Jonathan Edwards had long worried about the 'spirit of delusion' that led the 'wildest enthusiasts'"—Edwards, *Distinguishing Marks*, 55.

p. 141 "Let your auditors be awed with your flaming zeal, as if they heard a voice from the burning mountain"—Crawford, *Seasons of Grace*, 85.

p. 141 "yea, Negroes, have taken upon them to do the business of preachers"—Chauncy, *Seasonable Thoughts*, 226.

p. 141 "10 percent of Philadelphia's population was black and unfree—and 40 percent of the dock workers"—Nash, *Urban Crucible*, 109–110.

p. 141 "While most Quakers merchants had turned against slavery by this time"—Nash, "Slaves and Slave Owners," 226.

p. 141 "In New York, the enslaved made up one out of every five residents of the city"—Nash, *Urban Crucible*, 107.

p. 141   "Jonathan Edwards owned slaves and tried to justify the practice"—Minkema, "Edwards's Defense," 23–24.

p. 142   "New England ministers worried that 'slaves in a state of grace thought themselves above the laws'"—Lambert, "I Saw the Book Talk," 191.

p. 142   "poor Negroes have not been vindicated into the glorious liberty of the children of God"—Hall, *Contested*, 56.

p. 143   "Two years later a series of robberies and fires in New York City put residents on edge"—Zabin, *Conspiracy Trials*, 26–32; Lovejoy, *Religious Enthusiasm*, 202–03.

p. 143   "Ninety blacks and a dozen whites came under suspicion in this 'bloody and destructive conspiracy'"—Zabin, *Conspiracy Trials*, 175.

p. 143   "George Whitefield also came under suspicion in the conspiracy"—Lovejoy, *Religious Enthusiasm*, 204–205.

p. 144   "Whitefield and Davenport had drawn many Indians to the New Birth, as did other preachers"—Fisher, *Indian Great Awakening*, 71–73, 76–81.

p. 144   "In 1742 conversions spiked, as the radicals' freewheeling services attracted many" —ibid., 92.

p. 144   "itinerants, exhorters, prophets, and visionaries, embracing their own radical awakening"—Kidd, "Daniel Rogers," 113.

p. 144   "spurred his congregants to learn to read and study the Bible for themselves"—Fisher, *Indian Great Awakening*, 71–73.

p. 144   "Croswell delivered their petition to the Assembly himself"—ibid., 73.

p. 144   "they all gave praise to God in a great helter-skelter assembly where they 'sang, prayed, hugged, and fainted'"—Schmidt, "New Light Extremism," 238.

p. 145   "Yale rector Thomas Clap, in a letter to Jonathan Dickinson, linked Croswell to the maniacal excesses"—Webster, *History of the Presbyterian Church*, 204.

p. 145   "his encouragement of Davenport to go to Boston in 1741"—Schmidt, "New Light Extremism," 219.

p. 145   "Curse be that charity, for it is fierce, and that moderation, for it is cruel"—Croswell, *Heavenly Doctrine*, 11.

p. 145   "He envisioned nothing less than a second Reformation in the New World"—Schmidt, "New Light Extremism," 229–230.

p. 145   "God's order differs vastly from their nice and delicate apprehensions of it"—Winiarski, *Darkness Falls*, 318.

p. 146   "he claimed the author was leading his readers into hell"—Croswell, *Mr. Croswell's Reply*, 14, 23.

p. 146   "He wrote that the power and success of Christianity often depended on 'contention, persecution, and bloodshed'"—Schmidt, "New Light Extremism," 223.

p. 146   "my soul has heard the alarm of war; and the question is, Who will arise on the Lord's side?"—Croswell, *Mr. Croswell's Reply*, 18.

p. 146   "if they will keep hugging this monster, while I am killing it; what can I do?" —Croswell, *Second Defence*, 40n.

p. 147   "The truth is, every persecutor is a madman"—Croswell, *Advice to the Jaylor*, 7.

p. 147   "They believed the Lord had given them license to denounce anyone who stood in the way"—Winiarski, "Souls Filled," 14.

p. 147   "the revival had inspired waves of men and women to question everything they had been taught about God"—Bushman, *From Puritan to Yankee*, 267–268.

p. 147   "The radicals harnessed the fervent beliefs of their congregants"—Nash, *Urban Crucible*, 215.

p. 147   "the body of the ministers were never treated with more insult and contempt than by multitudes"—Chauncy, *Ministers Cautioned*, 12.

p. 148   "The country was never in a more critical state"—Letter from Charles Chauncy to Nathaniel Chauncy, Jan. 16, 1742.

p. 148   "Calvinism offered 'a radical, even democratic, social and political ideology'"—Heimert, *American Mind*, 15.

p. 148   "Wives rebuked husbands for their lack of piety; children evangelized their parents"—Brekus, *Strangers and Pilgrims*, 34.

p. 148   "a psychological earthquake had reshaped the human landscape"—Bushman, *From Puritan to Yankee*, 187.

CHAPTER 8: THE BOW OF JONATHAN

George Whitefield's return to America in 1744 was one of the most contentious episodes of the Great Awakening. His travels are not covered in the main body of his seven *Journals*, but are touched on in his *Unpublished Journal*, which was later published in *Church History* (7:4 (1938), 297–345). Unfortunately, the now more circumspect Whitefield does not make for a very revealing narrator of his journey, so other supplementary material provides a better window into this episode in his life. Douglas L. Winiarski, in "'A Jornal of a Fue Days at York': The Great Awakening on the Northern New England Frontier" (*Maine History* 42:1 (2004), 46–85), offers a useful look at his initial visit to York, and the potential revival he could have enflamed there. John Gillies, in the *Memoirs of Reverend George Whitefield* (Middletown: Hunt & Noyes, 1839), also illuminates this period, with much favorable treatment given to the reverend; while the more balanced Luke Tyerman, *The Life of the Reverend George Whitefield*, is a later and more useful source that offers criticism where needed. Contemporary, previously cited research is drawn from Harry Stout, *The Divine Dramatist: George Whitefield and the Rise of Modern Evangelicalism*; and Thomas Kidd, *George Whitefield: America's Spiritual Founding Father* and *The Great Awakening: The Roots of Evangelical Christianity in Colonial America*.

For a view of the controversial role Whitefield played in his own Anglican church, and the way that church turned against the revival in part because of the Itinerant's actions, see Gerald Goodwin, "The Anglican Reaction to the Great Awakening" and Martin Lodge, "The Crisis of the Churches in the Middle Colonies, 1720-1750." For a discussion of the contrast between the theology and practical application of the contrasting belief systems of Anglicanism and Puritanism/Congregationalism, see Alan Kantrow, "Anglican Custom, American Consciousness" (*The New England Quarterly* 52:3 (1979) 307–325).

A primary source that offers one of the most damning accounts of Whitefield's doings is *The Testimony of the President, Professors, Tutors and Hebrew Instructor of Harvard College in Cambridge, Against the Reverend Mr. George Whitefield, and His Conduct* (Boston: T. Fleet, 1744)—long-overdue revenge from that college for the brickbats the Itinerant had once given to it. Whitefield's response to his critics is offered in his various apologies (in the sources cited above), but particular attention should be given to his sermon *Britain's Mercies, and Britain's Duty* (Boston: S. Kneeland and T. Green, 1746), which isn't an apology per se, but does show how the minister had to adapt his rhetoric to be more acceptable to an American audience of the time—i.e., by issuing harsh anti-Catholic invective. For a different kind of response to criticism, see Gilbert Tennent, *The Necessity of Studying to Be Quiet, and Doing Our Own Business* (Philadelphia: William Bradford: 1744), the best example of that pastor's newfound turn toward moderation. Other valuable research on post-radical Tennent can be found in Milton Coalter, Jr., *Gilbert Tennent: Son of Thunder: A Case Study of Continental Pietism's Impact on the First Great Awakening in the Middle Colonies*; Janet Fishburn, "Gilbert Tennent, Established Dissenter"; and Frederick Brink, "Gilbert Tennent, Dynamic Preacher."

Another pastor who came to moderate his behavior after a radical phase was Hugh Bryan, whose troubles in South Carolina are covered in Leigh Eric Schmidt, "'The Grand Prophet,' Hugh Bryan: Early Evangelicalism's Challenge to the Establishment and Slavery in the Colonial South," and in Harvey Jackson, "Hugh Bryan and the Evangelical Movement in Colonial South Carolina." Whitefield's own problems in the South included others' attacks on his orphanage and his role as a budding slaveholder. For more on these issues, see Alfred Aldridge, "George Whitefield's Georgia Controversies" (*The Journal of Southern History* 9:3 (1943), 357–380), and Stephen Stein, "George Whitefield on Slavery: Some New Evidence." Whitefield's other significant Southern legacy was his tumultuous relationship with his own Anglican church; his struggles with Alexander Garden can be found in earlier chapters, but for the wider impact of his and others' anti-Anglican rhetoric, see Noah Hobart, *A Sermon Delivered at the Ordination of the Reverend Mr. Noah Welles* (Boston: D. Henchman, 1747), and Carl Bridenbaugh, *Mitre and Sceptre: Transatlantic Faiths, Ideas, Personalities, and Politics, 1689–1775* (New York: Oxford Univ. Press, 1962).

An adversary of Whitefield, Jonathan Mayhew is a critical figure in American political and religious history who begins his rise during this chapter, but his biographical sources remain thin—and none are contemporaneous. The best is still Charles Akers, *Called unto Liberty*, which puts him in the proper context as a theological maverick, and the more recent J. Patrick Mullins, *Father of Liberty: Jonathan Mayhew and the Principles of the American Revolution*, is also useful for fillings in the gaps with modern research. The outdated Alden Bradford, *Memoirs of the Life and Writings of Rev. Jonathan Mayhew, D.D.* (Boston: C.C. Little & Co., 1838), is a bit of a relic, though includes some helpful information and anecdotes. See also Clinton Rossiter, "The Life and Mind of Jonathan Mayhew," for an in-depth discussion of his philosophy and ministry; and the sermon of Ebenezer Gay, *The Alienation of Affections from Ministers Considered, and Improved* (Boston: Rogers and Fowle, 1747), which inaugurated Mayhew's career in controversy.

Supplementary sources that offer useful insights and details on the revival's peak and later decline include Harry Stout, *The New England Soul: Preaching and Religious Culture in Colonial New England* (New York: Oxford Univ. Press, 1986), one of the all-around best volumes on early American religion; Edwin S. Gaustad, *The Great Awakening in New England* (Gloucester, MA: Peter Smith, 1965), also excellent, and concisely written; the previously mentioned Frank Lambert, "The Great Awakening as Artifact: George Whitefield and the Construction of Intercolonial Revival, 1739–1745," regarding the publicity and marketing of evangelical religion in colonial America; and Eugene White, "Decline of the Great Awakening in New England," in which the major figures of the era are either forced to apologize, retreat into exile, or face consequences from the law.

Finally, incisive analyses of the transformation of religion, and its intertwining with the politics of the era, can be found in the following volumes: C. C. Goen, *Revivalism and Separatism in New England, 1740–1800: Strict Congregationalists and Separate Baptists in the Great Awakening*; Sydney Ahlstrom, *A Religious History of the American People*; Richard Bushman, *From Puritan to Yankee:*

Character and the Social Order in Connecticut, 1690–1765; and Gary Nash, *The Urban Crucible: Social Change, Political Consciousness, and the Origins of the American Revolution.*

CHAPTER 8 REFERENCES:

p. 149   "Its leaders followed that legal maneuver with another that revoked the toleration of dissenters"—Goen, *Revivalism and Separatism*, 63–64; Ahlstrom, *Religious History*, 290–291.

p. 149   "that colony's leaders outlawed missionaries to brought the gospel to . . . 'ignorant savages'"—Lovejoy, *Religious Enthusiasm*, 212.

p. 149   "perfect mess-medley of all kinds of disorder and error, enthusiastic wildness and extravagance"—Hall, *Contested Boundaries*, 69.

p. 150   "In Connecticut they formed a party that eventually wrested control"—Goen, *Revivalism and Separatism*, 64.

p. 150   "to make concerted attempts to remove their adversaries from political office"—Bushman, *From Puritan to Yankee*, 237–238.

p. 150   "as secular leaders increasingly meddled to control spiritual practices"—Nash, *Urban Crucible*, 202–204.

p. 150   "For the Anglican church had emerged as the foremost enemy of the revival"—Goodwin, "Anglican Reaction," 343.

p. 150   "Most Anglican clergymen were paid by the church as missionaries"—Lodge, "Crisis of the Churches," 592–593.

p. 150   "'visions and delusions' that appealed to the 'vanity and vapours of an empty skull'"—Kantrow, "Anglican Custom," 315.

p. 150   "They decried the extemporaneous preaching of the New Lights"—Goodwin, "Anglican Reaction," 353–354.

p. 150   "only served to create a climate of 'endless feuds, censoriousness, and uncharitableness'"—Kantrow, "Anglican Custom," 313.

p. 151   "Whitefield's arrival followed a flurry of newspaper reports of his travels"—Lambert, "Artifact," 238.

p. 151   "One writer in a Boston paper demanded he apologize for all the harm he had caused to colonial pulpits"—Kidd, *Great Awakening*, 169.

p. 151   "his old friends remained silent in response to the attacks"—White, "Decline of the Great Awakening," 48.

p. 151   "eight associations of New England ministers denounced him; many Old Side Presbyterians condemned him"—Hall, *Contested*, 69.

p. 152   "the detriment of religion, and the entire destruction of the order of [some] churches" to "an enthusiast, a censorious, uncharitable person"—Kidd, *Great Awakening*, 169–70.

p. 152   "In other cases his colleagues faced gunfire, beatings and (if female) rape and sexual abuse"—Stout, *Divine Dramatist*, 176.

p. 152   "At Moorfields, Whitefield faced off with stage actors, puppeteers and clowns"—Kidd, *America's Spiritual*, 148.

p. 152   "when he was staying at an inn and an intruder burst into his room"—Gillies, *Memoirs of Whitefield*, 99.

p. 152   "the body of the people into a national madness and frenzy in matters of religion"—Stout, *Divine Dramatist*, 180.

p. 153   "May the Crown long flourish on his Royal Head, and a Popish Pretender never be permitted to sit upon the English throne!"—ibid., 181.

p. 153   "his remaining New Light supporters flocked to his bedside with words of encouragement"—Winiarski, "Northern New England Frontier," 60.

p. 153   "the invisible realities of another world lay open to my view"—Gillies, *Memoirs of Whitefield*, 103.

p. 153   "preach the gospel of peace . . . and promote charity and love among all"—Whitefield, *Unpublished Journal*, 46.

p. 153   "I told them that these words were not wrote to imply that it was absolutely impossible"—ibid.

p. 153   "Some like Benjamin Colman even opened their meetinghouses to him"—Stout, *Divine Dramatist*, 189–190.

p. 154   "pious ancestors and the founders of Harvard College preached long before I was born"—ibid., 191–192.

p. 154   "Clap made the bold claim that Whitefield had secret plans to swap out the region's Old Light ministers"—Kidd, *America's Spiritual*, 183–184.

p. 154   "wild and extravagant people" to "In the end he won over men like Edwards, who saw that Whitefield had truly repented"—ibid., 186.

p. 155   "taking up evil reports against our brethren without sufficient evidence"—Tennent, *Necessity of Studying*, 11.

p. 155   "deluded votaries into the strangest absurdities in opinion"—Kidd, *Great Awakening*, 147.

p. 155   "the congregants of the New Building in Philadelphia had asked permission"—Coalter, *Son of Thunder*, 118.

p. 156   "As the leader of a parish of 140 souls, he continued to support the revival"—Brink, "Dynamic Preacher," 98.

p. 156   "He toned down his rhetoric, began preaching with notes"—Coalter, *Son of Thunder*, 121–22.

p. 156   "experimental knowledge was not enough to create a steadfast faith"—ibid., 123.

p. 156   "in a few years this son of Northern Ireland would hold formal services in an ornate, Anglican-style brick building"—Fishburn "Established Dissenter," 38–39.

p. 156   "I leave this place with no expectation of worldly comfort" to "I am fully persuaded that change of place and outward circumstances"—Coalter, *Son of Thunder*, 120–122.

p. 157   "an all-New England force of 3,600 soldiers and a thousand sailors" to "Christ leads! Never despair!"—Nash, *Urban Crucible*, 172; Stout, *New England Soul*, 234.

p. 157   "Many of the soldiers faced mounting debts and desperate conditions"—Nash, *Urban Crucible*, 170–171.

p. 158   "horrid plot, hatched in hell" to "How soon would that mother of harlots have made herself once more drunk"—Whitefield, *Britain's Mercies*, 9, 11, 15.

p. 158   "A few years before he had wed a woman named Elizabeth James, who was a decade older than him"—Kidd, *America's Spiritual*, 158–159.

p. 158   "He quickly became more interested in having her attend to his stateside affairs as a "ministry coordinator"—ibid., 246.

p. 159   "he sailed home without her, not even bothering to inform her of his departure"—ibid., 201–202.

p. 159   "a parcel of cant-phrases, trances, dreams, visions, and revelations"—Schmidt, "Grand Prophet," 242.

p. 159   "he came to working miracles and lived for several days in the woods barefooted" —ibid., 243.

p. 160   "An 'Angel of Light' ordered him to take a wooden rod"—Jackson, "Hugh Bryan," 608–609.

p. 160   "the dishonor I've done to God, as well as the disquiet which I may have occasioned to my country"—ibid., 610.

p. 160   "the workings of Whitefieldism in its native tendency"—ibid., 609.

p. 160   "through the badness of the institution, and the trustees' obstinacy in not altering it" —Aldridge, "Georgia Controversies," 370.

p. 160   "couldn't seem to silence his opposers, who claimed he had squandered money raised to support the orphans"—Aldridge, "Georgia Controversies," 370–373; Kidd, *America's Spiritual*, 193, 199.

p. 161   "He also began to see the answer to the orphanage's problems in the ownership of human beings"—Stein, "Whitefield on Slavery," 244–245.

p. 161   "impossible for [Georgia's] inhabitants to subsist without the use of slaves" to "one Negro has been given me"—Tyerman, *Life of the Reverend*, 169.

p. 162   "upon Whitefield's latest trip to America formally suspended him from the ministry" —Kidd, *America's Spiritual*, 192.

p. 162   "Whitefield has plagued us with a witness, especially his friends and followers"—Letter from Timothy Cutler to Zachary Grey, Sept. 29, 1743, quoted in Bridenbaugh, *Mitre and Sceptre*, 83–84.

p. 162   "During his New England trip, a public debate broke out"—Bridenbaugh, *Mitre and Sceptre*, 86–90.

p. 162   "'serious religion and practical godliness' of old-fashioned Calvinism"—Hobart, *Sermon Delivered*, 26.

p. 162   "has made herself drunken with the blood of the saints, and with the blood of the martyrs of Jesus"—ibid., 14.

p. 163   "a providential opportunity to divide and triumph"—Bridenbaugh, *Mitre and Sceptre*, 85.

p. 163   "inspiration, and the spirit of truth and wisdom, the vehicle of nonsense and contradiction"—Lovejoy, *Religious Enthusiasm*, 188.

p. 163   "chiefly of the more illiterate sort" to "as low, confused, puerile, conceited, ill-natured, enthusiastic"—Bradford, *Memoirs of Mayhew*, 102.

p. 163   "under the power of Satanical delusions"—Akers, *Liberty*, 35.

p. 163   "an uncharitable, censorious and slanderous man" and "a deluder of the people" —Harvard College, *Testimony Against Whitefield*.

p. 164   "He learned how Christian ethics and morality could reflect a devout faith in God" —Mullins, *Father of Liberty*, 27–29.

p. 164   "irreverent ideas made them seem like 'a pack of young heretics'"—Akers, *Liberty*, 40.

p. 164   "a questioner proposed that any religion that upheld an idea like original sin was not rational"—Mullins, *Father of Liberty*, 29.

p. 164   "Jonathan took his father's writings to one of his Harvard professors"—Akers, *Liberty*, 64–65.

p. 164   "Not only did he wish to expound on his ideas before a congregation, he also needed a steady income"—ibid., 41–42.

p. 165   "at West Church, a growing population of affluent merchants and upstarts looked to find an open-minded minister"—Akers, *Liberty*, 44–48, 53–55; Mullins, *Father of Liberty*, 30–31.

p. 166   "The *Boston Evening Post* accused establishment ministers of trying to undermine Jonathan"—Akers, *Liberty*, 67.

p. 166   "Be valiant for the truth against all opposition from the lusts of men"—Gay, *Alienation of Affections*, 27.

p. 166   "candid, sincere, diligent" to "Old Nick had thrown acid in his face"—Rossiter, "Life and Mind," 535.

p. 166   "His parishioners appreciated that he spoke in a clear and forceful manner"—Akers, *Liberty*, 57–58.

p. 166   "a merciful and faithful creator, a compassionate parent, a gentle master"—Rossiter, "Life and Mind," 542.

p. 167   "He described a new, modern God worthy of love and adoration"—ibid., 543–544.

p. 168   "I live very happily and contented without them"—Mullins, *Father of Liberty*, 31.

CHAPTER 9: THE REVOLT FROM WITHIN

The definitive volume on Separatism, and the way it transformed much of frontier and inner British North America, is C. C. Goen, *Revivalism and Separatism in New England, 1740–1800: Strict Congregationalists and Separate Baptists in the Great Awakening*. With countless case studies and examples of the growth of dissenting religion in the aftermath of the Great Awakening, Goen's work is still unparalleled. Also useful for illuminating different aspects of this transformation are Catherine Brekus, *Strangers and Pilgrims: Female Preaching America, 1740–1845*, with its emphasis on the social changes attendant in the post-Awakening years; and Rhys Isaac, "Evangelical Revolt: The Nature of the Baptists' Challenge to the Traditional Order in Virginia, 1765 to 1775" (*The William and Mary Quarterly* 31:3 (1974), 345–368), an excellent overview of just what made the sect so threatening to colonial powers, in advance of the revolution to come.

Related works already mentioned in these notes that provide further clarity on Separatism and the sects that arose from the revival include Sydney Ahlstrom, *A Religious History of the American People*; Patricia Bonomi, *Under the Cope of Heaven: Religion, Society, and Politics in Colonial America*; Richard Bushman, *From Puritan to Yankee: Character and the Social Order in Connecticut, 1690–1765*; David Lovejoy, *Religious Enthusiasm in the New World: Heresy to Revolution*; and Edmund Morgan, *Benjamin Franklin*.

Andrew Croswell's ministry did not end with the revival, and it took new and curious directions in the years to come. Still the best overview of his career is Leigh Eric Schmidt, "'A Second and Glorious Reformation': The New Light Extremism of Andrew Croswell," though it's also worthwhile to explore the startling invective and colorful language of the minister in his primary works. Some of these were mentioned in chapter 7, but those most relevant to his ministry in the mid-1740s include his *Narrative of the Founding and Settling of the New-Gathered Congregational Church in Boston* (Boston: Rogers and Fowles, 1749), *A Second Defence of the Old Protestant Doctrine of Justifying Faith*, and *The Apostle's Advice to the Jaylor Improved: Being a Solemn Warning Against the Awful Sin of Soul Murder*—still a jarring read for its scabrous tone and veiled attack on contemporary rulers as agents of sin.

Croswell was far from the only Northeasterner to decry British policy in the later 1740s, as the era became known for its turmoil in both spiritual and civic arenas. One of the best descriptions of the conflicts of major towns and cities is Gary Nash, *The Urban Crucible: Social Change, Political Consciousness, and the Origins of the American Revolution*, though other volumes also provide evidence of the shaky foundation of imperial rule. These include Edward Griffin, *Old Brick: Charles Chauncy of Boston, 1705–1787*, and J. Patrick Mullins, *Father of Liberty: Jonathan Mayhew and the Principles of the American Revolution*. See also Charles Chauncy, *Civil Magistrates Must Be Just, Ruling in the Fear of God* (Boston: Massachusetts Bay House of Representatives, 1747), as an early call for greater colonial liberties, and Chris Beneke, "The Critical Turn: Jonathan Mayhew, the British Empire, and the Idea of Resistance in Mid-Eighteenth-Century Boston" (*Massachusetts Historical Review* 10 (2008), 23–56), which summarizes many of the grievances colonists had against royal governors and magistrates, and the consequences of expressing them.

A good introduction to the controversy over the elevation of an Anglican bishop to the church in America can be found in Carl Bridenbaugh, *Mitre and Sceptre: Transatlantic Faiths, Ideas, Personalities, and Politics, 1689–1775*. Helpful background sources also include Joseph S. Tiedemann, "Presbyterianism and the American Revolution in the Middle Colonies" (*Church History* 74:2 (2005), 306–344), and Don R. Gerlach, "Champions of an American Episcopate: Thomas Secker of Canterbury and Samuel Johnson of Connecticut" (*Historical Magazine of the Protestant Episcopal Church* 41:4 (1972), 381–414).

The Knowles Riots are among the lesser known events that contributed to the growth of Anglo-American strife before the Revolution, at least for general readers. Still the best analysis of these riots is unquestionably John Lax and William Pencak, "The Knowles Riot and the Crisis of the 1740s in Massachusetts," in *Contested Commonwealths: Essays in American History*, ed. William Pencak (Bethlehem, PA: Lehigh Univ. Press, 2011), an article originally written in 1976. Denver Brunsman has also done commendable, more recent work and discovered additional sources that help to explain the riots; see his "The Knowles Atlantic Impressment Riots of the 1740s" (*Early American Studies* 5:2 (2007), 324–366), and "Subjects vs. Citizens: Impressment and Identity in the Anglo-American Atlantic" (*Journal of the Early Republic* 30:4 (2010), 557–586). Other worthy, if more general, perspectives can be found in Christopher Magra, "Anti-Impressment Riots and the Origins of the Age of Revolution" (*International Review of Social History*, 58:21 (2013), 131–151), and Pauline Maier, "Popular Uprisings and Civil Authority in Eighteenth-Century America" (*The William and Mary Quarterly* 27:1 (1970), 3–35). One key source of much of the tension that led to the violence was the Pyrrhic victory (for colonials, at least) at Louisbourg; a good overview of the conflict can be found in Douglas Edward Leach, "Brothers in Arms? Anglo-American Friction at Louisbourg, 1745–1746" (*Proceedings of the Massachusetts Historical Society* 3:89 (1977), 36-54). For a contemporaneous British view of these troubles, from the perspectives of the future and then-current governors, see Thomas Hutchinson, *The History of Massachusetts from the First Settlement Thereof in 1628 Until the Year 1750*, vol. 2 (Boston: Manning and Loring, 1795), and Charles Henry Lincoln, ed., *Correspondence of William Shirley, Governor of Massachusetts and Military Commander in America, 1731–1760* (New York: Macmillan, 1912). A more general treatment of the conflicts inherent to American colonial cities is laid out in Carl Bridenbaugh, *Cities in Revolt: Urban Life in America, 1743–1776* (New York: Knopf, 1955).

Aside from his Harvard thesis, which is lost to history, there is no better explication of the early thoughts of Samuel Adams than the piece he likely wrote under a pseudonym: Amicus Curiae, *An Address to the Inhabitants of the Province of the Massachusetts-Bay in New-England . . .* (Boston, 1747). Rare issues of the *Independent Advertiser* newspaper are also essential for their insight into the mind of the young protorevolutionary. For comprehensive biographies of the man, few modern works have the scope and sheer amount of quoted material found in William Wells, *The Life and Public Services of Samuel Adams*, vol. 1 (Boston: Little, Brown, and Co., 1865). However, one current volume well worth seeking out is John Alexander, *Samuel Adams: The Life of an American Revolutionary* (Lanham, MD; Rowman and Littlefield, 2011), a straightforward look at Adams's rise and the events that shaped his ideas of tyranny and rebellion. Also compelling is John Miller, *Sam Adams: Pioneer in Propaganda* (Stanford, CA: Stanford Univ. Press, 1936), which establishes Adams as a radical figure in enflaming public opinion before the war, using tactics that were both underhanded and brilliant.

CHAPTER 9 REFERENCES:

p. 169   "No fewer than one hundred Separatist churches opened their doors after the mid-1740s."—Brekus, *Strangers and Pilgrims*, 48–49.

p. 170   "the one denomination that prospered was Baptism"—Goen, *Revivalism and Separatism*, 206.

p. 170   "they rejected the 'Halfway Covenant' that allowed unconverted parents"—Kidd, *Great Awakening*, 184–186; Ahlstrom, *Religious History*, 292–293.

p. 170   "they poured into the frontier of New England and the isolated settlements"—Goen, *Revivalism and Separatism*, 243.

p. 170   "many itinerant Separatists descended into the Southern backcountry"—Ahlstrom, *Religious History*, 318–319.

p. 170   "in his case giving 2,400 sermons over nearly 15,000 miles"—Goen, *Revivalism and Separatism*, 222.

p. 170   "In Virginia, Baptists denounced the dancing, horse racing, and gambling"—Bonomi, *Under the Cope*, 184.

p. 170   "They renounced fine clothing and frivolities, spoke solemnly and called each other"—Isaac, "Evangelical Revolt," 353.

p. 171   "As one observer noted, in search of spiritual perfection, they 'cut off their hair'"—Bonomi, *Under the Cope*, 184.

p. 171   "solemn groans and lamentations" to "melt[ing] a whole concourse into tears by her prayers and exhortations"—Brekus, *Strangers and Pilgrims*, 62.

p. 171   "Slaves, too, found an emotional release through their testimony and rebirth in Baptism"—Isaac, "Evangelical Revolt," 355.

p. 171   "they became a key part of the vanguard of Americans who represented the 'revolt from within'"—ibid., 359.

p. 172   "Warning his presence would be 'offensive and dangerous' to the peace and stability of the town"—Schmidt, "New Light Extremism," 225.

p. 172   "GOD of his infinite mercy [to] cause poor people to separate from these men"—Croswell, *Second Defence*, 11.

p. 172   "Croswell's church was first called the 'Dear Society of Saints' before he renamed it"—Schmidt, "New Light Extremism," 226.

p. 173   "He was the apostle of true Calvinist faith, and they were the real Separatists"—Croswell, *Narrative of the Founding*, 7.

p. 173   "publicly pull down the Kingdom of Satan, and build up the Kingdom of Christ"—ibid., 4.

p. 173   "disputing about words and things which edify not" to "they appear to be incorrigible"—ibid., 6.

p. 173   "At the same time, he stressed that he preached 'the joyful religion of Jesus Christ'"—Schmidt, "New Light Extremism," 233.

p. 174   "Croswell attacked civic leaders as 'more fit for Bedlam than the Bench'"—Croswell, *Advice to the Jaylor*, 7.

p. 174   "They passed laws that forced Separatists to pay taxes"—Bushman, *From Puritan to Yankee*, 224.

p. 174   "Labeled as 'fraudulent dissenters,' many New Lights trundled off to prison"—Lovejoy, *Religious Enthusiasm*, 227.

p. 174   "Some Separatists went further and condemned any civil interference with religion whatsoever"—Bushman, *From Puritan to Yankee*, 228.

p. 174   "the illegal and discriminatory practices of government on behalf of the state Church"—Lovejoy, *Religious Enthusiasm*, 217.

p. 175   "This 'Gibraltar of the New World' enabled France, Britain's current enemy, to control the cod fisheries"—Nash, *Urban Crucible*, 168–171.

p. 175   "In Philadelphia, Benjamin Franklin, now clerk of the Pennsylvania Assembly"—Morgan, *Benjamin Franklin*, 63–64.

p. 175   "many New Englanders feared a debacle like Cartagena would ensue, in which 80 percent of the men who fought"—Nash, *Urban Crucible*, 172.

p. 175   "Some 3,600 men from Boston and other towns in the region took part in the campaign"—ibid.

p. 175   "the French booty and prizes they had been promised, which went into the coffers of the Royal Navy"—Leach, "Brothers in Arms," 54.

p. 176   "blacksmiths, tailors, barbers, shoemakers, and all the banditry them colonies affords"—Brunsman, "Impressment Riots," 355; Leach, "Brothers in Arms," 51–52.

p. 176   "War profiteers amassed fortunes through bribes and corruption"—Nash, *Urban Crucible*, 169.

p. 176   "lawmakers fearful of future rebellions demanded submission to the government"—Mullins, *Father of Liberty*, 49–50.

p. 176   "They warned that any act of subversion against the Crown would be treated with the severity"—Beneke, "The Critical Turn," 28.

p. 177   "His own financial condition was precarious, as he struggled on a meager salary"—Griffin, *Old Brick*, 101.

p. 177   "Chauncy used the sermon as an opportunity to scold the lawmakers for neglecting the needs"—Chauncy, *Civil Magistrates*, 59–60.

p. 177   "Rulers also should endeavor to keep the state from being embroiled in foreign war"—ibid., 43.

p. 177   "Tis the just exercise of power that distinguishes right from might"—ibid., 17.

p. 177   "They should not defraud or oppress the public, or use violence as a means"—ibid., 13–14.

p. 178   "preserve and perpetuate to every member of the community, so far as may be"—ibid., 33.

p. 178   "they claimed that colonial subjects who refused to submit to the Church of England"—Beneke, "The Critical Turn," 36.

p. 178   "obedience to God, king, lords and bishops—and in that order"—Tiedemann, "Presbyterianism and the American Revolution," 322.

p. 178   "to ordain ministers locally, instead of forcing them to sail back to Britain"—Griffin, *Old Brick*, 128.

p. 179   "Anglican clergymen openly argued that more needed to be done to advance the Church of England's cause"—Gerlach, "Champions of an American Episcopate," 384, 389.

p. 179   "a very great obstruction to the propagation of religion"—Bridenbaugh, *Mitre and Sceptre*, 86.

p. 179   "Thomas Secker, who had been calling for the creation of such a bishop since 1741"—ibid., 31.

p. 179   "in a few years time Episcopacy will generally prevail in this part of the world"—Beneke, "The Critical Turn," 35.

p. 179   "the first Anglican church in Boston, King's Chapel, erected its foundation on a hallowed burial ground"—ibid.

p. 181   "the navy . . . faced huge rates of desertion when its ships entered port"—Brunsman, "Impressment Riots," 39.

p. 181   "The practice of impressment had become critical for running a modern global empire"—Magra, "Anti-Impressment Riots," 135.

p. 181   "Britain deployed the practice ruthlessly and repeatedly in the Americas"—Brunsman, "Subjects vs. Citizens," 564.

p. 181   "Colonists saw impressment as a violation of their rights as British subjects"—ibid., 566.

p. 181   "Two years later, a parliamentary act upheld the old 'Sixth of Anne' policy"—Maier, "Popular Uprisings," 23.

p. 181   "the first victims destined to be sacrificed to a arbitrary and illegal power[.]"—Beneke, "The Critical Turn," 30.

p. 182   "He claimed they were exceptionally lazy and in camp they had used timber from the walls"—Lax and Pencak, "The Knowles Riot," 25.

p. 182   "Skilled sailors took the most precautions, refusing to man the private coasters"—Bridenbaugh, *Cities in Revolt*, 115–116.

p. 182   "his press-gang swept over the vessels in the harbor and snatched any men they could find"—Lax and Pencak, "The Knowles Riot," 26.

p. 182   "From there, the gang stormed into town, accosting sailors"—Bridenbaugh, *Cities in Revolt*, 115; Nash, *Urban Crucible*, 222.

p. 182   "Armed with sticks, cutlasses, clubs, and shipwrights' pitch mops, the hastily assembled crowd"—Hutchinson, *History of Massachusetts*, 387; Lincoln, *Shirley Correspondence*, 412.

p. 182   "First a lieutenant, then about a dozen other men of rank found themselves shackled"—Nash, *Urban Crucible*, 222; Lax and Pencak, "The Knowles Riot," 27.

p. 183   "The mob leaders blamed Shirley for the press gangs, but the governor claimed"—Lax and Pencak, "The Knowles Riot," 27–28.

p. 183   "the crowds moved on to the waterfront, where they burned a barge"—Brunsman, "Impressment Riots," 359.

p. 183   "He also called out the militia to suppress the crowds"—Lax and Pencak, "The Knowles Riot," 29.

p. 183   "Knowles refused and instead threatened to bombard the town with his cannons"—Lax and Pencak, "The Knowles Riot," 30; Hutchinson, *History of Massachusetts*, 388.

p. 183   "the impressed men would be released in exchange for the return of the British officers"—Lax and Pencak, "The Knowles Riot," 32.

p. 183   "foreign seamen, servants, Negroes, and other persons of mean and vile condition" —Nash, *Urban Crucible*, 222.

p. 183   "the insurrection was secretly countenanced and encouraged by some ill-minded inhabitants"—Lincoln, *Shirley Correspondence*, 406.

p. 184   "all of them enraged by the tactics of the British military and willing to risk their lives to stop it"—Brunsman, "Impressment Riots," 360.

p. 184   "what I think may be esteemed the principal cause of the mobbish turn in this town is its constitution"—Lincoln, *Shirley Correspondence*, 418.

p. 184   "he recommended changing the town's constitution to make it hospitable"—ibid.

p. 184   "The Knowles Riot was the greatest revolt against the power of the British state" —Brunsman, "Subjects vs. Citizens," 565.

p. 184   "Such bold defiance of the highest authorities, moreover, accorded well with the vision"—Nash, *Urban Crucible*, 223.

p. 185   "inspire in the minds of the people"—Amicus Curiae, *An Address to the Inhabitants*, 2–3.

p. 185   "the arbitrary, and illegal conduct, of those who have been the authors of our late sufferings"—ibid., 5.

p. 185   "had been popularly elected as a representative in the Boston Caucus by a town meeting"—Wells, *Life and Public Services of Adams*, 13.

p. 185   "Members of the caucus worked to protect the common people against abuses" —Alexander, *Samuel Adams*, 9.

p. 186   "Whether it be lawful to resist the Supreme Magistrate, if the Commonwealth"—Wells, *Life and Public Services of Adams*, 10–11.

p. 186   "an unprecedented act of incipient 'treason'"—ibid., 11.

p. 186   "Massachusetts land owners desperate for hard currency could mortgage their holdings"—Alexander, *Samuel Adams*, 6–7.

p. 186   "If the directors of the Land Bank could not pay it, they would be held liable for triple damages in court"—Alexander, *Samuel Adams*, 8–9; Miller, *Pioneer in Propaganda*, 15.

p. 186   "carnal wretches, hypocrites, fighters against God, children of the devil, cursed Pharisees" to "mutiny, sedition, and riots"—Nash, *Urban Crucible*, 215.

p. 187   "Parliament crushed the Land Bank and nearly destroyed the material wealth of Samuel Adams Sr."—Wells, *Life and Public Services of Adams*, 10.

p. 187   "For the next twenty years, Samuel Sr. and his successors would continue to be on the hook"—Miller, *Pioneer in Propaganda*, 15.

p. 187   "if he offered to advance upon the town, he should advance at his peril"—Lax and Pencak, "The Knowles Riot," 38.

p. 187   "He also compared Governor Shirley to King James II, who was widely seen as a tyrant"—ibid.

p. 188   "they had no other choice if their magistrates refused to protect them"—Beneke, "The Critical Turn," 33.

p. 188   "riots and other violent actions could be considered natural rights"—Brunsman, "Impressment Riots," 364.

p. 188   "the acts of the colony's General Court be given the same weight as those of the British Parliament"—Miller, *Pioneer in Propaganda*, 21.

p. 188   "'an itch for riding the beasts of the people' in order to subdue them"—ibid., 20.

p. 188   "despises his neighbors' happiness" to "struts immeasurably above the lower size of people"—Alexander, *Samuel Adams*, 10–11.

p. 188   "This experience had a profound impact, even for a scholar studying public affairs" —Miller, *Pioneer in Propaganda*, 7.

p. 188   "his first revolt was against materialism and his first hatreds were against those he believed hostile"—ibid., 19.

p. 189   "He lamented how Puritanism had declined and left 'our morals, our constitution, and our liberties'"—ibid., 18.

p. 189   "He claimed the new King's Chapel in Boston, being constructed over the burial ground"—Lax and Pencak, "The Knowles Riot," 39.

p. 189   "might be likely to disturb this people in the enjoyment of their inviolable liberties" ibid., 38.

CHAPTER 10: HOLY GROUND

Although *Sinners in the Hands of an Angry God* is the sermon that attracts most of the literary and theoretical commentary about Jonathan Edwards, many religious scholars and modern evangelicals consider *A Treatise Concerning Religious Affections* (Boston: S. Kneeland and T. Green, 1746) to be his most important work. This analysis of the role of the human mind and emotions in spiritual conversion continues to influence Christian philosophy and writing more than 270 years after it was written. Another classic volume from the post-revival period is Edwards's *Account of the Life of the Late Reverend Mr. David Brainerd* (Boston: D. Henchman, 1749), which shows its author using the biography of another minister to find a new balance between the religion of mind and the commitment of the heart. Both this and *Religious Affections* should be considered the starting points for any study of Edwards, along with his various works on the earlier revivals, including *Some Thoughts Concerning the Present Revival of Religion in New-England*. Also relevant to this chapter is *An Humble Inquiry into the Rules of the Word of God . . .* (Boston: S. Kneeland, 1749), especially interesting for its catalog of rules designed to measure true conversions, which put into practice encouraged Edwards's parishioners to relieve him of his duties as their pastor.

Supplemental works that offer useful perspectives on the reverend's ministry during this time include Nathan Hatch, "The Origins of Civil Millennialism in America: New England Clergymen, War with France, and the Revolution," in *Colonial America: Essays in Politics and Social Development*, 4th edition, ed. by Stanley Katz et al. (New York: McGraw-Hill (1993), 581–604), as well as Mark Valeri, "The Economic Thought of Jonathan Edwards," for Edwards's frustrations over, and reaction to, economic conditions in New England; and Kenneth Minkema, "Jonathan Edwards's Defense of Slavery," an illustration of his shameful role as a slave owner and his assorted justifications for it. Other helpful background sources include Harry Stout, *The New England Soul: Preaching and Religious Culture in Colonial New England*; and Douglas Winiarski, *Darkness Falls on the Land of Light: Experiencing Religious Awakenings in Eighteenth-Century New England*.

In contrast with Reverend Edwards, the "amiable heretic" Reverend Jonathan Mayhew has not attracted as much attention for his religious writing outside of Unitarian and other liberal circles in recent decades. However, his political sermons—of which there are several key examples—continue to draw interest from scholars. One of the most important is *A Discourse Concerning Unlimited Submission and Non-Resistance to the Higher Powers: with Some Reflections on the Resistance Made to King Charles I* (Boston: D. Fowle, 1750), the focus of Chapter 10, which laid down the gauntlet of resistance to future monarchs and justified it with copious references to British Whig theorists. Also useful for its blend of political criticism and liberal theology is the classic *Seven Sermons Upon the Following Subjects . . .* (Boston: Rogers and Fowle, 1749), which became a template for the kind of "natural religion" that would become prominent in the colonies, and the early United States, in years to come.

For worthy commentary and historic background on Mayhew's incendiary sermons, see Bernard Bailyn, *Pamphlets of the American Revolution, 1750–1776*, vol. 1 (Cambridge, MA: Harvard Univ. Press, 1965), as well as Chris Beneke, "The Critical Turn: Jonathan Mayhew, the British Empire, and the Idea of Resistance in Mid-Eighteenth-Century Boston," which puts the reverend in the context of the tumultuous period of the mid-18th century and all its economic miseries and social disorder. Also see Joseph Tiedemann, "Presbyterianism and the American Revolution in the Middle Colonies," for the Calvinist perspective on this era and the similar contentious reaction to it.

Biographies of Jonathan Mayhew from the 19th century are generally not helpful for understanding the minister, and offer little more than extended quotations from his work. Better are the contemporary sources such as J. Patrick Mullins, *Father of Liberty: Jonathan Mayhew and the Principles of the American Revolution*, the latest biography that brings the evidence up to date; and the classic by Charles Akers, *Called unto Liberty*, and Clinton Rossiter's "The Life and Mind of Jonathan Mayhew."

The growing hostility of American colonists toward the Church of England is a subject known to scholars of prerevolutionary America but has figured in almost no popular renderings of that history. Nonetheless, understanding how anti-Anglican feeling expanded in the 1740s is critical to any study of the era. The key volume for this is still Carl Bridenbaugh, *Mitre and Sceptre: Transatlantic Faiths, Ideas, Personalities, and Politics, 1689–1775*, a comprehensive view of how native ideas on Anglicanism bred revolutionary sentiments. Other useful sources for the time include Henry Wilder Foote, *Annals of King's Chapel, from the Puritan Age of New England to the Present Day*, vol. 2 (Boston: Little, Brown and Co., 1896), with mention of the construction of, and resistance to, that important structure; and John Beach, *A Calm and Dispassionate Vindication of the Professors of the Church of England . . .* (Boston: J. Draper, 1749), which provided the high church's defense of its expanding power, in an answer to Noah Hobart's controversial *Sermon Delivered at the Ordination of the Reverend Mr. Noah Welles*, mentioned in Chapter 8.

Other relevant secondary sources previously mentioned include Gary Nash, *The Urban Crucible: Social Change, Political Consciousness, and the Origins of the American Revolution*; Thomas Kidd, *The Great Awakening: The Roots of Evangelical Christianity in Colonial America*; and Patricia Bonomi, *Under the Cope of Heaven: Religion, Society, and Politics in Colonial America*. Furthermore, Alan Heimert, in *Religion and the American Mind: From the Great Awakening to the Revolution*, is particularly trenchant in writing about the intersection of evangelical radicalism and colonial stirrings of revolt, though he tends to unfairly dismiss the contributions of liberal ministers like Jonathan Mayhew in fostering revolutionary sentiments.

Finally, the scholarship on the English Civil War and Oliver Cromwell is obviously voluminous, and will not be mentioned in detail here. The sources for the Puritan Revolution and the Lord

Protector largely relate to their influence in America, both during the mid-17th century and in the century afterward. The best of these is Alfred Young, "English Plebeian Culture and Eighteenth-Century American Radicalism," in *The Origins of Anglo-American Radicalism*, ed. Margaret Jacob and James Jacob (London: Humanities Press Intl., 1991), an essential article on a little-known subject, and partly drawn from his equally influential "Pope's Day, Tar and Feathers, and Cornet Joyce, Jun.: From Ritual to Rebellion in Boston, 1745–1775" (*Bulletin of the Society for the Study of Labour History* 27 (1973), 27–59). Another useful study on Pope's Day, as a symbol of colonial ritual, is Francis Cogliano, "Deliverance from Luxury: Pope's Day, Conflict and Consensus in Colonial Boston, 1745–1765" (*Studies in Popular Culture* 15:2 (1993), 15–28).

The Puritan commander did not attract uniform praise in the colonies, especially outside New England, and for a look on the complex reaction to his legacy, see Rock Brynner, "Cromwell's Shadow over the Confederation: The Dread of Cyclical History in Revolutionary America" (*Proceedings of the Massachusetts Historical Society* 3:106 (1994), 35–52). For a look at how New Englanders returned to the home country to fight in his forces, Harry Stout, "The Morphology of Remigration: New England University Men and Their Return to England, 1640–1660" (*Journal of American Studies* 10:2 (1976), 151–172), is the definitive study. Background information on Massachusetts and the social conditions that burnished the legend of the Lord Protector include Thomas Hutchinson, *History of Massachusetts from the First Settlement Thereof in 1628, Until the Year 1750* (Boston: Thomas and Andrews, 1795), and Sydney Ahlstrom, *A Religious History of the American People*. For the second US president's quotations on Cromwell's long shadow, see John Adams, Diary, April 4–10, 1786, in Adams Family Papers, Massachusetts Historical Society, accessed at www.masshist.org/digitaladams/archive/diary.

CHAPTER 10 REFERENCES

p. 191   "effects on the animal spirits are more violent, and the mind more overpowered" —Edwards, *Religious Affections*, 6.

p. 191   "Separatists like Isaac Backus even claimed he understood Edwards's message better" —Stout, *New England* Soul, 211.

p. 191   "He painted Edwards as a milquetoast who valued 'ecclesiastical tranquility'" —Winiarski, *Darkness Falls*, 317–318.

p. 192   "The revival had not turned out as he had expected, but had become 'very sorrowful and dark'"—Hatch, "Civil Millennialism," 625.

p. 192   "he helped to foster a transatlantic network of faith seekers who knew no bounds of nationhood"—ibid.

p. 192   "Brainerd had gone from fiery young zealot who had been expelled from Yale"—Kidd, *Great Awakening*, 196–197.

p. 193   "false scheme of religion . . . gave men both an undue sense of their own importance" —Heimert, *American Mind*, 33.

p. 193   "greed and selfishness flourished in an unfettered market"—Valeri, "Economic Thought," 50.

p. 193   "he spurned other thinkers from the same movement who trafficked in market theories"—ibid., 51.

p. 193   "he also defended slavery and owned several humans himself"—Minkema, "Edwards's Defense," 42–43.

p. 193   "he put his faith in hopes that it might be abolished, in future 'glorious times'"—ibid., 42.

p. 193   "'jewelry, chocolate, Boston-made clothing, children's toys' and other luxuries"—ibid., 36.

p. 194   "tripling his salary to 870 pounds by 1748"—Valeri, "Economic Thought," 48.

p. 194   "He became further estranged from them when he realized many were tossing worthless old currency"—ibid.

p. 194   "none ought to be admitted as members of the visible church of Christ but visible saints"—Edwards, "Humble Inquiry," 11.

p. 194   "visible saints or converts are those who are so in the eye of man"—ibid., 15.

p. 195   "They didn't need 'skillful guides' to lead them toward the New Birth"—Bonomi, *Under the Cope*, 159.

p. 195   "Citing him with betraying the word of God and exploiting his position in the community"—Valeri, "Economic Thought," 51.

p. 195   "In an open rebuke, they denied him admittance to the Boston Association of Ministers"—Mullins, *Father of Liberty*, 51–52.

p. 196   "a merciful and faithful creator"—Mayhew, *Seven Sermons*, 106–107.

p. 196   "the splendid faculties of the mind to find true religion, which had nothing to do with 'vice, ignorance and superstition'"—Akers, *Liberty*, 72.

p. 196   "more readily embraced by a man after his brains are knocked out"—Mayhew, *Seven Sermons*, 63.

p. 196   "frequent raptures, and strange transports of mechanical devotion"—ibid., 153.

p. 196   "from predestination and human depravity to the election of the saints"—Rossiter, "Life and Mind," 542.

p. 196   "He exalted instead the 'natural religion' that showed 'beauty, order, harmony and design'"—Mullins, *Father of Liberty*, 32.

p. 196   "Christianity is principally an institution of life and manners"—Mayhew, *Seven Sermons*, 152.

p. 197   "in Britain, the sermons attracted great attention among nonconformists"—Mullins, *Father of Liberty*, 40–41.

p. 197   "they had cause to be shocked, and that it was akin to hearing 'good things coming out of Nazareth'"—Akers, *Liberty*, 76–77.

p. 197   "Among the recommendations Jonathan received for the degree was one from Governor William Shirley"—ibid., 77.

p. 197   "Governor Shirley had witnessed the ordination of Reverend Hooper"—ibid., 46.

p. 198   "he described a series of 'enemies' of liberty that deserved all the scorn he could muster"—Mullins, *Father of Liberty*, 36.

p. 198   "whose authority then is to be regarded, that of the King, or that of the Monarch of the Universe"—Mayhew, *Seven Sermons*, 82.

p. 199   "We have not only a right to think for ourselves in matters of religion"—ibid., 85.

p. 199   "Parliament had designated 183,000 pounds in silver specie to retire the old currency"—Nash, *Urban Crucible*, 224–225; Beneke, "Critical Turn," 29.

p. 199   "his house had taken flame while an angry crowd surrounded it, shouting 'Let it burn! Let it burn!'"—Nash, *Urban Crucible*, 226.

p. 199   "They felt it had been earned with 'the blood of the lower classes on the Canadian expeditions'"—ibid.

p. 200   "he proudly took credit for the currency replacement act and its approval by the king"—Beneke, "Critical Turn," 29.

p. 200   "The British state and its organs like the Board of Trade had been increasingly interfering"—ibid.

p. 200   "despite the efforts of Ben Franklin and countless others to enact laws to forbid the practice"—Morgan, *Benjamin Franklin*, 73–74.

p. 200   "'the ashes of the dead were inhumanely disturbed' to create the bulky stone Georgian edifice"—Beneke, "Critical Turn," 35–36.

p. 200   "Commodore William Knowles—cause of the eponymous riot—had even pledged one hundred pounds"—Beneke, "Critical Turn," 36; Foote, *Annals of King's Chapel*, 40.

p. 200   "the new church arose, to symbolize by the massive walls which made it a cathedral" —Foote, *Annals of King's Chapel*, 41.

p. 201   "'swifter than an eagle—stronger than a lion' but who was nonetheless murdered by 'vermin'"—Mullins, *Father of Liberty*, 50.

p. 201   "a disorderly rabble of enthusiasts scrambling for power in every part of the kingdom"—ibid.

p. 201   "He didn't consider himself a political philosopher but knew that history and politics would be essential"—Akers, *Liberty*, 83.

p. 201   "So he studied everything from John Locke"—Mullins, *Father of Liberty*, 52.

p. 202   "Twenty thousand dissenters from the state church awaited the outcome"—Stout, *New England* Soul, 50–51.

p. 202   "Economic conditions in New England were bleak and few jobs could be found amid the immigration surge of previous years"—ibid.

p. 202   "Ministers and Harvard graduates made up the bulk of returnees"—Stout, "Morphology," 156.

p. 202   "eight took positions in Parliament and ten held major roles in the New Model Army led by Oliver Cromwell"—Young, "English Plebeian Culture," 194–195; Stout, "Morphology," 155.

p. 202   "the foundation of the Church of England—its legal establishment and system of episcopacy"—Ahlstrom, *Religious History*, 94.

p. 202   "one prominent New England minister, John Cotton, commended him"—Young, "English Plebeian Culture," 194–195.

p. 203   "men who returned from New England after fighting in the New Model Army"—ibid.

p. 203   "he allowed the persecution of Anglicans in the New World, and when they complained"—Hutchinson, *History of Massachusetts*, 175.

p. 203   "He encouraged the banishment of rebels like Anne Hutchinson from Massachusetts"—ibid., 177.

p. 203   "that extraordinary privilege of having their goods imported into England"—ibid., 180.

p. 203   "the new royal government drove some two thousand nonconformist ministers" —Ahlstrom, *Religious History*, 95.

p. 204   "praise for Lord Protector Cromwell vanished from official circles"—Young, "English Plebeian Culture," 195–196.

p. 204   "Parents in New England named their children 'Oliver' in his honor"—ibid., 197.

p. 204　　"librarians in Massachusetts added books to their shelves written by sympathizers"
　　　　　—Brynner, "Cromwell's Shadow," 40–41.

p. 204　　"Cromwell's Head Inn forced visitors to bow to a giant sign"—Young, "English
　　　　　Plebeian Culture," 197.

p. 204　　"feathering the effigies of the pontiff and the devil, dragging them along in violent
　　　　　processions"—Cogliano, "Deliverance from Luxury," 16–17.

p. 204　　"the event evolved into 'a ritual of detestation of the Stuarts'"—Young, "English
　　　　　Plebeian Culture," 198.

p. 204　　"Ministers like John Dickinson openly defended the Puritan Revolution"—Heimert,
　　　　　American Mind, 375.

p. 204　　"Anonymous pamphlets called Charles I an 'execrable tyrant'"—Tiedemann,
　　　　　"Presbyterianism and the American Revolution," 320.

p. 204　　"Christ's ambassadors were represented by Calvinists in the image of Cromwell"
　　　　　—Heimert, *American Mind*, 151.

p. 205　　"And how much were the great things that Oliver Cromwell did, owing to these
　　　　　things!"—Edwards, *Some Thoughts*, 346.

p. 205　　"nearly every pietist in New England had secretly shared since the Great Awakening"
　　　　　—Young, "English Plebeian Culture," 196.

p. 205　　"[D]o Englishmen so soon forget the ground where liberty was fought for?"—Adams,
　　　　　Diary, April 4–10.

p. 206　　"the people's duty of passive obedience and nonresistance to tyrants"—Mullins, *Father
　　　　　of Liberty*, 46.

p. 206　　"disobedience to civil rulers in the due exercise of their authority"—Mayhew, *Unlimited
　　　　　Submission*, 10.

p. 206　　"James II 'was made to fly that country which he aimed at enslaving'"—ibid., 13.

p. 206　　"It is blasphemy to call tyrants and oppressors God's ministers"—ibid., 24.

p. 206　　"For a nation thus abused to arise unanimously, and to resist their prince"—ibid., 40.

p. 207　　"He called him an agent of oppression, a wretch who had married a French Catholic"
　　　　　—ibid., 41–42.

p. 207　　"They weren't any mere rebels, but 'the LORDS and COMMONS of England'"—ibid.,
　　　　　44.

p. 207　　"were not, properly speaking, guilty of rebellion; because he, whom they beheaded"
　　　　　—ibid., 48.

p. 208　　"a man black with guilt and laden with iniquity . . . and it was the oppression and
　　　　　violence"—ibid., 49.

p. 208　　"*Britons* will not be *slaves*; a warning to all corrupt councilors and ministers"—ibid., 54.

p. 208　　"They called the sermon a justification for murder and anarchy"—Akers, *Liberty*,
　　　　　89–90.

p. 208　　"Jonathan's longtime nemesis Charles Brockwell even called the sermon a work of
　　　　　treason"—Beneke, "Critical Turn," 44.

p. 208　　"urged the Bishop of London to have him arrested and shipped back to Britain"
　　　　　—Mullins, *Father of Liberty*, 61.

p. 209　　"He challenged his foes to put a name to any single criticism so he could answer it"
　　　　　—Akers, *Liberty*, 90.

p. 209   "he sent Hoadley a copy of the sermon along with a note thanking him for his influence"—Mullins, *Father of Liberty*, 60.

p. 209   "it set off a six-month battle in the press over the idea of citizens rebelling against their government"—Bonomi, *Under the Cope*, 197; Bridenbaugh, *Mitre and Sceptre*, 107.

p. 209   "the most famous sermon preached in pre-revolutionary America"—Bailyn, *Pamphlets*, 204.

p. 209   "a pre-eminent spokesman in the colonies for everything that was new, bold, and radically nonconformist"—ibid., 210–211.

p. 210   "till the substance of it was incorporated into my nature and indelibly engraved on my memory"—Mullins, *Father of Liberty*, 64.

p. 210   "the sermon 'was read by everybody; celebrated by friends, and abused by enemies'"—Beneke, "Critical Turn," 23.

p. 210   "He called it his own 'catechism' of revolution"—Stout, *New England Soul*, 240.

CHAPTER 11: THE AWAKENERS

The life of Jonathan Edwards was well chronicled, by himself and others, and he left a detailed record of his thoughts and beliefs. Unlike evangelists like George Whitefield, whose actions and motivations have been subject to continued speculation, those of Edwards are solid and well known. The best modern biography, and most detailed, is George Marsden's *Jonathan Edwards: A Life* (New Haven, CT: Yale Univ. Press, 2003), which offers a balanced and thoughtful perspective on his ministry. To delve into the theological implications of Edwards's work, consult Perry Miller's classic *Jonathan Edwards* (New York: William Morrow, 1949), though note that Miller's technical examination of the minister's theology is aimed more at scholars than general readers. An interesting alternative written by a primary source, is Samuel Hopkins, *The Life and Character of the Late Reverend Mr. Jonathan Edwards* (Boston: S. Kneeland, 1765), with the author having studied under the Calvinist master. Hopkins also wrote useful volumes on Sarah Osborn and Susanna Anthony, covered in earlier chapters.

If the details of Edwards's life are fairly well agreed upon, the import of his theology remains subject to debate. The reverend has been held up as an example of everything from early political liberalism and "Enlightenment" Calvinism to the rhetoric of religious terror and reactionary anti-intellectualism. An online search will deliver whatever version of Edwards you desire, but some of the better supplemental reading on the minister for this chapter includes Edwin Gaustad, "The Theological Effects of the Great Awakening in New England," a well-reasoned look at the results of his and other ministers' ideology of revival; Kenneth Minkema and Harry Stout, "The Edwardsean Tradition and the Anti-Slavery Debate, 1740–1865," following the long-term results of his preaching on subjects of slavery and liberation; and Rachel Wheeler, *To Live Upon Hope: Mohicans and Missionaries in the Eighteenth-Century Northeast* (Ithaca, NY: Cornell Univ. Press, 2008), putting his missionary work in context with that of others on the colonial frontier. For capsule biographies of Edwards as well as Aaron Burr Sr. in their educational roles, see the Trustees of Princeton University, "The Presidents of Princeton University: Jonathan Edwards," accessed at www.princeton.edu/pub/presidents/edwards/.

Ultimately the best approach to understand the great theologian is to read his work personally, without the filter of other interpreters. Most of it remains extant and can be found online or in divinity libraries. His key works mentioned in this chapter include *Misrepresentations Corrected, and*

Truth Vindicated, a defense against those who attacked him at Northampton; *The Great Christian Doctrine of Original Sin Defended* (Boston: S. Kneeland, 1758), a good late example of his Calvinist traditionalism; *A Careful and Strict Enquiry into the Modern Prevailing Notions of That Freedom of Will* (Boston: S. Kneeland, 1754), a rejoinder to those who elevate human free will over God's own powers; and *The Harmony of the Old and New Testament*, in Stephen R. C. Nichols, *Jonathan Edwards's Bible: The Relationship of the Old and New Testaments* (Eugene, OR: Pickwick, 2013), a fragmentary analysis of his notes in preparation for what might have been a towering work of theology. An even bigger undertaking, *The History of the Work of Redemption*, only exists in pieces, but the best modern discussion of it can be found in William Scheick, "The Grand Design: Jonathan Edwards' History of the Work of Redemption" (*Eighteenth-Century Studies* 8:3 (1975), 300–314)

Gilbert Tennent has attracted much less attention than Edwards, partly because of his glaring contradictions over the course of his life, and partly because his spiteful revival sermons remain distasteful to modern readers. The best overview of the Presbyterian stalwart is Milton Coalter Jr., *Gilbert Tennent: Son of Thunder: A Case Study of Continental Pietism's Impact on the First Great Awakening in the Middle Colonies*, supplemented by articles from Janet Fishburn, "Gilbert Tennent, Established Dissenter," and Frederick Brink, "Gilbert Tennent, Dynamic Preacher." The results of his ministry are also covered in the classic volumes by Sydney Ahlstrom, *A Religious History of the American People*; Charles Maxson, *The Great Awakening in the Middle Colonies*; and Alan Heimert, *Religion and the American Mind*. For a look at how his faith intersected with the politics of Anglicanism in the era, see Carl Bridenbaugh, *Mitre and Sceptre: Transatlantic Faiths, Ideas, Personalities, and Politics, 1689–1775*.

Some of Tennent's writings continue to impress, though he's not as fluid or accessible an author as Jonathan Edwards. For his defense of God's mystery after the lightning strike that nearly killed him, see *All Things Come Alike to All* (Philadelphia: William Bradford, 1745); for his attempt to reconcile the Presbyterian church, see *Irenicum Ecclesiasticum, or a Humble Impartial Essay Upon the Peace of Jerusalem* (Philadelphia: William Bradford, 1749); and for a review of his revised theology later in his career, and his defense of his ornate church, see *The Divine Government Over All Considered* (Philadelphia: William Bradford, 1752). His trip to Great Britain is covered in the biographical works mentioned above, though for the perspective of his traveling companion, see George William Pilcher, ed., *The Reverend Samuel Davies Abroad, The Diary of a Journey to England and Scotland, 1753–55* (Urbana, IL: Univ. of Illinois Press, 1967). Note that Davies also fueled the imagination and rhetoric of the young Patrick Henry (covered in the postscript to this book). Finally, a worthy investigation of how the united Presbyterian church encouraged rebellion in the colonies is laid out in Joseph S. Tiedemann, "Presbyterianism and the American Revolution in the Middle Colonies."

Edmund Morgan's *Benjamin Franklin* remains a favorite source for biographical data on the Founding Father, but for more detailed primary sources, see Leonard Labaree, ed., *The Papers of Benjamin Franklin, vol. 6, April 1755–September 1756* (New Haven: Yale Univ. Press, 1963), among other worthy volumes in the series. For a closer examination of the backbiting atmosphere in which he practiced politics, consult W. Shirley and James Hutson, "Benjamin Franklin and Pennsylvania Politics, 1751-1755: A Reappraisal" (*The Pennsylvania Magazine of History and Biography* 93:3 (1969), 303-371); and Theodore Thayer, *Pennsylvania Politics and the Growth of Democracy* (Harrisburg, PA: Pennsylvania Historical and Museum Commission, 1953). Further discussion of the tumultuous circumstances of poor government in the Middle Colonies can be found in Gary Nash, *The Urban Crucible: Social Change, Political Consciousness, and the Origins of the American Revolution*. A transcript of Franklin's interrogation in Parliament over colonists' views of the Stamp Act is included in David

NOTES

Brion Davis and Steven Mintz, eds., *The Boisterous Sea of Liberty: A Documentary History of America from Discovery through the Civil War* (New York: Oxford Univ. Press, 1998).

The friendship of Franklin and George Whitefield remains a puzzle to many scholars, and a source of speculation over how each may have affected the beliefs of the other, or not. The finest works that cover their relationship, from a variety of perspectives and in some detail, include Harry Stout, "George Whitefield and Benjamin Franklin: Thoughts on a Peculiar Friendship"; David T. Morgan, "A Most Unlikely Friendship—Benjamin Franklin and George Whitefield"; and Frank Lambert, "Subscribing for Profits and Piety: The Friendship of Benjamin Franklin and George Whitefield." Much of this information is similarly covered in Peter Charles Hoffer, *When Benjamin Franklin Met the Reverend Whitefield: Enlightenment, Revival, and the Power of the Printed Word*, which also offers extensive comments on the issues and controversies of the era.

George Whitefield attracted more attention in the 18th century than he did throughout most of the twentieth, but recent scholarship has shone more light on the most successful preacher of the New Birth. Among the better perspectives are those by Frank Lambert, *"Pedlar in Divinity": George Whitefield and the Transatlantic Revivals, 1737–1770*; Thomas Kidd, *George Whitefield: America's Spiritual Founding Father*; and *The Great Awakening: The Roots of Evangelical Christianity in Colonial America*; and Harry Stout, *The Divine Dramatist: George Whitefield and the Rise of Modern Evangelicalism*, each taking a particular thesis on the Grand Itinerant's success and backing it up with considerable research and cogent argument. For a view of Whitefield's troubled perspective and actions regarding slavery, see Jessica Parr, *Inventing George Whitefield: Race, Revivalism, and the Making of an American Icon*, while a summary view of his ministry, and its revision over time, is offered by David Ceri Jones, "'So Much Idolized by Some, and Railed At by Others': Towards Understanding George Whitefield" (*Wesley and Methodist Studies* 5 (2013), 3–29).

Some older sources on Whitefield provide valuable information, especially since they include extensive quoted material not often included in the works of modern authors. The best of these is Luke Tyerman, *The Life of the Reverend George Whitefield*, vols. 1 and 2, which also lobs criticism at the Itinerant for his actions to legalize slavery and does not downplay the controversies of his era. By contrast, John Gillies, *Memoirs of Reverend George Whitefield*, is a mostly sanitized memoir of the preacher, though it does speak with a certain moral urgency and formed the basis for his legendary reputation.

Whitefield's preaching in the Middle Colonies and New England in his later life was largely devoted to testaments to the New Birth and God's grace, and typical examples are covered in earlier chapters. More distinctive to the time is the upswelling in his martial rhetoric, for which see *A Short Address to Persons of All Denominations Occasioned by the Alarm of an Intended Invasion* (London: W. Strahan, 1756), occasioned by the nationalism of the French and Indian War. Other relevant works can be found in the earlier cited *Sermons on Important Subjects*.

Lastly, the quoted poems and rhymes that either praise or lampoon Whitefield can be found in the following: the broadside "A Poem, on the Joyful News of the Rev. Mr. Whitefield's Visit in Boston" (Boston: 1754), is accessible at the Library of Congress, www.loc.gov/item/rbpe.03501200; the doggerel "Friendly Advice for Dr. Squintum" is printed in Samuel Palmer, *St. Pancras; Being Antiquarian, Topographical, and Biographical Memoranda* (London: Samuel Palmer, 1870); and Phillis Wheatley's ode to the Itinerant, "An Elegiac Poem on the Death of That Celebrated Divine . . ." is in *The Poems of Phillis Wheatley*, ed. Julian Mason Jr. (Chapel Hill, NC: Univ. of North Carolina Press, 1966; reprinted 1988).

CHAPTER 11 REFERENCES:

p. 213   "the town folk claimed he had 'sinister views' and a 'tyrannical spirit'"—Marsden, *Edwards: A Life*, 363.

p. 213   "He said they meant to 'exhibit my scheme to the world in a ridiculous light'"—Edwards, *Misrepresentations*, 14.

p. 214   "Reverend Edwards's real problem was that he was a perfectionist"—Marsden, *Edwards: A Life*, 370.

p. 214   "Edwards consulted with his family and a ministerial council and accepted the role"—Hopkins, *Life of the Late Reverend*, 73–74.

p. 214   "He planned to educate the children of the Mohawk people in Christianity"—ibid., 74.

p. 214   "he saw many of his white peers as worse for having heard the gospel and rejecting it"—Marsden, *Edwards: A Life*, 385.

p. 214   "for as long as they keep you in ignorance . . . 'tis more easy to cheat you in trading with you"—ibid., 386–388.

p. 214   "Edwards oversaw a small group of Mohawk boys, as well as girls, and their instruction in reading, spelling, math and sacred music, as well as scripture."—ibid., 390.

p. 215   "had several young Indian friends and was better versed in Mahican and Mohawk than English"—Minkema and Stout, "Edwardsean Tradition," 51.

p. 215   "the reverend so lacked for writing paper that he was reduced to scrawling on their discarded scraps"—Marsden, *Edwards: A Life*, 391–392.

p. 215   "a sore scourge to use as a just punishment of our cruelty to their souls and bodies"—Wheeler, *To Live Upon Hope*, 212.

p. 215   "soldiers built a stockade surrounding it and prepared for an onslaught of enemy warriors"—Marsden, *Edwards: A Life*, 409–412.

p. 216   "God is indeed frowning upon us everywhere; our enemies get up above us very high"—Wheeler, *To Live Upon Hope*, 212.

p. 217   "Burr had been the president of the recently chartered College of New Jersey"—Trustees, "Presidents of Princeton."

p. 217   "childish weakness and contemptibleness of speech, presence and demeanor"—Hopkins, *Life of the Late Reverend*, 76.

p. 217   "he appeared uncommonly moved and affected with it, and fell into tears on the occasion"—ibid., 79.

p. 218   "Hopkins would carry the torch for Edwards's gospel for the next generation"—Gaustad, "Theological Effects," 699.

p. 218   "He girded up his loins, and set off from Stockbridge for Prince-Town in January"—Hopkins, *Life of the Late Reverend*, 79.

p. 218   "Edwards had warned of the liberalism of men like Jonathan Mayhew"—Marsden, *Edwards: A Life*, 435.

p. 218   "to sum up his career as a revivalist with his magnum opus"—ibid., 481–482.

p. 218   "Edwards didn't wish any of his other children to suffer the same fate, or worse" ibid., 493–494.

p. 219   "Many graduates and associates of the Log College became trustees of the new college"—Ahlstrom, *Religious History*, 273; Maxson, *Great Awakening*, 98.

p. 219   "the Church of England, which tried to prevent it from being chartered" —Bridenbaugh, *Mitre and Sceptre*, 129, 131.

p. 220   "The bolt sheared bricks off the chimney, tore through the house, melted his belt buckle"—Coalter, *Son of Thunder*, 126.

p. 220   "God's paths are in the great deep, and his footsteps are not known"—Tennent, *All Things Come Alike*, 11–12.

p. 220   "Gilbert preached to a congregation that included the governor of Pennsylvania" —Fishburn, "Established Dissenter," 37.

p. 220   "He spoke with extensive notes and reused many of his old sermons"—Coalter, *Son of Thunder*, 131.

p. 221   "He offered to assume control of the building for use as a proposed nondenominational college"—ibid., 138.

p. 221   "in cities where there is a greater resort of persons of honor, distinction, and polite taste"—Tennent, *Divine Government*, 64.

p. 221   "He created an alliance with other moderate revivalists to form the New York Synod" —Coalter, *Son of Thunder*, 129.

p. 222   "it was 'absurd and blasphemous' to accept divisions between people of faith" —Tennent, *Irenicum*, 39.

p. 222   "Schisms and divisions, my brethren, do not only expose the church to contempt and scorn"—ibid., 114.

p. 222   "wished only to unite Presbyterians once more in a spirit of 'humility, weakness and love'"—ibid., 92.

p. 222   "the visible church strikes a dread, a panic, into the hearts of all her foes"—ibid., 11; Heimert, *American Mind*, 150.

p. 222   "He began to preach of battle outside the pulpit, too, exhorting all Presbyterians" —Coalter, *Son of Thunder*, 132.

p. 222   "The trustees had tried to use public lotteries and domestic donations to fund the institution"—ibid., 146.

p. 223   "Even the quality of Presbyterianism seemed foreign to him—divided by liberal churchmen"—ibid., 149.

p. 223   "I never engaged in such a series of wasting fatigues and dangers as our present mission is attended with"—Pilcher, *Davies Abroad*, 88.

p. 223   "Their original goal had been to collect 300 pounds for the college"—Brink, "Dynamic Preacher," 105.

p. 223   "In 1745 the divided ranks of Presbyterian pastors were roughly equal"—Maxson, *Great Awakening*, 116.

p. 224   "all former differences and disputes are laid aside and buried"—Coalter, *Son of Thunder*, 156.

p. 224   "and approved of revivals as 'a blessed work of the Holy Spirit'"—Ahlstrom, *Religious History*, 274.

p. 224   "it graduated ninety-seven 'highly articulate and unusually vocal' Presbyterian ministers"—Coalter, *Son of Thunder*, 151.

p. 224   "ninety-four of its graduates would ultimately take arms against Britain"—Tiedemann, "Presbyterianism and the American Revolution," 339.

p. 224   "with five becoming members of the Constitutional Convention"—ibid., 338.

p. 225   "enabled him to eclipse his rival Andrew Bradford and retire from his print operation"—Morgan, *Benjamin Franklin*, 71–72.

p. 225   "Franklin tried to strip them of their power to spend money and appoint magistrates"—Shirley and Hutson, "Franklin and Pennsylvania Politics," 361.

p. 225   "the proprietors called Franklin 'the chief author and grand abettor' of sedition"—Thayer, *Pennsylvania Politics*, 90.

p. 225   "forced him out as president of the Academy of Philadelphia"—Nash, *Urban Crucible*, 269–270.

p. 225   "William Smith, so offended Quaker assemblymen that they had him arrested and jailed for libel"—ibid., 270.

p. 226   "now that he had mastered the physical world, encouraged him to explore the spiritual world"—Kidd, *America's Spiritual*, 210.

p. 226   "What a glorious thing it would be, to settle in that fine country a large strong body"—Letter from Franklin to George Whitefield, July 2, 1756, in Labaree, *Papers of Franklin*, vol. 6, 468.

p. 226   "these two oddly matched men had proved to be reliable stalwarts for each other"—Stout, "Peculiar Friendship," 15.

p. 226   "They despised privilege divorced from merit, and the way the colonies were often run"—ibid., 16–17.

p. 226   "With the aid of John Gillies, a historian and minister in the Church of Scotland"—Jones, "So Much Idolized," 13–16.

p. 227   "carefully removing the parts of his *Journals* that had infuriated his foes"—ibid., 15–16.

p. 227   "Is blessed Whitefield come again? / Our heart does now rejoice"—Anonymous, "A Poem, on the Joyful News."

p. 227   "He railed against 'an insulting, enraged and perfidious enemy'"—Whitefield, *A Short Address*, 3.

p. 227   "'horrid butcheries and cruel murders' using Indians to fight the battles of priests"—ibid., 7.

p. 228   "this here doctor is capable of seeing two sides of a thing at once"—Palmer, *St. Pancras*, 178.

p. 228   "Of all the knaves and all the fools / That ever left the public schools"—"Friendly Advice for Dr. Squintum," in Palmer, *St. Pancras*, 285–286.

p. 229   "I am now mimicked and burlesqued upon the public stage. . . . All hail such contempt!"—Kidd, *America's Spiritual*, 232.

p. 229   "Franklin took the lead against those he called 'Christian White Savages'"—Morgan, *Benjamin Franklin*, 131.

p. 230   "Franklin interpreted the melee as a disaster for civilized behavior and warned of 'violent parties and cruel animosities'"—Nash, *Urban Crucible*, 284.

p. 230   "his allies spread bile against their opposers, calling them reptiles and toads, liars and schemers"—ibid., 286.

p. 230   "religious groups split among political lines and clergymen became parapolitical leaders"—ibid., 270.

p. 230   "Franklin had proposed a clever scheme to Parliament creating a loan office"—Morgan, *Benjamin Franklin*, 150.

p. 231   "No, never . . . they will never do it, unless compelled by force of arms"—Davis and Mintz, *Boisterous Sea of Liberty*, 149–150.

p. 231   "He credited his friend with playing a major part in getting the Stamp Act repealed"—D. Morgan, "A Most Unlikely Friendship," 212.

p. 231   "Dr. Franklin has gained immortal honor by his behavior at the bar of the House" —Stout, *Divine Dramatist*, 263.

p. 232   "Franklin had made sure to have his notes and a transcript of his questioning published"—Hoffer, *When Benjamin Franklin*, 112.

p. 232   "saying he 'spoke very heartily and judiciously in his country's behalf'"—Lambert, *Pedlar in Divinity*, 222.

p. 232   "[W]ho would dare deny Mr. Whitefield's authority—will the Church? Will the Presbyterians?"—Stout, *Divine Dramatist*, 264.

p. 233   "they had continually pushed for the appointment of a bishop with broad powers" —Lambert, *Pedlar in Divinity*, 213.

p. 233   "young slaves would be taught to read and learn artisan skills"—Stout, *Divine Dramatist*, 272–273.

p. 233   "Forty percent of Savannah's population now included enslaved laborers"—Kidd, *America's Spiritual*, 249.

p. 234   "The orphanage took flame in 1773 after being hit by a lightning bolt"—Tyerman, *Life of the Reverend*, vol. 2, 584.

p. 234   "yoke-fellow" to "treasured but distant ally"—Stout, *Divine Dramatist*, 156, 170–171.

p. 234   "Shall I now sympathize with you, under the frequent and sometimes long absence of your dear husband?"—Kidd, *America's Spiritual*, 246.

p. 234   "Her death set his mind much at liberty"—Stout, *Divine Dramatist*, 171.

p. 234   "He preached to packed congregations in Philadelphia thick with mixed crowds of dissenters"—Tyerman, *Life of the Reverend*, vol. 2, 589.

p. 235   "'I have no wish about it,' Tennent said. 'No, sir, it is no pleasure to me at all'"—ibid., 591.

p. 235   "Poor New England is much to be pitied; Boston people most of all. How grossly misrepresented!"—Gillies, *Memoirs of Whitefield*, 209.

p. 235   "the great mischiefs the poor pious people suffered lately through the town's being disturbed by the soldiers"—Whitefield, *Sermons on Important Subjects*, 765.

p. 235   "He woke up in the night with 'a violent lax, attended with retching and shivering'" —Stout, *Divine Dramatist*, 277.

p. 235   "He drove himself to exhaustion repeatedly, became fatigued and breathed with difficulty"—Gillies, *Memoirs of Whitefield*, 210.

p. 236   "He met his end in the parsonage of a Presbyterian church and had asked to be buried"—Parr, *Inventing George Whitefield*, 119–121.

p. 236   "Six thousand people attended, a considerable turnout for an 18th-century funeral" —Tyerman, *Life of the Reverend*, vol. 2, 600–601.

p. 236   "integrity, disinterestedness, and indefatigable zeal in prosecuting every good work" —Kidd, *America's Spiritual*, 253.

p. 236   "Prominent figures like John Marrant, Olaudah Equiano, and Phillis Wheatley offered hearty praise"—Parr, *Inventing George Whitefield*, 148–150.

p. 236   "Thy lessons in unequal'd accents flow'd / While emulation in each bosom glow'd"
          —Wheatley, "An Elegiac Poem on the Death of That Celebrated Divine," in *Poems of
          Wheatley*, 133–134.

CHAPTER 12: THE NEW DIVINES

For much of the 19th and 20th centuries, one of the few resources available to study Sarah Osborn
was Samuel Hopkins's *Memoirs of the Life of Sarah Osborn*. Though Hopkins's work is compelling,
it has its flaws: too much emphasis on her saintly piety, and not enough about her social struggles,
as well as a dearth of information on controversies like her entanglements with Reverend Vinal and
contention with critics in Newport. More comprehensive, and offering a wider perspective on the
revivals she followed and led, is the excellent *Sarah Osborn's World: The Rise of Evangelical Christianity
in Early America* by Catherine Brekus. A shorter treatment of the same subject, and also taking a
modern view, is Charles Hambrick-Stowe, "The Spiritual Pilgrimage of Sarah Osborn (1714–1796),"
(*Church History*, 61:4 (1992), 408–421). For more on the intimate relation of Osborn and her friend
Susanna Anthony, see *Familiar Letters Written by Mrs. Sarah Osborn and Miss Susanna Anthony*, and
for a primary-source biography of her, see *The Life and Character of Miss Susanna Anthony*.

For a glimpse at how Osborn encountered, and responded to, criticism for her activities, especially
useful is Mary Beth Norton, "'My Resting Reaping Times': Sarah Osborn's Defense of Her 'Unfemi-
nine' Activities, 1767" (*Signs* 2:2 (1976), 515–529). Norton also offers a perspective on the lives of
colonial women in "The Evolution of White Women's Experience in Early America." The saga of
Osborn's relationship with the enslaved Phillis and her son Bobey is detailed in Caroline Wigginton,
"Vexing Motherhood and Interracial Intimacy in Sarah Osborn's Spiritual Diary," (*Early American
Literature* 47:1 (2012), 115–142).

Much valuable research on the slave population of colonial Newport has been uncovered in
recent years by Keith and Theresa Stokes. Their website "God's Little Acre: America's Colonial
African Cemetery" (www.colonialcemetery.com) provides interesting summaries of some of the
figures buried there and their position as slaves in that difficult time. See the subpages for "Naming
Traditions" (/names) and "Religion" (/religious-life) for research used in the current volume. Other
material unearthed by the Stokeses is examined in Keith Stokes, "R.I.'s Former Slaves Achieved
Great Things," *Providence Journal*, December 19, 2017; and in Andy Smith, "Couple's Burial Ground
Research Details Life in Colonial Newport," *Providence Journal*, Feb. 23, 2014. An earlier, more
detailed analysis of the same subject is Ann and Dickran Tashjian, "The Afro-American Section of
Newport, Rhode Island's Common Burying Ground," in *Cemeteries and Gravemarkers: Voices of American
Culture*, Richard E. Meyer, ed. (Logan, UT: Utah State Univ. Press, 1989).

Although significant data on the African Americans of early Newport has been lost, enough
factual fragments have been pieced together to provide a coherent view of the slavery and oppression
of the time. The socioeconomic foundation for the slave trade in town is laid out in John Michael
Ray, "Newport's Golden Age" (*Negro History Bulletin* 25:3 (1961), 51–57), while Sarah Deutsch, in
"The Elusive Guineamen: Newport Slavers, 1735–1774" (*The New England Quarterly*, 55:2 (1982),
229–253), details the background and financial motivations of the slavers themselves.

Some of the above sources contain accounts of the lives of individual slaves and freedmen in
Newport, and their struggles for abolition. More background on them can be found in Michael Barga,
"African Union Society (Founded 1780)," VCU Libraries Social Welfare History Project, accessed
at socialwelfare.library.vcu.edu/religious/african-union-society/, and in the wide-ranging Christy

Mikel Clark-Pujara, "Slavery, Emancipation and Black Freedom in Rhode Island, 1652–1842," PhD dissertation, University of Iowa, 2009. The extraordinary life of Newport Gardner is discussed in J. Southern, *The Black Perspective in Music*, 4:2 (1976), 202–207.

Samuel Hopkins remains one of the most important religious figures of the Revolutionary era. The most insightful primary source is Stephen West, ed., *Sketches of the Life of the Late Reverend Samuel Hopkins, D.D.* (Hartford, Conn.: Hudson and Goodwin, 1803), which details the highlights of his pastoral career and his ongoing self-effacement in the face of obstacles. Less useful is Edwards Park, *Memoir of the Life and Character of Samuel Hopkins, D.D.*, 2nd ed. (Boston: Doctrinal Tract and Book Society, 1854), though it does contain some interesting excerpts from his work. For a more contemporary perspective, see Joseph Conforti, *Samuel Hopkins and the New Divinity Movement: Calvinism and Reform in New England Between the Great Awakenings* (Eugene, OR: Wipf and Stock, 2008). An excellent insight into the New Divinity comes by way of Kenneth Minkema and Harry Stout, "The Edwardsean Tradition and the Anti-Slavery Debate, 1740–1865," showing the growth of Edwards's disciples in rejecting their leader's allowance for slavery. Also see Sydney Ahlstrom, *A Religious History of the American People*, for the relation of the New Divinity to other theological movements of the time.

Along with the testimony of African Americans, the alliance of Samuel Hopkins and Sarah Osborn became the driving force behind the movement of First Church toward abolition. A good overview of their bond is Sheryl Kujawa, "'The Path of Duty Plain': Samuel Hopkins, Sarah Osborn, and Revolutionary Newport" (*Rhode Island History* 58:3 (2000), 75–89), along with Catherine Brekus's *Sarah Osborn's World* cited earlier. For the view of Hopkins's friend and rival, see Edmund Morgan, *The Gentle Puritan: A Life of Ezra Stiles, 1727–1795*, and Stiles's own installment sermon for Hopkins, *A Discourse on Saving Knowledge, Delivered at the Instalment of the Reverend Samuel Hopkins, April 11, 1770* (Newport: Solomon Southwick, 1770).

Reverend Hopkins repeatedly offered jeremiads and denunciations of slavery which are illustrated in any number of contemporary sources, but the most important are those in which he implicates his listeners in the foul trade. A little-known but crucial document is in Jonathan Sassi, "'This Whole Country Have Their Hands Full of Blood This Day': Transcription and Introduction of an Antislavery Sermon Manuscript Attributed to the Reverend Samuel Hopkins" (*Proceedings of the American Antiquarian Society* 112:1 (2004): 29–92). A much more prominent treatise, and the sermon that made him famous as an early abolitionist, is *A Dialogue Concerning the Slavery of the Africans; Shewing It to Be the Duty and Interest of the American States to Emancipate All Their African Slaves* (Norwich, CT: Judah Spooner, 1776)—still potent for its graphic imagery and unhesitating condemnation of human bondage.

CHAPTER 12 REFERENCES:

p. 238   "In the 1750s she was well on her way toward writing, by the end of her life"
—Hambrick-Stowe, "Spiritual Pilgrimage," 410–411.

p. 238   "She led a crusade against theatrical entertainment in Newport, calling it a 'temple of wickedness'"—Brekus, *Sarah Osborn's World*, 236.

p. 238   "Such an awesome event was a sign of his 'adorable perfections'"—Wigginton, "Vexing Motherhood," 124.

p. 239   "More than a decade before, her only son Samuel died at the age of eleven"
—Hambrick-Stowe, "Spiritual Pilgrimage," 413.

p. 239   "she watched him wither away, rattling and choking to breathe and writhing in pain"
—Brekus, *Sarah Osborn's World*, 137, 148–149.

p. 239 "Her husband Henry could not work a regular job because of his lingering injuries"
—ibid., 197–198.

p. 239 "she finally resorted to raising the price of her tuition for teaching"—ibid., 200–201.

p. 239 "made her feel like 'a poor overloaded weak animal crouching and trembling under its
burden'"—Norton, "My Resting Reaping Times," 517–518.

p. 240 "John Osborn died fighting in the war, and left his father saddled with grief"—Brekus,
Sarah Osborn's World, 205, 222.

p. 240 "But she had owned him nearly all his life, from the time he was an infant"—ibid.,
174–75, 202.

p. 240 "Bobey's mother Phillis was a member of Sarah's church as well as her women's study
group"—Wigginton, "Vexing Motherhood," 117.

p. 240 "She reacted angrily, telling Sarah she was 'vexed' that she could even consider taking
the boy away"—ibid., 115–116.

p. 240 "She hid in a closet and wrote searching notes to herself"—ibid., 127.

p. 241 "In the spring of 1765 a group of free black residents of Newport"—Norton, "My
Resting Reaping Times," 519.

p. 241 "Sarah had already received a letter from a slave named Quaum"—Brekus, *Sarah
Osborn's World*, 252.

p. 241 "Expanding to Tuesday nights as well as Sundays, some forty-two slaves, a smaller
number of freedmen and women"—Hambrick-Stowe, "Spiritual Pilgrimage," 417.

p. 241 "Her life and home were now fully given over to religion: Sunday night for young
men"—ibid.

p. 242 "Many were Akan, a West African people from the Gold Coast (now Ghana)"—Stokes,
"God's Little Acre—Naming Traditions."

p. 242 "On boats known as 'rum vessels,' the captives would be tightly shackled and bound"
—Ray, "Golden Age," 52–54.

p. 242 "the captives were transferred to white owners who would shave their heads"—ibid.,
53.

p. 242 "As slaves they lived closely among whites in the city as forced laborers"—Tashjian,
"Afro-American Section," 165; Smith, "Couple's Burial Ground."

p. 242 "Those who were free had gained freedom from white Quakers in previous decades"
—Tashjian, "Afro-American Section," 169; Deutsch, "Elusive Guineamen," 233.

p. 242 "Ezra Stiles, counted numerous warehouses and businesses for spirits distillation"
—ibid., 230.

p. 243 "Newport's trade with Africa in liquor and slaves peaked, with new shippers and
investors"—ibid., 244, 247–248.

p. 243 "Almost one in seven residents of Newport was a slave, equating to more than 1,200
people"—Smith, "Couple's Burial Ground."

p. 243 "In the summer of 1766 Sarah hosted 500 people a week at her house"—Brekus, *Sarah
Osborn's World*, 254.

p. 244 "greatly feared that it would be as the river Jordan overflowing all the banks"—Norton,
"My Resting Reaping Times," 520.

p. 244 "Since the Ethiopian Society remained at the center of the movement"—Wigginton,
"Vexing Motherhood," 132; Brekus, *Sarah Osborn's World*, 254–255.

p. 244   "Man can't determine me . . . Man's opinion alone shant content me for or against" —Brekus, *Sarah Osborn's World*, 264.

p. 244   "She also defended her actions to her spiritual advisor, Reverend Joseph Fish"—Norton, "My Resting Reaping Times," 518–519.

p. 244   "a warrior who wore 'the whole armor of God' and wielded a 'shield of faith'—Brekus, *Sarah Osborn's World*, 264.

p. 244   "During the years preceding and during the Revolution, Americans argued about women's role"—Norton, "Evolution of White Women," 616.

p. 245   "more than 70 percent of the members were women"—Kujawa, "Path of Duty Plain," 87 n21.

p. 245   "Your zeal for God if you are not on your guard will carry you astray"—Brekus, *Sarah Osborn's World*, 258–259.

p. 245   "fired Vinal from the pulpit after twenty-two years, for 'bad habit of body' and other euphemisms"—ibid., 275.

p. 246   "a greater call for 'communalism, social responsibility, and moral reform'"—Hambrick-Stowe, "Spiritual Pilgrimage," 419.

p. 246   "They also had a reputation for being judgmental and censorious"—Ahlstrom, *Religious History*, 404–405.

p. 246   "He had learned Calvinism from Jonathan Edwards himself, arriving at his doorstep" —West, *Sketches of Hopkins*, 38–41.

p. 246   "Although there were only thirty families in the congregation, and life in the hinterlands was difficult"—ibid., 47–48.

p. 246   "He turned them down and instead recommended his mentor Edwards"—ibid., 53–54, 57.

p. 247   "he drawled and mumbled and had a difficult time pronouncing common words" —Brekus, *Sarah Osborn's World*, 277–279.

p. 247   "he preached a severe strain of Calvinism that emphasized human depravity" —Ahlstrom, *Religious History*, 408.

p. 247   "his congregants eventually became sick of him and fired him from his job"—Kujawa, "Path of Duty Plain," 77.

p. 247   "impressing enough of the all-male voters on the governing committee that he survived a narrow vote"—ibid., 78.

p. 247   "a number who appeared to be excellent Christians, and the best regulated church that I had seen"—West, *Sketches of Hopkins*, 69.

p. 247   "let it be known that he dreaded the arrival of Hopkins in Newport as his colleague" —Kujawa, "Path of Duty Plain," 78; Morgan, *The Gentle Puritan*, 172.

p. 248   "He will preach away all his congregation at Newport, or make them tenfold worse" —Morgan, *The Gentle Puritan*, 172.

p. 248   "the Quaker and Congregationalist faiths were declining at the hands of a revived Church of England"—Deutsch, "Elusive Guineamen," 251.

p. 248   "the congregants 'had appeared dissatisfied with my doctrines'"—West, *Sketches of Hopkins*, 69.

p. 248   "their consciences accused them so severely of their wickedness in what they had done"—ibid., 72.

p. 249   "I have been much dejected and sunk in my own mind"—Kujawa, "Path of Duty Plain," 79.

p. 249   "my preaching has always appeared to me as poor, low and miserable"—West, *Sketches of Hopkins*, 88.

p. 249   "Mrs. Osborn and the sorority of her meeting are violently engaged and had great influence"—Kujawa, "Path of Duty Plain," 80.

p. 249   "With the former he met regularly, sharing tea and prayer on Saturdays"—ibid., 80–81.

p. 250   "they found each other's company congenial and could regularly be spotted walking together"—Morgan, *The Gentle Puritan*, 207.

p. 250   "Hopkins assisted her by ministering to the still-numerous black students and congregants"—Brekus, *Sarah Osborn's World*, 281.

p. 250   "He heard his black congregants' stories of their cruel and despicable treatment"—Wigginton, "Vexing Motherhood," 133–134.

p. 250   "He witnessed the horror of the auction block in Newport"—Brekus, *Sarah Osborn's World*, 284.

p. 250   "saw the slave markets at Mill Street and at North Baptist streets"—Ray, "Golden Age," 55.

p. 250   "he met Obour Tanner, an enslaved woman active in women's gospel work"—Stokes, "R.I.'s Former Slaves."

p. 251   "he corresponded with Wheatley herself and other black evangelicals"—Brekus, *Sarah Osborn's World*, 286.

p. 251   "Newport Gardner, who learned to read and write in English"—Southern, *Black Perspective*, 203, 205; Barga, "African Union Society."

p. 251   "with Ezra Stiles did all he could to raise funds for their education at the College of New Jersey"—Stokes, "God's Little Acre—Religion"; Stokes, "R.I.'s Former Slaves."

p. 251   "He may have even seen the elaborate, joyous funerals of former slaves"—Tashjian, "Afro-American Section," 192–193.

p. 251   "carved by master stone mason Zingo Stevens"—Smith, "Couple's Burial Ground."

p. 251   "He knew this would set much of the white town folk against him, and would 'procure me many enemies'"—Sassi, "This Whole Country," 29.

p. 251   "many established falsehoods, as well as many vulgar errors"—ibid., 43.

p. 251   "The majority of his hearers were astounded that they, of themselves, had not long before seen"—Kujawa, "Path of Duty Plain," 81.

p. 252   "Ezra Stiles, cooperated with Hopkins and tried to raise funds for a missionary society"—Minkema and Stout, "Edwardsean Tradition," 52.

p. 252   "he banned slave holders from becoming members of First Church"—Barga, "African Union Society."

p. 252   "opening of the prison to the bound" to "If it be lawful and right for us to reduce the Africans"—Minkema and Stout, "Edwardsean Tradition," 53.

p. 252   "thousands of blacks in slavery, who have an equal right to freedom with ourselves"—Hopkins, *A Dialogue*, 9.

p. 253   "Who can realize all this, and not feel a mixture of grief, pity, indignation and horror, truly ineffable!"—ibid., 20.

p. 253   "inexpressible unjust, inhuman and cruel [and] glaringly contrary to the whole tenor"—ibid., 26.

p. 253   "He said the promoters of slavery had twisted and misrepresented passages from the Bible"—ibid., 28–30.

p. 253   "Are you willing to be the instruments of bringing judgments and ruin on this land" —ibid., 63.

p. 253   "Newport Gardner and Zingo Stevens founded the African Union Society"—Barga, "African Union Society."

p. 253   "Obour Tanner launched the Free African Female Benevolent Society"—Barga, "African Union Society"; Stokes, "R.I.'s Former Slaves"; Smith, "Couple's Burial Ground."

p. 254   "would create organizations like the Society for the Promotion of Freedom"—Minkema and Stout, "Edwardsean Tradition," 57.

p. 254   "first banning the internal trade in human cargo to the colony in 1774"—Clark-Pujara, "Slavery, Emancipation and Black Freedom," 131–135.

p. 254   "Hopkins often gave Sunday services in her home so she could participate in them" —Kujawa, "Path of Duty Plain," 80.

p. 255   "Those we see here who once have been / Made slaves to man by horrid sin"—Hopkins, *Osborn Memoirs*, 378.

p. 255   "Sarah's release from her own suffering came in 1796, at the age of eighty-three" —ibid., 362.

p. 255   "I therefore, the prisoner of the Lord, beseech you, that you walk worthy of the vocation"—Ephesians 4:1, quoted in Hopkins, *Osborn Memoirs*, 362.

CHAPTER 13: THE BLACK REGIMENT

The revolutionary impulses of Separatist Baptists are one of the lesser-known aspects of the movement toward independence in British North America. However, though the evangelical revolt came late to the South, it had an even more lasting effect than it did in the North, and a more direct impact on the revolution. The best overview of this spiritual movement is in Rhys Isaac, "Evangelical Revolt: The Nature of the Baptists' Challenge to the Traditional Order in Virginia, 1765 to 1775," still the essential study of how Separatism undermined Southern class hierarchies. Also valuable, though more general, is Ross Phares, *Bible in Pocket, Gun in Hand: The Story of Frontier Religion* (New York: Doubleday, 1964), and David Lovejoy, "'Desperate Enthusiasm'; Early Signs of American Radicalism," in *The Origins of Anglo-American Radicalism*, ed. Margaret Jacob and James Jacob (London: Humanities Press Intl., 1991). Lovejoy's wider look at enthusiastic spiritual practices is *Religious Enthusiasm in the New World: Heresy to Revolution*, still the definitive study. For a comprehensive view of how Separatism operated in the North, and especially on the frontier, see C. C. Goen, *Revivalism and Separatism in New England, 1740–1800: Strict Congregationalists and Separate Baptists in the Great Awakening*. For the role of itinerant preaching in forcing social change, see Timothy Hall, *Contested Boundaries: Itinerancy and the Reshaping of the Colonial American Religious World*; and for how the mechanisms of revival translated into political restructuring in one colony, see Richard Bushman, *From Puritan to Yankee: Character and the Social Order in Connecticut, 1690–1765*.

    Previously cited books that provide further context to the revolutionary impact of the revivalists and their former foes include Sydney Ahlstrom, *A Religious History of the American People*; Thomas Kidd, *The Great Awakening: The Roots of Evangelical Christianity in Colonial America*; Patricia Bonomi, *Under the Cope of Heaven: Religion, Society, and Politics in Colonial America*; and Harry Stout, *The New England Soul: Preaching and Religious Culture in Colonial New England*. The seminal volume by

Alan Heimert, *Religion and the American Mind: From the Great Awakening to the Revolution*, is a great resource for showing how New Light rhetoric fed the desire for revolt.

Andrew Croswell's actions as a Boston preacher after the revival are little known, partially because of his status as an outcast, and partially because he doesn't fit comfortably into standard narratives. Still, he was prescient in his social gospel and commanded a small legion of followers. Some of his history is laid out in Robert Cray, Jr., "James Davenport's Post-Bonfire Ministry, 1743–1757," which also covers Croswell; and the best current study, Leigh Eric Schmidt, "'A Second and Glorious Reformation': The New Light Extremism of Andrew Croswell." For a glimpse of how Croswell denounced his enemies at midcentury such as Jonathan Mayhew, see his Preface to Abraham Taylor, *The Insufficiency of Natural Religion* (Boston: J. Draper, 1755) or any of his sermons of the era.

Jonathan Mayhew was widely known throughout the North in the years before the Revolutionary War and a few decades afterward, though his name has since fallen into obscurity among the wider public. A few biographers have tried to rectify this, among them Charles Akers, in *Called unto Liberty*, and J. Patrick Mullins, in *Father of Liberty: Jonathan Mayhew and the Principles of the American Revolution*, as well as Clinton Rossiter's article, "The Life and Mind of Jonathan Mayhew." The biographies of Mayhew from the era are either hagiographies or document collections, so they aren't terribly useful. More valuable are the works of the preacher himself, including *A Sermon Preached in the Audience of His Excellency William Shirley, Esq.* (Boston: S. Kneeland, 1754), known as the 1754 election sermon, which heightened his reputation as a threat to the Crown; and *A Discourse on Rev. XV 3rd, 4th, Occasion by the Earthquakes in November 1755* (Boston: Edes and Gill, 1755), in which he channeled Whitefield in threatening God's punishment by seismic revenge. A more sedate sermon, and eulogy, is his *Discourse Occasioned by the Death of King George II* (Boston: Edes and Gill, 1761), which includes his high, unrealized hopes for his son as monarch.

The complex and convoluted saga of colonial episcopacy cannot be fully laid out in the current book, but for those with an interest in the long-forgotten controversy, see the definitive study, Carl Bridenbaugh, *Mitre and Sceptre: Transatlantic Faiths, Ideas, Personalities, and Politics, 1689–1775*. A shorter look at the same subject is Joseph Henry Allen, "The Ecclesiastical Situation in New England Prior to the American Revolution" (67–77), in *Papers of the American Society of Church History* (New York: G. P. Putnam's Sons, 1897), which also refers to the writings of East Apthorp. Mayhew's response to Apthorp and harsh judgment of Anglican missionaries is revealed in his *Observations on the Charter and Conduct of the Society for the Propagation of the Gospel in Foreign Parts* (Boston: Edes and Gill, 1763).

Unfortunately, one of Mayhew's most important sermons, just before the second round of Stamp Act riots, is lost to history. Historians have pieced together some of what he said to his congregation from a variety of sources. These include his Letter to Thomas Hutchinson, August 27, 1765, in "Second Stamp Act Riots," Colonial Society of Massachusetts, accessed at https://www.colonialsociety.org/node/2532#chsect1701, and his Letter to Richard Clarke, September 3, 1765, in the *New-England Historical and Genealogical Register*, vol. 46 (Boston: New England Historic Genealogical Society, 1892). Thomas Hutchinson's feelings on the matter are discussed in his *History of Massachusetts from the First Settlement Thereof in 1628 Until the Year 1750*, vol. 3, while the best study of the whole affair is Howard Lubert, "Jonathan Mayhew: Conservative Revolutionary" (*History of Political Thought* 32:4 (2011), 589–616).

The larger scope of revolutionary activity in Boston is familiar to generations of American history students; for Samuel Adams' unique role during the era, see the biographies by John Alexander, *Samuel Adams: The Life of an American Revolutionary*, which depicts him as a powerful force against injustice, and John Miller, *Sam Adams: Pioneer in Propaganda*, which sees him as a clever manipulator.

A broader view of the tumultuous and violent spirit of the times can be found in Gary Nash, "The Transformation of Urban Politics, 1700–1764," in *Colonial America: Essays in Politics and Social Development*, 4th edition, ed. by Stanley Katz, et al. (New York: McGraw-Hill (1993), 523–552), and the same author's *The Urban Crucible: Social Change, Political Consciousness, and the Origins of the American Revolution*. Another worthy perspective on how feelings of revolt affected colonial life is in Bruce Tucker, "The Reinvention of New England, 1691–1770" (*New England Quarterly* 59:3 (1986), 315–340), and the groundbreaking study *The Ideological Origins of the American Revolution*, by Bernard Bailyn. Edmund Morgan also provides an excellent overview of how the Calvinists of the past affected those of the 1770s in "The Puritan Ethic and the American Revolution" (*William and Mary Quarterly* 24:1 (1967), 3–43).

Charles Chauncy remains a lodestar for the formation of the liberal religious tradition in New England, for both Universalism (which adheres to many of his views) and Unitarianism (which takes them quite a bit further). For a deeper look at his theology, see Edward Griffin, *Old Brick: Charles Chauncy of Boston, 1705–1787*, and Conrad Wright, *The Beginnings of Unitarianism in America*. His sermons and writings also serve to show just how radical "Old Brick" had become by the time of revolution. For his innovative theology, created at mid-century but not revealed until after the war, see his critical works *Salvation for All Men* (Boston: T. and J. Fleet, 1782); *The Benevolence of the Deity, Fairly and Impartially Considered* (Boston: Powars and Willis, 1784); and his magnum opus, *The Mystery Hid from Ages and Generations, Made Manifest by the Gospel Revelation* (London: Charles Dilly, 1784). All became foundational documents for New England liberalism.

Chauncy's scathing attacks on British policies and the events of the day are evident in just about any major sermon he preached in the years before the war. He was particularly enflamed over the progress of Anglican episcopacy and missionary efforts, and a series of sermons and tracts show his bitter judgments: *The Appeal to the Public Answered, in Behalf of the Non-Episcopal churches in America* (Boston: Kneeland and Adams, 1768); *A Compleat View of Episcopacy, as Exhibited from the Fathers of the Christian Church* (Boston: D. Kneeland, 1771); and *Letter to a Friend, Containing Remarks on Certain Passages in a Sermon . . .* (London: S. Bladon, 1768). Perhaps the most potent piece appeared after the Boston Massacre, for which Chauncy reserved some of his strongest rhetoric, *Trust in God, The Duty of a People in a Day of Trouble* (Boston: D. Kneeland, 1770).

John Adams was one of the keenest of the founders in analyzing the role of religion and politics in colonial America, and several of his writings are mentioned in the chapter. For his understanding of religious enthusiasm, see "A Dissertation on the Canon and Feudal Law," in *The Works of John Adams, Second President of the United States*, vol. 3 (Boston: Little and Brown, 1851). For his laudatory view of Jonathan Mayhew and the revolutionary impulses of the era, see the Letter to Hezekiah Niles, February 13, 1818 (National Archives, Founders Online, accessed at founders.archives.gov /documents/Adams/99-02-02-6854); and the Letter to the Inhabitants of the Colony of Massachusetts-Bay, February 6, 1775 (National Archives, Founders Online, founders.archives.gov /documents/Adams/06-02-02-0072-0004). His wife's witness to a sermon by Charles Chauncy can be found in her Letter to John Adams, August 14, 1776, in Charles Francis Adams, *Familiar Letters of John Adams and His Wife Abigail Adams, During the Revolution* (New York: Houghton Mifflin, 1875).

CHAPTER 13 REFERENCES:

p. 256   "Barefaced attempts to manipulate the electorate resulted in the passage of laws"
           —Bushman, *From Puritan to Yankee*, 268–269.

p. 256 "One observer asked 'how ridiculous is the sight and sound' of clergymen"—Nash, "Transformation," 543.

p. 257 "the poor and working classes became energized in the pews"—ibid., 544.

p. 257 "many drifted toward New Light evangelism, and still others embraced Separatist Baptism"—Goen, *Revivalism and Separatism*, 202–203.

p. 257 "the Separatist Baptists worshipped in two and a half times more churches"—Ahlstrom, *Religious History*, 293.

p. 257 "They conquered the frontier and built meetinghouses"—Goen, *Revivalism and Separatism*, 298–299.

p. 257 "By the 1760s the Separatist Baptists had perfected a system for seeding the countryside"—Hall, *Contested Boundaries*, 123–124.

p. 257 "especially in Virginia, where they battled mobs and hostile authorities"—Kidd, *Great Awakening*, 246–248.

p. 258 "the Anglican gentry, who charged them with being 'ignorant enthusiasts'"—Hall, *Contested Boundaries*, 125–126.

p. 258 "Black and Indian preachers, too, served as deacons and exhorters"—Kidd, *Great Awakening*, 250.

p. 258 "everything from extensive feet-washing and laying on of hands to 'kisses of charity'" —Bonomi, *Under the Cope*, 184.

p. 258 "some roaring on the ground, some wringing their hands, some in ecstasies"—Phares, *Bible in Pocket*, 80.

p. 258 "it appealed to rural Christians who had little interest in formal sermonizing"—Isaac, "Evangelical Revolt," 354.

p. 258 "the radical Baptists demanded the Church of England be disestablished over the colonies"—Bailyn, *Ideological Origins*, 257–259.

p. 259 "Some pastors saw the conflicts with royal officials through the lens of apocalyptic Millenarianism"—Lovejoy, "Desperate Enthusiasm," 221.

p. 259 "I believe it will be found universally true, that no great enterprise for the honor" —J. Adams, "Dissertation," 452.

p. 259 "champion a radical, experiential faith . . . defiantly outside the religious mainstream"—Cray, "Post-Bonfire Ministry," 69.

p. 259 "He had few allies in town, and regularly heard 'the ministers are all against you,'" —Schmidt, "New Light Extremism," 242.

p. 260 "his attacks on the liberalism of colleges like Harvard"—ibid., 241.

p. 260 "had since tied his own theology to the rationalism of Isaac Newton and Enlightenment philosophers"—Akers, *Called Unto Liberty*, 114–115.

p. 260 "Christ acted as a mediator between humans and God, and was his subordinate" —ibid., 116–118.

p. 260 "daring attempts to confute and ridicule the doctrines once delivered to the saints" —Croswell, Preface to *Insufficience*.

p. 261 "divine right of monarchy [and] . . . the despotic, unlimited power of kings"—Mayhew, *Sermon Preached to William Shirley*, 4.

p. 261 "loyalty and slavery mean the same thing. . . . to prepare us for the dutiful reception" —ibid., 20–21.

p. 261 "Do I see Christianity banished for Popery! The Bible, for the Mass book!"
—ibid., 37–38.

p. 262 "these sermons would stand as the apotheosis of revolutionary preaching in New England"—Stout, *New England Soul*, 242.

p. 262 "a nation where infidelity, irreligion, corruption and venality, and almost every kind of vice"—Mayhew, *Discourse on Earthquakes*, 66.

p. 262 "dogs, and sorcerers, and whoremongers, and murderers, and IDOLATERS"—ibid., 47.

p. 263 "he became stricken with smallpox and survived, then faced painful kidney stones" —Akers, *Called Unto Liberty*, 105.

p. 263 "He grieved the loss of his father and sometimes mentor Experience Mayhew" —ibid., 111.

p. 263 "lamented the demise of one of the good ones in his *Discourse Occasioned by the Death of King George II*"—Mullins, *Father of Liberty*, 92–93.

p. 263 "confirm the apprehensions which I have all along had concerning the [king]"—ibid., 155.

p. 263 "he overheard a rumor of Governor Francis Bernard accepting a small bribe from a petitioner"—ibid., 97, 103–106.

p. 264 "dagger aimed at the heart of Puritan tradition in America'"—Akers, *Called unto Liberty*, 181.

p. 264 "he saw a great opportunity to proselytize to Indians who lived there"—Griffin, *Old Brick*, 132.

p. 265 "equating New England nonconformity not only with superstition"—Bailyn, *Ideological Origins*, 255.

p. 265 "narrow, censorious and bitter spirit that prevails in too many of the Episcopalians among us"—Mayhew, *Observations*, 155.

p. 265 "recalled how 'furious episcopal zealots' had done the same thing in the previous century"—ibid., 157.

p. 265 "this blind bigot is for setting up an Inquisition against the religion of the nation" —Mullins, *Father of Liberty*, 133; Akers, *Called unto Liberty*, 185, 190.

p. 265 "a most foul-mouthed bespatterer of our church and our missionaries in print"—Akers, *Called unto Liberty*, 177.

p. 265 "rope of sand; there is no union, no authority among us; we cannot even summon a convention"—Griffin, *Old* Brick, 132.

p. 266 "they would act tactfully and respect the native traditions and faiths of the king's subjects"—Mullins, *Father of Liberty*, 140.

p. 266 "high churchmen compared his work to 'the devil's thunderbolt'"—ibid.

p. 266 "won for himself a transatlantic reputation as the champion of British Nonconformity"—Bridenbaugh, *Mitre and Sceptre*, 242.

p. 266 "Mayhew's controversies 'spread an universal alarm against the authority of Parliament'"—J. Adams, Letter to Hezekiah Niles.

p. 267 "By the summer boycotts against British-made products became widespread" —Morgan, "Puritan Ethic," 8.

p. 267 "turmoil erupted when a mob of Bostonians hung effigies of the colony's stamp collector"—Nash, *Urban Crucible*, 293–294.

p. 267   "but did use passages from the Bible to tell his congregation that in any nation"
—Mullins, *Father of Liberty*, 160.

p. 267   "slaves are bound to labor for the pleasure and profit of others"—ibid., 161; Lubert,
"Conservative Revolutionary," 599–600.

p. 267   "For colonists to be stripped of their rights by the imperial overlords or distant
legislature"—Akers, *Called unto Liberty*, 203–204.

p. 268   "This time the angry masses broke into the homes of several royal officials and
ransacked them"—Nash, *Urban Crucible*, 294.

p. 268   "The lieutenant governor was inside dining with his family when the mob approached"
—Hutchinson, *History of Massachusetts*, 124; Alexander, *Samuel Adams*, 32.

p. 268   "elite bankers and royal officials, who called them a 'herd of fools, tools and
sycophants'"—Nash, *Urban Crucible*, 297.

p. 268   "he was excited to [violence] by this sermon, and that he thought he was doing God
service"—Hutchinson, *History of Massachusetts*, 123.

p. 268   "one of the most seditious sermons ever delivered, advising the people to stand up"
—Mullins, *Father of Liberty*, 164–165.

p. 269   "I had rather lose my hand, than be an encourager of such outrages"—Akers, *Called
Unto Liberty*, 206.

p. 269   "He warned against 'abusing liberty to licentiousness'"—ibid.

p. 269   "[I]f his zeal, at any time, betrayed him into too great a severity of expression"—
ibid., 221.

p. 269   "he was a shining example for his brethren in the ministry to follow"—ibid., 222.

p. 270   "a Whig of the first magnitude, a clergyman equaled by very few of any denomination
in piety"—J. Adams, Letter to the Inhabitants.

p. 270   "to draw the character of Mayhew would be to transcribe a dozen Volumes"—J. Adams,
Letter to Hezekiah Niles.

p. 270   "Adams would later claim that there were five critical figures who drove America toward
revolution"—Rossiter, "Life and Mind," 531.

p. 270   "many in the British government saw him as nothing less than 'the most dangerous
man in America'"—Nash, *Urban Crucible*, 352.

p. 270   "many of his artisan and shipyard worker allies in the Sons of Liberty had rioted in
recent months"—Miller, *Pioneer in Propaganda*, 52.

p. 270   "he was hardly their puppet master, and was careful not to call for outright violence"
—Alexander, *Samuel Adams*, 34.

p. 270   "the Loyal Nine, a group of upper-middle-class merchants"—Miller, *Pioneer in
Propaganda*, 52–53.

p. 270   "the religion and public liberty of a people are so intimately connected"—Heimert,
American Mind, 359.

p. 270   "He aimed his message at the commoners of Boston, lauding their struggle for
liberty"—Nash, *Urban Crucible*, 361.

p. 271   "mankind is governed more by their feelings than by reason"—Lovejoy, *Religious
Enthusiasm*, 225–226.

p. 271   "Americans from a variety of backgrounds and beliefs invested the age-old Puritans"
—Morgan, "Puritan Ethic," 7.

p. 271   "there is no truth, no mercy, nor knowledge of God in the land"—Tucker, "Reinvention," 338.

p. 271   "scarcely a patriot club was without a divine who lent an odor of sanctity"—Miller, *Pioneer in Propaganda*, 37.

p. 271   "RIGHTS that had been dearly paid for by a vast expense of blood, treasure and labor"—Griffin, *Old Brick*, 140.

p. 272   "That fine preacher, called a teacher / Of Old Brick Church the First"—ibid., 141.

p. 272   "He exalted 'the power and wisdom of the infinitely benevolent Creator'"—Chauncy, *Benevolence*, 203.

p. 272   "who the author of this controversial tract was, along with Chauncy's code word for it: 'the pudding'"—Wright, *Unitarianism*, 191.

p. 272   "all of life and part of life after death is a process of trial and discipline"—ibid., 195.

p. 273   "an occasion of pride, haughtiness, tampering with princes, and advising and helping forward"—Chauncy, *Letter to a Friend*, 21.

p. 273   "reminding readers of the growing threat to their liberties"—Bridenbaugh, *Mitre and Sceptre*, 308.

p. 273   "scuffles between Boston rope makers and the occupying British army led to crowds hurling taunts"—Alexander, *Samuel Adams*, 104–106.

p. 273   "Figures at the highest levels of the British government blamed Sam Adams for the Boston Massacre"—Miller, *Pioneer in Propaganda*, 186.

p. 274   "Sam Adams, however, tried the soldiers in the *Boston Gazette* under the name 'Vindex,'"—ibid., 188–189.

p. 274   "if I was to be one of the jury upon [a soldier's] trial, I would bring him in guilty"—Griffin, *Old Brick*, 146.

p. 274   "the streaming blood of many slaughtered, and wounded innocents"—Chauncy, *Trust in God*, 35.

p. 274   "God would not suffer the town and land to lie under the defilement of blood!"—ibid., 36.

p. 274   "advise, persuade, propagandize, comment on the times, and lend the influence of his position"—Griffin, *Old Brick*, 151.

p. 275   "an increasing number of Americans who no longer saw themselves as colonists"—ibid., 152.

p. 275   "Adams excerpted the most controversial parts and had them read before the Massachusetts assembly"—Miller, *Pioneer in* Propaganda, 280–281.

p. 275   "rebels realized it immediately, calling it 'parliamentary despotism'"—ibid., 284.

p. 275   "on December 16, 1773, some sixty or more Bostonians dressed as Indians clambered aboard ships"—Alexander, *Samuel Adams*, 162, 170–174.

p. 275   "calling itself the Solemn League and Covenant after a Puritan alliance"—ibid., 175.

p. 276   "to frustrate the designs of those who would rule [Americans] with a rod of iron"—Griffin, *Old Brick*, 174–175.

p. 277   "The Continental Congress arranged for the nonimportation and nonconsumption"—ibid., 158.

p. 277   "Chauncy concluded the reading and 'lifted his eyes and hands to heaven'"—Abigail Adams, in *Familiar Letters*, 212.

p. 277   "The crowd answered him,—'Amen'"—Griffin, *Old Brick*, 164.

NOTES

POSTSCRIPT: NOTES ON LIBERTY AND DEATH

p. 279   "Henry saw Davies as 'the greatest orator he ever heard'"—Charles Cohen, "The 'Liberty or Death' Speech: A Note on Religion and Revolutionary Rhetoric" (*The William and Mary Quarterly* 38:4 (1981), 712).

p. 280   "There is a just God who presides over the destinies of nations"—William Wirt, *Sketches of the Life and Character of Patrick Henry* (Philadelphia: James Webster, 1817), 123.

p. 280   "With its effective mixing of Revolutionary and biblical themes, the 'Liberty or Death' speech"—Cohen, "The 'Liberty or Death' Speech," 709.

p. 280   "None of Henry's revolutionary orations survive in print"—David McCants, "The Authenticity of William Wirt's Version of Patrick Henry's 'Liberty or Death' Speech" (*The Virginia Magazine of History and Biography* 87:4 (1979), 389).

p. 280   "Wirt relied heavily on the recollections of a lawyer named St. George Tucker"—ibid., 395–96, 398.

p. 281   "Masonry was 'at war with the fundamental principles of the social compact'"—William Wirt, Letter to the Convention of the Anti-Masonry Party, September 28, 1831.

p. 282   "called him everything from a 'roaring demagogue' to a 'pocket-sized Paul Bunyan' to 'a frontier bully'"—Michael Fellman, "The Earthbound Eagle: Andrew Jackson and the American Pantheon" (*American Studies* 12:2 (1971), 69).

p. 282   "he broke treaties protecting Native American land rights and oversaw 'the forced relocation'"—Alfred Cave, "Abuse of Power: Andrew Jackson and the Indian Removal Act of 1830" (*The Historian* 65:6 (2003), 1331–1332).

p. 282   "It hit its peak from the 1820s to the 1840s and spread widely across the country"—Michael Barkun, "The Awakening-Cycle Controversy" (*Sociological Analysis* 46:4 (1985), 431–432).

p. 282   "others called it 'an expansion of religious feeling unknown in American history'"—Donald Mathews, "The Second Great Awakening as an Organizing Process, 1780–1830: An Hypothesis" (*American Quarterly* 21:1 (1969), 23).

p. 283   "Professional organizers and formal literature helped drive conversions"—ibid., 26, 37, 43.

p. 283   "He even dismissed hoary Calvinism with his book on free will, *Sinners Bound to Change Their Own Hearts*"—James Bratt, "The Reorientation of American Protestantism, 1835–1845" (*Church History* 67:1 (1998), 58–59).

p. 283   "'chaos as the birthpangs of a new and perfect era' in predicting the end of the world"—Barkun, "The Awakening-Cycle Controversy," 441.

p. 284   "the Presbyterian church once again split over the practices of revivalism"—Bratt, "The Reorientation of American Protestantism," 67.

p. 285   "the flames and smoke surged amongst the burning buildings, like ocean waves"—John Hight, *History of the Fifty-Eighth Regiment of Indiana Volunteer Infantry* (Princeton, N.J.: Clarion Press, 1895), 411.

INDEX